Presented to Purchase College
by
Gary Waller, PhD Cambridge

State University of New York
Distinguished Professor

Professor
of Literature & Cultural
Studies, and Theatre &
Performance, 1995-2019
Provost 1995-2004

Richard Tottel's
Songes and Sonettes
The Elizabethan Version

MEDIEVAL AND RENAISSANCE
TEXTS AND STUDIES
VOLUME 338

RENAISSANCE ENGLISH TEXT SOCIETY
SEVENTH SERIES
VOLUME XXXII (FOR 2007)

Richard Tottel's
Songes and Sonettes

The Elizabethan Version

edited by
Paul A. Marquis

ACMRS
(Arizona Center for Medieval and Renaissance Studies)
in conjunction with
Renaissance English Text Society
Tempe, Arizona
2007

Library of Congress Cataloging-in-Publication Data

Tottel's miscellany
  Richard Tottel's Songes and sonettes : the Elizabethan version / edited by
Paul A. Marquis.
  p. cm. -- (Medieval and Renaissance texts and studies ; v. 338) (Renaissance
English Text Society ; 7th ser., v. 32)
  Includes bibliographical references and index.
  ISBN 978-0-86698-386-0 (alk. paper)
  1. English poetry--Early modern, 1500-1700. I. Tottel, Richard, d. 1594. II.
Marquis, Paul A. III. Title. IV. Title: Songes and sonettes.

  PR1205.T6 2007
  821'.208--dc22

                                                          2007039230

∞
This book is made to last.
It is set in ITC Berkeley Oldstyle,
smyth-sewn and printed on acid-free paper
to library specifications.
Printed in the United States of America

For Anne,

David and Sarah

TABLE OF CONTENTS

Acknowledgments   *ix*

Abbreviations   *xiii*

Textual Introduction   *xv*
     The First Quarto   *xvi*
     The Second Quarto   *xx*
     The Third Quarto   *xxiii*
     Manuscript Sources   *xxvi*
     Subsequent Elizabethan Editions   *xxxiv*
     Note on the Text   *xxxvi*
Critical Introduction   *xxxvii*
     Order of Poems in Q1   *xxxix*
     Order of Poems in Q2   *xlvi*
     Textual Variants between Q1 and Q2   *liv*
     Textual Variants between Q2 and Q3   *lviii*

Songes and Sonettes Q2
Contents: Sequence of poems in Q2 (first lines)
Poems by Henry Howard, the Earl of Surrey   2
Poems by Sir Thomas Wyatt, the Elder   35
Poems by Uncertain Auctours   95
Poems by Nicholas Grimald   217

Annotations and Glossary   229
Appendix 1: Possible manuscript sources for poems in Q2   239
Appendix 2: Poems in Q3 significantly changed from Q2   243

List 1: Substantive variants between Q1 and Q2   253
List 2: Substantive variants between Q2 and Q3   271
List 3: Accidental variants between Q1 and Q2   277
List 4: Press variants in Q2   291

Index 1: Sequence of poems in Q1 (first lines) with the nos. of poems in Q2   295
Index 2: Alphabetical Sequence of Headings in Q2   303
Index 3: Alphabetical Sequence of poems in Q2 (first lines)   311

ACKNOWLEDGMENTS

Those who have left lasting impressions on me, whose work I have appreci-
ated because of its uncanny knack for conveying fact with economy and el-
egance, are now, or have been, editors. I owe much to A. C. Hamilton, Steve
Lukits, George Whalley, and Barbara Rooke.

This project began as part of a larger plan to investigate the influence of
Richard Tottel's *Songes and Sonettes* on poetic anthologies in the Elizabethan
period. Supported in part by a Social Sciences Humanities Research Council
of Canada grant, I embarked in 1994/95 *en famille* for a year's research at Cam-
bridge University, where I had the good fortune to meet Michael Schoenfeldt,
then a fellow at Clare Hall. I benefited repeatedly from the many conversa-
tions we had over the year and especially from his comments on an earlier
abstract of my project. I am also grateful for the hospitality of Anne Barton,
John Kerrigan, and Jeremy Maule who urged attendance and participation in
the fortnightly graduate seminar in Renaissance English literature at Trinity
College; for discussions with Frank Kermode and Helen Vendler whose in-
terest in Tottel inspired me to pursue the topic with renewed vigor; and for
the friendship of Andy, Heather, Jack, and Spencer Martin who welcomed us
warmly into the neighborly enclave of Owlstone Road.

While presenting my argument to audiences at conferences hosted by the
Association of Canadian Colleges and University Teachers of English, the Ca-
nadian Society for Renaissance Studies, and the Renaissance Society of Amer-
ica, from 1995 to 1997, I began to see the need for a new edition of *Songes and
Sonettes*, based on the arrangement of poems published on 31 July 1557. This
text, and not the arrangement in the first edition, 5 June 1557, had been re-
printed numerous times in the Elizabethan period and had left its imprint
on Googe, Turbervile, Gascoigne, Spenser, Sidney, Shakespeare, Donne, and
many others. A conversation with Arthur Kinney and Arthur Marotti in Van-
couver led me to submit a proposal to the Renaissance English Text Society
to edit Tottel's second edition. Since then I have profited enormously from an
advisory committee established by RETS, whose directive it was to guide this
book through to its publication. David Freeman, Elizabeth H. Hageman, W.
Speed Hill, and George Walton Williams have shown patience, generosity,
and grace while instructing me in the mysteries of early modern printing and

publishing. If this work proves valuable to future students and scholars, I have the committee to thank. I also acknowledge with gratitude the helpful advice of Craig Ferguson who assisted me at a time when circumstance put me at a distance from the committee.

I gratefully acknowledge the Folger Shakespeare Library and the Folger Institute for inviting me to participate in a seminar on the theory and practice of scholarly editing, directed by W. Speed Hill. My thanks for the friendship of Jennifer Abeles, Nick Clulee, Jeremy Ehrlich, K.C. Elliott, Susan Iwanisziw, Patricia Lennox, Eric Lindquist, Robert Madison, Bill Rivers, and Sarah Werner whose collective experience in the field of editing was of great assistance. Speed Hill aided me on a weekly basis and in particular in my discussion of variants in Q1–Q3. Barbara Mowat, Kathleen Lynch, Laetitia Yeandle, Peter Blayney, Ben Griffith, Carol Brobeck, along with the efficient and professional Folger staff, lent credence to the report that the Folger Library is one of the greatest research institutions on earth. I owe a special debt to Steven May who assisted me on numerous occasions, especially in tracking down possible manuscript sources for Tottel's compilation of poems. I am grateful also to Georgiana Ziegler and Richard Kuhta for introducing me to Mr. James Edwards, of Washington, DC, then owner of the former Houghton copy of Tottel's third edition of *Songes and Sonettes*. Mr. Edwards was kind enough to allow me to examine this very valuable book for a short time at the Folger Library during which I was able to transcribe marginalia in Elizabethan script, including a continuation of one of the printed poems. Research at the Library also afforded me the pleasure of meeting Vincent Carey whose eloquent and insightful observations on Tudor history and literature, impressive knowledge of the Folger archives, and infectious spirit of community transformed the library into a Renaissance academy of higher learning. I acknowledge also the assistance of the staffs of the Bodleian Library, the British Library, the Wren Library, Trinity College, Cambridge, and the University Library, Cambridge.

Among the many colleagues from whose questions about Tottel this project has benefited, I wish to single out David Carlson, Jim Taylor, Phil Milner, Douglas Burnet Smith, Earla Wilputte, Pamela Black, Richard Nemesvari, Maureen Moynaugh, Jeanette Lynes, and Jonathan Boulter. I especially wish to thank the late Hubert Spekkens who has lent me more books from his personal collection than I care to remember and without whose vigilance to all matters Tottelian and to the history of print I would be the poorer. Derek Wood's exemplary commitment to academic research and his vast knowledge of early modern European literature has helped to sustain me through the years. Particular mention must be made of the debt I owe to Peter Clancy and Mary McGillivray whose intelligence, wit, and sense of social justice provided an imperative that guided this work to its completion. I am indebted also to members of both the Southeastern and the South-Central Renaissance Societies of America, especially to John Shawcross, Boswell Jackson, George Klawitter, Donald Dickson, Donald Stump, John Ford, Marguerite Tassi, and Martha Oberle for their intellectual and moral support. Moreover, conversations about literature with Gary Bynkoski, René Hogue, David Lush, Marilyn Allen, David Solie, Gordon Johnson, and Richard Dellamora lie at the foundation of this edition. The cheerful disposition of Marie Gillis enabled me to rely on her technical expertise too often in the past. The careful proofreading of Trudy McCormick improved an earlier draft of the introduction. Thanks also to Anna O'Leary for accommodating my requests to photocopy numerous copies of this edition in its various states. I wish also to acknowledge the University Council for Research at St. Francis Xavier University, and in particular, the Dean of Arts, Robert E. Hawkins, who had the vision to see the value of this work and the means to help facilitate its completion.

There are also those friends who have been patient over the years in allowing me to dominate too many conversations in my attempts to describe the curious activities in Tottel's printing shop in the summer of 1557, especially Kate Crawford, Jovita MacPherson, Anne Camozzi, Alison Mathie, Tiiu Poder, Jay Ross, Peter Jackson, Bill Faulkner, Dave and Mary Coyle. Finally, I want to thank David and Chris Baird, Bruce Griffen, Grant Heckman, and Geoffrey McKay who have taught me much about the relation between language and music.

I would also like to thank the editorial staff at the Arizona Center for Medieval and Renaissance Studies, including Robert E. Bjork, William Gentrup, and, Roy Rukkila for assisting in the final preparation of the text. I would especially like to thank Dr. Leslie S. B. MacCoull for her careful reading of the text and her learned contributions to the annotations and glossary.

I dedicate this book to my wife Anne, and to our children David and Sarah, whose patience, good humor, faith, and encouragement provided the support necessary to bring this work to fruition.

ABBREVIATIONS

Manuscripts

Add.	British Library, Additional 15225; 18752; 23971; 26737; 28636; 30513; 36529; 37529; 38599; 60577
Arundel Harington	British Library, Additional 28635, a transcript of the MS made by George F. Nott, c. 1810. Folio enteries in Appendix 1 are to Ruth Hughey's transcript of the manuscript owned by the Duke of Norfolk, Arundel Castle, MSS (Special Press), 'Harington MS. Temp. Eliz.' (*The Arundel Harington Manuscript of Tudor Poetry*, 2 vols. [Columbus, OH: Ohio State University Press, 1960]).
Ash.	Bodleian Library, Ashmole 48 (6933); Ashmole 176 (part 3)
Blage	Trinity College, Dublin 160 (D.2.7)
Devonshire	British Library, Additional 17492
Egerton	British Library, Egerton 2711
Harl.	British Library, Harley 78
Osborn	Yale University, Osborn music 13. The Braye Lute Book
PRO. SP	Public Record Office, London, SP 1/246
Rawl. Poet.	Bodleian Library, Rawlinson Poetry 32; 82; 85;172
Royal	British Library, Royal 7.C.ix

Books / Journals

Beal	Peter Beal, *Index of English Literary Manuscripts, Volume I: 1450–1625, Part 2: Douglas-Wyatt*. London: Mansell / New York: R.R. Bowker, 1980.
Bennett	H. S. Bennett. *English Books and Readers 1475-1557: Being a Study in The History of the Book Trade from Caxton to the Incorporation of the Stationers' Company*. 2nd ed. Cambridge: Cambridge University Press, 1969.

ELH	*English Literary History*
ELR	*English Literary Renaissance*
EMS	*English Manuscript Studies 1100-1700*
ES	*English Studies*
JMRS	*Journal of Medieval and Renaissance Studies*
MLN	*Modern Language Notes*
MLR	*Modern Language Review*
PMLA	*Publications of the Modern Language Association*
Q1	*Songes and Sonettes*. London: Richard Tottel, Colophon 5 June 1557. (STC 13860): Bodleian Library [Arch.G.f.12.1].
Q2	*Songes and Sonettes*. London: Richard Tottel, Colophon 31 July 1557. (STC 13861): British Library [Grenville 11170]; Huntington Library [no. 59482].
Q3	Songes and Sonettes. London: Richard Tottel, Colophon 31 July 1557. (STC 13862): Wren Library, Trinity College, Cambridge [Capell W.1]; Pforzheimer Collection, University of Texas at Austin [no. 506].
Ren&Ref	*Renaissance and Reformation*
RES	*Review of English Studies*
Rollins	*Tottel's Miscellany 1557–1587*. Ed. Hyder E. Rollins. 2 vols. 1928-1929; rev. ed. Cambridge, MA: Harvard University Press, 1965.
SEL	*Studies in English Literature*
SP	*Studies in Philology*
STC	*A Short-Title Catalogue of Books Printed in England, Scotland, & Ireland and of English Books Printed Abroad 1475-1640*, 2nd edition. Eds. W. A. Jackson, F.S. Ferguson, and Katharine F. Pantzer. 3 vols. London: The Bibliographical Society, 1986.
TEXT	An Interdisciplinary Annual of Textual Studies published by the Society for Textual Studies

RICHARD TOTTEL'S *SONGES AND SONETTES*: THE ELIZABETHAN VERSION

Textual Introduction

Songes and Sonettes, the first printed anthology of English poetry, was published by Richard Tottel in 1557, the same year the Stationers' Company received its royal charter, but before its later practice of licensing and listing entries of new publications in an official capacity.[1] The first reference to the title appears in the Stationers' Register in February 1583, when Tottel recorded a number of books on the subject of English common law, as well as several works of literature which he had previously printed.[2] The first quarto of *Songes and Sonettes* (STC 13860) was published on 5 June 1557; the second revised quarto (STC 13861) was published eight weeks later on 31 July

---

[1] The first clerk of the Stationers' Company, appointed in 1571, was charged with the responsibility of ensuring that the rights of stationers to copy certain books were recorded in the Company's Register. As Cyndia Susan Clegg points out, "the company clerk recorded the license in the company Register, in which each entry records the title of the copy, the namé of the stationer holding the license, the entry date, and the entrance fee" ("The Stationers' Company of London," in *The Dictionary of Literary Biography*, vol. 170, *The British Literary Book Trade, 1475–1700*, ed. James K. Bracken and Joel Silver [Detroit, Washington, DC, and London: Bruccoli Clark Layman, 1996], 275–91, here 278).

[2] Along with the law books, Tottel also registered *Songes and Sonettes* and Grimald's translation of Cicero's *De officiis*, or *Thre bokes of Duties*. Tottel seems to have been motivated to register these texts as a safeguard against piracy. "Since printing monopolies were under attack at the time by under-employed Stationers and others, perhaps Tottel wished to safe-guard his interests" (*STC*, 3: 198, Appendix B). See also Christopher A. Knott, "Richard Tottell," in *The British Literary Book Trade 1475–1700*. ed. Bracken and Silver, 308–13.

1557; and the third quarto (*STC* 13862), though also dated 31 July 1557, was published after the second and before the fourth quarto (*STC* 13863), which was published in 1559. The most recent edition of the *STC* lists the following surviving copies: one copy of Q1 in the Bodleian Library (Arch. G.f. 12.1); two copies of Q2, one in the British Library (Grenville 11170), and one in the Huntington Library (no. 59482, with C_{2-3}, O_{1-4}, P_1, Y_{2-3} replaced by leaves of Q4 [*STC* 13863], and F_{2-3}, Gg_4 in pen facsimile); and three copies of Q3: one in the Wren Library, Trinity College, Cambridge (Capell W.1), one in the Pforzheimer collection at the University of Texas at Austin, Harry Ransom Center for the Humanities (no. 506), and one in the private library of James Edwards, Washington, DC (some leaves in facsimile). By the time Tottel died in 1593, *Songes and Sonettes* had gone through eleven printings: twice in 1557; once between 1557 and 1559; twice in 1559; twice in 1565; and once each in 1567, 1574, 1585, and 1587. The standard twentieth-century edition by Hyder E. Rollins is *Tottel's Miscellany 1557–1587*, 2 vols. (Cambridge, MA: Harvard University Press, 1928–1929; rev. ed. 1965). Rollins used Q1 as his copy text and appended to it "Poems Added in the Second Edition." The present edition uses as its copy text Q2, a version distinctly different from Q1, with changes in punctuation and diction, and a new arrangement of poems. As all subsequent editions in the sixteenth century follow the arrangement of Q2, this is the version of *Songes and Sonettes* known to most Elizabethans.[3]

The First Quarto

Q1: Collation: $4°$: A–Dd_4. [\$4 signed — A_4, B_4, E_4, H_3, H_4, L_4, O_3, S_4, V_4, X_4, Y_3, Y_4, Z_4, Aa_4, Bb_4, Cc_3, Cc_4, Dd_3, Dd_4.] 108 leaves, excluding letters J, U, and W. Variants: the numeral ".i." is omitted on the first leaf of B, E, F, M, and P; K_4 is missigned as K_3; and Bb_3 is missigned as B_3. Not paginated.

   Contents: A_1^v. Title: **SONGES AND SONETTES,| written by the ryght honourable Lorde | Henry Haward late Earle of Sur-| rey, and other. |** *Apud Richardum Tottel.* **| 1557 |** *Cum privilegio.* A_1^r. "The Printer to the Reader." A_2^r– D_4^r contain poems by Surrey, with "*SVRREY.*" at the foot of D_4^r; D_4^v–M_2^v contain poems by Wyatt, with "*T. VVYATE the elder.*" following the final poem on M_2^v; M_3^r–P_4^v contain poems by Nicolas Grimald, advertised on M_3^r with the heading, "*Songes written by Nicolas Grimald.*", and concluded on P_4^v with

---

[3] For a review of the critical literature on Tottel's *Songes and Sonettes*, see Paul A. Marquis, "Recent Studies in Richard Tottel's *Songes and Sonettes*," *ELR* 28 (1998): 299–313. More recent are S. Hamrick, "Tottel's Miscellany and the English Reformation," *Criticism* 44 (2002): 329–61, and G. Waller, *Writing Under Tyranny: English Literature and the Henrician Reformation* (Oxford: Oxford University Press, 2005), chap. 17, "Wyatt, Surrey, and the Reinvention of English Poetry," 414–32.

initials "*N.G.* " at mid-page; Q_1^r–Cc_3^r contain poems by anonymous authors, introduced by the heading, "*Vncertain auctours.*"; Cc_3^v–Dd_1^v contain additional poems by Surrey introduced as "*Other Songes and Sonettes written by | the earle of Surrey.*", and followed by "*finis*" on Dd_1^v; and finally, beginning on Dd_2^r–Dd_3^r, there is a cluster of six poems by Wyatt, introduced by "*Other Songes and Sonettes written by Sir Thomas wiat the elder.*", followed by "FINIS". The colophon is found on Dd_3^v: **Imprinted at London in flete strete | within temple barre, at the sygne of the | hand and starre, by Richard Tottel | the fift day of June | An. 1557. | *Cum privilegio ad impri- | mendum solum.***

Q1 contains 271 poems, numbered 1 to 271 in Rollins's edition, a scheme that will be used in this Introduction when referring to Q1. The poems are divided into four large sections and two smaller sections. Poems by Henry Howard, the Earl of Surrey, begin the compilation (1–36); followed by poems by Thomas Wyatt, the Elder (37–127); by Nicholas Grimald (128–167); by the Uncertain Auctours (168–261); before two short clusters by Surrey and Wyatt (262–265 and 266–271).

Running-titles: After A_2^r, the full running-title, "*Songes and Sonettes.*", is divided so that "*Songes*" is found on verso leaves, while "*and Sonettes.*" is found on recto leaves. On pages with section headings, namely M_3^r, Q_1^r, and Cc_3^v, there are no running titles, with the exception of Dd_2^r. There are numerous instances when "*Songes*" is printed with a point: A_2^v, A_3^v, A_4^v, B_1^v, B_2^v, B_3^v, B_4^v, D_3^v, D_4^v, E_1^v, E_2^v, E_3^v, E_4^v, G_1^v, G_2^v, G_3^v, G_4^v, H_1^v, H_2^v, H_3^v, H_4^v, K_1^v, K_2^v, K_3^v, K_4^v, L_1^v, L_2^v, L_3^v, L_4^v, M_1^v, M_3^v, N_1^v, N_2^v, N_3^v, N_4^v, O_1^v, O_2^v, O_3^v, O_4^v, P_1^v, P_2^v, P_3^v, Q_3^v, R_1^v, R_2^v, R_3^v, R_4^v, S_3^v, S_4^v, T_1^v, T_2^v, T_3^v, T_4^v, V_3^v, V_4^v, X_1^v, X_2^v, X_3^v, X_4^v, Y_1^v, Y_4^v, Z_1^v, Z_2^v, Z_3^v, Z_4^v, Aa_1^v, Aa_2^v, Bb_1^v, Bb_2^v, Bb_3^v, Bb_4^v, Cc_2^v, and Dd_2^v. There are several instances where "*and Sonettes*" is printed without a point: R_1^r, R_2^r, T_1^r, T_2^r, Xi^r, X_2^r, Z_1^r, Z_2^r, Bb_1^r, Bb_2^r, and Dd_1^r. The running-titles are reversed on D_1^r and D_2^v, and on D_1^v and D_2^r, with the verso titles appearing on the recto pages and the recto titles on the verso pages. "*Songes*" appears, sometimes pointed, sometimes not, on both the recto and verso leaves of the section of poems by Nicolas Grimald, from M_4^r to P_4^v. Irregularities in the running-titles are caused by idiosyncrasies in composing, though the absence of points could be explained by their failure to ink.

Identification of the skeletons has been based on an analysis of the running titles, with or without points.

I:	A (o/i) B (o/i) D (o/i) E (o/i) G (o/i) H (o/i) K (o/i) L (o/i)
II:	C (o/i) F (o/i) I (o/i)
III:	M (o)
IV:	M (i)
V:	N (o/i) O (i) P (i)
VI:	O (o) P (o)
VII:	Q (o/i) S (o/i) V (o/i) Y (o/i) Aa (o/i) Cc (o/i)
VIII:	R (o/i) T (o/i) X (o/i) Z (o/i) Bb (o/i) Dd (o/i)

Eight skeletons in total were used to print the text. A schedule of the skeletons of the outer and inner formes based on the running-titles suggests that the printing process of the text employed two presses and two compositors. Skeleton I, used for the outer and inner formes, prints two quires for each one pressed by skeleton II. This 2:1 ratio continues until the end of the Wyatt section and the beginning of the Grimald section at M_2^v and M_3^r. Two new skeletons (III and IV) are used for the transition from Wyatt's to Grimald's poems, then two more skeletons (V and VI) continue the regular pattern of printing Grimald's poems in four quires, which the compositor thought consisted only of songs and not of sonnets. The poems by Uncertain Auctours are printed without interruption in skeletons VII and VIII, accommodating the inclusion of the two short clusters of poems by Surrey and Wyatt at the end of Q1.

It appears that the sequence of skeletons is not related to the sequence of authors in the book. Poems by Surrey and the Uncertain Auctours conclude on recto leaves, D_4^r and Cc_3^r, respectively, while poems by Wyatt, and again by Surrey near the end of the text, begin at the top of verso leaves D_4^v and Cc_3^v, respectively. The printer of Q1 is not practising good form when he begins a major section on a verso, though he is saving paper, and thus avoiding unnecessary expense by using the white space of what would otherwise have been an empty verso leaf. A more careful printer would have ensured that authorial sections commenced on recto leaves and concluded on verso leaves, and that the running-titles reflected these changes. Such is not the case with Q1, in which the running-titles run along in their curious way with little or no reference to the poems that appear on the pages they head. The evidence, then, supports the claim that once Tottel committed himself to the task of printing a collection of poems, he acquired a number of lyrics by Surrey, Wyatt, and Grimald, then added the lyrics by the Uncertain Auctours, before acquiring several more poems by Surrey and Wyatt. No wonder Q2 followed shortly on the heels of Q1; the collection needed an editor to straighten it out.

Catchwords in Q1 are employed on every page, except on Z_3^v and on the pages at the end of each authorial section: D_4^r, M_2^v, P_4^v, Cc_3^r, and Dd_1^v. The following discrepancies occur:

Signature	Catchword/Text	Forme	Skeleton
F_1^v / F_2^r	if / In	inner	II
G_4^v / H_1^r	Since / Sins	inner	I
L_3^r / L_3^v	I am / I can	outer/inner	I
M_4^v / N_1^r	Or / Oh	outer	III and V
T_1^r / T_1^v	Nothing/ Thus	outer/inner	VIII
X_3^r / X_3^v	Says / Say	outer/inner	VIII

The text is correct in all cases, and the catchwords are incorrect, with one possible exception. While "Nothing" on T_1^r would have in some sense strengthened the line on T$_1$^{v}: "Nothing am I bothe in ioye and in distresse" (187.11), the text's "Thus" indicates a logical turn to the argument. Further, when the compositor sets the word "Sins" on H$_1$^{r} for the catchword "Since" on G4v, he provides further resonance to three other uses of the word "sins" in the poem. "Sins"—like "syth"—is old-fashioned, but preferred by one compositor. The correction of the catchword "Says" on X$_3$^{r} to "Say" on X$_3$^{v} indicates the compositor's respect for the relation between grammatical form and prosodic sense. At least half of the discrepancies between catchwords and text occur at the point of transition between the outer and inner formes of leaves, while one occurs between skeletons III and IV.

The size of the press run invites consideration, for it could explain in part why Q2 followed so soon after Q1. W.W. Greg reminds scholars of an ordinance by the Stationers' Company some thirty years later, in 1587, which limited "the number of copies to be printed from one setting to 1250 for ordinary works." He suggests that this ordinance "very possibly did nothing more than give binding force to a generally recognized custom."[4] H.S. Bennett finds that while secular works could run from 100 to 1000,[5] until well into the sixteenth century "only very special reasons" would "persuade a printer to print more than 600–700 copies of any ordinary work."[6] A modest press run of *Songes and Sonettes* made good business sense; it would have taken less time to impress and would have cost less to produce. It would also allow Tottel an opportunity to test the public's interest in the compilation, which, if vigorous enough, he would satisfy expeditiously with a second edition—"in more hereafter," as he states in his preface to the reader.

---

[4] W.W. Greg, "Tottel's Miscellany," *The Library*, n.s. 5 (1904): 113–33, here 123.

[5] In the preface (K$_4$r) to John Dee's *General and rare memorials pertayning to the perfecte arte of navigation* in 1577, the author states that only 100 copies were printed of this work. This number is amended in the manuscript of the Huntington Library copy to 50 (*STC* 6459). In 1493–1494, Richard Pynson printed 600 copies of five books, including *Dives and pauper*, the *Fall of princes*, and *Festial*, a service book (H. R. Plomer, "Two Lawsuits of Richard Pynson," *The Library*, n.s. 10 [1909]: 115–33). Works that had a higher number of copies printed were either commissioned by a patron, small in size, or propaganda for a smear campaign of some sort (Bennett, 225–28). Wendy Wall suggests that in England in the mid-sixteenth century "the average print run consisted of only 300 to 400 copies" ("Authorship and the Material Conditions of Writing," in *The Cambridge Companion to English Literature 1500–1600*, ed. Arthur F. Kinney [Cambridge and New York: Cambridge University Press, 2000], 64–89, here 72). See also R. B. McKerrow, *An Introduction to Bibliography for Literary Students* (Oxford: Clarendon Press, 1927), 130–33.

[6] "Matthew's version" of the Bible in 1537 was provided a press run of 1500 copies (J. A. Kingdom, *Incidents in the Lives of T. Poyntz and R. Grafton* [1895], part ii, 29), cited in Bennett, 225.

The Second Quarto

In Q2, published eight weeks later, the order of poems is altered significantly. Six sections of poems are reduced to four. Thirty-nine new poems by Uncertain Auctours are added, and the entire section moved to the penultimate position in the text. Thirty poems by Nicholas Grimald included in Q1 are omitted in Q2, while his ten remaining poems are transferred to the end of the text and his initials are substituted for his name at the beginning of the group. Four poems by Surrey, and six by Wyatt placed at the end of Q1 are rearranged and incorporated into the main body of poems by their respective authors. The significance of the rearrangement of these poems is discussed fully in the Critical Introduction below.

Q2 Collation: 4°: A–Gg$_4$ [$2 signed – A$_1$] + A$_3$, C$_3$, C$_4$, Cc$_3$, Ee$_3$, Ff$_3$. 120 leaves, excluding letters J, U, and W. Variants occur with T.$_2$, ; Y$_{11}$.; and Dd. Paginated.

Contents: A$_1$^{r}. Title: **SONGES AND SONETTES, | written by the right honorable Lorde | Henry Haward late Earle of Sur-| rey, and other. |** *Apud. Richardum Tottel. | Cum privilegio ad impri- | mendum solum.*. A$_1$^{v}. "*To the reder.*"; A$_2$^{r}–E$_2$^{v} contain Surrey's poems, with "*SVRREY.*" at the foot of E$_2$^{v}; E$_3$^{r}–N$_1$^{v} contain poems by "*T. VVYATE the elder.*", designated at the foot of N$_1$^{v}; N$_2$^{r} to the top of Ff$_1$^{r} contain poems by "Uncertain Auctours," introduced on N$_2$^{r} by the heading, "*Songes and Sonettes of | Uncertain auctours.*"; and finally, Ff$_1$^{r}–Gg$_1$^{v} contain poems by Nicolas Grimald, introduced by "*Songes written by N.G.*" and concluded with initials "*N.G.*"; Gg$_2$^{r} to Gg$_3$^{v} contain "*The table.*", and G$_4$^{r}, the Colophon: **[ornament] Imprinted at London in flete | strete within Temple barre, at the | sygne of the hand and starre, | by Richard Tottell | the .xxxi. day of July. | An. 1557. | *Cum privilegio ad impri-| mendum solum.***

Q2 contains 280 poems, which have been numbered 1 to 280 and reproduced in the following edition: poems by Henry Howard, the Earl of Surrey (1–41); by Thomas Wyatt, the Elder (42–137); by Uncertain Auctours (138–270); and by Nicolas Grimald (271–280). "*The table*" in Q2 lists the opening phrase of the first line of each poem in alphabetical order, followed by the folio page on which the poem commences.

Running-Titles: The full title, "*Songes and Sonettes* ", is found on A$_1$^{r}; thereafter, "*Songes*" is found on all verso leaves, except on A$_2$^{v}, C$_1$^{v}, and C$_2$^{v}, where "*Songes.*" is pointed. On all recto leaves, the running title, "*and Sonettes.*", is found, except on C$_4$^{r}, D$_3$^{r}, D$_4$^{r}, E$_2$^{r}, G$_3$^{r}, G$_4$^{r}, H$_1$^{r}, K$_3$^{r}, K$_4$^{r}, L$_1$^{r}, N$_4$^{r}, O$_1$^{r}, O$_2$^{r}, Q$_3$^{r}, Q$_4$^{r}, R$_1$^{r}, and R$_2$^{r}, where "*and Sonettes*" is not pointed. Variants in pointing of the running title occur on Z$_1$^{r}, Z$_2$^{r}, and Dd$_3$^{r}, as "*and Sonettes,*". Spelling variants of the running-title occur on A$_3$^{r}, as "*Sonnets.*"; on B$_1$^{r} and B$_2$^{r}, as "*and Sonnettes.*"; on C$_3$^{r}, as "*and Sone*"; and on X$_4$^{r}, where a possessive form of the title occurs, "*and Sonette's.*" Finally, on Gg$_2$^{r} and Gg$_2$^{v}, the title "*Tbe table*" is given, whereas on G$_3$^{r} and G$_3$^{v} it is corrected to "*The table*".

Identification of the skeletons has been based on an analysis of the running titles, with or without points, and on the use of *Fo.*; *Fo* ∧; *Fol.*; and *Fol* ∧. Missing points after words in the running titles and in the various forms of the abbreviated folio references are caused by idiosyncrasies in composing, which could include inadequate inking.

I:	A (o)
II:	A (i)
III:	B (o) D (o) E (o) G (o) H (o) K (o) L (o) N (o) O (o) Q (o) R (o) S (o) V (o) X (o) Z (o) Bb (o) Dd (o) Ee (o)
IV:	B (i) D (i) E (i) G (i) H (i) K (i) L (i) N (i) O (i) Q (i) R (i) S (i) V (i) X (i) Z (i) Bb (i) Dd (i) Ee (i)
V:	C (o)
VI:	C (i)
VII:	F (o) I (o) M (o) P (o) T (o) Y (o) Aa (o) Cc (o) Ff (o) Gg (o)
VIII:	F (i) I (i) M (i) P (i) T (i) Y(i) Aa (i) Cc (i) Ff (i) Gg (i)

Eight separate skeletons can be identified, but the skeletons used in A (o/i) and in C (o/i) are used nowhere else in the text. After sheet A, the compositors apparently had a sense of how the whole text would be impressed. Skeletons III and IV alternate uniformly in the setting of the outer and inner formes of twice as many sheets as skeletons VII and VIII, which were sorted more slowly. Another press was opened for sheet C, of which anomalies include badly inked running titles, missing type from the title of C_3^r, and a crowded text on the left hand margin on C_3^r and C_4^r. This new press was probably used again, with different compositors and different skeletons, for sheet F. The decision seems to have been made to regularize this second press that was to machine 8 out of the remaining 24 sheets. To achieve a textual sequence from one skeleton to another, casting off—the division of the text into page units before composition began, not necessarily with regard to the poetical content of the poems—would have been desirable. One could surmise, then, that two principal compositors were involved in composing Q2. They would have been responsible for setting formes with skeletons III, IV, VII, and VIII, with minor assistance provided by one, or perhaps two different compositors, responsible for skeletons I and II, and VII and VIII. This analysis suggests that the printing process of Q2 was more deliberate than that of Q1.

Pagination: Commencing on A_2^r, leaves are numbered in the upper right corner of recto pages, designated *Fo.* or *Fol.* from 2 to 117, with "*The table*" pages not foliated. Pointing is either complete or incomplete: *Fo.* appears with a period after the abbreviation and the number, on pages *2, 13–20, 26, 28–32, 37–39, 41–44, 49, 50, 53–56, 61–62, 65–67, 69, 77–78, 81–82, 89–90, 99, 106–108, 110–112,* and *117*; *Fo.,* with a period after the abbreviation, but not after the number, appears on pages *4, 70, 79–80, 91–92, 100* and *109*; *Fo* ∧, without a period after the abbreviation, but with a period following the number, appears on pages *27, 40, 51, 52, 63–64, 71–72, 83–84, and 97–98; Fo* $_{\wedge}$, without a period after the abbreviation and without a period after the number, appears on page *68; Fol.*, with a period after the abbreviation and the number, appears on pages *6, 8, 21, 34, 48, 74, 85–86, 93, 96, 101–102,* and *113–116; Fol.*, with a period after the abbreviation, but not after the number, appears on pages *24, 36, 45–47, 57–58, 60, 73, 75–76, 87, 94, 103, 104* and *105; Fol* $_{\wedge}$, without a period after the abbreviation but with one following the number, appears on pages *22, 23, 59,* and *88;* and *Fol* $_{\wedge}$, without a period after the abbreviation or the number, appears on page *95.* One notes the curious error in the folio of G_1^r: the numbers 2 and 5 have been reversed, and the period has been placed between them and not after *Fo.* Also, *Fol. 31.* has been used for *Fol. 33.*, and *Fol. 33.* has been used for *Fol. 35.* Finally, folio numbers *3, 5, 7, 9, 10, 11, 12, 118, 119,* and *120* are missing.

Catchwords are employed on every page, except on E_2^v, H_4^r, Ee_1^r, and Gg_1^v. The following discrepancies occur:

Signature	Catchword/Text	Forme	Skeleton
C_2^v / C_3^r	Yo / Your	outer	V
H_3^r / H_3^v	Since / Sins	outer/inner	III and IV
H_3^v / H_3^r	Ye / Yee	outer/inner	III and IV
I_3^r / I_3^v	You / Then	outer/inner	VII and VIII
R_4^v / S_1^r	Away / A way	outer	III
Ff_2^r / Ff_2^v	Doe / Doway	inner/outer	VIII and VII
Ff_3^v / Ff_4^r.	A match / Amatch	inner	VIII

While most of the discrepancies between catchwords and text in Q1 have been corrected in Q2, other inconsistencies occur. While the compositor of the inner forme of skeleton IV, signature H_3^v, exploits the pun in the word "Sins" in the text of poem 84, the compositor of the outer forme of skeleton III, signature H_3^r, links the catchword with the adverb in (84.3), "since," spelled "sins" in Q1. In most cases, the text in Q2 corrects the catchword. From a compositor's perspective, however, "Doe" could have been a legitimate mnemonic key for "Doway." The discrepancy between the outer and inner formes of skeletons VII and VIII, "You" and "Then," may have been caused by a miscalculation which occurred in casting off the number of lines that would fit on I_3^r, for the catchword, "You," keys the word on the second line of I_3^v. There is one clear case in which the text is incorrect. While the inner forme of skeleton VIII records the key, "A match," the compositor incorrectly condenses the phrase into a compound word in the text.

The bibliographical differences between Q1 and Q2 suggest that the second edition of Tottel's *Songes and Sonettes* eliminates most of the inconsistencies in the signatures and running-titles and provides pagination. Q2 is a more accessible text than Q1. For example, the 26 variant signatures in Q1 are reduced to 9 in Q2. There are approximately 50 mispointed running-titles in Q1; only 22 in Q2. In Q1, there are 108 leaves and 6 variant catchwords, while Q2 has 120 leaves and 7 variant catchwords. The compositors of Q2 had an advantage in that they were able to work with Q1 before them; nevertheless, given the large number of revisions that were introduced to Q2, including the rearrangement of lyrics, the vigilance and professionalism of Tottel's editorial staff must be recognized.[7] The greatest assistance to the reader was the inclusion of the pagination throughout the text, and *The Table* appended to Q2.

The Third Quarto

Q3: Collation: $4°$: A–Gg$_4$ [\$2 signed – A$_1$ and Gg$_2$; +A$_3$, B$_3$, C$_3$, C$_4$]. 120 leaves, excluding J, U, and W. Variants occur between the fonts used for T$_1$^{r}. and T$_2$^{r}, and the punctuation of Bb.$_2$^{r}, and Dd,$_2$^{r}. Paginated.

Contents: A$_1$^{r}: Title: **SONGES AND SONETTES | written by the right honorable Lorde | Henry Haward late Earle of Sur- | rey, and other. |** *Apud Richardum Tottell. | Cum privilegio ad imprimendum | solum.* 1557.; A$_1$^{v}. "*To the reader.*"; A$_2$^{r}–E$_2$^{v} contain Surrey's poems, with "*SVRREY.*" at the foot of E$_2$^{v}; E$_3$^{r}–N$_1$^{v}, poems by *T. VVYATE the elder.*", designated at the foot of N$_1$^{v}; N$_2$^{v} to the top of Ff$_1$^{r}, poems by "Uncertain Auctours," introduced at the top of N$_2$^{r} by "*Songes and Sonettes of Vncertain auctours.*"; and finally, "*Songes written by N.G.*" introduces poems by Nicolas Grimald on Ff$_1$^{r}, which conclude on Gg$_1$^{v} after the initials "N.G."; Gg$_2$^{r} to Gg$_3$^{v} contain "*The table.*", and G$_4$^{r}, the Colophon: **Imprinted at London in fletestreet | within Temple barre. at the signe of the | hand and starre, by Richard Tot-| till, the .xxxi. day of July. | Anno.** 1557. *Cum privilegio ad impri- | mendum solum.*

The relation between the colophon of Q3, which lists 31 July 1557 as its date of publication, and the text of Q3, requires explanation.[8] From an analysis

---

[7] In 1556, Tottel's compositors produced an impressive printing of Grimald's translation of Cicero's *Duties*. Gerald O'Gorman suggests that the "textual uniformity" of Grimald's translation of Cicero's *Duties* depended on the fact that Tottel's compositors were "trained to respond to the exacting requirements of law texts," and so "by temperament and experience were faithful to copy-text accidentals" (*Marcus Tullius Ciceroes thre bokes of duties, to Marcus his sonne, turned oute of latine into english, by Nicolas Grimalde*, ed. Gerald O'Gorman, RETS [London and Toronto: Associated University Presses, 1990], 18). Given the importance of accuracy and uniformity in law texts, and the fact that his reputation as a printer of legal texts depended on the quality of accurate printing, Tottel could well have directed his most experienced compositors to his law texts.

[8] W.W. Greg suggests that as far as Q2 and Q3 are concerned there are either "two successive editions, one a close reprint of the other, or else a work set up in duplicate"

of entries in the *STC*, it is clear that Tottel's standard practice was to reprint books, especially calendars of English common law, yearbooks, statutes, and books of tenures, using the colophons of those titles printed at earlier dates. At least two of the books by Tottel, the colophons of which claim 1557 as the date of publication, were printed in later years, but impressed with colophons of the original 1557 date.[9] This practice continued throughout Tottel's career, for, as the listings in the *STC* reveal, forty-four texts were reprinted using colophons from earlier editions, twenty of which were published initially in 1556.[10] These were small books of a few pages, but essential reading for those employed in the law profession or simply curious about the constantly changing legal environment in Tudor England.[11] By retaining the original date of the colophon in later reprints of law books, Tottel most likely assumed he was insuring his copyright and providing a sense of authenticity for his reader. One can argue, then, that when Tottel wished to reprint *Songes and Sonettes* after 31 July 1557, and before 1559, a slightly revised Q2 was given to his compositor to reprint,

---

("Tottel's Miscellany," 120–23). If the editions are "successive," then, as Rollins points out, the colophon of Q3 "may possibly be only a mechanical reproduction of the colophon" of Q2 (2: 13, 19). Indeed, it is difficult to see how Q3 could be a "duplicate" of Q2, given that many readings in Q2 are discarded in Q3 in favor of the old readings of Q1.

[9] I wish to acknowledge with thanks the assistance of Dr. Peter Blayney in calling to my attention Tottel's practice of reprinting the dates of earlier colophons in later editions. The two texts printed after 1557, but employing colophons of books published in 1557 are *STC* 9809 and *STC* 9863, both printed first in 1557 and again in 1566.

[10] These forty-four texts are interspersed between *STC* numbers 9582 to 9967, the entries of which record the publication of yearbooks, and *STC* 15737 and 15774, where the record of translations of French law books by Sir Thomas Littleton, published by Tottel and various other printers, is recorded. These entries by no means exhaust Tottel's record in the *STC*. For a complete list, see the *STC*, Vol. 3, Index 1: "Printers and Publishers," under Richard Tottell (169–70), where no fewer than 719 entries are recorded in his name. As the editors of the *STC* acknowledge, "The date of some of Tottell's editions is often repeated in subsequent ones or is entirely erroneous. Although an attempt to establish the true dates has been made with the yearbooks (*STC* numbers between 9551 and 9967), multiple editions of the same date under other headings have not been re-examined" (169).

[11] In 1553, four years before the publication of *Songes and Sonettes*, Tottel had secured the license to publish books pertaining to English common law. The income generated by the license would have afforded him the opportunity to publish works of literature for which an audience was less assured.

and that following what he took to be the house style in the matter of the colophon, the compositor carefully set the date that was before him.[12]

Running-Titles: The full title, "*Songes and Sonettes*", is not found on any of the leaves after the title page. "*Songes*" is found on A_2^v, and thereafter on the verso leaves, and "*and Sonettes.*" is found on A_2^r, and thereafter on the recto leaves (but without a point on R_1^r, R_2^r, X_1^r, X_2^r, Bb_1^r, Bb_2^r, Ff_1^r, Ff_2^r, and with a comma following "*Sonettes,*" on C_3^r, C_4^r, E_1^r, K_1^r and K_2^r). The section heading, "*Songes and Sonettes of Uncertain auctours.*", is found on N_2^r, but not the running-title. On Gg_2^r to Gg_3^v, the title, "*The table.*", is found.

Identification of the skeletons has been based on an analysis of the running-titles, with or without points, and on the use of folio abbreviations *Fo,* with or without points, followed by the numbers of the page, with or without points. Missing points after words in the running titles and in the various forms of the abbreviated folio references are caused by idiosyncrasies in composing, which could include inadequate inking. The schedule of the punctuation of the running-titles and the folio abbreviations and numbers listed in the skeletons of inner and outer formes of Q3 reads as follows:

I:	A (o)
II:	A (i) N (i)
III:	B (o)
IV:	B (i) D (o) E (o/i) F (o/i) N (o) T (o)
V:	C (o) T (i)
VI:	C (i) I (o/i) K (o/i) P (o/i) R (o/ i) X (o/i) Bb (o/i) Ff (i/o)
VII:	D (i)
VIII:	G (o/i) H (o/i) L (o/i) M (o/i) O (o/i) Q (o/i) S (o/i) V (o/i) Y (o/i) Z (o/i) Aa (o/i) Cc (o/i) Dd (o/i) Ee (o/i) Gg (o/i)

Pagination: Commencing on A_2^r, leaves are numbered in the upper right corner of recto pages, designated *Fo.,* or *Fo* $_\wedge$, with or without a point after the abbreviation, followed by numbers, with or without punctuation, from 2 to 117, with the pages on which "*The table*" is printed, not foliated. *Fo.,* with a period after the number, appears on folios *2, 4, 6, 8, 13–14, 23–30, 32–33, 35–36, 41–43, 45–46, 55, 60, 63–64, 75, 78–[76], 87–90, 93–94, 105–106, 108–112;* *Fo.,* with a period after the abbreviation but no period after the number, appears on folios *9–12, 17–22, 33–34, 37–40, 47, 49–53, 56–58, 61–62, 65–68,*

---

[12] Tottel did not publish as many yearbooks in 1557 as in 1556, but it was a busy year for the publication of literature. As well as the nine yearbooks published in 1557, Tottel also printed and published two editions of *Songes and Sonettes;* books 2 and 4 of Surrey's translation of Virgil's *Aeneid;* Thomas More's *Works,* a massive project of 1458 leaves, all of which—except the first quire which was produced by the printer Cawood—were printed by Tottel; as well as Rastell's *Correccion of all the Statutes,* amounting to 550 folios.

71–74, 76–77, 80–84, 91–92, 95–100, 103–104, 107, and 113–116 . Fo $_\wedge$, not followed by a period after the abbreviation, but with a period after the number, appears on folios 16, 31, 54, 59, 69, 70, 85, 86, 101–102, and 117. Fo $_\wedge$, with neither a period following the abbreviation, nor one following the number, appears on folios 44 and 48. Incorrectly printed: Fo. 79. is misnumbered Fo. 76.; numbers Fo. 114. and Fo. 116 are interchanged. Incompletely inked: 15 after Fo. is all but invisible. Finally, there is no pagination on leaves 3, 5, 7, 118, and 119.

Catchwords are employed on every page, except E_2^v, N_1^v, Gg_1^v, and Gg_2^r. The following discrepancies occur:

Signature	Catchword/Text	Forme	Skeleton
B_1^r / B_1^v	Flowe / flowring	outer/inner	III and IV
E_3^v / E_4^r	Tye / The	inner	IV
I_3^r / I_3^v	You / Then	outer/inner	VI
O_4^v / P_1^r	Whic / which	outer	VI
R_4^v / S_1^r	A way / Away	outer	VI and VIII
Aa_2^v / Aa_3^r	An /Another	outer	VIII
Ee_4^v / Ff_1^r	On / One	outer	VIII
Ff_2^r / Ff_2^v	Doe /Doway	outer/inner	VI
Ff_3^v / Ff_4^r	A match /Amatch	inner	VI

Several discrepancies between catchwords and the text of Q2 were corrected in Q3, though there are four instances where Q3 corresponds to Q2. Most of the uncorrected discrepancies occur in skeleton VI, whose compositor apparently was less attentive to the task of correction. There are five new inconsistencies between catchword and text in Q3, and in each case, the text corrects the catchword.

Manuscript Sources

Of the 280 poems in the collection, seven are to be found also in printed sources; the great majority come — so far as we now know — from manuscript sources.[13] There are three main manuscripts that contain versions of many of the poems found in *Songes and Sonettes*:[14] the Egerton MS; the Devonshire MS; and the Arundel Harington MS. In the Egerton MS, there are 120 poems

---

[13] Wyatt's poems 70, 84, and 91, in Q2, appeared in the first edition of *The Court of Venus*, circa 1538 (Beal, 596, 606–7). As elaborated below, Surrey's poems 31, 33, and 35, in Q2, were printed before 1557. Q2's poem 207 was printed earlier in editions of Chaucer's poems by Pynson (1526), and Thynne (1532, 1542, and 1545).

[14] As indicated below, several scholars have argued for a direct link between these manuscripts and *Songes and Sonettes*, though none has established the manuscripts as

by Wyatt, loosely arranged according to genre and theme, with several poems revised in his hand.[15] Sometime before Wyatt's death in 1542, the manuscript came into the possession of John Harington of Stepney, who not only collected the works of early sixteenth-century poets, but "improved" them through revision.[16] The Devonshire MS, at one time a possession of the Howard family,[17] contains the work of approximately two dozen poets whose poems were gathered over a period of 35 years, from 1525 to 1559.[18] Only one poem by Surrey can be found in the manuscript, but as many as 122 poems have been attributed to Wyatt, which lends credence to A. K. Foxwell's earlier claim that the

---

the copy texts for Tottel's book. It is probable, however, that Tottel had access to a number of poems that were copied from the manuscripts themselves.

[15] Sonnet translations are generally followed by epigrams, epitaphs, elegies, satires, and Psalm translations, voicing a trajectory of concerns, from secular love to spiritual salvation, which loosely parallels the thematic contours of Petrarch's *Rime Sparse*. See especially Joost Daalder, "Are Wyatt's Poems in Egerton MS 2711 in Chronological Order?" *ES* 69 (1988): 205–23. Also see R.A. Rebholz, *Sir Thomas Wyatt: The Complete Poems* (New Haven and London: Yale University Press, 1978), 12.

[16] In fact, Nicolas Grimald's hand can be seen in the revisions of at least ten poems at the beginning of the manuscript. Grimald may have acted as an intermediary between Harington and Tottel.

[17] Henry Howard, the Earl of Surrey, or perhaps Henry Fitzroy, the illegitimate son of Henry VIII, likely had access to the manuscript during their time at Windsor Castle, in 1531 and early 1532 (Raymond Southall, "The Devonshire Manuscript Collection of Early Tudor Poetry 1532–41," *RES* 15 [1964]: 145). The hands of three women who attended the Henrician court have been identified in the manuscript: Lady Margaret Douglas, the niece of Henry VIII; Mary Shelton, the cousin of Anne Boleyn; and Mary Howard, Duchess of Richmond, sister of the poet. See Helen Baron, "Mary (Howard) Fitzroy's Hand in the Devonshire Manuscript," *RES*, n.s. 45 (1944): 318–35; and Elizabeth Heale, "Women and the Courtly Love Lyric: The Devonshire MS (BL Additional 17492)," *MLR* 90 (1995): 296–313. Paul G. Remley argues that "as a private document in which some of Henry [VIII's] disillusioned subjects were able to give voice to their dissent," the Devonshire manuscript circulated quietly among a small circle of friends as a private collection ("Mary Shelton and Her Tudor Literary Milieu," in *Rethinking the Henrician Era: Essays on Early Tudor Texts and Contexts*, ed. Peter C. Herman [Urbana and Chicago: University of Illinois Press, 1994], 54). See also Agnes K. Foxwell, *A Study of Sir Thomas Wyatt's Poems* (London: University of London Press, 1911).

[18] The contents involve approximately 184 courtly verses in various states: fragmented jottings, ciphers, anagrams, and expressions of praise. There is still some dispute about how many poems exist in the manuscript, a problem caused by the fact that the ends of some poems and the beginnings of others are not clear. Julia Boffey, for example, suggests that there are 167 courtly lyrics (*Manuscripts of English Courtly Love Lyrics in the Later Middle Ages*, Manuscript Studies 1 [Woodbridge, Suffolk: D.S. Brewer, 1985], 8–9).

Devonshire MS was originally Wyatt's.[19] The Arundel Harington MS, containing approximately 324 poems, under the direction of the same John Harington, is the most important manuscript source for *Songes and Sonettes*.[20] The manuscript is arranged authorially, with poems by Harington, Surrey, Wyatt, and anonymous authors.[21] In the Surrey section, poems are arranged so that secular themes are followed by translations of Psalms and Ecclesiastes.

Some of the poems in *Songes and Sonettes* are found nowhere else but Tottel's text. Of the forty-one poems attributed to Surrey in Q2, for example, fourteen are currently unlocated in early manuscript copies: nos. 2, 5, 10, 14, 20, 21, 22, 23, 25, 26, 28, 39, 40, and 41. Versions of the remaining twenty-seven poems are found in sixteen manuscripts, none of which is a direct source for any one of the poems in Tottel.[22] Q2's poem 33 appears with variants in the

---

[19] Beal, 589. Foxwell's account of the origins of the manuscript are found in her *A Study of Sir Thomas Wyatt's Poems*, Appendix A. See also Arthur Marotti, *Manuscript, Print, and the English Renaissance Lyric* (Ithaca and London: Cornell University Press, 1995), who suggests that the Devonshire manuscript "best demonstrates the immersion of [Wyatt's] verse in a collection of miscellaneous poetry developing within a distinct social group" (38).

[20] Conceived around 1540, the Arundel Harington MS was used as a storehouse of mid-Tudor and Elizabethan verse until about 1600. In his comparison of the Arundel Harington MS with the Egerton MS and *Songes and Sonettes*, Richard Harrier argues that John Harington of Stepney most likely also edited the collection of poems eventually printed by Tottel in 1557 (*The Canon of Sir Thomas Wyatt's Poetry* [Cambridge, MA: Harvard University Press, 1975], 19–20).

[21] Ruth Hughey argues that this manuscript plays a pivotal role in the relation between Tottel's *Songes and Sonettes* and the Devonshire and Egerton manuscripts. As the poems are revised and copied from one manuscript to another, Hughey argues, they undergo a process of selection and distillation. An analysis of the variants among the poems in the Egerton and the Arundel Harington manuscripts reveals a "progressive continuity in editorial principle" (58), which leads to the development of the iambic line that emerges strongly in Tottel's *Songes and Sonettes*. Hughey suggests that alterations between the Egerton and the Arundel Harington manuscript were made by "someone with a definite theory about rhythm" which changed the line most often into more regular iambics (49). "In other words, the Tottel text may have emerged by a kind of school, or group, with the revisions of the AH text contributing" (*The Arundel Harington Manuscript of Tudor Poetry*, ed. Ruth Hughey, 2 vols. [Columbus, OH: Ohio State University Press, 1960], 1:58).

[22] Seven British Library manuscripts have been identified by F. M. Padelford: Egerton; Harl. 78; Hargrave 205; Devonshire; Arundel Harington; Add. 28636; and Add. 36529 ("The Manuscript Poems by Henry Howard, Earl of Surrey," *Anglia* 29 [1906]: 273–337). William A. Ringler, Jr., has identified five manuscripts: Osborn MS; Royal MS; Add. MS 30513; Blage MS; and PRO. SP (*Bibliography and Index of English Verse in Manuscript 1501–1558* [London: Mansell, 1992]). Manuscripts and print copies of Surrey's poems in Q2 are listed in Beal (533–42). Beal also notes that British

Egerton MS; poems 17, 32, 35, 232, are found in Harl. 78; poem 17 is found again in the Devonshire MS and parts of it are found, accompanied by musical notations, in Add. MS 30513 and PRO. SP; nos. 1, 4, 9, 19, 27, 29, and 38 are in the Arundel Harington MS; while poems 1 and lines 1–30, 33–50 of poem 4 are found also in Add. MS 36529, which contains versions of fourteen other poems by Surrey: nos. 3, 6, 7, 8, 11, 12, 13, 15, 24, 31, 33, 34, 36, and 37. Poem 4 is also found in the Blage MS. The Osborn MS contains the beginning of Surrey's poems 16, 18, and 30, while the Royal MS contains the first two stanzas of poem 18. The Hargrave MS. 205 contains Surrey's translation of Book IV of Virgil's *Aeneid*. Though Tottel obviously valued the poems he included in *Songes and Sonettes*, he did not include all the works by the authors available in print. He applied selective principles even here. [23]

In Q2's poem 35, Surrey's persona proclaims that Wyatt was the premier poet of the age, rivaling Chaucer in "what might be said in rime" (Q2 35.13). Where Surrey provides 15 percent of the poems in *Songes and Sonettes*, Wyatt provides about 36 percent, the largest group of poems by one single author in the anthology. Possible sources suggest that poems were carefully selected from an extensive network of manuscripts and commonplace-books. As with the Surrey section, Tottel tended not to print poems that had already been printed. For example, Tottel printed Wyatt's secular poems, but did not include his paraphrases of the seven Penitential Psalms, published in *Certain Psalms* (1549). Wyatt's translations of Petrarch's sonnets and canzoni were included, as were his experiments with the rondeaux of Jean Marot; the strambotti, ballades, and epigrams of Serafino d'Aquilano; and the epistolary satires of Luigi Alamanni. Of the one hundred twenty poems by Wyatt in the Egerton MS, ten are included with variants in Q2 but not found elsewhere: nos. 65, 66, 75,

---

Library Stowe MS. 389 contains a version of poem 30; Add. 30513 and Cotton Titus A. 24 contain a version of poem 31; Cotton MS. Titus A. 24 contains a version of poem 38, lines 1–12; and Ash. MS. 176 contains a version of Q2's poem 30.

[23] Of Surrey's four published works available before 1557, Tottel includes three and excludes one. "An excellent Epitaffe of syr Thomas Wyatt," published anonymously shortly after Wyatt's death in 1542, appears again in *Songes and Sonettes* in Surrey's cluster of poems devoted to Wyatt, where it is headed *Of the same* (poem 35), which refers to the theme of the preceding epitaph *Of the death of the same sir. T. w*; Surrey's encomia, in *Praise of certain psalmes of David, translated by sir T. w. the elder* (poem 33), which commences this cluster, was published in 1549. Peter Beal notes that poem 31 was first published at the end of Book III of William Baldwin's *A treatise of Morrall phylosophye*, 1547/8 (538). Tottel does not print Surrey's translation of Book 4 of the *Aeneid*, however, which appeared in 1554, nor does he print Surrey's translation of Book 2 of the *Aeneid*, which he most likely had in hand, because a few weeks later, on 21 June 1557 he published Surrey's translations of Book 2 and 4 of the *Aeneid* (*STC* 24798).

87, 89, 114, 115, 130, 131, and 133. From the one hundred twenty-two poems by Wyatt in the Devonshire MS, versions of three are included in *Songes and Sonettes* but not in any other manuscript: in Q2, nos. 80, 93, and 94. From the Arundel Harington MS, copies of three poems by Wyatt are included that can be found in no other manuscript: in Q2, nos. 105, 106, and 128.[24] Versions of the twenty-three remaining poems in *Songes and Sonettes* are in eight other manuscripts.[25] Finally, fifteen poems by Wyatt in Tottel's text are currently unlocated in early manuscript copies: in Q2, nos. 81, 85–86, 88, 109–113, 117, 121–122, 124, 127, and 129. It is noteworthy that of the 154 poems attributed to Wyatt in the sixteenth century, only ninety-six are included in Tottel's compilation.

Poems by Uncertain Auctours comprise approximately 33 percent or 94 of the 271 poems in Q1, and an even greater 48 percent or 134 poems of 280 in Q2. An analysis of the possible sources of poems by Uncertain Auctours in *Songes and Sonettes* again reveals an expansive network of manuscripts. The Arundel Harington MS has versions of twenty-one poems of the 134 found in

---

[24] The Egerton and Devonshire MSS share versions of nine poems by Wyatt found in *Songes and Sonettes*: in Q2, nos. 50, 57, 64, 67, 70, 74, 90, 107, and 116. The Egerton and Arundel Harington MSS share twenty-three poems found in Tottel's compilation: nos. 42, 43, 47–49, 52–53, 55–56, 59, 61–62, 69, 71, 78, 98–102, 118, 136, and 137. Versions of nine poems in the Egerton, Devonshire, and Arundel Harington MSS are found in *Songes and Sonettes*: nos. 45–46, 51, 72–73, 103–104, 108, and 134. There are no poems in the Wyatt section of Tottel's compilation that are found only in the Devonshire and Arundel Harington manuscripts.

[25] In the Blage MS, three poems with variants are found that appear in Q2 but are found in no other manuscripts: nos. 79, 82, and 83. Versions of Q2's poems 58, 63, and 68 can be found in the Egerton and Blage MSS; versions of 95 and 132 are in the Devonshire and Blage MSS; the Egerton, Devonshire, and Blage MSS contain versions of Q2's poem 91, while the Egerton, Devonshire, Blage, and Harl. 78 MSS have versions of Q2's poem 92. The Devonshire, Egerton, Arundel Harington, and Blage MSS have versions of no. 44. Add. 36529 and Blage MSS contain Q2's poem 97, while the Egerton, Devonshire, and Add. 36529 MSS contain versions of poems 54 and 60, while the Egerton, Devonshire, and Add. 37529 contain versions of poem 77. The Egerton, Devonshire, Add. 36529, and Harl. 78 MSS have versions of poem 119, while the Egerton, Devonshire, Arundel Harington, and Harl. 78 MSS have versions of poem 76; the Add. MS. 36529 contains a version of 96, while Add. MS. 18752 contains a version of poem 84. The Egerton and Harl. 78 MSS contain versions of poem 125, while on its own, Harl. 78 MS. contains a version of poem 126. The Arundel Harington and Rawl. Poet. 172 MSS contain versions of poem 120, while Q2's poem 123 is found in the Parker MS. 168, Corpus Christi College, Cambridge. The Egerton, Devonshire, Arundel Harington, Add. 36529, and Corpus Christ College, Cambridge 168 MSS have versions of poem 135. According to Ringler, Osborn MS has a version of poem 95, with tablatures for lute.

Q2: nos. 27, 140–142, 145, 149, 153, 156, 169, 176, 186, 187, 189, 196, 198, 212, 214, 222, 227, 229 and 242. Cotton Titus MS. A 24 has versions of five poems that are also found in Q2: nos. 139, 152, 166, 242, and 243. The Ash. MS. 48 has two poems with variants found in Q2: nos. 141 and 182; and Lansdowne MS. 98 has copies of three poems that are also found in Q2: nos. 197, 239, and 240. Poem 218 is also found in Sloane MS. 1896. The Devonshire MS has two poems that are also found with variants in Q2: nos. 177 and 195; while Harl. MS. 78 has two poems that are also found with variants in Q2: nos. 156 and 232. Sloane MS. 1896 is the possible source for two poems in Q2: nos. 254 and 257. A version of poem 257 is also found in PRO SP. Sloane MS. 159 has a variant of Q2, no. 144, and Sloane MS. 1207 has a variant of Q2, no. 239. Rawl. Poet. MS. 85 has a version of Q2, no. 144, and Rawl. Poet. MS. 82 has a version of Q2, no. 234. Add. MS. 23971 contains a variation of Q2, no. 175; Add. MS. 15225 has a version of Q2, no. 218; and Add. MS. 60577 has a version of poem 234. The Blage MS. has a copy of Q2's poems 140, 195, and 255. Given that in Q2 there are 134 poems by Uncertain Auctours, and that only 39 poems have possible sources in the manuscripts listed above, approximately 71 percent, or 95 poems are currently unlocated in early manuscript copies.[26]

As far as authorship of poems by the Uncertain Auctours is concerned, there is very little to go on. It may be that Tottel was not concerned about who the "other" poets were; as long as he had possession of their poems, he was free to publish them.[27] There are several poems in Q2 whose authorship is identified in sixteenth-century manuscripts: poem 182, in Ash. MS. 48, for example, concludes with "quod lord Vaux," and poem 187, in the Arundel Harington MS, concludes with "L vawse," both signatures suggesting Thomas Vaux, second Baron of Harrowden (1510–1556). A version of Q2's poem 239 found in Sloane MS. 1207 is headed "Epitaph by Will Gray made by himself." In Cotton Titus MS. 48, a version of poem 242 is followed by "finish Norton," while a version of poem 243 is followed by "Norton."[28] But one needs

---

[26] Poems by the Uncertain Auctours not found in manuscripts are nos. 138, 143, 146–148, 150–151, 154–155, 157–165, 167–168, 170–174, 178–181, 183–185,188, 190–192, 194, 198–211, 213, 215–217, 219–221, 223–226, 228, 230–231, 233, 235–238, 241, 244–253, 256, 258–270.

[27] As Adrian Johns points out, "publication without express authorial consent seems to have been an acknowledged reality" (*The Nature of the Book: Print and Knowledge in the Making* [Chicago and London: University of Chicago Press, 1998], 228).

[28] Further claims are advanced by Ruth Hughey, who proposes the authorship of John Harington, especially for poems in close proximity in the Arundel Harington manuscript. Though Harington played a significant role in the collecting of poems in various manuscripts in the mid-1550s, his authorship cannot be confirmed for any one poem in Tottel's text. See Hughey's comments to poems in her edition of *The Arundel Harington Manuscript of Tudor Poetry*, vol. 2, especially notes to poems

to follow a strict set of guidelines to avoid the problem of allowing a poem to be attributed to one author whose source could be elsewhere. [29] One should note, for example, that though Tottel's Q2, no. 139, is not signed, Sir John Harington claimed in 1602 that his grandfather, John Harington, wrote the poem. Another poem not signed by John Harington in the Arundel Harington MS. Add. MS. 28635, but later claimed as his own, is Q2's no. 141. [30] In fact, if one works through the information available on the Uncertain Auctours, the authorship of very few poems can be authenticated. [31] Even though there

---

15, and 17–19 (17–22). Rollins entreats readers not to doubt the claim by Thomas Churchyard in his preface to *Churchyard's Challenge* (1593) that "many things in the booke of songs and Sonets, . . . were of my making", and that "an infinite number of other Songes and Sonets, [were] given where they cannot be recovered, or purchase any favour when they are craved." Of this statement Rollins says: "Churchyard was an honest man, if a poor poet. His word cannot be doubted" (2: 83), but we have as yet no way of verifying Churchyard's claim.

[29] I appreciate Rebholz's arguments that if the poet's handwriting can be identi-fied, as can Wyatt's in the Egerton manuscript, one can be fairly certain of his author-ship of the poem which he inscribes to himself in a certain manuscript. If revisions are found in a poet's hand, one can be fairly certain that the poem is that poet's, though this does not apply in Grimald's case in the Egerton manuscript, where he revises poems not written by him. If the initials of the poet are inscribed beside the poem or beneath it in the manuscript, one can presume the poem can be attributed to that poet. But, if the name or initials can be proven to have been entered into the man-uscript after the actual inscription of the poem in the manuscript, then there is cause for doubt. Another piece of evidence not considered by Rebholz is sometimes pro-vided in headings where the author is identified. For example, the heading of poem 69 informs readers that it is *Wiates complaint upon Love to Reason: with Loves answer.* See Rebholz, *Sir Thomas Wyatt: The Complete Poems*, 9–10.

[30] In a later miscellany of the Harington family, *Nugae Antiquae*, published in 1779, a version of Tottel's Q2, no. 141, is ascribed to John Harington, and titled to indi-cate that it was written by him in 1554 while imprisoned in the Tower. The title does not appear in the Arundel Harington MS., however, but was entered later by Henry Harington in *Nugae Antiquae*. See also Rollins, 2: 257–59. Other examples of later attribution of authorship are in Q2, nos. 147 and 149, which are both attributed to J. Canand, by Joseph Lilly, in his printing of *A Collection of Seventy-nine Black-letter Bal-lads and Broadsides, Printed in the Reign of Queen Elizabeth* (London: J. Lilly, 1867). In Q2, poem 234 is anonymous, but in the Rawl. Poet. MS. 82, the poem is apparently ascribed by Gabriel Harvey to Sir John Cheke, at least, that is the claim made by the compiler of the Bodleian *Summary Catalogue of Western Manuscripts*, vol. 3 (Oxford: Clarendon Press, 1895; repr. Munich: Kraus-Thompson, 1980), 299.

[31] See Rollins, 2:79–85. For an interesting perspective on the significance of ano-nymity in English Renaissance literature, see Marcy L. North, "Anonymity's Revela-tions in *The Arte of English Poesie*," *SEL* 39 (1999): 1–18; and "Ignoto in the Age of Print: The Manipulation of Anonymity in Early Modern England," *SP* 91 (1994): 390–416.

is some evidence that signatures could have been provided, Tottel did not take the trouble to ascertain authorship to specific poems in manuscript or print sources. For example, though Q2's poem 207 had already been printed with some variation in earlier editions of Chaucer (Pynson's 1526 edition, and Thynne's 1532, 1542, and 1545 editions), and Chaucer's authorship widely known, Tottel does not record his signature. [32]

The sources for Nicholas Grimald's poems are slightly less elusive. Tottel and Grimald had a close professional relationship. Tottel published Grimald's translation of *Marcus Tullius Ciceroes Three bokes of duties* in 1556, and again in 1558, 1568, 1574, and 1583. [33] As Grimald had spent much of his life affiliated with the Universities of Oxford and Cambridge, both as a tutor and lecturer in classics and as a Latin dramatist, he was certainly qualified for the task of translating Cicero. [34] He also knew Wyatt's translations well. According to John Bale's *Index Britanniae Scriptorum*, in his *Restitutionem psalmorum Thome Viati* (now lost), Grimald edited Wyatt's psalm translations, which had been corrupted by copyists. [35] The probable source for Grimald's own verses in Tottel's compilations is also mentioned in *Index Britanniae Scriptorum*,

---

[32] Also, poem 156, a riddle that is now attributed to Wyatt, is placed by Tottel among the Uncertain Auctours section, followed by another riddle, which appears in the same sequence in the Arundel Harington MS where it also serves as a conclusion (see Rebholz, *Sir Thomas Wyatt: The Complete Poems*, 498). Beal (620), points out that poem 195 has been attributed to Sir Francis Bryan, in A. Stuart Daley, "The Uncertain Author of Poem 225 [Q1], *Tottel's Miscellany*," *SP* 47 (1950): 485–93.

[33] Curiously, Grimald's motives for translating and publishing Cicero's text echo Tottel's comments in the preface to *Songes and Sonettes*. Grimald says that he has made "this latine writer english" to bring "into light" what was hidden from the reader for so long: he has "caused an auncient wryting to beecomme, in a maner, newe agayne: and a boke, vsed but of fewe, to wax common to a great many" [A₃r–A₃v] (*Marcus Tullius Ciceroes thre bokes of duties*, ed. O'Gorman, 38).

[34] He was known at the Inns of Court and by the students and fellows at Oxford and Cambridge, as well as in Germany, for his Latin resurrection-play, *Christus Redivivus*, published in Cologne in 1543, and his Latin tragedy, *Archipropheta* (1546–1547), on the life of the arch-prophet, John the Baptist. These works secured his reputation as a dramatist of the new learning. By 1557, others knew him as an apostate who had abandoned his position as a cleric in the Church of England and had, at least outwardly, turned to the Roman Church (LeRoy Merrill, "Nicholas Grimald, the Judas of the Reformation," *PMLA* 37 [1922]: 216–27); see also *The Life and Poems of Nicholas Grimald,* Yale Studies in English 69 [Cambridge and New York: Yale University Press, 1925; repr. New York: Archon Press, 1969]).

[35] Merrill, *Nicholas Grimald*, 20. See also John Bale, *Index Britanniae Scriptorum*, ed. Reginald Lane Poole and Mary Bateson (Oxford: Oxford University Press, 1902); a new edition is in preparation by J. Christopher Warner for the MRTS series published by ACMRS.

where Bale lists thirty-one works by Grimald. [36] If Bale's list is accurate, two
of these works (now lost) could have contained poems found in *Songes and
Sonettes*. Shortly after April 1551 Grimald published a book of congratulatory
poems on the release from prison of the Duke of Somerset. *Congratulatorium
carmen* contained 150 poems, and though one may assume that not all were
on the subject of Somerset, certainly those in Tottel's Q1 (but omitted in Q2)
addressed to the Mistresses Seymour, the daughters of Somerset, could have
been from this text. [37] A more promising title listed by Bale is a two-volume
work by Grimald, *Carmina et Epigrammata*, from which some of the poems
in Tottel editions may have had their source. Since *Index Britanniae* was pub-
lished in 1556, Bale does not list the 40 poems published in Q1, but most
likely they were selected from these lost texts.

Subsequent Elizabethan Editions

After Q3, *Songes and Sonettes* received inconsistent editorial attention. In
Q4, 1559, for example, misprints, typographical errors, broken fonts, and
unaligned leaves are more prominent than in earlier editions, which suggests
that vigilant proofreading had become less of a priority. [38] Q5, also dated 1559,
has more variant catchwords than any other edition. [39] In subsequent editions,
errors occur when words receive extra syllables, and when lines from poems
are dropped. [40] In Q7, 1567, more dramatic changes begin, with the altering
of the lineation of 17 out of 280 titles; Q8, 1574, varies significantly from the
wording of poems in Q2, a fact which invites further attention. [41] Q9, colophon

---

[36] L.R. Merrill suggests that Bale was probably accurate in his assessment of
Grimald's work. As Cambridge men with similar interests in the classics, Bale and
Grimald were quite close, even though Bale spent the years of Mary Tudor's reign on
the Continent (Merrill, "Nicholas Grimald," 33).

[37] After the publication of Q1, it may have been thought unpropitious to allot
much space to poems honoring the family of the man who was the mortal enemy of
the Earl of Surrey, the only author whose name is privileged on the title page, and
who had earlier brought great anxiety to Mary Tudor. In the summer of 1549, Edward
Somerset, in his capacity as Protector of Edward VI, tried to force Mary into comply-
ing with the king's council to forgo hearing mass at Kinninghall (David Loades, *Mary
Tudor: A Life* [Cambridge and Oxford: Blackwell, 1989], 143–48).

[38] Rollins, 2: 23.

[39] Q1 has 6 variant catchwords; Q2 has 6; Q3 has 9; Q4 has 7; Q5 has 17.

[40] In Q6, for example, "enmy" in 9.11 is changed to "enemy," and "blames" in 51.9
is changed to "blame men." Further examples are found in Rollins, vol. 2: 263–325.

[41] Rollins has argued that the extent of the word variance between Q2 and Q8
(1574) makes the latter a "much less interesting text". He responds to an earlier claim
by Thomas Grenville that the variants in Q8 make that text the most interesting and

1585, is a few pages shorter than earlier texts because of reduced font size for headings, though Q10, 1587, condenses headings even further, and corrects folio numbers. Rollins concludes that on account of the accumulated mistakes from other editions, the Elizabethan reader "must frequently have had difficulty in understanding what the poets really meant."[42]

It is difficult to believe that after 1587, *Songes and Sonettes* was not printed again until the eighteenth century. Most likely there were editions that have disappeared.[43] In the eighteenth century, editors published Tottel's compilation according to author: in 1717, Henry Curll reprinted Surrey's forty-one poems; in 1728 he included Wyatt's poems, using Q2 as copy-text; in 1793, Robert Anderson printed the poems by Surrey, Wyatt, and Grimald, but only a selection of fourteen poems by the Uncertain Auctours; the Percy-Stevens edition of 1808 was destroyed by fire in the printing shop before it reached the book-stalls; Alexander Chalmers's 1810 *Works of the English Poets*, Vol. 2, followed Q3, but supplemented the Surrey and Wyatt sections with poems not published in *Songes and Sonettes*; G. F. Nott's 1814 edition followed Q2 but modernized spelling and punctuation and appended the thirty poems by Grimald found in Q1. In 1815–1816, Nott published the poems of Surrey and Wyatt; in 1819 Ezekiel Sanford devoted two volumes in his fifty volumes on the works of British poets to the selected works of Surrey and Wyatt; Nicholas Harris Nicolas, the editor of the Aldine edition (1831), was the first to attack Nott's obsession to prove that Surrey's poems were written to the "fair Geraldine." Robert Bell's annotated edition in 1854 followed Q2 in the printing of poems by Surrey, but also included works by Thomas Sackville, Lord Buckhurst, and contemporary poets. Wyatt's poems are found in Vol. 2 of Bell's edition, though only fourteen poems by the Uncertain Auctours—the same as in Anderson's 1793 edition—are included. The first American edition of 1854 printed the works of Surrey and Wyatt, based on the Aldine edition (1831).

John Payne Collier's 1867 edition of *Seven English Poetical Miscellanies 1557–1602* was the first to reprint *Songes and Sonettes* Q1. Edward Arber's 1870 *English Reprints*, Vol. 6, is also based on Q1, though collated in part with Q2, and supplemented by notes to draw attention to the variants between Q1 and Q2. Biographical, bibliographical, and historical information is provided, along with an index of first lines, though Arber carelessly omits words and

---

important in relation to all the Elizabethan editions (2:32). Perhaps the quotient of interest will increase when it is pointed out that the 1574 edition was among the books recorded in the catalogue of the Sidney family library of Penshurst Place (Germaine Warkentin, "Sidney's Authors," in *Sir Philip Sidney's Achievement,* ed. M. J. B. Allen, Dominic Baker-Smith, and Arthur Kinney [New York: AMS Press, 1990], 89).

[42] Rollins, 2:36.

[43] Rollins lists editions in the seventeenth century mentioned by later editors, though these texts are no longer extant (2: 36–37).

alters spelling and punctuation. For more than fifty years, however, the Arber edition reigned supreme, making *Songes and Sonettes* the most popular poetic miscellany of the Tudor period. After Rollins's publication of *Tottel's Miscellany*, the Scolar Facsimile Press, in 1966, published Richard Tottel's *Songes and Sonettes* 5 June 1557, and again in 1970, prefacing the latter edition with a list of supposed contributing authors, annexing the title page of Q2, copies of poems printed for the first time in Q2, and a colophon.

Note on the Text

The present edition provides a critical text based on Q2 (British Library copy, Grenville 11170) with emendations of substantives and accidentals as necessary (see Lists 1 and 2 for substantives, List 3 for accidentals, and List 4 for press corrections in the two extant copies of Q2).[44] Except for these emendations, the spelling and punctuation of Q2 have been retained. No formal system of punctuation has been imposed. The punctuation of Q2 could be to some extent compositorial, and compositors, being busy people, punctuated according to house rules, to what made sense to them, and to what they were told. Where it does not make sense, the punctuation has been revised. The aim is to avoid ambiguity, though where ambiguity seems to be what is wanted in the poem, the punctuation is left untouched. Possessive forms are retained as originally printed, that is, without apostrophes. The colonlike pointing devices (:), that functions variously as a comma, a semi-colon or a colon, and the sign (?), signaling interrogation or exclamation, has likewise been retained, at least when their effect is not confusing. Whenever possible, the habit, inherited from the manuscript tradition, of not marking the end of lines with punctuation, has been retained, since the line ending itself is considered sufficient indication of a pause or an end point.[45] The phrasing has often been allowed to speak for itself, without punctuation; and whenever possible, the exchange of modern conventions of punctuation for early modern habits, has been avoided, as variable and inconsistent as these habits may seem. Since the lineation, word-division, and accidentals of the headings are a part of the entire *mise en scène* of the volume, they have been retained as they stand in Q2.

---

[44] The collation of texts Q1, Q2, and Q3 is the result of a close analysis of microfilms and photocopies.

[45] Ted-Larry Pebworth, "Manuscript Transmission and the Selection of Copy-Text in Renaissance Coterie Poetry," in *TEXT* 7, ed. D.C. Greetham, W. Speed Hill, Edward L. Burns, and Peter Shillingsburg (Ann Arbor: University of Michigan Press, 1991), 250.

Silent emendations to the text include the replacement of black-letter type with roman. Where Q2 differentiates the roman of headings from the black-letter in the verses, this edition italicizes the headings and romanizes the verses. The alternative forms of the letters *r* and *s* have been silently emended, and *u* and *v*, and *i* and *j* regularized; the contraction *ye* has been expanded to *the,* and *yt* to *that* or sometimes *yet,* the ampersand *&* to *and;* for macron and tilde vowels and consonants have been provided. No record has been kept in this edition of either the original pagination of Q2 or the signatures on recto leaves. Poem numbers (1–280), added in the present edition, are placed in square brackets. Although the stanzaic distinctions and line indentations of Q2 are preserved, the oversized initial capital and indentation often found on the second line of each verse have been reduced to uniformity.

Critical Introduction

The order of poems in Q2 differs from that of Q1 in 27 places.[46] Each change involved two alterations—taking the poem or cluster of poems out of the place it occupied in Q1 and inserting it into a new position in Q2—amounting to

---

[46] That the editor of *Songes and Sonettes* attended to the order of poems in both Q1 and Q2 is not surprising. The anthologic genre had been identified long before the sixteenth century as an appropriate vehicle for lyric arrangements that could provide cultural and political commentary on the age. Recent scholarship has shown that the classical Latin compilations of Statius and Martial, and to a lesser extent of Propertius, Catullus, and Tibullus – which were the staples of English schoolboys in the early sixteenth-century humanist revival – comprised clusters of arranged poems that criticized the changing social and historical content of the Roman Empire. In her analysis of how specific ideological assumptions toward the state are revealed by Roman poets, Elaine Fantham points out that "infinite varieties of arrangement" emerge between "individual poems separated from each other" and draw upon "the pleasures of comparison and contrast, expectation and surprise." Roman readers found that poems could "be related in so many ways – theme, meter, length, tone – it is as misguided for the modern reader to expect a single reason for a sequence as it is certain that there will be a fluid design unifying the whole" (*Roman Literary Culture: From Cicero to Apuleius* [Baltimore: Johns Hopkins University Press, 1996], 65–66).

Also part of the literary heritage of mid-Tudor lyric anthologies, medieval manuscripts comprising multiple texts reveal organizing principles that show that the "whole book" had a specific function to speak about the cultural "moment of its inscription." As Stephen G. Nichols and Siegfried Wenzel argue, such considerations as the layout, the arrangement of each volume, how it is gathered, subscribed, and bound, its colophon, with what works it is preserved, and the nature of its variants when it is copied by scribes, provide information on the cultural and political milieu of a text, its readers, its purpose as conceived in the mind of the author who composed the text and the scribe who compiled it with other texts. "Beyond transmitting basic information about a given text, [these features] speak to us about its social, commercial, and intellectual organization at the moment of its inscription" (*The Whole Book: Cultural Perspectives on the Medieval Miscellany* [Ann Arbor: University of Michigan Press, 1996], 1–2).

Commonplace books, in which students compiled and arranged fragments of literary works, were also important to the early sixteenth century as reservoirs of new humanist learning. Fragments of lyric poems, for example, or excerpts from prose tracts and spiritual treatises emphasize the struggle between virtue and vice encountered in the lives of early modern individuals. These books, Ann Moss suggests, map the moral extremes of Renaissance culture, the strategies of persuasive thinking, and the methods of transmitting knowledge. "The order suggested for organizing the common-place book," Moss argues, "presupposes a universe of knowledge and moral activity in which everything is loosely connected by association of ideas, by similarity and difference" (*Printed Commonplace-Books and the Structuring of Renaissance Thought* [Oxford: Clarendon Press, 1996] 122–23). Also see Paul A. Marquis, "Politics and Print: The Curious Revisions to Tottel's *Songes and Sonettes*," *SP* 97 (2000): 145–64.

A selection of other studies on the issues of arrangement of poems in printed anthologies and manuscripts follows: Mieke Bal, "Telling Objects: A Narrative Perspective on Collecting," in *The Cultures of Collections*, ed. John Elsner and Robert Cardinal (London: Reaktion Books, 1994), 97–115; Jean Baudrillard, "The System of Collecting," in *The Cultures of Collections*, ed. Elsner and Cardinal, 7–24; Mary Thomas Crane, *Framing Authority: Sayings, Self, and Society in Sixteenth-Century England* (Princeton: Princeton University Press, 1993); Elizabeth H. Hageman and Andrea Sununu, "New Manuscript Texts of Katherine Philips, 'The Matchless Orinda'," *EMS* 4 (1993):174–216; and "'More Copies of It Abroad than I Could Have Imagin'd': Further Manuscript Texts of Katherine Philips's, 'The Matchless Orinda'," *EMS* 5 (1995):127–69. S. K. Heninger, Jr., "Sequences, Systems, Models: Sidney and the Secularization of Sonnets," in *Poems in their Place: The Intertextuality and Order of Poetic Collections,* ed. Neil Fraistat (Chapel Hill: University of North Carolina Press, 1986), 66–94; Mary Hobbs, *Early Seventeenth-Century Verse Miscellany Manuscripts* (London: Scholar Press, 1992); Arthur F. Marotti, "'Love is not Love': Elizabethan Sonnet Sequences and the Social Order," *ELH* 49 (1982): 396–428; Richard C. Newton, "Making Books From Leaves: Poets Become Editors," in *Print Culture in the Renaissance: Essays on the Advent of Printing in Europe*, ed. Gerald P. Tyson and Sylvia S. Wagonheim (Newark: University of Delaware Press, 1986), 246–264; Anthony Allan Shelton, "Cabinets of Transgression: Renaissance Collections and the Incorporation of the New World," in *The Cultures of Collections*, ed. Elsner and Cardinal, 177–203; Michael R.G. Spiller, *The Development of the Sonnet: An Introduction* (London and New York: Routledge, 1992); Gary A. Stringer, "Evidence for an Authorial Sequence in Donne's Elegies," *TEXT* 13 (2000): 175–196; Wendy Wall, *The Imprint of Gender: Authorship and Publication in the English Renaissance* (Ithaca and London: Cornell University Press, 1993); Germaine Warkentin, "The Meeting of the Muses: Sidney and the Mid-Tudor Poets," in *Sir Philip Sidney and the Interpretation of Renaissance Culture*, ed. Gary F. Waller and Michael D. Moore (London: Croom Helm, 1984), 17–33; and "'Love's sweetest part, variety': Petrarch and the Curious Frame of the Renaissance Sonnet Sequence," *Ren&Ref* 11 (1975): 14–23.

54 changes in the sequence of the poems. A further 39 new poems were added to the Uncertain Auctours section in Q2, and 30 poems by Grimald omitted. Finally, over 400 substantive emendations to words and phrases in the poems were provided. As Hyder Rollins points out, in the eight short weeks between Q1 to Q2, *Songes and Sonettes* was "completely changed" and "thoroughly revised."[47]

Order of poems in Q1

In the manuscript sources from which the poems in *Songes and Sonettes* were ultimately derived, there are few headings, or titles, to the poems. Significantly, in Q1, the poems are provided headings and also grouped according to lyric genre, prosodic measure, line length, and *topoi*, which range from the private concerns of the poet-lover to public exhortations on the role of virtuous action in the human community. A simple tally of Q1 reveals that some variant of the word *love* is found in the headings of 143 poems. In each of the groups of poems by Surrey (1–36) and Wyatt (37–127), *love* appears consistently in the first half of the poems before being replaced by morally educative poems.[48] This topic is thoroughly outnumbered in the Grimald section by meditations on classical principles of virtue, and almost equally matched in the Uncertain Auctours section by concerns relating to the transience of all human experience.[49] Poems dealing with love employ Petrarchan conventions and generally take the form of songs, ballads, sonnets, and canzone; poems on public and political issues generally take the form of epigrams, epitaphs, elegies, and satires.

The Surrey section begins with a display of lyric virtuosity. Surrey's first poem is a terza rima in 55 lines that provides an *excusatio*, a justification for writing in which the persona hopes that his "carefull song" will "print

---

[47] Rollins, 2:10, 13.

[48] Unless otherwise stated, the numbers to the poems in this section of the Introduction on Q1 are 1 to 271, a scheme also used by Rollins, though the poems are not numbered in the 5 June 1557 edition.

[49] In Q1, with the exception of poems 9 and 15, *love* appears in the headings of Surrey's poems 1 to 26, then disappears until the final poem 36. In the Wyatt section, *love* appears in the headings of most poems from 37 to 113, before the political and social commentary in the final 14 epigrams and three epistles. Only the first three headings of Grimald's 40 poems refer to *love*, while in the Uncertain Auctours section, 39 of the 94 headings cite *love*, until the final 16 poems, where only three references are found. Three of the 10 poems in the two clusters by Surrey and Wyatt at the end of Q1 refer to *love*.

in [her] hart some parcell of [his] tene [i.e., grief]" (1.51–52).[50] Poem 2 is a
sonnet in two rhymes; poem 3 is a song in eight quatrains of alternate rhymes
which describes the *innamoramento*, the moment of falling in love; poems 4
and 5 are in poulter's measure of nearly 50 lines each. A cluster of sonnets
follows (nos. 6 to 14), arranged according to rhyme scheme.[51] The elegy in
poem 15 introduces political and historical motifs that increase in importance
in the latter part of the Surrey section. Cluster 16 to 26 is interwoven with
issues of Petrarchan love in a variety of lyric forms. The feminine personae in
poems 17 and 19 both complain *of the absence of her lover upon the sea*, as their
headings suggest. The persona in poem 18 admits that he has not learned the
"unjoynted" style of a lover, but instead has become a victim of *the injust mis-
taking of his writyng* (18.20). He grows disaffected with the whole of woman-
kind (poem 22), and finally in the *commiato* of poem 23, he *forsaketh love*.

Poems 27 and 28, translations of epigrams by Martial and Horace respec-
tively, advance an ethos of classical Roman rationality and personal control,
and provide a simple remedy to suffering caused by the vagaries of courtly
love. Poems 29 to 31 praise Wyatt as a poet and a man of virtue, an exemplar
of personal control.[52] The final poems, 33 to 36, are composed in a variety of
lyric genres: an elegy, a psalm paraphrase, an epigram, and a sonnet, the voices
of which urge the reader toward a life of virtue. Thematically and historically,
these poems can be related to the end of Surrey's career.[53] Finally, the heading
of Surrey's sonnet 36: *The fansie of a weried lover*, recalls the Petrarchan con-
text, but the speaker actually leaves unspecified the "fansie" that has always

---

[50] William Sessions points out that readers see in this poem the "musical distil-
lation of forms, themes, and motifs" that reveals Surrey's debt to Dante, Chaucer, and
Wyatt, and presents "a powerful model of love poetry for the English Renaissance."
"It is a small wonder," Sessions continues, "that this poem is the first in *Tottel's Mis-
cellany*" (*Henry Howard, Earl of Surrey*, Twayne's English Author Series [Boston: G.K.
Hall, 1986], 81). The high poetic standard of this poem allows the reader to anticipate
the quality of the following verses, which upon reading proves Tottel's claim in the
preface that English poets are equal to the best on the Continent.

[51] Sonnets 6 to 8, in seven rhymes, *abab cdcd efef gg*, contain Surrey's experi-
ments with what becomes known later as the English sonnet form; sonnets 9 and 10
in three rhymes, *abab abab abab cc*, are variations on the Italian form; and sonnets 11
to 14 are further experiments in seven rhymes.

[52] Surrey's "worthy sepulchre" (29.5) in Wyatt's honor is an elegy of 39 lines rep-
resenting the age of the poet at his death.

[53] Physical decay overcomes the speaker in poem 33, and his anticipated death
is contemplated. Poem 34 is a paraphrase of Psalm 119, verse 71, a meditation on the
value of affliction and persecution: *Bonum est mihi quod humiliasti me* translates as "It
is good that thou hast afflicted me." According to G. F. Nott, Surrey's son claimed that
his father composed this poem in prison between December 1546 and January 1547,
when he was executed (cited in Rollins, 2:159).

been an enemy to his "ease" (36.2). Be it amorous, political, or moral, what he had hoped for in life, as in the preceding poems, remains unattainable.

The Wyatt section also displays virtuosity. It opens with an arrangement of fifteen sonnets,[54] after which small clusters of epigrams, ballads, songs, and canzone are found in repeated patterns until poem 93.[55] Sonnets 94 to 103 are in the Italian forms of octaves and sestets, though poems 100 to 103, including the double sonnet 101, scan irregularly. These poems are followed by a cluster of ten lyrics of various kinds (104–113), ten epigrams (114–123), three verse epistles (124–126), and an unfinished song (127). Through much of the section, the caustic and witty tone of the epigrams responds to the amorous flourishes by the speakers in sonnets, ballads, and songs. The final cluster of epigrams, however, indicates that the Petrarchan narrative has ended, and the focus of the personae has shifted to issues of cultural and political importance. The over-arching narrative trajectory of *topoi* in the Wyatt section, then, passes from the private suffering of the Petrarchan lover to a lament for the absence of virtue in the public arena. The link among specific lyrics is based on the principle of *variatio* in which particular ideas or experiences are represented from a variety of perspectives often separated by lyrics in other genres on different topics.[56] The distinct lyric voice in each poem speaks in relation to ideas and concerns expressed in other poems in its immediate context. As important as the individual voice is in specific poems, so too are the dramatic verbal relations between clusters of poems, and the *discordia concors* in the tonal variations of the architectural score in the entire text.[57]

---

[54] Sonnets 37 to 51 are imitations of Petrarch which mostly follow the Italian octave and sestet division, with a rhyme scheme of *abba abba cdc cdd*, though the pattern is interrupted by the English three quatrains and couplet structure, poems 41 to 44.

[55] Exceptions occur in sonnets 69–70, revisions of Wyatt's rondeaux, and sonnet 84.

[56] Though poems in clusters may be linked structurally through types of genre, stanzaic form, prosodic measure, or line length, topical links emerge in contrast to amplify or oppose themes found in other clusters in earlier parts of the text, or anticipate poems found later in the text. Germaine Warkentin identifies the principle of *variatio* in the classical compilations of Latin poets and traces its importance as a linking device in Italian and Elizabethan sonnet sequences ("'Love's sweetest part, variety': Petrarch and the Curious Frame of the Renaissance Sonnet Sequence," 18). See also Paul Veyne, *Roman Erotic Elegy: Love, Poetry and the West*, trans. David Oellauer (Chicago: University of Chicago Press, 1988), 3–4.

[57] Several critics have noted the emergence of the metaphysical style in mid-Tudor poetry. For example, see William A. Sessions, "*Tottel's Miscellany* and the Metaphysical Poets," in *Approaches to Teaching the Metaphysical Poets*, ed. Sidney Gottlieb (New York: MLA America, 1990), 48–53. Though Sessions does not emphasize the use of *discordia concors* in *Songes and Sonettes*, he does point out similarities in metaphysical

There are two cycles of Petrarchan experience, from the *innamoramento* to the *commiato*, poems 40 to 87, and 89 to 99. In the context of these experiences, there is also a debate about the negative effect of love on the poet. In "hindryng" him, the beloved has "made a gap where was a style" (60.15–16). Cupid, in contrast, claims that he has transformed the lover from a "clatteryng knight" who "selleth wordes" (64.76) to a poet with a "frame" (64.81), with wings so that he "might upflie | To honor, and fame . . . higher | Than mortall thinges" (64.128–130). The *excusatio* aims not merely to seduce the lady, then, but to construct verse that profits the reader and immortalizes the poet. Just how important the Petrarchan narrative is to Tottel's editor is clear in the latter section of Wyatt's poems, where a number of headings announce the topic of *love* even though the poems do not address the subject.[58] In the final epigrams, love is abandoned, words have lost their meaning, and a withdrawal from the world is advised and enacted. The *courtiers life* is "fettred with cheines of gold" (119.7), the persona claims, and in the verse satires, he bids farewell to courtly life. John Poins is advised to embrace the life of moderation, the "quiet life" (124.74), where one can seek one's "selfe to finde | The thing" that has been "sought so long" (124.97–98). In the court one must learn to "cloke the truth" and "prayse [courtiers] without desert" (125.20), but there is peace in the country, quiet in "kent and christendome: | Among the Muses, where [he] read[s] and ryme[s]" (125.100–101). Wyatt himself was living in

---

poetry and several lyrics in Tottel's text. See also W. J. Courthope (*A History of English Poetry*, 6 vols. [New York: Macmillan and Co., 1895–1910; repr. (New York: Russell and Russell, 1962]), who claims that "the pedantry and learned allusion which characterize [Grimald's "The death of Zoroas" and "Marcus Tullius Ciceroes death"] are perhaps the earliest notes in English poetry of that manner which culminated in the 'metaphysical' style of Cowley and his contemporaries" (2:51). I propose that *discordia concors*, at least in terms of the importance of juxtaposition of *topoi* in poems, is evident in the structural composition of *Songes and Sonettes*.

[58] Epigrams 71 to 74, whose headings refer to *love*, do not in fact mention "love." At least three of the four epigrams have been given an historical context by editors who suggest that in these poems the poet is concerned about political opportunism (Rebholz, ed., *Sir Thomas Wyatt: The Complete Poems*, 374, 366, 381). Similar observations have been made about poems 101, 102, and 108. Muir and Thompson suggest a composition date for poem 108: "during one of the periods" when Wyatt "was in danger of his enemies in 1536, 1538, or 1540" (*Collected Poems of Sir Thomas Wyatt* [Liverpool: Liverpool University Press, 1969], 435). The heading, *Complaint of the absence of his love*, is provided to poem 104, though in the Egerton manuscript Wyatt himself titles the poem *In Spain*. That Tottel's editor had his eye out for thematic links between poems is evident again at the end of poem 104 and the commencement of poem 105. In the former, the lover is certain that his beloved will be so enchanted by his letter that she will put it between her breasts for safe-keeping. In the latter, he roundly criticizes her for tearing up his letters.

Kent when he composed the poem. Finally, the unfinished *Song of Jopas* pro-
vides a cosmological account of aberrations among planets that parallels the
varied experiences of personae in socially and politically charged environ-
ments, such as those displayed at court in the preceding poems.

The Grimald section of Q1 (128–167) is even more obviously arranged
according to lyric genres: three love songs (128–130); two companion pieces
on marriage (131–132); a cluster of encomia, epigrams, riddles, and sonnets
(133–138); a long section of occasional poems (139–147); another cluster of
encomia and epigrams (150–155); a final group of epitaphs and elegies (156–
166), and a concluding epigram (167). In contrast to the Surrey and Wyatt
sections in Q1, didactic poems far outnumber love poems in the Grimald sec-
tion. Poems 128 to 130 provide a portrait of the poet's *true love* (128.01), while
the dialogue between N. Vincent and G. Blackwood in poems 131 and 132
expresses contrary perspectives on marriage.[59] Grimald's strength, however,
is in classical scholarship, and thus in poem 133, the poet praises the muses,
the sources of inspiration for various styles of writing and performance, while
the epigrams that follow examine the classical principles that "work well" in
the representation of "noble vertues" (134.1, 12).

In the cluster of "occasional poems" addressed to Grimald's personal
acquaintances (139–147), the virtue of moderation is valued over impas-
sioned desire. The poet or artisan has a moral obligation to provide "no image
carved with coonnying hand" because "such gear" does not allure "hevenly
herts" (148.1–3).[60] In the encomia of poems 154 and 155, an alternative to
the imbalance between court and commons is provided in a period beyond
time, in an image of friendship that never fails (154.38), and in the "the bliss-
ful plott of garden" (155.2), which of course, recalls Eden. The final clus-
ter of epitaphs and elegies, 156 to 164, laments the loss of exemplars of vir-
tue largely from Grimald's pre-Marian past. The encomia for these personal

---

[59] That these poems were included in Grimald's section, even though they were
apparently not composed by Grimald, raises interesting questions. If the editor of Q1
believed the poems were by Grimald, he would have noticed how the dialogical oppo-
sition of the personae regarding the state of marriage effectively concludes further dis-
cussions of love in the Grimald section. If the editor knew the poems were by Vincent
and Blackwood, the fact that he inserted them into the Grimald's section is further
evidence of the value he placed on the trajectory of *topoi* in the compilation.

[60] This aesthetic is clarified in epigram 150, in *Prayse of measure kepying*, where
virtue is the mean arbiter of both right and wrong, an advocate of the "mid way"
(150.5). The "mid way" is achieved on a political level in the epigram *Of lawes*, where
the state joins with the Church to rule the commonwealth. L. R. Merrill suggests that
the poem refers to Thomas Wyatt the Younger's rebellion against Mary Tudor because of
his objection to her pending marriage to the Catholic Philip II of Spain in 1554, which led
to Wyatt's execution (*Nicholas Grimald*, 432).

acquaintances exemplify friendship and community, for which the poet shows an understandable nostalgia.[61] The long narrative poems in blank verse that follow (165–166) portray the courageous resolve of two virtuous figures that chose the honorable path of martyrdom.[62] The final epigram celebrates the immortality of Cicero and the immutability of art. Cicero lives, the speaker is told by the god of poetry, and "and styll alyve shall bee" (167.4).

The neat structural and thematic design in the Grimald section of Q1 is followed by the expansive Uncertain Auctours section (168–261), poems arranged according to lyric genres, stanzaic structure, prosodic measure, and line lengths. From the perspective of *topoi*, the narrative of the Petrarchan lover is interwoven in a larger context of morally didactic poems, including elegies and epitaphs, encomia, negative exempla, poems on *contemptus mundi*, and on the mean estate. The section commences with a display of the major lyric genres and themes: a Petrarchan complaint, an elegy, a moral epigram, a ballad, and a tale. The *innamoramento* and *excusatio* are provided in poem 168, in which the reader is told that the verse is meant to "perce her hert" to evoke pity in the beloved (168.68). The description of virtue in poem 169 and the *meane estate* in epigram 170 infantilize the amorous claims in the preceding complaint and provide an educative response to its obsession with private suffering. The speaker of Pygmalion's tale in poem 172 advocates the pursuit of fame by exploring how "fansie" can be infused in form, a theme that is explored in the poems that follow.

In the encomia of poem 186, the beloved *White* has the right combination of beauty and virtue. Like Pygmalion's statue, she has a mythical power to illuminate the world: "in dark night, [she] can bring day bright againe" (186.4), but because she is alive, her beauty has the power to restore those who gaze on her (186.10). The aesthetic motif is thus followed by other examples of virtue, in the life of Sir James Wilford (elegy 189), and in the philosophy of moderation espoused in the epigrams (191, 194) and translations (196–197)

---

[61] In Q1, 40 percent of the poems in the Grimald section have as their subjects historical figures, mostly personal acquaintances of the poet. At least three poems are in praise of Damascene Audley of the great Staffordshire family, by whom Grimald was likely befriended in his pre-Marian days, when he preached in the impressive country church. At least five poems are devoted to the Seymour sisters, Jane, Margaret, Katherine, and Elizabeth, the daughters of Edward Seymour, the Duke of Somerset. Only one poem praises a figure from Mary's court, Lord Mautravers, who died in Brussels in 1556 from a fever while employed as ambassador.

[62] Grimald's translation of these two poems continues an earlier interest in martyrology apparent in his Oxford dramas: *Archipropheta*, on the life of John the Baptist; and the lost *Protomartyr*, assumed to dramatize the life of St. Stephen, traditionally regarded as the first Christian martyr (Howard B. Norland, "Grimald's *Archipropheta*: A Saint's Tragedy," *JMRS* 14 [1984]: 63–76).

on the "mean estate." The question, then, is whether the lover can exorcise his "wanton will" (204.18) by writing alone, believing as he does that "truth it will trye in time" (204.26). It becomes a matter of priorities. In poem 211, Cupid has pierced the lover's heart which now lies wounded in the fort of reason, but in poem 212, the poet bids farewell to love because in part, he finds he can no longer compose: "My hand and pen are not in plight, | As they have bene of yore" (212.15–16).

The danger of finding an ideal woman is inherent in the desire to deify her. "I carde for her so much alone," the speaker admits, "that other God I carde for none" (226.39–40). Though he may be as constant as Troilus (237), he nevertheless lives in a world unsympathetic to love; as the translation of Chaucer's "Truthe" contests: "Here is no home, here is but wildernesse" (238.18). Near the end of the Uncertain Auctours, a heated dialogue emerges between the sexes (241–244). Positive and negative *exempla* follow, in which the virtues and vices of women are disclosed (poems 245–248). Another cluster suggests that the violent and destructive relationship between the sexes is merely part of the entropy of the natural world, the "canker" that leads to decay and dissolution. "Every thing that nature wrought, | Within it self his hurt doth beare" (249.8, 13–14). In such a world, "no frendship can be founde," for people look elsewhere for the root of their own suffering (253.19). The motif of the "gaze" that leads to enthrallment and death is developed in poem 259. In the blazon of poem 260, however, eyes are used to accentuate an image of the beloved whose beauty is "sure excedyng all the rest." In fashioning her, the poet concludes, nature "frame[d] a thing that God could not amende" (260.7, 27).

All that remains in Q1 are those poems attached to the end that have affiliations to earlier parts of the compilation. Poem 261, which provides an *answere* to poem 178, was perhaps acquired after the inner forme of sheet R was printed, on which poem 178 appears. The editor may have added poem 261 to sheet Cc, anticipating that in a possible later edition—which he announces in the preface to Q1—the poem would be inserted into its rightful position, beside the poem it "answers." Similar arguments can be advanced for the final two groups of poems, Surrey's 262 to 265, and Wyatt's 266 to 271. Given the earlier evidence of the editor's attention towards textual design in Q1, and the absence of significant structural and thematic linkage among the poems in these two small clusters, it is difficult to conclude that the editor placed these poems at the end of the compilation for any other reason than because he came into their possession after the earlier sections of poems by Surrey and Wyatt had been printed.

In Q1, then, in contrast to the arrangement of poems in the sections by Surrey, Wyatt, and Grimald, where attention shifts from the self-interested Petrarchan lover to didactic and morally educative poems, the Uncertain Auctours section is without a sense of an ending or closure. This is apparent even though the preceding lyric genres are clustered and arranged according to type and *topoi*. The desire for personal fulfillment in love leads to displays of agony, and fits of despair over the power of beauty. Poems on moderation and the "mean estate" are offered as antidotes to excessive desire, but followed by questions about the value of women in general and expressions of contempt for the transience of all earthly things. There is no suggestion here, however, that love can be transformed by virtuous action in the community (as in Surrey's poems) or that sensual love will be rejected and replaced by a spiritual retreat (as in Wyatt's poems) or that love naturally leads to self-sacrifice and martyrdom (as in Grimald's poems). Q1 ends fragmented by several clusters of poems that are obviously out of place.

Order of poems in Q2

Eight weeks later, the editor published a revised second edition of these poems. In the next twenty-five years, Q2 was reprinted at least nine times. George Puttenham alludes to it frequently in *The Arte of English Poesie* (1589), hailing many of its verses as examples worthy of emulation by the Elizabethan poets. Slender, in Shakespeare's *Merry Wives of Windsor*, regards it affectionately as a primer of love poems. Indeed, Tottel's success was followed by a number of editors and authors who compiled and published their own verse anthologies. Barnabe Googe, George Turbervile, George Gascoigne, Edmund Spenser, Sir Philip Sidney, and William Shakespeare, as well as numerous other lesser-known writers, experimented with gathering and arranging lyric poems into single books. If Tottel had not been in some way concerned with the compilation as a unified text, he would have replicated the first edition, simply attaching the small clusters of new poems by Surrey and Wyatt to their respective authorial sections, and the new poems by the Uncertain Auctours to their section. Instead he incorporated the additions by Surrey and Wyatt into appropriate places, and rearranged a number of poems by the Uncertain Auctours whose section he enlarged by 39 poems. What had the greatest impact in the new edition was the culling of 30 poems by Grimald and the repositioning of his remaining 10 translations to the end of the volume. By moving the poems of the Uncertain Auctours from the final position in the text to the penultimate position and concluding with Grimald's 10 poems, the editor ensured that Grimald's work would have a culminating influence on the compilation and provide an effective closure to the entire text. This form of *Songes and Sonettes*, reissued repeatedly in the following twenty-five years, was the one that the Elizabethans knew and admired.

In Q2, an early example of editorial attentiveness is evident when poem 243 of Q1 is moved from its position in the Uncertain Auctours section to the position following Surrey's poem 26 in Q2.[63] In poem 26, the lover berates women for their *subtle usage. . .toward their lovers*; in Q2's new poem 27, the feminine persona defends the actions of women towards incompetent and self-serving men. Other examples of attentive rearrangement occur in the four poems by Surrey at the end of Q1. Poem 262 in Q1 is inserted into position 28 in Q2, answering "fortune's wrath" with a gesture of complete submission: "What would ye more of me?" the speaker asks his beloved (28.1, 24). The response follows in poem 264 from Q1, where, in terms of the allegory, she does not want "more" of him, but less: "go range about where thou mayst finde some meter fere for thee" (29.22). Understandably, Q2's editor inserts Q1's poem 263, in which Wyatt's learning is praised, at the end of the cluster of elegies and epitaphs by Surrey on Wyatt, and provides the heading, *Of the same*, to indicate its topical link. Thus the rearrangement of Surrey's poems in Q2 contributes to the lover's sense of desperation and enhances the argument that Wyatt, as a poet and man of virtue, is worthy of emulation.

Wyatt's final cluster, poems 266 to 271 in Q1, is inserted after poem 117 in Q2.[64] In this position, the six short poems are linked to the large cluster of epigrams that precede the final verse epistles in Q2. They expand the sense of suffering brought on by love and introduce the prospect of engaging in more virtuous action. In poem 118, *Of his loue called Anna*, the poet is reminded by the palindrome of how his love "changeth not | Though it be turned and made in twaine" (118.1–2). His beloved has the power to cure or destroy him, as the speaker claims in the next poem, "since every woe is joyned with some wealth" (119.8). In poem 123, the choices are simplified metaphorically: enthrallment or death? unending desire or the end of love? "What say ye lovers?", the poet asks his readers, "which shall be the best?" (123.25). The reader is thus drawn into the debate between sensual love and virtuous action. In the final ten epigrams, three verse satires, and the unfinished *Song of Jopas*, we have seen Wyatt define his response to the conflict when he withdraws from court and community and retreats to his estate in Kent.

Most of the reshaping of Q2 occurs in the last two authorial sections. With 39 new poems added to the Uncertain Auctours section, there is even more of an opportunity for dialogic interchange among the speakers. Added to the existing 94 poems from Q1, the new poems, including poem 82 from the Wyatt section, provide a total of 134, or almost half of the poems in Q2. From a generic perspective, the new poems include songs, laments, encomia,

---

[63] References to Q2 will be to the present edition, with the poem number followed by line number(s) where appropriate in parentheses.

[64] Poem 82 from Q1 is omitted from Wyatt's section of Q2 and placed among the Uncertain Auctours as poem 255.

complaints, epigrams, sonnets, epitaphs, and epistles. *Topoi* favor Petrarchan conventions, with more than half about a lover wanting, having, or recalling that he once had his beloved. The remaining poems provide morally educative alternatives to the repetitive cycle of love and despair. Other changes include poems shifted from their place in Q1 and repositioned in Q2 to form companion pieces that amplify or oppose attitudes and opinions already voiced.

Q2 prints the first 10 poems in the Uncertain Auctours section of Q1 without interruption, Q2's 138 to 147: here we have seen an elaboration of the *excusatio*, in which the personae debate the aesthetics of composition in writing and sculpting, and the importance of finding a "subject" to inspire work that brings fame and immortality, especially in a world of social corruption and physical decay. Poem 148, however, is not Q1's 178, but its 179,[65] after which Q2 follows Q1 for twenty-three poems (148–170), in which Petrarchan motifs are more than equally matched by epigrams on the "mean estate," epitaphs on virtuous men and women, and poems of *contemptus mundi*. Inserted after poem 170, however, is poem 234 from Q1, which answers a lover's complaint in the preceding poem. Then Q2 follows Q1 for thirty-nine poems in which the personae ponder a number of ultimately irreconcilable issues, including the desire for sexual and spiritual fulfillment, its relation to truth, constancy, virtue, infidelity, mutability, and death (172–210).[66] The parallel between Q2 and Q1 continues for nine poems, in which readers hear a vigorous debate between the sexes, and accusations of slander and seduction, followed by a positive *exemplum* for women, two meditations on natural decay and communal discord, and a lover's complaint (211–219).[67] Finally, Q2's 220 and 221 correspond to poems 259 and 260 from Q1; in the former, the lover's desire to know her beloved ends in her slaughter, while in the latter, the beloved rises like a "Phenix" (221.1) in a body blazoned by the poet.

Seventeen new poems are then inserted into Q2 (222–238) in an arrangement of songs, epitaphs, epistles, and sonnets, whose *topoi* recall the preceding pattern, in which love poems are followed by moral and didactic exhortations. The political complaint of poem 229 links the pursuit of sensual pleasure that led to the fall of Troy, and that now occupies the lover, to the

---

[65] Why was poem 178 extracted from the sequence? From a structural perspective, Q2's 147 and 148 are sonnets. The repositioned 178 is a long poem in poulter's measure that precedes another poem in the same measure which "answers" it.

[66] At this point, there is a hiatus of two poems from Q1 which are repositioned in Q2; no. 242 is placed later in Q2, and no. 243 answers Surrey's poem 26.

[67] After poem 219, the next six poems from Q1 have been moved to a later section in Q2.

recent disturbances in England's commonwealth.[68] As joy, when it is found in these poems, is soon followed by sorrow, we are provided several *contemptus mundi* poems with an underlying political context.[69] In poem 234, as the heading states, *Totus mundus in maligno positus*, "the whole world is set on mischief" (1 John 5:18 [Vulgate]). In the preceding poem, hope provides fruit, but now "hope is nye gone" (234.2), nothing is certain; the ship of state sails on aimlessly; natural order is subverted: "Trouth is folly: and might is right" (234.30–32). From a religious perspective, "Mens harts are burnde with sundry sectes | and to echeman his way is best" (234.55–56). The metaphor of burning "sects" alludes to the passions of opposing religious factions, spurred on by Queen Mary's attempt to turn England back to the Church of Rome after the Church of England was established by her father, Henry VIII, and advanced by her half-brother, Edward VI. In the summer of 1557, the phrase would also remind readers of the martyrs who burned at the stake under Mary's policy of religious intolerance, which, as far as the poet is concerned, the Lord needs "tamend" (234.62).[70] If the human community tends towards "mischief," how can one survive with integrity? The answers are provided in the epigrams that follow in which readers are encouraged to act always with the end of life in mind, and to trust those whose friendship has been "tried," that is, proven in action (235.1–6). *Wisdome*, readers are told in the heading, is revealed by those who speak *few wordes* and *work much quiet* (236.01–02).

Poems 237 to 248, mostly repositioned from Q1 to form companion pieces with new poems, accelerate and intensify the dialogic exchange among

---

[68] Rollins suggests that the poem refers to the younger Wyatt's challenge to the throne on hearing of Mary's intended marriage to Philip II (2:322). Though it was likely written shortly after the younger Wyatt's execution in April 1544, the parallels drawn in the poem between the excesses of Troy and the English court would be obvious by 1557. "Such was the time," the poet argues, "Troy trembled not so careles were the men | Like to our time, wherin hath broken out, | The hidden harme" (229.31–32, 37–38).

[69] A copy of poem 234 is found in Rawl. Poet. MS. 32 in which Gabriel Harvey indicates that it was composed by Sir John Cheke, a well-known proponent of Protestantism.

[70] Rollins points out that *Songes and Sonettes* was published amid the Marian Counter-Reformation, when English dissenters were tortured and burned in the streets where booksellers sold their wares: "To the accompaniment of fire and martyr's shrieks the epoch-making book. . .made its appearance" (2:3). The commentary in the poem challenges the laws on dissent during the last year of Mary's reign when government bodies were established "to enquire concerning all heresies, heretical and seditious books and all conspiracies against the King and Queene. . .with power to seize such books and writings" (*Calendar of Patent Rolls: Mary and Philip* [London: 1936–1939], 3:24).

the personae on topics of infidelity and greed. The increasingly misogynistic tone towards women is disrupted by epitaphs that praise the courage and virtue of Master Henry Williams, a soldier in the court of Edward VI.[71] The six poems that follow illustrate unresolved differences between the sexes. Poems 249 to 254, new to Q2, encapsulate the preceding discordant *topoi*, with a staccato-like version of the Petrarchan affair. An *innamoramento* (250), followed by a *commiato* (252), before epigrams of moral advice on the "mean estate" (253) and the importance of the virtue of friendship (poem 254), provide an alternative to the apparently futile prospects of the lovers. The next two poems from Q1 (nos. 82 and 242), resume the debate on infidelity.

Q2's poems 257 to 270, the last fourteen new poems by the Uncertain Auctours, are comprised of songs, ballads, and laments in a variety of trimeter, tetrameter, and poulter's measure. The *topoi* commence with a portrayal of the contemptible nature of human existence, *the vanitie of mans lyfe*. The conflict between desire inspired by beauty and the transience of life soon drives the poet to despair. When he gazes on her "excellence divine," he despises "all earthly things" (260.7–10), and though he craves death, "yet [he] cannot dye" (261.3). A last will and testament is provided in poem 262, by an emotionally exhausted speaker, while poem 263 begins, "Adieu desert, how art thou spent?" He has failed to move his beloved to mercy, though he has spent his best years, "the flowryng time" (263.20), lamenting his plight.[72] The final poems oscillate thematically between disdain and praise for the beloved.[73]

To summarize, then, the new poems added to Q2 intensify the unresolved relationships between the lovers and the world depicted in Q1. The excesses of passion are amplified and opposed in the newly formed "companion poems," which disclose the problems encountered by personae enthralled by beauty and obsessed by desire, whose frustration leads in the extreme to either misogyny or deification. Antidotes to the endless cycle of suffering are

---

[71] Though the heading of poem 242, *Another of the same*, implies that a second epitaph follows on Williams, we find instead a meditation on death and immortality.

[72] Poems 264 and 265 wittily evoke the "flowryng time", when he was young and in love: the first involves a bay tree, the second a laurel tree.

[73] In poem 266, the beauty of his mistress brings discord to the community. "Her limmes so answeryng were," we are told, that old men felt a "rage of flame" for that "paradice. . .to behold" (266.21, 26–29). In poem 267, an old man quips to a young beauty: "I know a key can pick your locke | And make you runne your selves on ground" (267.15–16). In the *commiato* following, the aged lover criticizes her immaturity: "Thou lackest yeres to understand the grefe that I did fele" (268.2). In poem 269, the speaker prays that "her goddesse face | might never change" or cease to exemplify "how vertue can with beauty beare degree" (269.39–42), but in the final poem by the "Uncertain Auctours" the woman is subjected to the ravages of time and dies, though memory of that "old love" renews his desire for her.

provided in the morally educative poems that remind us that lovers aim too high, that this world "is set on mischief" (poem 234), and that we do well to live moderately and with discipline, by recalling those in the past whose virtues are worth emulating. The positive *exempla* provide a nostalgic strain that acts as a counterpoint to despair.

In the radically condensed closing section of poems by Grimald, the editor extends the instructive reach of Q2. The selection and arrangement of ten specific poems from Q1, mostly translations from Theodore Beza's *Poemata Juvenilia* (1548), and the omission of thirty others, serve to answer the major concerns expressed earlier in the poems. First, the subject of physical love is all but dismissed earlier in the book when the editor of Q2 omits five poems from the beginning of the Grimald section in Q1. He opens with Grimald's catalogue of the muses, in which the mythical sources of inspiration for poets are invoked. The speaker calls upon "Phebus," the patron of poetry, to lead the graces forth, dressed as muses, "so that men in maze they fall" (271.24). But clearly this obsequious response is inadequate. The epigram that follows clarifies the choices available to the poet and the reader, according to the philosophy of Musonius. "Working well" allows one to endure suffering lightly and achieve glory among "worthy wightes" (272.1–4); in contrast, "working wrong" is exemplified by those who seek pleasure and are "fowl defame[d]." We are urged finally to flee pleasure and pursue "noble vertues" (272.5–12).

But what kind of work is virtuous? The next three poems provide various responses to this question.[74] Virtue is allegorized in poem 273. Careless of life's pleasures and tolerant of pain, which comes with disciplining the "mindes rage," she can "teach [us] above the starres to flye." There is no other way to immortality: "I onely cannot dye" (273.5–8). How is virtue accomplished or exemplified? By keeping measure, especially in matters of the heart. In poem 274, we are encouraged to "worship not Jove with curious fansies vain," nor "him despise," but "hold right atween these twain" (274.15–16). In the middle, we are positioned to see when certain choices are wrong, leading to "no life," or right, leading to a prolonged life, not free from death but only "soon to dye" (275.10; 276.10). Death cannot be avoided, but acknowledging it helps us to choose rightly and prolong life.

In the context of death, one's life is best defined through friendship. The panegyric, *Of frendship*, is a celebration of a classical virtue that, if realized, stabilizes the relationship between the individual and his or her community: "eche house, eche towne, ech realm" flourishes with "stedfast love" (277.19). Friendship is a "heavenly gift" (277.1), like grace, and therefore it does not

---

[74] By excluding epigrams 135 to 138, from Q1, and the ten occasional poems to personal acquaintances, 139 to 148, the editor of Q2 avoids digression and focuses specifically on the topic of virtue.

rely on human passion. The catalogue of famous friends is a testimony to the eternalizing potential of the virtue: for they "no terme of time, no space of place, no storme. . .can deface" (277.8). If Tottel's editor had concluded Q2 with poem 277, the reader would have been left with positive *exempla* as models for action in the mid-Tudor world; however, he did not.[75] Instead, he follows this poem with two other translations of Beza, in which friendship is betrayed for political ends. They recall the numerous *contemptus mundi* poems earlier in Q2, where we have heard, for example, that "no state on earth may last" (152.11), and the political poems which lament that "signes of our decay, which tong dares not expresse, . . .which never were before this time, no not this thousand yeres," are now apparent (218.22–24), and that "hope is nye gone" (234.2).

The slaughter of Zoroaster and Cicero depicts those moments in history when "frenship fayl[ed]" (277.38). In the midst of the fray between the Egyptians and the Greeks, Zoroaster wounds Alexander and is destroyed. Martyrdom, however, assures Zoroaster immortality, as he is set free from the "dark oblivion of devouring death" (278.115). His execution is linked by the connective "therefore," commencing poem 279, to the political assassination of Cicero. Cicero's countrymen repay him for saving them from the "civill swoord" (279.5) by executing him.[76] At his death, "the latine Muses, and the Grayes [Graces]. . .wept" (279.78), and then Pitho, the goddess of persuasion, accompanied Cicero as he departed from the earth, "ne will no more return" (179.85). Nevertheless, in the final translation from Beza, poem 280, Q2 reaffirms the importance of virtue and the role of the poet in relation to the community. Poetry matters, we are told, because in it, Cicero "lives, and styll alyve shall bee" (280.4). Cicero lives in his letters, his theories of rhetoric, and, paradoxically, because he tried to civilize the community that eventually sent him to his death.

---

[75] Tottel's editor omits a number of poems from Q1, including poem *Of lawes*, and *The Garden*, and nine epitaphs and elegies (156–164 Q1), the effect of which is to enhance the dramatic importance of the final three poems by Grimald in Q2.

[76] Cicero chooses the most honorable path, according to a treatise written by Nicholas Ridley, a celebrated martyr who burned at the stake in 1555. According to Ridley, fleeing to the Continent was an acceptable response to Mary's reversion of the state to the Catholic faith, but to "ask pardon" by conforming outwardly to Catholicism while remaining inwardly a believer in the Church of England was unacceptable. Such hypocrites were guilty of "wily ways with the word of God" (*The Works of Nicholas Ridley*, ed. Henry Christmas [Cambridge: 1841], 68. See also John R. Knott, *Discourse of Martyrdom in English Literature 1564–1694* (Cambridge: Cambridge University Press, 1993), 85; *A View from the Palatine: The Iuvenilia of Théodore de Bèze*, ed. K.M. Summers, MRTS (Tempe: ACMRS, 2001), 10–15.

Standing back from the entire text of Q2, one can assess the impact of the revisions. Surrey praises Wyatt as an exemplar of virtue and criticizes the barbarism of the age, which has, from king to courtier, occupied itself with the excessive pursuit of pleasure. Wyatt portrays political treachery in the court and eventually withdraws into a quiet life where virtuous action is at least possible. There is a clear moral trajectory in the arrangement of poems by these Henrician poets. In contrast, the voices of the Uncertain Auctours—largely Marian poets, it can be assumed, who preferred to remain anonymous, or who were granted that privilege by the editor—provide a much less certain view of the world and the place of virtue in it. Some comfort is found, however, in the numerous encomia of virtuous men and women whose lives are celebrated and praised in this section. Largely from the courts of Henry VIII and Edward VI, these figures remind us of what virtue is and how it should be practised: Master Devorox, the lord Ferres' son; Sir James Wilforde; Thomas Audley; Philip van Wilder; Lady Anne Wentworth; Sir Anthony Deny; the Countess of Pembroke; Sir Thomas Wyatt the elder; Henry Williams; and Mistress White. These poems are complemented by encomia for the gift of "good will"; the joy that accompanies generosity; the temperament of the "mean estate," the style of Petrarch, and the virtue of Laura; the liberating nature of truth; the comfort of a faithful wife; the wisdom of silence; and the importance of friendship. One could argue, then, that the prominence of these poems in the Uncertain Auctors section of Q2 provides a series of portraits with an educative potential to inspire readers to virtuous action. As moral *exempla*, these lyrics accumulate in effect to provide a measurement against which all examples of self-interested action in the text are judged.

If the revised Grimald section had remained where it is found in Q1, lodged between the long Wyatt section and the even longer section by Uncertain Authors, it would have been all but invisible to the reader. In their new position in Q2, Grimald's final translations of Beza explore the complex nature of virtuous action, its importance to the survival of the human community, and its relationship to martyrdom and immortality. By excluding Grimald's personal poems, the editor ensures that the reader focuses exclusively on his translations of Beza. The significance of this gesture would not have gone unnoticed. Beza was an active participant in the Reformation; as John N. King points out, "as Calvin's chaplain and the continuator of Marot's French Psalter, Beza was a sanctioned neo-classical model for the Protestant poet."[77] The

---

[77] J. N. King, *English Reformation Literature: The Tudor Origins of the Protestant Tradition* (Princeton: Princeton University Press, 1995), 243. Also see Hoyt Hopewell Hudson, "Grimald's Translations From Beza," *MLN* 39 (1924): 388–94; and S. Laigneau, "La mort de Cicéron chez Théodore de Bèze (Juvenilia): une silve entre épopée et tragédie," in *Acta Conventus Neo-Latini Bonneusis*, ed. R. Schnur, MRTS 315 (Tempe: ACMRS, 2006), 449–56

argument in the final poems in Q2 urges the reader to admire and appreciate the courageous resolve of classical figures that chose the honorable path of martyrdom instead of a life of subjection to the forces of oppression. Tottel's editor anticipates John Foxe's *Acts and Monuments* (1563), which emphasizes the triumphs of faith of the Protestant martyrs. The suffering and death of Zoroaster and Cicero provide a secular dramatization of the passion, death, and ascension of Christ.[78]

Grimald's translations also remind us of the difficulties involved in attempting to revive the voices of those trying to contribute to the construction of an improved human community. In spite of the endeavor in the early sixteenth century to inculcate classical ideals in the young through the study of Latin authors, mid-Tudor culture was no less vicious. Parallels can be drawn between the execution of Zoroaster and that of Surrey in 1547, and Cicero's murder and Grimald's brush with public execution at the stake, shortly after Mary assumed the throne in 1553. In these ritual acts of violence, the voice of the poet as prophet and cultural critic is immortalized by the society that he has criticized and helped to sustain. The second edition of *Songes and Sonettes* is a text in which lyric voices explore the volatile and socially unstable world of the Tudor monarchy. The revised arrangement of poems in Q2 suggests that the quest for personal and poetic fulfillment leads not to recantation, as in Petrarch, but to questions about political authority and personal censorship, which set the stage for the cultural criticism of the later Elizabethan period.

Textual Variants between Q1 and Q2

While the rearrangement of poems in Q2 has a significant effect on the reader's response to the whole compilation, analysis of the variants in particular poems reveals an editorial attention focused mostly on tonal and prosodic "corrections."[79] In other words, there are few poems that are radically altered, and fewer still whose revisions advance clear and sustained ideological positions. The substantive and accidental variants in Q2 are recorded in lists appended to this text, the former in List 1, and the latter in List 3. The variants of Q3, which reveal a curious privileging of the readings of Q1 over Q2, are recorded in List 2. One can see from List 1 that substantive changes,

---

[78] R. D. Kendall, *The Drama of Dissent* (Chapel Hill: University of North Carolina Press, 1986) emphasizes the parallels between the inquisitor's examination for heresy and the tyrant play of the mystery cycles. He calls the former "displaced dramas" of Christ's trials. The final two elegies of Grimald's revised poems, one could also suggest, are "displaced dramas" of Christ's passion.

[79] The term "correction" does not mean right over wrong; it simply refers to the change that the compositor or editor made thinking he was correcting the text.

where the meaning of words in Q2 are different from those of Q1, could have been caused by simple typographical oversights: in 209.20, for example, the word "clarke" in Q2 replaces "clacke" in Q1. In other instances, emendations are more deliberate: the heading for the preface of Q2, for example, reads *To the reder* instead of *The Printer to the Reader*, as in Q1, which suggests that the revised arrangement of Q2 was produced by someone other than the printer.

In Q2, there are three kinds of variants: transposition of letter types, which involve the exchange of letters in a word or words on the page; the obvious substitution of entire words in the diction of Q2 over that of Q1; and the revision of prosody that alters the scansion of the verse. The emendations may be the result of a curious blend of idiosyncratic impressions and stylistic preferences left over from the compositors and the editor. But careful attention to the differences between Q2 and Q1 reveals the importance of the emendations to individual poems and to the text as a whole. Examples of transpositional variants are found in the Surrey section, in 5.34 where "Unwittingly" replaces "Unwillingly"; in the Wyatt section, in 119.1, where "thrones" replaces "thornes"; in the Uncertain Auctours section, in 156.02 where "*stare*" replaces "*state*"; and in the Grimald section, in 278.66, where "martiall" replaces "Martiall."[80] There are some instances when the editor effects a grammatical emendation in Q2 in an attempt to "correct" an apparent mistake in Q1; in 26.1 "walkt" replaces "walke"; in 107.2 "with" replaces "which"; and in 171.32 "were" replaces "where."[81] Further alterations in grammar are produced when plural forms of words are exchanged in Q2 for singular forms in Q1, or vice-versa; for example, in 5.6 "woes" replaces "woe"; in 81.2 "mindes" replaces "mynde"; in 212.16 "dede" replaces "dedes"; and in 271.16 "rankes" replaces "renke."[82]

---

[80] In Q2, there are approximately 58 variants that involve the exchange or inversion of letters: 7 in Surrey's poems, 16 in Wyatt's, 34 in poems by the "Uncertain Auctours," and 1 in Grimald's poems. Other such variants involve the addition or omission of vowels or consonants that emend the meaning of the word and possibly its measure in the line; for example, in the Surrey section, at 6.7, "restraine" replaces "refraine"; in the Wyatt section, at 134.100, "Made" replaces "Madde"; and finally, in the Grimald section, at 279.76, "lothy" replaces "lothly". There are 9 typographical variants of this kind in the Surrey section; 10 in the Wyatt section; and 14 in the Uncertain Auctours section, with a curious run at 159.15, 207.15 and 21, 208.8, 212.15 and 27, where "thee" replaces "the".

[81] There are 8 grammatical emendations in the Surrey section; 10 in the Wyatt section; and 13 in the Uncertain Auctours section.

[82] There are 5 emendations in plural and singular forms in the Surrey section; 3 in the Wyatt section; 4 in the Uncertain Auctours section; and one in the Grimald section.

Matters of diction involve several kinds of variants in Q2, including the substitution of an archaic word for a modern word in Q1, or vice versa. Examples of the former are evident in 13.8, where "Sins that" replaces "Yet, since"; and in 213.2 "hath" replaces "had."[83] As one would expect, however, Q2's editor is more apt to modernize an archaic form of a word than not: for example, in 72.3 and 107.4 "heard" replaces "herd"; in 154.299 "would" replaces "wold"; and in 278.23 "shinyng" replaces "shinand."[84] Other changes in diction occur when spacing is altered, either causing or eliminating a compound word, such as in 5.7 where "A brode" replaces "Abrode"; in 137.77 where "to the" replaces "tothe"; and in 213.7 where "a row" replaces "arow."[85] Words are also substituted in Q2 that have no obvious link with those words they replace in Q1, but which significantly alter the meaning of the line. In the Surrey section, for example, in 13.12, "corner" replaces "cornet"; in the Wyatt section, in 69.89, "honour" replaces "nurture," and in 136.89, "guift" replaces "thing"; in the Uncertain Auctours section, in 158.10, "fame" replaces "praise," and in 244.10, "rote" replaces "frute"; and finally, in the Grimald section, in 271.5, "all" replaces "old"; and in 278.2, "dredfull trompets" replaces "taratantars".[86]

Finally, the editor of Q2 also emends the prosodic phrasing of lines in Q1. In the Surrey section, for example, in 8.8, "With a kings child, who tasteth ghostly food" replaces "With kinges child, where she tasteth costly food." In the Wyatt section, in 98.3, "With doubtful love that but increaseth pain" replaces "That love or wait it, alike doth me payne"; and in 136.45, "But if thou can" replaces "By which returne." In the Uncertain Auctours section, changes are found in 213.22, where "The noise did cease, the hall was stil" replaces "The audience ceased with the same"; and in 154.162, "Those shining" replaces "I mean, those." Finally, in Q2 there are no prosodic variants in Grimald's poems.[87]

---

[83] There are 14 instances where an archaic word is emended in Q2 to replace a modern version of the word in Q1, with almost half the instances involving "sins" which replaces "since" at 1.5, 104.11, 106.9, 108.5, 108.35, and 178.5.

[84] There are approximately 36 instances in which Q2's editor modernizes archaic words in Q1, including 2.1, 76.5, 164.25, 166.13, where "forth" replaces "furth"; and at 126.4, 159.7, 161.13, 175.15, where "poore" replaces "pore."

[85] There are 13 instances in Q2 where alterations in spacing substantively alter Q1. Words can also change when sorts are inadvertently mistaken; for example, "u" when used for the modern "v" could be turned and mistaken for "n", such as at 279.21, where "proue" replaces "prone." In total, there are 10 instances of such inversions of sorts in Q2.

[86] There are approximately 20 emendations of this kind to Surrey's diction in Q1: 21 in the diction of Wyatt; 31 in that of the Uncertain Auctours; and 5 in Grimald's diction.

[87] In Q2, there are a total of 11 prosodic changes in phrasing in the Surrey section; 24 changes in the Wyatt section; and 26 in the Uncertain Auctours section.

Thus, in more than 400 instances in Q2, the editor changes the substantive wording of Q1. Much attention is given to Surrey: of his 40 poems, 7 receive three or more substantive revisions, for a total of 40 substantive variants. Wyatt receives the least attention: of his 96 poems, 13 receive three or more substantive revisions, for a total of 55 variants. Of the 94 poems by Uncertain Auctours in Q1, 29 poems receive three or more substantive revisions in Q2, for a total of 145 emendations. Of the 22 emendations in Grimald, the final two poems, both elegies and both in unrhymed iambic pentameter, receive 20 substantive emendations. Moreover, though variants in punctuation are usually considered accidental—the work of compositors and not the work of the author or editor—patterns in the emended punctuation of Q2 parallel patterns in the substantive emendations. Q2's editor apparently conducted his revisions of the punctuation as an author might prepare his revisions for the press. For example, there are more than 650 changes in punctuation from Q1 to Q2. Surrey's poems reveal 46 new instances of punctuation; 60 alterations from a comma to a period, and 21 cases where no punctuation mark is used in Q2 though it is present in Q1. In contrast, Wyatt's poems in Q2 are proportionately the least punctuated. Whereas Surrey's 40 poems have emended punctuation in 127 places, Wyatt's 96 poems receive a mere 119 changes: 9 new instances of punctuation; 55 cases of different punctuation, and 55 instances where no punctuation mark is used in Q2, though it is present in Q1. Punctuation in the Uncertain Auctours section is vigorously emended: 134 poems receive 409 changes in punctuation; 180 cases of new punctuation; 163 cases of different punctuation; and 69 cases of lines not punctuated. Grimald's 10 poems in Q2 are not without emended punctuation: 6 new marks; 11 altered; and 16 instances where no punctuation is used in Q2, though it is present in Q1. Of the 10 poems by Grimald in Q2, the final two elegies receive most attention.

To conclude, then, analysis of the substantive and accidental variants between Q2 and Q1 indicates that the editor did not engage in full-scale revisions of each poem. Apparently, he emended words, phrases, and punctuation as seemed appropriate to his ear in his attempt to produce a strong iambic line and still remain committed to the issues addressed by the speaker of each poem.[88] While specific poems may have ideological significance, one cannot

---

[88] William A. Sessions argues that the variants in Surrey's poem (8.7–8) are ideologically significant. In Q2, the lines read: "From tender yeres, in Britain did she rest, | With a kinges child, who tasteth ghostly food"; while in Q1 they read: "From tender yeres, in Britain she doth rest, | With a kinges child, where she tasteth costly food." Sessions suggests that "ghostly food" refers to the "Eucharist or Holy Communion acting as *synecdoche* (the part for the whole) for religious instruction and proof of the young woman's careful education" (*Henry Howard: The Poet Earl of Surrey: A Life* [Oxford and New York: Oxford University Press, 1999], 192–93). Historically, Surrey's

conclude that Q2 is a pro-Marian text, especially if statements in the 39 new poems by the Uncertain Auctours are considered which could be read as political criticism of the Marian regime. In particular, in poem 229, we hear that the "hidden harme" has "broken out" in "our time" (229.37–38), and in poem 234, "the whole world is set on mischief," "measure and mean" are absent, "trouth is folly" and "mens harts are burnde with sundry sectes" (234.30–32, 55–56). These statements, combined with the claim by the persona in poem 218 that in this age "such troubles still apperes, | Which never were before this time, no not this in thousand yeres" (23–25), suggest that at least some of the poems by the Uncertain Auctours are particularly critical of Mary's reign. But Tottel was a political survivor. His ability to maintain his monopoly as a printer of law books during the reigns of Edward VI and Mary Tudor meant that he was not likely to forfeit his flourishing career in 1557 by publishing an anthology of poems that could be censored, or for which he would be prosecuted and sent to prison, if not worse. Tottel's book sold in 1557, and continued selling through the Elizabethan period most likely because it included a large variety of poems reflecting a breadth of private and public perspectives on the individual and the community in the mid-Tudor world.

Textual Variants between Q2 and Q3

The editor of Q3, using Q2 as a copy text, also reveals an interest in providing a text accessible to the reader. This is evident in the impression of the first few leaves. In contrast to pages A_1r and A_1v in Q2, which provide the title page and the preface *To the Reder*, crowded to the left and right margin respectively, Q3's type is recast to compose pages that are centered and more graphically shaped. The prefatory remarks on A_1v are designed as a column or monument that funnels at the bottom to a fine point, which pivots on the word "delight." Compared to the elongated rectangular shape of the preface in Q1 and Q2, the editorial design of the opening leaves of Q3 is strong and impressive. The change in format projects the book as a monument of literary significance.[89]

Geraldine, Elizabeth Fitzgerald, shared a Catholic upbringing with her cousin, Princess Mary, at Hunsdon, the old Howard estate, where she was sent in 1534 and where Geraldine remained until 1539. According to Sessions's argument, one could suggest that the editor of Q2 aligned the titular poet of *Songes and Sonettes* with the Marian Counter-Reformation by reminding the reader not only that Surrey's beloved Geraldine was Catholic but also that his family had earlier provided a refuge for the reigning Queen Mary, both at Hunsdon and at Kenninghall.

[89] The editor of Q3 was a literary man, of some surprising literary taste. He did not concern himself with catchwords or signatures, though possibly with the lining of the titles. It seems likely that he worked with copies of Q2 and Q1 before him. Wendy

An analysis of the substantive variants of Q3 suggests that this concern for the graphic effect of the book is also present in the revision of the verses.

In Q3, Surrey's poems 7, 8, and 13, are revised significantly; in every instance, Q2's reading is replaced by Q1's. Sonnet 7 is altered in nine places; sonnet 8 has five alterations; and sonnet 13 has four alterations. These poems receive more attention in Q3 than any others in the collection.[90] Indeed, most of the revisions in Q3 seem motivated by matters of diction and prosody. The task, vigorously embraced by the editor of Q2, to ensure that Tottel's verses conformed to iambic scansion, is continued in Q3. What the editor rejects, for the most part, are those instances where the revisions in Q2 exceed the measure of the iambic line. A number of other instances occur in which Q3 abandons the wording of Q2 in favor of Q1. Some changes involve transposition, the substitution, inversion, addition, or omission of one letter or two in certain words to provide another word with a different meaning. Revisions are also grammatical, where the editor of Q3 corrects what he considers a mistake in Q2. In 2.1, for example, Q3 recalls Q1's "soote" to replace Q2's "foote"; in 119.1, "thornes" replaces "thrones"; and in 190.4, "untruth" replaces "but truth." A number of other instances occur in which Q3 abandons the wording of Q2 in favor of Q1. Some changes involve capitalizing nouns to enhance their importance or placing them in small caps to diminish their importance; for example, in 29.57, "nature" replaces "Nature." Plural nouns are also replaced by the singular form;

Wall has argued that the presentation of title pages and prefaces authorizes the legitimacy of the contents of books. Her comments on the first few leaves of the 1598 *Arcadia* are relevant to Tottel's Q3: "The trappings of the 1598 *Arcadia*—the title page and the two prefaces—helped to create and monumentalize the literary reputation that the combined works established" (*The Imprint of Gender: Authorship and Publication in the English Renaissance* [London and Ithaca: Cornell University Press, 1993], 151).

[90] Versions of the poems are also found in the Arundel Harington MS, but no attempt is made in Q3 to return the poems to the readings in that manuscript. Why would the editor emend the revisions of these poems provided by the editor of Q2 back to the readings in Q1? If we accept Sessions's claim that "ghostly food" in poem 8 is a synecdoche for the Holy Eucharist that recalls Mary Tudor's religious education and instruction in the Roman Church, one might argue that Q3's emendation of the text back to the Q1 reading of "costly food" eliminates the subtle allusion to the Catholicism of both Mary and Henry Howard, the Earl of Surrey, the author of the poem. Was Q3 edited in the early years of Elizabeth's reign, during a time when it was thought wise to eliminate such allusions? A marshalling of evidence in the revisions to Q3 might provide a sound basis for dating that text as Elizabethan, but such evidence must be based as much on bibliographical analysis as on the presence or absence of literary devices such as synecdoche. Indeed, why the editor of Q3 made substantive changes to Q2 that recalled the readings of Q1 is a question that Rollins concluded was a "mystery" that he was "incompetent to solve" (2: 99). Since then, no one has been more competent.

in 15.4, "feast" replaces "feastes"; and in 15.40, "night" replaces "nightes." At times, spacing between letters is altered to produce or eliminate a compound; in 154.143, "forelore" replaces "for lore"; in 172.9, "Away" replaces "A way"; and in 213.41, "a side" replaces "aside." In matters of diction, the editor of Q3 sometimes replaces words or phrases to correct what were to him unsound alterations in Q2, by employing either archaic words to replace modern ones, or vice versa: for example, in 12.1, "doth" replaces "do"; in 30.5, "hath" replaces "have"; and in 178.5, "since" replaces "sins." These changes suggest that in certain instances, Q3's editor had a fastidious allegiance to Q1, recalling the iambic scansion of the lines, and resorting to the editorial authority of that text over Q2.

Instances also occur where Q3 abandons both readings of Q2 and Q1 and provides a variant of its own. Here again is evidence of editorial principles in play: for example, in 23.2, "hard" replaces "herd"; in 162.02, "and" replaces "or"; and in 243.8 and 244.10, "roote" replaces "rote." In all but a few cases, the editor of Q3 provides an improvement over Q2.[91] Further revisions appear in Q3, where the editor rejects the archaic diction of Q2 and Q1: for example, in 1.1 and 4.26, "forth" replaces "furth"; in 108.97, "read" replaces "red"; and in 178.28, "serves" replaces "sarves."[92] When the archaic spellings of words in Q2 are replaced by modernized equivalents, the historical ambivalence of the diction is diminished, but a more accessible text is produced for the "unlearned" reader for whom, in part, Tottel publishes his book, as he suggests in his preface. In short, he updates the spelling for current tastes.[93] There are 15 instances in Q3 where the thematic thrust of the lyric voices in the verses is sharpened, revealing the attentive, though idiosyncratic, reading of Q3's editor. In some cases, it is merely a matter of correcting grammar, but elsewhere the editor apparently attempts to fill what he sees as an absence of consistency in the thematic action of the verse. The result is often a verbal clarity that is missing in Q2 and Q1: for example, in 20.30, "sunne" replaces "sonne"; in 167.42, "Nor aging" replaces "No raging"; in 213.15, "pase" replaces "prease"; and in 278.70, "workes" replaces "wordes."

The editor also made changes to the 39 new poems added to Q2 (222–238, 242, 246, 249–254, 257–270). In Q3, variants to fifteen poems are made in grammar and diction which alter the prosody and tone of the lyrics: in 226.12, for example, "thus" replaces "this"; in 268.29, "not" replaces "no"; and in 270.40, "grace" replaces "grave." Q3 continues the general initiative in Q2 towards impersonalization. In the few instances when Q2 opts for a more

---

[91] There are 20 instances in Q3 where the text is not obviously improved, as in 128.8, 192.22, and 241.1.

[92] There are 14 instances of modernization in Q3.

[93] There are also a few instances in which emendations do produce alternate meanings, though a consistent policy concerning titles and compound nouns is not apparent in Q3.

personal reference than Q1, the editor of Q3 reverts to the impersonal reading of Q1. For example, in 14.9, Q3 reinstates Q1's "Ladie" to replace Q2's "Garret," a reference to the family name of Elizabeth Fitzgerald, Surrey's idealized subject in 1542, the year he likely penned the sonnet.[94] Further, Q2 emphasizes the acrostic in poem 169, when the first letters of each line followed by a space spelling vertically the letters in the name "Edward Somerset," until the last line emphasizes the final letter by setting it apart spatially from the word to which it belongs ("bes T") at the end of the line. The editor of Q3, however, omits the emphasis by eliminating the spacing and allows the name to retreat back into the poem, erasing its significance to all but the keenest reader.

What can be inferred from the preceding discussion of the variants in Q3 in relation to those in Q2? First, that the variants in Q3 do not radically alter the text of Q2. Indeed, the editor clearly accepted the most significant changes in Q2, that is, the revised arrangement of authors, the exclusion of Grimald's 30 poems, the inclusion of 39 new poems by the Uncertain Auctours, and the shuffling of poems from one position to another, especially in the Uncertain Auctours section. Nevertheless, Q3 differs from Q2 substantively in approximately 140 instances: Surrey's poems receive 37 substantive variants; Wyatt's poems, 17 variants; the Uncertain Auctours, 79 variants (with one-third of the changes occurring in the 39 new poems); while the remaining 10 poems by Grimald have 7 substantive variants. Fewer than one-third of the total substantive changes in Q3 revert to Q1. Thus, though Q3's editor respected the readings of Q1, he was motivated less by a need to restore that text than by a desire to continue the initiative, evident from the beginning of the project, to provide a consistent tone to individual poems and a uniform iambic measure to the verses as a whole, that is, to create a text more accessible to the reader.

To conclude, *Songes and Sonettes* provides the first example in English of an editor's canonization in a printed book of poems by a group of authors whose works had been circulating largely in manuscripts. As announced in Tottel's preface, the anthology presents to the reader the "honorable stile of the noble Earle of Surrey and the weightinesse of the depewitted Sir Thomas Wiatt the Elders verse." The book also shows that the works of living authors, reflected in the poems by the Uncertain Auctours and by *N.G.*, could compete with the technical and verbal accomplishments of Latin and Italian verse: "our tong is able in that kinde to do as praise worthelye as the rest," the preface asserts. The careful editing of Q2 and Q3 demonstrates a belief in the value of the anthology as a literary genre and the importance of its aesthetic presentation to the public. In the mid-Tudor period, the advantage of publishing a compilation of poems by other people was that once the poems were arranged, the lyric voices would speak for themselves, leaving virtually no

---

[94] By 1552, through several successful marriages, Elizabeth Fitzgerald had become the enormously wealthy Countess of Lincoln, a figure the editor of Q3 might well have chosen not to disturb after 1557.

trace of editorial presence, and thus little room for recrimination. The arrangement of poems in Q2 traces the plight of the personae from the private world of courtly love to the public world of politics and religion. But no one particular position is valorized, for the personae merely record and observe various attitudes towards their relations with others and the political, religious, moral or amoral world in which they live. In the end, however, the new revised order of Q2 does celebrate the poet for immortalizing the selfless deeds of those who have suffered injustice in the attempt to construct a more civilized human community. The editor of Tottel's revised *Songes and Sonettes*, then, assumes the role of the author in the arrangement of a compilation of poems in which the personae provide cultural commentary on the mid-Tudor world. This anthology thus anticipated and inspired numerous works by Elizabethan writers, including George Gascoigne's *A Hundreth Sundrie Flowres* (1573) and *Posies* (1575), Edmund Spenser's *The Shepheardes Calendar* (1579), and Sir Philip Sidney's *Certain Sonnets* (ca 1581), which in turn initiated the fashion for sonnet sequences that culminated in *Shake-speares Sonnets* (1609).

SONGES AND SONETTES

written by the right honorable Lorde
Henry Haward late Earle of Sur-
rey, and other.

Apud Richardum Tottel.
Cum privilegio ad impri
mendum Solum.
.1557.

Contents
The sequence of poems in Q2 (first lines)

1. The sunne hath twise brought furth his tender grene
2. The soote season, that bud and blome forth brings
3. When youth had led me half the race
4. Such waiward waies hath love, that most part in discord
5. When sommer toke in hand the winter to assail
6. Love, that liveth, and raigneth in my thought
7. In Ciprus, springes (where as dame Venus dwelt)
8. From Tuskane came my Ladies worthy race
9. Brittle beautie, that nature made so fraile
10. Alas so all things now do hold their peace
11. When Windsor walles susteyned my wearied arme
12. Set me wheras the Sunne do parche the grene
13. I never saw my Ladie laye apart
14. The golden gift that nature did thee geve
15. So cruell prison how could betide, alas
16. When raging love with extreme payne
17. O happy dames, that may embrace
18. In winters just returne, when Boreas gan his raigne
19. Good Ladies: ye that have your pleasures in exile
20. Geve place ye lovers, here before
21. Although I had a check
22. To dearely had I bought my grene and youthfull yeres,
23. O lothsome place where I
24. As oft as I behold and see
25. Though I regarded not
26. Wrapt in my carelesse cloke, as I walke to and fro
27. Girt in my giltles gowne as I sit here and sow
28. Sins fortunes wrath envieth the wealth
29. Eche beast can chose his fere according to his minde
30. If care do cause men cry, why do not I complaine
31. Martial, the thinges that do attain
32. Of thy life, Thomas, this compasse wel mark
33. The great Macedon, that out of Persie chased
34. Dyvers thy death do diversly bemone
35. W. resteth here, that quick could never rest
36. In the rude age when knowledge was not rife
37. Thassirian king in peace, with foule desire
38. Layd in my quiet bed, in study as I were
39. The stormes are past these cloudes are overblowne
40. My Ratclif, when thy retchlesse youth offendes
41. The fansy, which that I have served long
42. The long love, that in my thought I harber
43. Yet was I never of your love agreved
44. Was never file yet half so well yfiled

45. The lively sparkes, that issue from those eyes

46. Such vain thought, as wonted to mislead me

47. Unstable dreame according to the place

48. Ye that in love finde luck and swete abundance

49. If waker care: if sodayn pale colour

50. Cesar, when that the traitour of Egipt

51. Eche man me telth, I change most my devise

52. Some fowles there be that have so perfit sight

53. Because I stil kept thee fro lyes, and blame

54. I finde no peace, and all my warre is done

55. My galley charged with forgetfulnesse

56. Avisyng the bright beames of those fayre eyes

57. They flee from me, that sometime did me seke

58. Madame, withouten many wordes

59. Alas, Madame, for stealing of a kisse

60. The wandring gadling, in the summer tide

61. What nedes these threatning wordes, and wasted wynd

62. Right true it is, and sayd full yore ago

63. It may be good like it who list

64. Resownde my voyce ye woodes, that heare me plain

65. In faith I wot not what to say

66. Farewell the hart of crueltie

67. The restfull place, renewer of my smart

68. From these hie hilles as when a spring doth fall

69. Mine old dere enmy, my froward maister

70. Marvell no more altho

71. Where shall I have, at mine owne wyll

72. She sat, and sowed: that hath done me the wrong

73. What man hath heard such cruelty before

74. Behold, Love, thy power how she despiseth

75. What vaileth troth? or by it, to take payn

76. Somtime I fled the fire, that me so brent

77. He is not dead, that somtime had a fall

78. The furious goonne, in his most raging yre

79. Accused though I be, without desert

80. My love to skorne, my service to retayne

81. Within my brest I never thought it gain

82. Passe forth my wonted cries

83. Your lokes so often cast

84. Disdaine me not without desert

85. For want of will, in wo I plain

86. If every man might him avaunt

87. The answere that ye made to me my dere

88. Such is the course, that natures kinde hath wrought

89. The enmy of life, decayer of all kinde

90. Once as me thought, fortune me kist

91. My lute awake performe the last

92. Nature that gave the Bee so feate a grace

93. Unwarely so was never no man caught
94. Al in thy loke my life doth whole depende
95. Perdy I sayd it not
96. Lux, my faire fawlcon, and thy felowes all
97. A face that should content me wonderous wel
98. Ever my hap is slack and slowe in comming
99. Love, Fortune, and my minde which do remember
100. How oft have I, my deare and cruel fo
101. Lyke unto these unmesurable mountaines
102. If amorous fayth, or if an hart unfained
103. Farewell, Love, and all thy lawes for ever
104. My hart I gave thee, not to do it pain
105. The flaming sighes that boyle within my brest
106. The piller perisht is wherto I lent
107. Go burning sighes unto the frosen hart
108. So feble is the threde, that doth the burden stay
109. Suffised not (madame) that you did teare
110. When first mine eyes did view, and marke
111. Synce love will nedes, that I shall love
112. Mystrustfull mindes be moved
113. Lover. It burneth yet, alas my hartes desire
114. Of purpose, love chose first for to be blinde
115. What rage is this: what furor: of what kinde

116. Desire (alas) my master, and my fo
117. I see, that chance hath chosen me
118. What word is that, that changeth not
119. Venemous thrones that are so sharp and kene
120. A Lady gave me a gift she had not
121. Speake thou and spede where will or power ought helpth
122. If thou wilt mighty be, flee from the rage
123. Lyke as the birde within the cage enclosed
124. For shamfast harm of great, and hatefull nede
125. Vulcane begat me: Minerva me taught
126. Syghes are my foode: my drink are my teares
127. Throughout the world if it wer sought,
128. Stond who so list upon the slipper wheele
129. In court to serve decked with fresh aray
130. Of Carthage he that worthy warriour
131. Tagus farewell that Westward with thy stremes
132. Driven by desire I did this dede
133. In doubtfull breast whiles motherly pity
134. My mothers maides when they do sowe and spinne
135. Myne owne Jhon Poins: sins ye delite to know
136. A spendyng hand that alway powreth out
137. When Dido feasted first the wandring Trojan knight

138. If ever wofull man might move your hartes to ruthe
139. Who justly may rejoyce in ought under the skye
140. If right be rackt, and overronne
141. The life is long, that lothsomly doth last
142. In Grece somtime there dwelt a man of worthy fame
143. Lyke as the Larke within the Marlians foote
144. The lenger lyfe, the more offence
145. To thys my song geve eare, who list
146. The plage is great, where fortune frownes
147. O evyll tonges, which clap at every winde
148. The restlesse rage of depe devouryng hell
149. By fortune as I lay in bed, my fortune was to finde
150. Phylida was a fayre mayde
151. Lo, here the end of man the cruell sisters three
152. Who list to live upright, and holde him self content
153. Unto the living Lord for pardon do I pray
154. Syth singyng gladdeth oft the harts
155. Full faire and white she is, and White by name
156. What thing is that which I both have and lacke
157. It is no fire that geves no heate
158. Alas that ever death such vertues should forlet
159. Shall I thus ever long, and be no whit the neare
160. The doutfull man hath fevers strange
161. Sith that the way to wealth is wo

162. A studient at his boke so plast
163. Who craftly castes to stere his boate
164. I lent my love to losse and gaged my life in vaine
165. When dredful swelling seas, through boisterous windy blastes
166. The winter with his griesly stormes ne lenger dare abide
167. In seking rest, unrest I finde
168. Geve place you Ladies and be gone
169. E xperience now doth shew what God us taught before
170. Thestilis, a sely man, when love did him forsake
171. Thestilis, thou sely man, why dost thou so complayne
172. Nature that taught my silly dog god wat
173. Since thou my ring mayst go where I ne may
174. For that a restles hed must somwhat have in ure
175. When Audley had run out his race, and ended wer his daies
176. Eche thing I see hath time, which time must try my truth
177. My youthfull yeres are past
178. Behold my picture here well portrayed for the nones
179. Bewaile with me all ye that have profest
180. I see there is no sort
181. When Cupide scaled first the fort
182. I lothe that I did love
183. To live to dye and dye to live againe
184. The smoky sighes the bitter teares
185. As Cypres tree that rent is by the roote

186. The shining season here to some
187. O temerous tauntres that delights in toyes
188. O Petrarke hed and prince of poets al
189. With Petrarke to compare ther may no wight
190. Cruel unkinde whom mercy cannot move
191. If it were so that God would graunt me my request
192. To love, alas, who would not feare
193. In fredome was my fantasie
194. Among dame natures workes such perfite law is wrought
195. To my mishap alas I finde
196. All you that frendship do professe
197. Death and the king did as it were contend
198. Lyke as the brake within the riders hand
199. Such grene to me as you have sent
200. As I have bene so will I ever be
201. The golden apple that the Troyan boy
202. The Cowerd oft whom deinty viandes fed
203. Though in the waxe a perfect picture made
204. Lyke as the rage of raine
205. At libertie I sit and see
206. I read how Troylus served in Troy
207. Flee from the prease and dwell with sothfastnes
208. Sins Mars first moved warre or stirred men to strife
209. The dolefull bell that still doth ring
210. For love Apollo (his Godhed set aside)

211. As Lawrell leaves that cease not to be grene
212. False may be he, and by the powers above
213. I heard when fame with thundring voice did sommon to appere
214. I ne can close in short and cunning verse
215. Yet once againe my muse I pardon pray
216. Why fearest thou thy outward fo
217. The flickeryng fame that flieth from eare to eare
218. Who loves to live in peace, and marketh every change
219. Walkyng the pathe of pensive thought
220. Procryn that somtime served Cephalus
221. Lyke the Phenix a birde most rare in sight
222. The soules that lacked grace
223. Lo dead he lives, that whilome lived here
224. What harder is then stone, what more then water soft
225. O lingring make Ulisses dere, thy wife lo sendes to thee
226. You that in play peruse my plaint, and reade in rime the smart
227. It was the day on which the sunne deprived of his light
228. The Sunne when he hath spred his raies
229. The secret flame that made all Troy so hot
230. The bird that somtime built within my brest
231. Not like a God came Jupiter to woo
232. I that Ulysses yeres have spent

233. Thou Cupide God of love, whom Venus thralles do serve
234. Complaine we may: much is amisse
235. Do all your dedes by good advise
236. Who list to lead a quiet life
237. A kinde of coale is as men say
238. Your borrowd meane to move your mone, of fume withouten flame
239. Lo here lieth G. under the ground
240. If that thy wicked wife had spon the thread
241. From worldly wo the mede of misbelefe
242. Stay gentle frend that passest by
243. A man may live thrise Nestors life
244. The vertue of Ulisses wife
245. To false report and flying fame
246. Whom fansy forced first to love
247. To walke on doutfull ground, where daunger is unsene
248. To trust the fayned face, to rue on forced teares
249. Ah love how waiward is his wit what panges do perce his brest
250. The blinded boy that bendes the bow
251. I wold I found not as I fele
252. No joy have I, but live in heavinesse
253. The wisest way, thy bote, in wave and winde to guie
254. Who so that wisely weyes the profite and the price
255. Some men would think of right to have
256. Such waiward waies have some when folly stirres their braines
257. Vaine is the fleting welth
258. Do way your phisike I faint no more

259. A cruell Tiger all with teeth bebled
260. Ah libertie now have I learnd to know
261. Holding my peace alas how loud I crye
262. I sely Haw whose hope is past
263. Adieu desert, how art thou spent
264. In Bayes I boast whose braunch I beare
265. When Phebus had the serpent slaine
266. In court as I behelde, the beauty of eche dame
267. Ye are to yong to bryng me in
268. Farewell thou frosen hart and eares of hardned stele
269. Resigne you dames whom tikelyng brute delight
270. Alas when shall I joy
271. Imps of king Jove, and quene Remembrance lo
272. In working well, if travell you sustain
273. What one art thou, thus in torn weed yclad
274. The auncient time commended, not for nought
275. What path list you to tread? what trade will you assay
276. What race of life ronne you? what trade will you assay
277. Of all the heavenly giftes, that mortall men commend
278. Now clattering armes, now ragyng broyls of warre
279. Therfore, when restlesse rage of winde, and wave
280. For Tullie, late, a tomb I gan prepare

To the reder.

That to have wel written in verse, yea and in small parcelles,
deserveth great praise, the workes of divers Latines, Italians,
and other, doe prove sufficiently. That our tong is able in that
kinde to do as praise worthelye as the rest, the honorable stile
5 of the noble earle of Surrey, and the weightinesse of the
depewitted sir Thomas Wiat the elders verse, with several graces
in sondry good Englishe writers, do show abundantly.
It resteth now (gentle reder) that thou thinke it not evil don, to
publishe, to the honor of the english tong, and for profit of the
10 studious of Englishe eloquence, those workes which the
ungentle horders up of such tresure have heretofore envied the.
And for this point (good reder) thine own profit and pleasure,
in these presentlye, and in moe hereafter, shal answer for my
defence. If parhappes some mislike the statelinesse of stile
15 removed from the rude skil of common eares: I aske help of
the learned to defende their learned frendes, the authors of this
woork: And I exhort the unlearned, by reding to learne to bee
more skilfull, and to purge that swinelike grossenesse, that
maketh the swete majerome not to smell to their delight.

[1] *Descripcion of the restlesse state*
of a lover, with sute to his
ladie, to rue on his di-
yng hart.

   The sunne hath twise brought furth his tender grene,
   Twise clad the earth in lively lustinesse:
   Ones have the windes the trees despoiled clene,
   And ones again begins their cruelnesse,
5 Sins I have hid under my brest the harm,
   That never shal recover healthfulnesse.
   The winters hurt recovers with the warm:
   The parched grene restored is with shade.
   What warmth (alas) may serve for to disarm
10 The frosen hart, that mine in flame hath made?
   What cold againe is able to restore
   My fresh grene yeres, that wither thus and fade?
   Alas, I see nothing hath hurt so sore,
   But time in time reduceth a returne:
15 In time my harm encreaseth more and more,
   And semes to have my cure alwaies in scorne.
   Strange kindes of death, in life that I do trie:
   At hand to melt, farre of in flame to burne.
   And like as time list to my cure apply,
20 So doth eche place my comfort cleane refuse.
   Al thing alive, that seeth the heavens with eye,
   With cloke of night may cover, and excuse
   It self from travail of the daies unrest,
   Save I, alas, against all others use,
25 That then stirre up the tormentes of my brest,
   And curse eche sterre as causer of my fate:
   And when the sunne hath eke the dark opprest,
   And brought the day, it doth nothing abate
   The travailes of mine endlesse smart and pain.
30 For then as one that hath the light in hate,
   I wish for night, more covertly to plain,
   And me withdraw from every haunted place,
   Lest by my chere my chaunce appere to plain:
   And in my minde I measure pace by pace,
35 To seke the place where I my self had lost,
   That day that I was tangled in the lace,
   In semyng slack that knitteth ever most:
   But never yet the travaile of my thought

Of better state coulde catch a cause to bost.
40 For if I found sometime, that I have sought,
Those sterres by whom I trusted of the port:
My sailes do fall, and I advance right nought,
As ankerd fast: my sprites do all resort
To stand agazed, and sink in more and more
45 The deadly harme which she doth take in sport.
Lo, if I seke, how I do finde my sore:
And if I flee, I cary with me still
The venomd shaft, which doth his force restore
By haste of flight, and I may plaine my fill
50 Unto my self unlesse this carefull song
Print in your hart some parcell of my tene.
For I, alas, in silence all to long,
Of mine old hurt yet fele the wound but grene.
Rue on my life: or els your cruel wrong
55 Shall well appere, and by my death be sene.

[2] *Description of Spring, wherin eche*
thing renewes, save onely
the lover.

The soote season, that bud and blome forth brings,
With grene hath clad the hill, and eke the vale:
The nightingale, with fethers new she sings:
The turtle to her make hath tolde her tale:
5 Somer is come, for every spray now springs,
The hart hath hong his old hed on the pale:
The buck in brake his winter coate he flings:
The fishes flete with new repayred scale:
The adder all her slough away she slings:
10 The swift swallow pursueth the flies smalle:
The busy bee her hony now she minges:
Winter is worne that was the flowers bale:
And thus I see among these pleasant things,
Eche care decayes, and yet my sorow springs.

[3] *Description of the restlesse state*
of a lover.

When youth had led me half the race,
That Cupides scourge had made me runne:
I loked backe, to mete the place,
From whence my wery course begonne.
5   And then I saw how my desire,
Misguidyng me, had led the way:
Mine eyen, to gredy of their hyre,
Had made me lose a better pray.
For when in sighes I spent the day
10   And could not cloke my grief with game:
The boylyng smoke did still bewray
The persant heat of secrete flame.
And when salt teares do bain my brest,
Where love his pleasant traines hath sowen:
15   Her beauty hath the frutes opprest,
Ere that the buds were sprong and blowne.
And when mine eyen did styll pursue
The fliyng chace of their request
Their gredy lokes did oft renew
20   The hidden wound within my brest.
When every loke these chekes might staine,
From deadly pale to glowyng red:
By outward signes appeared plaine,
To her for help my hart was fled.
25   But all to late love learneth me,
To paint all kinde of colors new:
To blinde their eyes that els should see
My specled chekes with Cupides hewe.
And now the covert brest I claime,
30   That worshipt Cupide secretely,
And nourished his sacred flame:
From whence no blasyng sparkes do flye.

[4] *Desciption of the fickle affec-*
tions, panges, and sleightes
of love.

Such waiward waies hath love, that most part in discord
Our willes do stand: whereby our harts but seldom do accord.

Deceit is his delight, and to begile, and mock
The simple hartes, whom he doth strike with froward divers stroke.
5   He causeth thone to rage with golden burning dart,
And doth alay with leaden cold again the other hart.
Whote glemes of burning fire, and easy sparkes of flame
In balaunce of unegal weight he pondereth by aime.
From easy ford, where I might wade and passe ful wel,
10   He me withdrawes, and doth me drive into a depe dark hel,
And me withholdes, wher I am cald, and offred place:
And willes me that my mortall foe I doe beseke of grace.
He lettes me to pursue a conquest welnere wonne,
To folow where my paines were lost, ere that my sute begonne.
15   So by this meanes I know how soone a hart may turne,
From warre to peace, from truce to strife, and so againe returne.
I know how to content my self in others lust:
Of litle stuffe unto my self to weave a web of trust:
And how to hide my harmes with soft dissembling chere,
20   When in my face the painted thoughtes would outwardly apere.
I know how that the blood forsakes the face for dred:
And how by shame it staines again the chekes with flaming red.
I know under the grene the serpent how he lurkes.
The hammer of the restles forge I wote eke how it workes.
25   I know and can by roate the tale that I would tel:
But oft the words come furth awrie of him that loveth wel.
I know in heat and cold the lover how he shakes:
In singing how he doth complain, in sleping how he wakes:
To languish without ache, sicklesse for to consume:
30   A thousand things for to devise, resolving all in fume.
And though he list to see his ladies grace full sore,
Such pleasures, as delight his eye, do not his health restore.
I know to seke the track of my desired foe:
And fear to finde that I do seke. But chiefly this I know,
35   That lovers must transforme into the thing beloved,
And live (alas who would beleve?) with sprite from life removed.
I know in harty sighes, and laughters of the splene,
At ones to change my state, my will, and eke my color clene.
I know how to deceave my self with others help:
40   And how the Lion chastised is by beating of the whelp.
In standing nere my fire, I know how that I freze:
Far of I burne: in both I wast: and so my life I leze.
I know how love doth rage upon a yelding minde:
How smal a net may take and meash a hart of gentle kinde:

45   Or els with seldom swete to season heapes of gall:
      Revived with a glimse of grace old sorowes to let fal,
         The hidden traines I know, and secret snares of love:
      How soone a loke wil print a thought, that never may remove.
         The slipper state I know, the sodein turnes from wealth,
50   The doubtful hope, the certain woe, and sure despeire of health.

[5] *Complaint of a lover, that defied*
love, and was by love after
the more tor-
mented.

     When sommer toke in hand the winter to assail,
     With force of might, and vertue gret, his stormy blasts to quail,
        And when he clothed faire the earth about with grene,
     And every tree new garmented, that pleasure was to sene:
5   Mine hart gan new revive, and changed blood did stur
     Me to withdrawe my winter woes, that kept within the dore.
        A brode, quod my desire: assay to set thy fote,
     Where thou shalt finde the savour swete: for sprong is every rote.
        And to thy health, if thou were sick in any case,
10 Nothing more good, than in the spring the aire to fele a space.
        There shalt thou heare and se all kindes of birdes ywrought,
     Well tune their voice with warble smal, as nature hath them tought.
        Thus pricked me my lust the sluggish house to leave:
     And for my health I thought it best such counsail to receave.
15   So on a morow furth, unwist of any wight,
     I went to prove how well it would my heavy burden light.
        And when I felt the aire so pleasant round about,
     Lord, to my self how glad I was that I had gotten out.
        There might I se how Ver had every blossom hent:
20 And eke the new betrothed birdes ycoupled how they went.
        And in their songes me thought they thanked nature much,
     That by her licence all that yere to love their happe was such,
        Right as they could devise to chose them feres throughout:
     With much rejoysing to their Lord thus flew they al about.
25   Which when I gan resolve, and in my head conceave,
     What pleasant life, what heapes of joy these litle birdes receave,
        And saw in what estate I wery man was brought,
     By want of that they had at will, and I reject at nought:
        Lord how I gan in wrath unwisely me demeane.
30 I cursed love and him defied: I thought to turne the streame.

But when I well beheld he had me under awe,
I asked mercy for my fault, that so transgrest his lawe.
    Thou blinded God (quod I) forgeve me this offence,
Unwittingly I went about, to malice thy pretence.
35 Wherwith he gave a beck, and thus me thought he swore,
Thy sorowe ought suffice to purge thy fault, if it were more.
    The vertue of which sound mine hart did so revive,
That I, me thought, was made as whole as any man alive,
    But here I may perceive mine errour all and some,
40 For that I thought that so it was: yet was it still undone.
    And all that was no more but mine expressed minde,
That faine would have some good reliefe, of Cupide well assinde.
    I turned home forthwith, and might perceve it well,
That he agreved was right sore with me for my rebell.
45 My harmes have ever since, encreased more and more,
And I remaine without his help, undone for evermore,
    A mirror let me be unto ye lovers all:
Strive not with love, for if ye do, it will ye thus befall.

[6] *Complaint of a lover*
rebuked.

Love, that liveth, and raigneth in my thought,
That built his seat within my captive brest,
Clad in the armes, wherin with me he fought,
Oft in my face he doth his banner rest.
5   She, that me taught to love, and suffer payne,
My doutfull hope, and eke my hot desire,
With shamefast cloke to shadow and restraine,
Her smiling grace converteth straight to yre.
And coward love then to the hart apace
10 Taketh his flight, wheras he lurkes and plaines
His purpose lost, and dare not shew his face.
For my lordes gilt thus faultlesse bide I paines.
Yet from my lorde shall not my foote remove.
Swete is his death, that takes his end by love.

[7] *Complaint of the lover disdained.*

In Ciprus, springes (where as dame Venus dwelt)
A Well so hotte is, that who tastes the same,
Were he of stone, as thawed yse should melt,

And kindeled finde his brest with fired flame.
5 Whose moist poyson dissolved hath my hart.
With crepyng fire my colde lyms ar supprest,
Feeleth the hart that harborde freedome smart,
Endlesse dispaire long thraldome hath imprest.
An other well of frozen yse is founde,
10 Whose chilling venome of repugnant kinde
The fervent heat doth quenche of Cupides wounde:
And with the spot of change infectes the minde:
Whereof my dere hath tasted, to my paine.
Wherby my service growes into disdaine.

[8] *Description and praise of his*
love Geraldine.

From Tuskane came my Ladies worthy race:
Faire Florence was sometime her auncient seate:
The Western yle, whose pleasant shore doth face
Wilde Cambers clifs, furst gave her lively heate:
5 Fostred she was with milke of Irishe brest:
Her sire, an Earle: her dame, of princes blood.
From tender yeres, in Britain did she rest,
With a kinges child, who tasteth ghostly food.
Honsdon did first present her to mine iyen:
10 Bright is her hewe, and Geraldine she hight.
Hampton me taught to wishe her first for mine:
And Windsor, alas, doth chase me from her sight.
Her beauty of kinde, her vertues from above.
Happy is he, that can obtaine her love.

[9] *The frailtie and hurtfulnes*
of beautie.

Brittle beautie, that nature made so fraile,
Wherof the gift is small, and short the season,
Flowring to day, to morowe apt to faile,
Tickell treasure abhorred of reason,
5 Dangerous to dele with, vaine, of none availe,
Costly in keping, past not worthe two peason,
Slipper in sliding as is an eles taile,
Hard to attaine, once gotten not geason,
Jewel of jeopardie that perill doth assaile,

10   False and untrue, enticed oft to treason,
     Enmy to youth: that most may I bewaile.
     Ah bitter swete infecting as the poyson:
     Thou farest as frute that with the frost is taken,
     To day redy ripe, to morowe all to shaken.

[10] *A complaint by night of the lover*
not beloved.

     Alas so all things now do hold their peace.
     Heaven and earth disturbed in nothing:
     The beasts, the ayre, the birdes their song do cease:
     The nightes chare the starres about doth bring:
5   Calme is the Sea, the waves worke lesse and lesse:
     So am not I, whom love alas doth wring,
     Bringing before my face the great encrease
     Of my desires, whereat I wepe and sing,
     In joy and wo, as in a doutfull ease.
10   For my swete thoughtes sometime do pleasure bring:
     But by and by the cause of my disease
     Geves me a pang, that inwardly doth sting.
     When that I thinke what griefe it is againe,
     To live and lacke the thing should ridde my paine.

[11] *How eche thing save the lover*
in spring reviveth to
pleasure.

     When Windsor walles susteyned my wearied arme,
     My hand my chin, to ease my restles hed:
     The pleasant plots revested green with warme,
     The blossomd bowes with lusty Ver yspred,
5   The flowred meades, the wedded birdes so late
     Mine eyes discover: and to my minde resorte
     The joly woes, the hatelesse shorte debate,
     The rakehell life that longes to loves disporte.
     Wherewith (alas) the heavy charge of care
10   Heapt in my brest breakes forth against my will,
     In smoky sighes, that overcast the ayre.
     My vapord eyes suche drery teares distill,
     The tender spring which quicken where they fall,
     And I halfbent to throw me down withall.

[12] *Vow to love faithfullie how-*
soever he be re-
warded.

Set me wheras the Sunne doth parche the grene,
Or where his beames do not dissolve the yse:
In temperate heat where he is felt and sene:
In presence prest of people madde or wise.
5   Set me in hye, or yet in low degree:
In longest night, or in the shortest day:
In clearest skie, or where clowdes thickest be:
In lusty youth, or when my heares are gray.
Set me in heaven, in earth, or els in hell,
10 In hill, or dale, or in the foming flood:
Thrall, or at large, alive where so I dwell:
Sicke, or in health: in evyll fame, or good,
Hers will I be, and onely with this thought
Content my selfe, although my chaunce be nought.

[13] *Complaint that his ladie after she*
knew of his love kept her face
alway hidden from
him.

I never saw my Ladie laye apart
Her cornet blacke, in cold nor yet in heate,
Sith first she knew my griefe was growen so great,
Which other fansies driveth from my hart.
5   That to my selfe I do the thought reserve,
The which unwares did wounde my woful brest,
For on her face mine eyes mought never rest,
Sins that she knew I did her love and serve,
Her golden tresse is clad alway with blacke,
10 Her smiling lokes to hide thus evermore,
And that restraines which I desire so sore.
So doth this corner governe my alacke:
In somer, sunne: in winter, breath of frost:
Wherby the light of her faire lokes I lost.

[14] *Request to his love to joyne*
bountie with beautie.

The golden gift that nature did thee geve
To fasten frendes, and feede them at thy wyll,
With fourme and favour, taught me to beleve,
How thow art made to shew her greatest skill.
5 Whose hidden vertues are not so unknowen,
But lively domes might gather at the furst
Where beauty so her perfect seede hath sowen,
Of other graces folow nedes there must.
Now certesse Garret, sins all this is true,
10 That from above thy giftes are thus elect:
Do not deface them than with fansies newe,
Nor change of mindes let not thy minde infect:
But mercy him thy frende, that doth thee serve,
Who seekes alway thine honour to preserve.

[15] *Prisoned in windsor, he recoun-*
teth his pleasure there
passed.

So cruell prison how could betide, alas,
As proude Windsor? where I in lust and joy,
With a kinges sonne, my childishe yeres did passe,
In greater feastes than Priams sonnes of Troy:
5 Where eche swete place returns a taste full sower,
The large grene courtes, where we were wont to hove,
With eyes cast up into the maydens tower.
And easie sighes, such as folke drawe in love:
The stately seates, the ladies bright of hewe:
10 The daunces short, long tales of great delight:
With wordes and lokes, that tigers could but rewe,
Where eche of us did pleade the others right:
The palme play, where, dispoiled for the game,
With dazed eies oft we by gleames of love,
15 Have mist the ball and got sight of our dame,
To baite her eyes, which kept the leads above:
The gravell ground, with sleves tied on the helme:
On foming horse, with swordes and frendly hartes:
With cheare, as though one should another whelme:
20 Where we have fought, and chased oft with dartes,

With silver droppes the meade yet spred for ruth,
In active games of nimblenes, and strength,
Where we did straine, trained with swarmes of youth.
Our tender limmes, that yet shot up in length:
25 The secret groves, which oft we made resound
Of pleasaunt plaint, and of our ladies praise,
Recording oft what grace eche one had found,
What hope of spede,what dread of long delaies:
The wilde forest, the clothed holtes with grene:
30 With rains availed, and swift ybreathed horse,
With crie of houndes, and mery blastes betwene,
Where we did chase the fearfull hart of force,
The wide vales eke, that harborde us ech night,
Wherwith (alas) reviveth in my brest
35 The swete accord, such slepes as yet delight:
The pleasant dreames, the quiet bed of rest:
The secrete thoughtes imparted with such trust:
The wanton talke, the divers change of play:
The frenship sworne, eche promise kept so just:
40 Wherwith we past the winter nightes away.
And, with this thought, the bloud forsakes the face,
The teares beraine my chekes of deadly hewe:
The which as soone as sobbing sighes (alas)
Upsupped have, thus I my plaint renew:
45 O place of blisse, renuer of my woes,
Geve me accompt, where is my noble fere:
Whom in thy walles thou doest eche night enclose,
To other leefe, but unto me most dere.
Eccho (alas) that doth my sorow rewe,
50 Returns therto a hollow sound of plaint.
Thus I alone, where all my freedome grewe,
In prison pyne, with bondage and restraint,
And with remembrance of the greater griefe
To banish the lesse, I finde my chief reliefe.

[16] *The lover comforteth himselfe*
with the worthinesse of
his love.

When raging love with extreme payne
Most cruelly distrains my hart:
When that my teares, as floods of rayne,

Beare witnes of my wofull smart:
5   When sighes have wasted so my breath,
That I lye at the point of death.
    I call to minde the navie great,
That the Grekes brought to Troye town:
And how the boysteous windes did beate
10 Their ships, and rent their sayles adown,
Till Agamemnons daughters blood
Appeasde the Gods, that them withstood.
    And how that in those ten yeres warre,
Full many a bloodie dede was done,
15 And many a lord, that came full farre,
There caught his bane (alas) to soone:
And many a good knight overron,
Before the Grekes had Helene won.
    Then thinck I thus: sithe such repaire,
20 So long time warre of valiant men,
Was all to winne a lady faire:
Shall I not learne to suffer then,
And thinck my life well spent to be,
Serving a worthier wight than she?
25 Therfore I never will repent,
But paines contented still endure.
For like as when, rough winter spent,
The pleasant spring straight draweth in ure:
So after raging stormes of care
30 Joyfull at length may be my fare.

[17] *Complaint of the absence of*
her lover being upon
the sea.

O happy dames, that may embrace
The frute of your delight,
Help to bewaile the wofull case,
And eke the heavy plight
5   Of me, that wonted to rejoyce
The fortune of my pleasant choyce:
Good Ladies, help to fill my moorning voyce.
    In ship, freight with remembrance
Of thoughts, and pleasures past,
10 He sailes that hath in governance

My life, while it will last:
With scalding sighes, for lack of gale,
Furdering his hope, that is his sail
Toward me the swete port of his avail.
15   Alas, how oft in dreames I see
Those eyes that were my food,
Which somtime so delited me,
That yet they do me good.
Wherwith I wake with his returne,
20   Whose absent flame did make me burne.
But when I finde the lack, Lord how I mourne?
    When other lovers in armes acrosse,
Rejoyce their chiefe delight:
Drowned in teares to mourne my losse,
25   I stand the bitter night,
In my window, where I may see,
Before the windes how the clowdes flee.
Lo, what a Mariner love hath made me.
    And in grene waves when the salt flood
30   Doth rise by rage of winde:
A thousand fansies in that mood
Assaile my restlesse minde.
Alas, now drencheth my swete fo,
That with the spoyle of my hart did go,
35   And left me but (alas) why did he so?
    And when the seas ware calme againe,
To chase fro me annoye.
My doutful hope doth cause me plaine:
So dread cuts of my joye.
40   Thus is my wealth mingled with wo,
And of eche thought a dout doth growe,
Now he comes, will he come? alas, no no.

[18] *Complaint of a diyng lover refused
upon his ladies injust mista,
king of his wri-
ting.*

In winters just returne, when Boreas gan his raigne,
And every tree unclothed fast, as nature taught them plaine:
    In misty morning darke, as sheepe are then in holde,
I hyed me fast, it sat me on, my sheepe for to unfolde.

5   And as it is a thing, that lovers have by fittes,
Under a palme I heard one cry, as he had lost his wittes.
    Whose voyce did ring so shrill, in uttering of his plaint,
That I amazed was to heare, how love could him attaint.
    Ah wretched man (quod he) come death, and ridde this wo:
10   A just reward, a happy end, if it may chaunce thee so.
    Thy pleasures past have wrought thy wo, without redresse.
If thou hadst never felt no joy, thy smart had bene the lesse,
    And retchlesse of his life, he gan both sighe and grone,
A rufull thing me thought, it was, to hear him make such mone,
15   Thou cursed pen (sayd he) wo worth the bird thee bare,
The man, the knife, and all that made thee, wo be to their share.
    Wo worth the time, and place, where I so could endite.
And wo be it yet once againe, the pen that so can write.
    Unhappy hand, it had ben happy time for me,
20   If, when to write thou learned first, unjoynted hadst thou be.
    Thus cursed he himself, and every other wight,
Save her alone whom love him bound, to serve both day and night.
    Which when I heard, and saw, how he himself fordid,
Against the ground with bloody strokes, himself even ther to rid:
25   Had ben my heart of flint, it must have melted tho:
For in my life I never sawe a man so full of wo.
    With teares, for his redresse, I rashly to him ran.
And in my armes I caught him fast, and thus I spake him than.
    What woful wight art thou, that in such heavy case
30   Tormentes thy selfe with such despite, here in this desert place?
    Wherwith, as al agast, fulfild with ire, and dred,
He cast on me a staring loke, with colour pale, and ded.
    Nay, what art thou (quod he) that in this heavy plight,
Doest find me here, most wofull wretch, that life hath in despight?
35   I am (quoth I) but poore, and simple in degre:
A shepardes charge I have in hand, unworthy though I be.
    With that he gave a sighe, as though the skie shold fall:
And lowd (alas) he shriked oft, and Shepard, gan he call,
    Come, hie the fast at ones, and print it in thy hart:
40   So thou shalt know, and I shall tell the, giltlesse how I smart.
    His back against the tree, sore febled al with faint,
With weary sprite he stretcht him up: and thus hee told his plaint.
    Ones in my hart (quoth he) it chaunced me to love
Such one, in whom hath nature wrought, her cunning for to prove.
45   And sure I can not say, but many yeres were spent,
With such good will so recompenst, as both we were content
    Wherto then I me bound, and she likewise also,

The sunne should runne his course awry, ere we this faith forgo.
Who joyed then, but I? who had this worldes blisse?
50 Who might compare a life to mine, that never thought on this?
But dwelling in this truth, amid my greatest joy,
Is me befallen a greater losse, then Priam had of Troy.
She is reversed clene, and beareth me in hand,
That my deserts have geven her cause to breke this faithful band.
55   And for my just excuse availeth no defence,
Now knowest thou all: I can no more, but shepheard hie the hence
And geve him leave to dye, that may no lenger live:
Whose record lo I claime to have, my death, I do forgeve.
And eke when I am gone, be bolde to speake it plaine:
60 Thou hast seen dye the truest man, that ever love did paine.
Wherwith he turned him round, and gaspyng oft for breath,
Into his armes a tree he raught, and said welcome my death:
Welcome a thousand folde, now dearer unto me,
Than should without her love to live, an emperour to be.
65   Thus, in this wofull state, he yelded up the ghost:
And little knoweth his lady, what a lover she hath lost.
Whose death when I beheld, no marvail was it, right
For pitye though my hart did blede, to se so piteous sight,
My blood from heat to colde oft changed wonders sore:
70 A thousande troubles there I found I never knew before.
Twene drede and dolour, so my sprites were brought in feare,
That long it was ere I could call to minde, what I did there.
But, as ech thing hath end, so had these payns of myne:
The furies past, and I my wits restord by length of tyme.
75   Then as I could devise, to seke I thought it best,
Where I might finde some worthy place, for such a corse to rest.
And in my minde it came: from thence not far away,
Where Creseids love, king Priams sonne, the worthy Troilus lay.
By him I made his tomb, in token he was true:
80 And as to him belongeth well, I covered it with blew.
Whose soule by angels power, departed not so sone,
But to the heavens, lo it fled, for to receive his dome.

[19] *Complaint of the absence of
her lover being upon
the sea.*

Good Ladies: ye that have your pleasures in exile,
Step in your fote, come take a place, and moorne with me a while
   And such as by their lordes do set but little price,
Let them sit still: it skilles them not what chance come on the dice.
5   But ye whom love hath bound by order of desire,
To love your lords, whose good deserts none other wold require:
   Come ye yet once again, and set your fote by mine,
Whose wofull plight and sorowes great no tong may well define,
   My love and lorde alas, in whom consistes my wealth,
10 Hath fortune sent to passe the seas in hazarde of his health.
   Whom I was wont tembrace with well contented minde
Is now amid the fomyng floods at pleasure of the winde.
   Where God well him preserve, and sone him home me send,
Without which hope, my life (alas) were shortly at an end.
15   Whose absence yet, although my hope doth tell me plaine,
With short returne he comes anone, yet ceaseth not my payne,
   The fearefull dreames I have, oft times do greve me so:
That when I wake, I lye in dout, where they be true, or no.
   Sometime the roaring seas (me semes) do grow so hye:
20 That my dere Lord (ay me alas) me thinkes I see him dye.
   An other time the same doth tell me: he is come:
And plaieng, where I shall him find with his faire little sonne.
   So forth I go apace to se that leefsom sight.
And with a kisse, me think, I say: welcome my lord, my knight:
25   Welcome my swete, alas, the stay of my welfare.
Thy presence bringeth forth a truce atwixt me, and my care.
   Then lively doth he loke, and salveth me againe,
And saith: my dere, how is it now, that you have all this payne?
   Wherwith the heavy cares: that heapt are in my brest,
30 Breake forth, and me dischargen clene of all my huge unrest.
   But when I me awake, and find it but a dreme:
The anguish of my former wo beginneth more extreme:
   And me tormenteth so, that unneath may I find
Sum hidden place, wherein to slake the gnawing of my mind
35   Thus every way you se, with absence how I burn:
And for my wound no cure I find, but hope of good return.
   Save whan I think, by sowre how swete is felt the more:
It doth abate som of my paines, that I abode before.
   And then unto my self I say: when we shal meete.

40 But litle while shal seme this paine, the joy shal be so sweete.
    Ye windes, I you conjure in chiefest of your rage,
That ye my lord me safly sende, my sorowes to asswage:
    And that I may not long abide in this excesse.
Do your good wil, to cure a wight, that liveth in distresse.

[20] *A praise of his love: wherin he*
reproveth them that compare
their Ladies with his.

    Geve place ye lovers, here before
That spent your bostes and bragges in vaine:
My Ladies beawtie passeth more
The best of yours, I dare wel sayen,
5 Than doth the sonne, the candle light:
Or brightest day, the darkest night.
    And thereto hath a troth as just,
As had Penelope the faire.
For what she saith, ye may it trust,
10 As it by writing sealed were.
And vertues hath she many moe,
Than I with pen have skill to showe.
    I could reherse, if that I wold,
The whole effect of natures plaint,
15 When she had lost the perfite mould,
The like to whom she could not paynt:
With wringyng handes how she did cry,
And what she said, I know it, I.
    I know, she swore with ragyng minde:
20 Her kingdome onely set apart,
There was no losse, by lawe of kinde,
That could have gone so nere her hart.
And this was chefely all her paine:
She could not make the like againe.
25   Sith nature thus gave her the praise,
To be the chefest worke she wrought:
In faith, me thinke some better wayes
On your behalf might well be sought,
Then to compare (as ye have done)
30 To matche the candle with the sonne.

[21] *To the ladie that
scorned her
lover.*

    Although I had a check,
To geve the mate is hard,
For I have found a neck,
To kepe my men in gard.
5   And you that hardy ar
To geve so great assay
Unto a man of war,
To drive his men away,
    I rede you take good hede,
10 And marke this folish verse,
For I will so provide,
That I will have your ferse,
    And when your ferse is had,
And all your war is done:
15 Then shall your self be glad
To end that you begon.
    For if by chance I winne
Your person in the felde:
To late then come you in
20 Your selfe to me to yeld.
    For I wil use my power,
As captain full of might,
And such I will devour,
As use to shew me spight.
25   And for because you gave
Me checke in such degre,
This vantage loe I have:
Now checke, and garde to the.
    Defend it, if thou may:
30 Stand stiffe, in thine estate.
For sure I will assay,
If I can give the mate.

[22] *A warning to the lover*
how he is abused by
his love.

To dearely had I bought my grene and youthfull yeres,
If in mine age I could not finde when craft for love apperes.
And seldom though I come in court among the rest:
Yet can I judge in colours dim as depe as can the best.
5   Where grefe tormentes the man that suffreth secret smart,
To breke it forth unto som frend it easeth well the hart.
So standes it now with me for my beloved frend,
This case is thine for whom I fele such torment of my mind.
And for thy sake I burne so in my secret brest
10   That till thou know my hole disseise my hart can have no rest.
I see how thine abuse hath wrested so thy wittes,
That all it yeldes to thy desire, and folowes the by fittes.
Where thou hast loved so long with hart and all thy power,
I se thee fed with fained wordes, thy fredom to devoure.
15   I know, (though she say nay, and would it well withstand)
When in her grace thou held the most, she bare the but in hand.
I see her pleasant chere in chifest of thy suite:
Whan thou art gone, I se him come, that gathers up the fruite.
And eke in thy respect I se the base degre
20   Of him to whom she gave the hart that promised was to the.
I se (what would you more) stode never man so sure
On womans word, but wisedome would mistrust it to endure.

[23] *The forsaken lover describeth*
and forsaketh love.

O lothsome place where I
Have sene and herd my dere,
When in my hert her eye
Hath made her thought appere,
5 By glimsing with such grace
As fortune it ne would,
That lasten any space
Betwene us lenger should.
As fortune did avance,
10 To further my desire:
Even so hath fortunes chaunce
Throwen al ammides the mire.

And that I have deserved
With true and faithfull hart,
15 Is to his handes reserved
That never felt the smart.
    But happy is that man,
That scaped hath the griefe
That love wel teche him can
20 By wanting his reliefe.
A scourge to quiet mindes
It is, who taketh hede,
A common plage that binds,
A travell without mede.
25   This gift it hath also,
Who so enjoies it most,
A thousand troubles grow
To vexe his weried ghost.
And last it may not long
30 The truest thing of all
And sure the greatest wrong
That is within this thrall.
    But sins thou desert place
Canst give me no accompt
35 Of my desired grace
That I to have was wont,
Farewel thou hast me tought
To thinke me not the furst,
That love hath set aloft,
40 And casten in the dust.

[24] *The lover describes his*
restlesse state.

    As oft as I behold and see
The soveraigne beauty that me bound:
The nyer my comfort is to me,
Alas the fresher is my wound.
5   As flame doth quench by rage of fire,
And runnyng stremes consume by raine:
So doth the sight, that I desire,
Appease my grief and deadly payne.
    First when I saw those cristall streames,
10 Whose beauty made my mortall wound:

I little thought within her beames
So swete a venom to have found.
    But wilfull will did prick me forth,
And blinde Cupide did whippe and guide:
15 Force made me take my grief in worth:
My fruteles hope my harme did hide.
    As cruel waves full oft be found,
Against the rockes to rore and cry:
So doth my hart full oft rebound
20 Against my brest full bitterly.
    I fall, and see mine owne decay,
As one that beares flame in his brest,
Forgets in payne to put away,
The thing that bredeth mine unrest.

[25] *The lover excuseth himself*
of suspected change.

    Though I regarded not
The promise made by me,
Or passed not to spot
My faith and honestee:
5 Yet were my fancy strange,
And wilfull will to wite,
If I sought now to change
A falkon for a kite.
    All men might well disprayse
10 My wit and enterprise,
If I estemed a pese
Above a perle in prise:
Or judged the owle in sight
The sparehauke to excell,
15 Which flieth but in the night,
As all men know right well:
    Or if I sought to sayle
Into the brittle port,
Where anker hold doth faile,
20 To such as do resort.
And leave the haven sure,
Where blowes no blusteryng winde,
Nor fickelnesse in ure
So farforth as I finde.

25   No, thinke me not so light,
       Nor of so churlish kinde,
       Though it lay in my might
       My bondage to unbinde.
       That I would leve the hinde
30   To hunt the ganders fo.
       No no I have no minde
       To make exchanges so:
          Nor yet to change at all,
       For think it may not be
35   That I should seke to fall
       From my felicitie,
       Desirous for to win,
       And loth for to forgo,
       Or new change to begin:
40   How may all this be so?
          The fire it can not frese:
       For it is not his kinde,
       Nor true love can not lese
       The constance of the minde.
45   Yet as sone shall the fire,
       Want heat to blase and burn,
       As I in such desire,
       Have once a thought to turne.

           [26] *A carelesse man scorning and*
              describing the suttle u-
                sage of women to-
                  warde their lo-
                    vers.

     Wrapt in my carelesse cloke, as I walke to and fro:
     I se, how love can shew, what force ther reigneth in his bow
       And how he shoteth eke, a hardy hart to wound:
     And where he glanceth by againe, that litle hurt is found.
5   For seldom is it sene, he woundeth hartes alike.
     The tone may rage, when tothers love is often farre to seke.
       All this I see, with more: and wonder thinketh me:
     How he can strike the one so sore, and leave the other free.
     I see, that wounded wight, that suffreth all this wrong:
10   How he is fed with yeas, and nayes, and liveth all to long.
     In silence though I kepe such secretes to my self:

Yet do I see, how she somtime doth yeld a looke by stelth:
    As though it seemd, ywys I will not lose thee so,
When in her hart so swete a thought did never truely grow.
15   Then say I thus: alas, that man is farre from blisse:
That doth receive for his relief, none other gaine but this.
    And she, that fedes him so, I fele, and finde it plain:
Is but to glory in her power, that over such can reign.
    Nor are such graces spent, but when she thinkes, that he,
20 A weried man is fully bent, such fansies to let flie:
    Then to retain him still, she wrasteth new her grace,
And smileth lo, as though she would forthwith the man embrace.
    But when the proofe is made, to try such lookes withall:
He findeth then the place all voyde, and freighted ful of gall.
25   Lord what abuse is this? who can such women praise?
That for their glory do devise, to use such craftie wayes.
    I, that among the rest do sit, and marke the row,
Finde, that in her is greater craft, then is in twenty mo.
    Whose tender yeres, alas, with wyles so well are sped:
30 What will she do, when hory heares are powdred in her hed?

[27] *An answer in the behalfe of a woman of an*
uncertain aucthor.

Girt in my giltles gowne as I sit here and sow,
I see that thinges are not in dede as to the outward show.
And who so list to looke and note thinges somewhat nere:
Shall finde wher plainesse semes to haunt nothing but craft appere.
5 For with indifferent eyes my self can well discerne,
How some to guide a ship in stormes seke for to take the sterne,
Whose practise if were proved in calme to stere a barge,
Assuredly beleve it well it were to great a charge.
And some I see againe sit still and say but small,
10 That could do ten times more than they that say they can do all.
Whose goodly giftes are such the more they understand,
The more they seke to learn and know and take lesse charge in hand.
And to declare more plain the time fleetes not so fast:
But I can beare full well in minde the song now soung and past.
15 The authour whereof came wrapt in a crafty cloke:
With will to force a flaming fire where he could raise no smoke,
If power and will had joynde as it appeareth plaine,
The truth nor right had tane no place their vertues had ben vain.
  So that you may perceive, and I may safely se,
20 The innocent that giltlesse is, condemned should have be.

[28] *The constant lover la-*
menteth.

Sins fortunes wrath envieth the wealth,
Wherein I raigned by the sight:
Of that that fed mine eyes by stelth,
With sower swete, dread and delight.
5   Let not my griefe move you to mone,
For I will wepe and waile alone.
Spite drave me into Borias raigne,
Where hory frostes the frutes do bite,
When hilles were spred and every plaine:
10   With stormy winters mantle white.
And yet my dere such was my heate,
When others freze then did I sweate.
And now though on the sunne I drive,
Whose fervent flame all thinges decaies,
15   His beames in brightnesse may not strive,
With light of your swete golden rayes,
Nor from my brest this heate remove,
The frosen thoughtes graven by love.
Ne may the waves of the salt flood,
20   Quenche that your beauty set on fire,
For though mine eyes forbeare the foode,
That did releve the hot desire.
Such as I was such will I be,
Your own, what would ye more of me?

[29] *A song written by the earle of Sur-*
rey to a ladie that refused to
daunce with him.

Eche beast can chose his fere according to his minde,
And eke can shew a frendly chere like to their beastly kinde.
A Lion saw I late as white as any snow,
Which semed well to lead the race his port the same did show.
5   Upon the gentle beast to gaze it pleased me,
For still me thought he semed wel of noble blood to be,
And as he praunced before, still seking for a make,
As who wold say there is none here I trow will me forsake.
I might perceive a Wolfe as white as whales bone,
10   A fairer beast of fresher hue beheld I never none.
Save that her lookes were coy, and froward eke her grace,

Unto the which this gentle beast gan him advance apace.
   And with a beck full low he bowed at her feete,
In humble wise as who would say I am to farre unmeete.
15   But such a scornefull chere wherewith she him rewarded,
Was never sene I trow the like to such as well deserved.
   With that she start aside welnere a foote or twaine,
And unto him thus gan she say with spite and great disdaine.
   Lion she sayd if thou hadst knowen my minde before,
20 Thou hadst not spent thy travail thus nor all thy paine forlore.
   Doway I let thee wete thou shalt not play with me,
Go range about where thou maiest finde some meter fere for thee.
   With that he bet his taile, his eyes began to flame,
I might perceive his noble hart much moved by the same.
25   Yet saw I him refraine and eke his wrath aswage,
And unto her thus gan he say when he was past his rage.
   Cruell, you do me wrong to set me thus so light,
Without desert for my good will to shew me such despight.
   How can ye thus entreat a Lion of the race,
30 That with his pawes a crowned king devoured in the place:
   Whose nature is to pray upon no simple food,
As long as he may suck the flesh, and drink of noble blood.
   If you be faire and fresh, am I not of your hue?
And for my vaunt I dare well say my blood is not untrue.
35   For you your self have heard it is not long agoe,
Sith that for love one of the race did end his life in woe
   In tower strong and hie for his assured truth,
Whereas in teares he spent his breath, alas the more the ruth.
   This gentle beast so dyed whom nothing could remove,
40 But willingly to lese his life for losse of his true love.
   Other there be whose lives do lingre still in paine,
Against their willes preserved ar that would have died faine.
   But now I do perceave that nought it moveth you,
My good entent, my gentle hart, nor yet my kinde so true.
45   But that your will is such to lure me to the trade,
As other some full many yeres to trace by craft ye made.
   And thus behold our kindes how that we differ farre.
I seke my foes: and you your frendes do threaten still with warre.
   I fawne where I am fled: you slay that sekes to you,
50 I can devour no yelding pray: you kill where you subdue.
   My kinde is to desire the honour of the field:
And you with blood to slake your thirst on such as to you yeld.
   Wherefore I would you wist that for your coyed lookes,

I am no man that will be trapt nor tangled with such hookes.
55   And though some lust to love where blame full well they might,
And to such beasts of currant sort that would have travail bright.
    I will observe the law that Nature gave to me,
To conquer such as will resist and let the rest go fre.
    And as a Faucon free that soreth in the ayre,
60 Which never fed on hand nor lure, nor for no stale doth care,
    While that I live and breath such shall my custome be,
In wildnes of the woods to seke my pray where pleaseth me,
    Where many one shall rue, that never made offence.
Thus your refuse against my power shall bote them no defence.
65   And for revenge therof I vow and swere therto,
A thousand spoiles I shall commit I never thought to do.
    And if to light on you my lucke so good shall be,
I shall be glad to fede on that that would have fed on me.
    And thus farewell unkinde to whom I bent and bow,
70 I would ye wist the ship is safe that bare his sailes so low.
    Sith that a Lions hart is for a Wolfe no pray,
With bloody mouth go slake your thirst on simple shepe I say,
    With more dispite and ire than I can now expresse,
Which to my paine though I refrain, the cause you may wel gesse.
75   As for because my self was aucthor of the game,
It bootes me not that for my wrath I should disturbe the same.

[30] *The faithfull lover declareth his paines*
and his uncertein joyes, and with
only hope recomforteth
somwhat his wo-
full heart.

    If care do cause men cry, why do not I complaine?
If eche man do bewaile his wo, why shew not I my paine?
    Since that amongst them all I dare well say is none,
So farre from weale, so full of wo, or hath more cause to mone.
5   For all thinges having life sometime have quiet rest.
The bearing Asse, the drawing Oxe, and every other beast.
    The peasant and the post, that serve at all assayes,
The shipboy and the galley slave have time to take their ease,
    Save I alas whom care of force doth so constraine
10 To waile the day and wake the night continually in paine,
    From pensivenes to plaint, from plaint to bitter teares,
From teares to painfull plaint againe: and thus my life it weares.

No thing under the sunne that I can heare or se,
But moveth me for to bewaile my cruell destenie.
15   For where men do rejoyce since that I cannot so,
I take no pleasure in that place, it doubleth but my wo.
    And when I heare the sound of song or instrument,
Me think eche tune there dolefull is and helps me to lament.
    And if I see some have their most desired sight,
20 Alas think I eche man hath weal save I most wofull wight.
    Then as the striken Dere withdrawes him selfe alone,
So do I seke some secrete place where I may make my mone.
    There do my flowing eyes shew forth my melting hart,
So that the stremes of those two welles right well declare my smart.
25   And in those cares so colde I force my selfe a heat,
As sick men in their shaking fittes procure them self to sweat,
    With thoughtes that for the time do much appease my paine,
But yet they cause a farther feare and brede my woe againe.
    Me thinke within my thought I se right plaine appere,
30 My hartes delight my sorowes leche mine earthly goddesse here,
    With every sondry grace that I have sene her have.
Thus I within my wofull brest her picture paint and grave.
    And in my thought I roll her bewties to and fro,
Her laughing chere her lovely looke my hart that perced so.
35   Her strangenes when I sued her servant for to be,
And what she said and how she smiled when that she pitied me.
    Then comes a sodaine feare that riveth all my rest
Lest absence cause forgetfulnes to sink within her brest.
    For when I think how far this earth doth us devide,
40 Alas me semes love throwes me downe I fele how that I slide,
    But then I think againe why should I thus mistrust,
So swete a wighte so sad and wise that is so true and just,
    For loth she was to love, and wavering is she not.
The farther of the more desirde thus lovers tie their knot.
45   So in dispaire and hope plonged am I both up an doune,
As is the ship with wind and wave when Neptune list to froune.
    But as the watery showers delay the raging winde,
So doth good hope clene put away dispaire out of my minde.
    And biddes me for to serve and suffer paciently,
50 For what wot I the after weale that fortune willes to me.
    For those that care do know and tasted have of trouble,
When passed is their wofull paine eche joy shall seme them double.
    And bitter sendes she now to make me tast the better,
The pleasant swete when that it comes to make it seme the sweter.
55   And so determine I to serve until my breath,

Ye rather die a thousand times then once to false my faithe.
    And if my feble corps through weight of woful smart,
Do faile or faint my wyll, it is that still she kepe my hart.
    And when thys carcas here to earth shalbe refarde,
60 I do bequeth my weried ghost to serve her afterwarde.

[31] *The meanes to attain
happy life.*

Martial, the thinges that do attain
The happy life, be these, I finde.
The richesse left, not got with pain:
The frutefull ground: the quiet minde:
5 The egall frend, no grudge, no strife:
No charge of rule, nor governance:
Without disease the healthful life:
The houshold of continuance:
The meane diet, no delicate fare:
10 Trew wisdom joyned with simplenesse:
The night discharged of all care,
Where wine the wit may not oppresse:
The faithfull wife, without debate:
Such slepes, as may begile the night:
15 Contented with thine own estate,
Ne wish for death, ne feare his might.

[32] *Praise of meane and
constant estate.*

Of thy life, Thomas, this compasse wel mark:
Not aye with ful sailes the hye seas to beat:
Ne by coward dred, in shonning stormes dark,
On shalow shores thy keel in peril freat.
5 Who so gladly halseth the golden meane,
Voide of daungers advisdly hath his home
Not with lothsome muck, as a den unclean:
Nor palacelike, wherat disdain may glome.
The lofty pyne the great winde often rives:
10 With violenter swey falne turrets stepe:
Lightnings assault the hie mountains, and clives,
A hart wel stayd, in overthwartes depe,
Hopeth amendes: in swete, doth feare the sowre.

God, that sendeth, withdraweth winter sharp.
15   Now il, not aye thus: once Phebus to lowre
With bowe undent shal cesse, and frame to harp
His voice. In straite estate appere thou stout:
And so wisely, when lucky gale of winde
All thy puft sailes shal fill, loke well about:
20   Take in a ryft: hast is wast, profe doth finde.

[33] *Praise of certaine psalmes*
of David, translated by
sir T.w. the elder.

The great Macedon, that out of Persie chased
Darius, of whose huge power all Asie rong,
In the rich ark dan Homers rimes he placed,
Who fayned gestes of heathen princes song.
5   What holy grave? what worthy sepulture
To Wiattes Psalmes should Christians then purchase?
Where he doth paint the lively faith, and pure,
The stedfast hope, the swete returne to grace
Of just David, by perfite penitence.
10   Where rulers may see in a mirrour clere
The bitter frute of false concupiscence:
How Jewry bought Urias death full dere.
In princes harts Gods scourge imprinted depe,
Ought them awake, out of their sinfull slepe.

[34] *Of the death of the same*
sir T.w.

Dyvers thy death do diversly bemone.
Some, that in presence of thy livelyhed
Lurked, whose brestes envy with hate had swolne,
Yeld Ceasars teares upon Pompeius hed,
5   Some, that watched with the murdrers knife,
With eger thirst to drink thy giltlesse blood,
Whose practise brake by happy end of life,
With envious teares to heare thy fame so good.
But I, that knew what harbred in that hed:
10   What vertues rare were temperd in that brest:
Honour the place, that such a jewell bred,
And kisse the ground, whereas thy corse doth rest,

With vapord eyes: from whence such streames avail,
As Pyramus did on Thisbes brest bewail.

[35] *Of the same.*

    W. resteth here, that quick could never rest:
Whose heavenly giftes encreased by disdain,
And vertue sank the deper in his brest.
Such profit he by envy could obtain.
5   A head, where wisdom misteries did frame:
Whose hammers bet still in that lively brain,
As on a stithe: where that some work of fame
Was dayly wrought, to turne to Britaines gaine.
    A visage, stern, and mylde: where both did grow,
10 Vice to contemne, in vertue to rejoyce:
Amid great stormes, whom grace assured so,
To live upright, and smile at fortunes choyce.
    A hand, that taught, what might be said in rime:
That reft Chaucer the glory of his wit:
15 A mark, the which (unparfited, for time)
Some may approch, but never none shal hit.
    A toung, that served in forein realmes his king:
Whose courteous talke to vertue did enflame.
Eche noble hart: a worthy guide to bring
20 Our English youth, by travail, unto fame.
    An eye, whose judgement none affect could blinde,
Frendes to allure, and foes to reconcile:
Whose persing loke did represent a minde
With vertue fraught, reposed, void of gile.
25 A hart, where dreade was never so imprest,
To hide the thought, that might the trouth avance:
In neither fortune loft, nor yet represt,
To swel in wealth, or yeld unto mischance,
    A valiaunt corps, where force, and beawty met:
30 Happy, alas, to happy, but for foes:
Lived, and ran the race, that nature set:
Of manhodes shape, where she the mold did lose.
    But to the heavens that simple soule is fled:
Which left with such, as covet Christ to know,
35 Witnesse of faith, that never shall be ded:
Sent for our helth, but not received so.
Thus, for our gilte, this jewel have we lost:
The earth his bones, the heavens possesse his gost.

[36] *Of the same.*

In the rude age when knowledge was not rife,
If Jove in Create and other were that taught,
Artes to convert to profit of our life,
Wend after death to have their temples sought,
5   If vertue yet no voide unthankfull time,
Failed of some to blast her endles fame,
A goodly meane both to deterre from crime:
And to her steppes our sequele to enflame,
In daies of truth if Wiates frendes then waile,
10 The only det that dead of quick may claime:
That rare wit spent employd to our availe.
Where Christ is taught we led to vertues traine.
His lively face their brestes how did it freat,
Whose cindres yet with envy they do eate.

[37] *Of Sardanapalus dishonora-*
ble life, and miserable
death.

Thassirian king in peace, with foule desire,
And filthy lustes, that staind his regal hart
In warre that should set princely hartes on fire:
Did yeld, vanquisht for want of marciall art.
5   The dint of swordes from kisses semed strange:
And harder, than his ladies side, his targe:
From glutton feastes, to souldiars fare a change:
His helmet, farre above a garlands charge.
Who scace the name of manhode did retain,
10 Drenched in slouth, and womanish delight,
Feble of sprite, impacient of pain:
When he had lost his honor, and his right:
Proud time of wealth, in stormes appalled with dred,
Murthered himself, to shew some manful dede.

[38] *How no age is content with his*
owne estate, and how the age
of children is the happiest,
if they had skill to
understand it.

Layd in my quiet bed, in study as I were,
I saw within my troubled head, a heape of thoughtes appere:
    And every thought did shewe so lively in myne eyes,
That now I sighed, and then I smilde, as cause of thought dyd rise.
5   I saw the litle boy in thought, how oft that he
Did wish of god, to scape the rod, a tall yongman to be.
    The yongman eke that feles, his bones with paines opprest
How he would be a rich olde man, to lyve, and lye at rest.
    The rych oldman that sees his end draw on so sore,
10 How he would be a boy again, to live so much the more.
    Wherat full oft I smilde, to se, how all these three,
From boy to man, from man to boy, would chop and change degree.
    And musing thus I think, the case is very strange,
That man from welth, to live in wo, doth ever seke to change.
15   Thus thoughtfull as I lay, I saw my witherd skyn,
How it doth show my dented chewes, the flesh was worne so thyn:
    And eke my tothelesse chaps, the gates of my rightway,
That opes and shuts, as I do speake, doe thus unto me say:
    Thy white and horish heares, the messengers of age,
20 That shew, like lines of true belief, that this life doth asswage,
    Byds thee lay hand, and fele them hanging on thy chin:
The which do write two ages past, the third now comming in.
    Hang up therfore the bit of thy yong wanton time:
And thou that therin beaten art, the happiest life define,
25   Wherat I sighed, and sayd, farewell, my wonted joy:
Trusse up thy pack, and trudge from me to every litle boy:
    And tell them thus from me, their time most happy is:
If, to their time, they reason had to know the trueth of this.

[39] *Bonum est mihi quod*
humiliasti me.

The stormes are past these cloudes are overblowne,
And humble chere great rigour hath represt:
For the defaute is set a paine fore knowne,
And pacience graft in a determed brest.

5   And in the hart wher heapes of griefes were growne,
    The swete revenge hath planted mirth and rest,
    No company so pleasant as mine owne.
    Thraldom at large hath made this prison fre,
    Danger wel past remembred workes delight:
10 Of lingring doubtes such hope is sprong pardie,
    That nought I finde displeasaunt in my sight:
    But when my glasse presented unto me
    The curelesse wound that bledeth day and night,
    To think (alas) such hap shoud graunted be
15 Unto a wretch that hath no hart to fight,
    To spill that blood that hath so oft bene shed,
    For Britannes sake (alas) and now is ded.

[40] *Exhortacion to learne by o-*
thers trouble.

My Ratclif, when thy retchlesse youth offendes:
Receve thy scourge by others chastisement.
For such calling, when it workes none amendes:
Then plages are sent without advertisement.
5   Yet Salomon said, the wronged shall recure:
But Wiat said true, the skarre doth aye endure.

[41] *The fansie of a weried*
lover.

The fansy, which that I have served long,
That hath alway bene enmy to myne ease,
Semed of late to rue upon my wrong,
And bad me flye the cause of my misease.
5   And I forthwith did prease out of the throng,
That thought by flight my painfull hart to please
Som other way: tyll I saw faith more strong:
And to my self I said: alas, those daies
In vayn were spent, to runne the race so long.
10 And with that thought, I met my guyde, that playn
Out of the way wherin I wandred wrong,
Brought me amiddes the hilles, in base Bullayn:
Where I am now, as restlesse to remayn,
Against my will, full pleased with my payn.

SURREY.

[42] *The lover for shamefastnesse hideth*
his desire within his faith-
full hart.

The long love, that in my thought I harber,
And in my hart doth kepe his residence,
Into my face preaseth with bold pretence,
And there campeth, displaying his banner.
5 She that me learns to love, and to suffer,
And willes that my trust, and lustes negligence
Be reined by reason, shame, and reverence,
With his hardinesse takes displeasure.
Wherwith love to the hartes forest he fleeth,
10 Leaving his enterprise with paine and crye,
And there him hideth and not appeareth.
What may I do: when my maister feareth,
But in the field with him to live and dye,
For good is the life, ending faithfully.

[43] *The lover waxeth wiser, and*
will not die for affec-
cion.

Yet was I never of your love agreved,
Nor never shall, while that my life doth last:
But of hating my self, that date is past,
And teares continuall sore hath me weried.
5 I will not yet in my grave be buried,
Nor on my tombe your name have fixed fast,
As cruel cause, that did my sprite sone hast.
From thunhappy boones by great sighes stirred.
Then if an hart of amorous faith and will
10 Content your minde withouten doing grief:
Please it you so to this to do relief,
If otherwise you seke for to fulfyll
Your wrath: you erre, and shall not as you wene.
And you your self the cause therof have bene.

[44] *The abused lover seeth his folie,*
and entendeth to trust
no more.

Was never file yet half so well yfiled,
To file a file for any smithes entent,
As I was made a filing instrument,
To frame other, while that I was begiled.
5   But reason loe, hath at my foly smiled,
And pardoned me, sins that I me repent
Of my lost yeres, and of my time mispent.
For youth led me, and falshod me misguided.
Yet, this trust I have of great apparence:
10   Sins that disceit is ay returnable,
Of very force it is agreable,
That therwithall be done the recompence.
Then gile begiled playnd should be never,
And the reward is little trust for ever.

[45] *The lover describeth his being*
striken with sight of
his love.

The lively sparkes, that issue from those eyes,
Against the which there vaileth no defence,
Have perst my hart and done it none offence,
With quaking pleasure, more then once or twise.
5   Was never man could any thing devise,
Sunne beames to turne with so great vehemence
To dase mans sight, as by their bright presence
Dased am I, much like unto the gise
Of one striken with dint of lightening,
10   Blinde with the stroke, and crying here and there,
So call I for helpe, I not when, nor where,
The paine of my fall paciently bearing.
For streight after the blase (as is no wonder)
Of deadly noyse heare I the fearfull thunder.

[46] *The wavering lover willeth,*
and dreadeth, to move
his desire.

Such vain thought, as wonted to mislead me
In desert hope by well assured mone,
Makes me from company to live alone,
In folowing her whom reason bids me flee.
5 And after her my hart would faine begone:
But armed sighes my way do stop anone,
Twixt hope and dread lacking my libertie.
So fleeth she by gentle crueltie.
Yet as I gesse under disdainfull brow
10 One beame of ruth is in her cloudy looke:
Which comfortes the minde, that erst for feare shooke.
That bolded straight the way then seke I how
To utter forth the smart I bide within:
But such it is, I not how to begin.

[47] *The lover having dreamed enjoying*
of his love, complaineth that
the dreame is not either
longer or truer.

Unstable dreame according to the place,
Be stedfast ones, or els at least be true.
By tasted swetenesse, make me not to rew
The soden losse of thy false fained grace.
5 By good respect in such a daungerous case
Thou broughtest not her into these tossing seas,
But madest my sprite to live my care tencrease,
My body in tempest her delight timbrace,
The body dead, the sprite had his desire.
10 Painlesse was thone, the other in delight.
Why then alas did it not kepe it right,
But thus returne to leape into the fire:
And where it was at wish, could not remaine?
Such mockes of dreames do turne to deadly paine.

[48] *The lover unhappy biddeth happy*
lovers rejoice in Maie, while he
waileth that month to him
most unlucky.

    Ye that in love finde luck and swete abundance,
    And live in lust of joyfull jolitie,
    Arise for shame, doway your sluggardy:
    Arise I say, do May some observaunce.
5   Let me in bed lye, dreaming of mischance.
    Let me remember my mishappes unhappy,
    That me betide in May most commonly:
    As one whom love list little to advance,
    Stephan said true, that my nativitie
10 Mischanced was with the ruler of May.
    He gest (I prove) of that the veritie.
    In May my wealth, and eke my wittes, I say,
    Have stand so oft in such perplexitie.
    Joye: let me dreame of your felicitie.

[49] *The lover confesseth him in love*
with Phillis.

    If waker care: if sodayn pale colour:
    If many sighes, with litle speche to plaine:
    Now joye, now wo: if they my chere distaine:
    For hope of small, if much to feare therfore,
5   To haste, or slack: my pace to lesse, or more:
    Be signe of love: then do I love againe.
    If thou aske whom: sure sins I did refraine
    Brunet, that set my welth in such a rore,
    Thunfayned chere of Phillis hath the place,
10 That Brunet had: she hath, and ever shall:
    She from my self now hath me in her grace:
    She hath in hand my wit, my will, and all
    My hart alone wel worthy she doth stay,
    Without whose helpe skant do I live a day.

[50] *Of others fained sorrow, and*
the lovers fained
mirth.

Cesar, when that the traitour of Egipt
With thonorable hed did him present,
Covering his hartes gladnesse, did represent
Plaint with his teares outward, as it is writ.
5   Eke Hannibal, when fortune him out shit
Clene from his reigne, and from all his entent,
Laught to his folke, whom sorow did torment,
His cruel despite for to disgorge and quit.
So chanceth me, that every passion
10   The minde hideth by colour contrary,
With fained visage, now sad, now mery.
Wherby, if that I laugh at any season:
It is because I have none other way
To cloke my care, but under sport and play.

[51] *Of change in minde.*

Eche man me telth, I change most my devise:
And, on my faith, me thinke it good reason
To change purpose, like after the season.
For in eche case to kepe still one guise
5   Is mete for them, that would be taken wise.
And I am not of such maner condicion:
But treated after a divers fashion:
And therupon my diversnesse doth rise.
But you, this diversnesse that blamen most,
10   Change you no more, but still after one rate
Treat you me well: and kepe you in that state.
And while with me doth dwell this weried gost,
My word nor I shall not be variable,
But alwaies one, your own both firme and stable.

[52] *How the lover perisheth in his*
delight, as the flie in
the fire.

Some fowles there be that have so perfit sight,
Against the sunne their eies for to defend:
And some, because the light doth them offend,
Never appeare, but in the darke, or night.
5 Other rejoyce, to se the fire so bright,
And wene to play in it, as they pretend:
But find contrary of it, that they intend.
Alas, of that sort may I be, by right.
For to withstand her loke I am not able:
10 Yet can I not hide me in no dark place:
So foloweth me remembrance of that face:
That with my teary eyen, swolne, and unstable,
My desteny to behold her doth me lead:
And yet I know, I runne into the glead.

[53] *Against his tonge that failed to*
utter his sutes.

Because I stil kept thee fro lyes, and blame,
And to my power alwayes thee honoured,
Unkind tongue, to yl hast thou me rendred,
For such desert to do me wreke and shame.
5 In nede of succour most when that I am,
To aske reward: thou standst like one afraied,
Alway most cold: and if one word be said,
As in a dreame, unperfit is the same.
And ye salt teares, against my wyll eche nyght,
10 That are with me, when I would be alone:
Then are ye gone, when I shold make my mone.
And ye so ready sighes, to make me shright,
Then are ye slacke, when that ye should outstart.
And onely doth my loke declare my hart.

[54] *Description of the contra-*
rious passions in a
lover.

I finde no peace, and all my warre is done:
I feare, and hope: I burne, and frese like yse:
I flye aloft, yet can I not arise:
And nought I have, and all the world I season.
5 That lockes nor loseth, holdeth me in prison,
And holdes me not, yet can I scape no wise:
Nor lettes me live, nor dye, at my devise,
And yet of death it geveth me occasion.
Without eye I se, without tong I playne:
10 I wish to perish, yet I aske for helth:
I love another, and thus I hate my selfe.
I fede me in sorow, and laugh in all my paine.
Lo, thus displeaseth me both death and life.
And my delight is causer of this strife.

[55] *The lover compareth his state*
to a ship in perilous storme
tossed on the sea.

My galley charged with forgetfulnesse,
Through sharpe seas, in winter nightes doth passe,
Twene rocke, and rocke: and eke my fo (alas)
That is my lord, stereth with cruelnesse:
5 And every houre, a thought in readinesse,
As though that death were light, in such a case.
An endlesse wind doth teare the saile apace
Of forced sighes, and trusty fearefulnesse.
A rayne of teares, a clowde of darke disdaine
10 Have done the weried coardes great hinderance,
Wrethed with errour, and with ignorance.
The starres be hidde, that leade me to this payne.
Drownde is reason that should be my comfort:
And I remayne, dispearing of the port.

[56] *Of doutful love.*

Avisyng the bright beames of those fayre eyes,
Where he abides that mine oft moistes and washeth:
The weried mynde streight from the hart departeth,
To rest within his worldly Paradise,
5   And bitter findes the swete, under his gise.
What webbes there he hath wrought, well he perceaveth
Whereby then with himself on love he plaineth,
That spurs with fire, and bridleth eke with yse.
In such extremitie thus is he brought:
10   Frosen now cold, and now he standes inflame:
Twixt wo and wealth: betwixt earnest and game:
With seldome glad, and many a divers thought:
In sore repentance of his hardinesse,
Of such a roote lo cometh frute frutelesse.

[57] *The lover sheweth how he is for-*
saken of such as he som-
time enjoyed.

They flee from me, that sometime did me seke
With naked foote stalking within my chamber.
Once have I seen them gentle, tame, and meke,
That now are wild, and do not once remember
5   That sometime they have put them selves in danger,
To take bread at my hand, and now they range,
Busily seking in continuall change.
Thanked be fortune, it hath been otherwise
Twenty times better: but once especiall,
10   In thynne aray, after a pleasant gise,
When her loose gown did from her shoulders fall,
And she me caught in her armes long and small,
And therwithall, so swetely did me kisse,
And softly sayd: deare hart, how like you this?
15   It was no dreame: for I lay broade awaking.
But all is turnde now through my gentlenesse,
Into a bitter fashion of forsaking:
And I have leave to go of her goodnesse,
And she also to use newfanglenesse.
20   But, sins that I unkindly so am served:
How like you this, what hath she now deserved?

[58] *To a ladie to answer directlie*
with yea or naie.

Madame, withouten many wordes:
Once I am sure, you will, or no.
And if you will: then leave your boordes,
And use your wit, and shew it so:
5 For with a beck you shal me call.
And if of one, that burns alway,
Ye have pity or ruth at all:
Answer him faier with yea, or nay.
If it be yea: I shall be faine.
10 Yf it be nay: frendes, as before.
You shall another man obtain:
And I mine owne, and yours nomore.

[59] *To his love whom he*
had kissed against
her will.

Alas, Madame, for stealing of a kisse,
Have I so much your minde therin offended?
Or have I done so grevously amisse:
That by no meanes it may not be amended?
5 Revenge you then, the rediest way is this:
Another kisse my life it shal have ended.
For, to my mouth the first my hart did suck:
The next shal clene out of my brest it pluck.

[60] *Of the Jelous man that loved*
the same woman and espied
this other sitting
with her.

The wandring gadling, in the summer tide,
That findes the Adder with his rechlesse foote
Startes not dismaid so sodeinly aside,
As jealous despite did, though there were no boote,
5 When that he sawe me sitting by her side,
That of my health is very crop, and roote,
It plesed me then to have so faire a grace,
To stynge the hart, that would have had my place.

[61] *To his love from whom he had*
her gloves.

What nedes these threatning wordes, and wasted wynd?
All this can not make me restore my pray.
To robbe your good ywis is not my mynde:
Nor causelesse your faire hand did I display,
5 Let love be judge: or els whom next we finde:
That may both hear, what you and I can say.
She reft my hart: and I a glove from her:
Let us se then if one be worth the other.

[62] *Of the fained frend.*

Right true it is, and sayd full yore ago:
Take hede of him, that by the backe thee claweth.
For, none is worse, then is a frendly fo.
Though he seme good, all thinge that thee deliteth:
5 Yet know it well, that in thy bosome crepeth.
For, many a man such fire oft times he kindleth:
That with the blase his berd him self he singeth.

[63] *The lover taught, mistrusteth*
allu;rementes.

It may be good like it who list:
But I do dout, who can me blame?
For oft assured, yet have I mist:
And now againe I feare the same.
5 The wordes, that from your mouth last came,
Of sodain change make me agast.
For dread to fall, I stand not fast.
Alas I tread an endlesse mase:
That seke taccord two contraries:
10 And hope thus still, and nothing base:
Imprisoned in liberties,
As one unheard, and still that cries:
Alwayes thirsty, and naught doth taste,
For dreade to fall, I stand not fast.
15 Assured I dout I be not sure,
Should I then trust unto such suretie?
That oft have put the proofe in ure,

And never yet have found it trustie?
Nay syr in fayth, it were great folly.
20   And yet my life thus do I wast,
For dread to fall I stand not fast.

[64] *The lover complaineth that his
love doth not pitie him.*

Resownde my voyce ye woodes, that heare me plain:
Both hilles and vales causing reflexion,
And rivers eke, record ye of my paine:
Which have oft forced ye by compassion,
5   As judges lo to heare my exclamacion.
Among whom, ruth (I finde) yet doth remaine.
Where I it seke, alas, there is disdaine.
    Oft ye rivers, to heare my wofull sounde,
Have stopt your cours, and plainely to expresse,
10   Many a teare by moysture of the ground
The earth hath wept to heare my heavinesse:
Which causelesse I endure without redresse.
The hugy okes have rored in the winde,
Eche thing me thought complayning in their kind.
15   Why then alas doth not she on me rew,
Or is her hart so hard that no pitie
May in it sinke, my joye for to renew?
O stony hart who hath thus framed thee
So cruell? that art cloked with beauty,
20   That from thee may no grace to me procede,
But as reward death for to be my mede.

[65] *The lover rejoyseth against fortune
that by hindering his sute had
happily made him forsake
his folly.*

In faith I wot not what to say,
Thy chaunces ben so wonderous,
Thou fortune with thy divers play
That makst the joyful dolourous,
5   And eke the same right joyous.
Yet though thy chaine hath me enwrapt
Spite of thy hap, hap hath wel hapt.

Though thou hast set me for a wonder,
And sekest by change to do me paine:
10   Mens mindes yet maist thou not so order.
For honestie if it remaine,
Shal shine for all thy cloudy raine.
In vaine thou sekest to have me trapt,
Spite of thy hap, hap hath well hapt.
15   In hindring me, me didst thou further,
And made a gap where was a stile.
Cruel willes ben oft put under.
Wening to lower, then didst thou smile.
Lord, how thy selfe thou didst begile,
20   That in thy cares wouldst me have wrapt?
But spite of hap, hap hath wel hapt.

[66] *A renouncing of hardly*
escaped love.

Farewell the hart of crueltie.
Though that with paine my libertie
Deare have I bought, and wofully
Finisht my fearful tragedy,
5   Of force I must forsake such pleasure:
A good cause just, sins I endure
Therby my wo, which be ye sure,
Shal therwith go me to recure.
I fare as one escapt that fleeth,
10   Glad he is gone, and yet still feareth
Spied to be caught, and so dredeth
That he for nought his paine leseth.
In joyfull paine rejoice my hart,
Thus to sustaine of ech a part.
15   Let not this song from thee astart,
Welcome among my pleasant smart.

[67] *The lover to his bed, with*
describing of his unqui-
et state.

The restfull place, renewer of my smart:
The labours salve, encreasing my sorow:
The bodies ease, and troubler of my hart:

Quieter of minde, mine unquiet fo:
5 Forgetter of paine, remembrer of my wo:
The place of slepe, wherin I do but wake:
Besprent with teares, my bed, I thee forsake.
    The frosty snowes may not redresse my heat:
Nor heat of sunne abate my fervent cold.
10 I know nothing to ease my paines so great.
Eche cure causeth encrease by twenty fold,
Renewing cares upon my sorowes old.
Such overthwart effectes in me they make.
Besprent with teares my bed for to forsake.
15   But all for nought: I finde no better ease
In bed, or out. This most causeth my paine:
Where I do seke how best that I may please,
My lost labour (alas) is all in vaine.
My hart once set, I can not it refraine.
20 No place from me my griefe away can take.
Wherfore with teares, my bed I thee forsake.

[68] *Comparison of love to a streame*
falling from the Alpes.

From these hie hilles as when a spring doth fall,
It trilleth downe with still and suttle course,
Of this and that it gathers ay and shall,
Till it have just down flowed to streame and force:
5 Then at the foote it rageth over all.
So fareth love, when he hath tane a sourse.
Rage is his raine. Resistance vaileth none.
The first eschue is remedy alone.

[69] *Wiates complaint upon Love*
to Reason: with Loves
answere.

    Mine old dere enmy, my froward maister,
Afore that Quene, I causde to be acited,
Which holdeth the divine part of our nature,
That, like as golde, in fire he mought be tried.
5 Charged with dolour, there I me presented
With horrible feare, as one that greatly dredeth
A wrongfull death, and justice alway seketh.

And thus I sayd: Once my left foote, Madame,
When I was yong, I set within his reigne:
10   Wherby other then fiercely burning flame
I never felt, but many a grevous pain.
Torment I suffred, angre, and disdain:
That mine oppressed pacience was past,
And I mine own life hated, at the last.
15   Thus hitherto have I my time passed
In pain and smart. What waies profitable:
How many pleasant daies have me escaped,
In serving this false lyer so deceavable?
What wit have wordes so prest and forceable,
20   That may contain my great mishappynesse,
And just complaintes of his ungentlenesse?
So small hony, much aloes, and gall,
In bitternesse, my blinde life hath ytasted.
His false semblance, that turneth as a ball:
25   With faire and amorous daunce, made me be traced,
And, where I had my thought, and minde araced,
From earthly frailnesse, and from vain pleasure,
Me from my rest he toke, and set in errour:
God made he me regardlesse, than I ought,
30   And to my self to take right litle hede:
And for a woman have I set at nought
All other thoughtes: in this onely to spede.
And he was onely counseler of this dede:
Whetting alwaies my youthly fraile desire
35   On cruell whetston, tempered with fire.
But (Oh alas) where had I ever wit?
Or other gift, geven to me of nature?
That sooner shalbe changed my weried sprite:
Then the obstinate will, that is my ruler.
40   So robbeth he my freedom with displeasure,
This wicked traytour, whom I thus accuse:
That bitter life hath turned in pleasant use.
He hath me hasted, through divers regions:
Through desert woods, and sharp hye mountaines:
45   Through froward people, and through bitter passions:
Through rocky seas, and over hilles and plaines:
With wery travell, and with laborous paines:
Alwaies in trouble and in tediousnesse:
All in errour, and dangerous distresse.
50   But nother he, nor she, my tother fo,

For all my flight, did ever me forsake:
That though my timely death hath been to slow
That me as yet, it hath not overtake:
The heavenly Gods of pitie do it slake.
55 And, note they this his cruell tiranny,
That feedes him, with my care, and misery.
    Sins I was his, hower rested I never,
Nor looke to do: and eke the waky nightes
The baneshed slepe may in no wise recover.
60 By guile, and force, over my thralled sprites,
He is ruler: sins which bell never strikes,
That I heare not as sounding to renue
My plaintes. Himself, he knoweth, that I say true.
    For never wormes old rotten stocke have eaten:
65 As he my hart, where he is resident
And doth the same with death dayly threaten,
Thence come the teares, and thence the bitter torment:
The sighes: the wordes, and eke the languishment:
That noy both me, and paraventure other.
70 Judge thou: that knowest the one, and eke the tother.
    Mine adversair, with such grevous reproofe,
Thus he began. Heare Lady, thother part:
That the plain troth, from which he draweth aloofe,
This unkinde man may shew, ere that I part.
75 In his yong age, I toke him from that art,
That selleth wordes, and makes a clattering knight:
And of my wealth I gave him the delight.
    Now shames he not on me for to complain,
That held him evermore in pleasant gaine,
80 From his desire, that might have been his pain.
Yet therby alone I brought him to some frame:
Which now as wretchednes, he doth so blame:
And toward honour quickned I his wit:
Whereas a daskard els he mought have sit.
85   He knoweth, how great Atride that made Troy freat,
And Hanniball, to Rome so troubelous:
Whom Homer honored, Achilles that great,
And Thaffricane Scipion the famous:
And many other, by much honour glorious:
90 Whose fame, and actes did lift them up above:
I did let fall in base dishonest love.
    And unto him, though he unworthy were:
I chose the best of many a Milion:

That, under sunne yet never was her pere,
95   Of wisdome, womanhod, and of discrecion:
And of my grace I gave her such a facion,
And eke such way I taught her for to teache,
That never base thought his hart so hye might reache.
     Evermore thus to content his maistresse,
100 That was his onely frame of honesty,
I stirred him still toward gentlenesse:
And causde him to regard fidelity.
Pacience I taught him in adversity.
Such vertues learned he in my great schoole:
105 Wherof repenteth now the ignorant foole.
     These were the same deceites, and bitter gall,
That I have used, the torment and the anger:
Sweter, then ever did to other fall,
Of right good sede yll fruite lo thus I gather.
110 And so shall he, that the unkinde doth further.
A Serpent nourish I under my wing:
And now of nature, ginneth he to sting.
     And for to tell, at last, my great servise.
From thousand dishonesties have I him drawen:
115 That, by my meanes, him in no maner wise.
Never vile pleasure once hath overthrowen.
Where, in his dede, shame hath him alwaies gnawen:
Douting report, that should come to her eare:
Whom now he blames, her wonted he to feare.
120   What ever he hath of any honest custome:
Of her, and me: that holdes he every whit,
But, lo, yet never was there nightly fantome
So farre in errour, as he is from his wit.
To plain on us, he striveth with the bit,
125 Which may rule him, and do him ease, and pain:
And in one hower, make al his grief his gain.
     But, one thing yet there is, above all other:
I gave him winges, wherwith he might upflie
To honour and fame: and if he would to higher
130 Then mortal thinges, above the starry skie:
Considering the pleasure, that an eye
Might geve in earth, by reason of the love:
What should that be that lasteth still above?
     And he the same himself hath sayd ere this.
135 But now, forgotten is both that and I,
That gave her him, his onely wealth and blisse.

And, at this word, with dedly shreke and cry.
Thou gave her once: quod I, but by and by
Thou toke her ayen from me: that wo worth the.
140 Not I but price: more worth than thou (quod he.)
 At last: eche other for himself, concluded:
I, trembling still: but he, with small reverence.
Lo, thus, as we eche other have accused:
Dere Lady: now we waite thine onely sentence.
145 She smiling, at the whisted audience:
It liketh me (quod she) to have heard your question:
But, lenger time doth ask a resolucion.

  [70] *The lovers sorowfull state maketh*
   him write sorowfull songes, but
    (Souche) his love may
    change the same.

 Marvell no more altho
The songes, I sing do mone:
For other life then wo,
I never proved none.
5 And in my hart also,
Is graven with letters depe
A thousand sighes and mo:
A flood of teares to wepe.
 How may a man in smart
10 Finde matter to rejoyce?
How may a moorning hart
Set foorth a pleasant voyce.
 Play who so can, that part:
Nedes must in me appere:
15 How fortune overthwart
Doth cause my moorning chere.
 Perdy there is no man,
If he saw never sight:
That perfitly tell can
20 The nature of the light.
 Alas: how should I than,
That never taste but sowre:
But do, as I began,
Continually to lowre.
25 But yet perchance some chance

May chance to change my tune:
And when (Souch) chance doth chance:
Then shall I thank fortune.
    And if I have (Souch) chance:
30 Perchance ere it be long:
For (Souch) a pleasant chance,
To sing some pleasant song.

[71] *The lover complaineth him-*
self forsaken.

Where shall I have, at mine owne wyll,
Teares to complain? Where shall I fet
Such sighes? that I may sigh my fill:
And then againe my plaintes repete.
5 For, though my plaint shall have none end:
My teares cannot suffise my wo.
To mone my harm, have I no friend,
For fortunes friend is mishaps fo.
Comfort (God wot) els have I none:
10 But in the winde to wast my wordes,
Nought moveth you my deadly mone:
But still you turne it into bordes.
I speake not, now, to move your hart,
That you should rue upon my pain:
15 The sentence geven may not revert:
I know, such labour were but vain.
But sins that I for you (my dere)
Have lost that thing, that was my best:
A right small losse it must appere,
20 To lese these wordes, and all the rest.
But, though they sparkle in the winde:
Yet, shall they shew your falsed faith:
Which is returned to his kinde:
For like to like: the proverb saith,
25 Fortune, and you did me avance.
Me thought, I swam, and could not drown:
Happiest of all, but my mischance
Did lift me up, to throw me down.
And you, with her, of cruelnesse,
30 Did set your foote upon my neck,
Me, and my welfare to oppresse:

Without offence your hart to wreck,
Where are your pleasant wordes? alas:
Where is your faith? your stedfastnesse?
35 There is no more: but all doth passe:
And I am left all comfortlesse.
But sins so much it doth you greve,
And also me my wretched life:
Have here my troth: Nought shall releve,
40 But death alone my wretched strife.
Therfore, farewell my life, my death
My gain, my losse: my salve, my sore:
Farewell also, with you my breath:
For, I am gone for evermore.

[72] *Of his love that pricked*
her finger with
a nedle.

She sat, and sowed: that hath done me the wrong:
Wherof I plain, and have done many a day:
And, whilst she heard my plaint, in piteous song:
She wisht my hart the samplar, that it lay.
5 The blinde master, whom I have served so long:
Grudging to heare, that he did heare her say:
Made her own weapon do her finger blede:
To fele, if pricking were so good in dede.

[73] *Of the same.*

What man hath heard such cruelty before?
That, when my plaint remembred her my wo,
That caused it: she cruell more and more,
Wished eche stitche, as she did sit and sow,
5 Had prickt my hart, for to encrease my sore,
And, as I think, she thought it had been so.
For as she thought, this is his hart in dede:
She pricked hard: and made her self to blede.

[74] *Request to Cupide for re-*
venge of his unkinde
love.

Behold, Love, thy power how she despiseth:
My grevous pain how litle she regardeth,
The solemne othe, wherof she takes no cure,
Broken she hath: and yet, she bydeth sure,
5 Right at her ease, and litle thee she dredeth.
Weaponed thou art, and she unarmed sitteth:
To thee disdainfull, all her life she leadeth:
To me spitefull, without just cause, or measure.
Behold Love, how proudly she triumpheth,
10 I am in hold, but if thee pitie meveth:
Go, bend thy bow, that stony hartes breaketh:
And with some stroke revenge the great displeasure
Of thee, and him that sorow doth endure,
And as his Lord thee lowly here entreateth.

[75] *Complaint for true love*
unrequited.

What vaileth troth? or by it, to take payn
To strive by stedfastnesse, for to attain
How to be just: and flee from doublenesse?
Since all alyke, where ruleth craftinesse,
5 Rewarded is both crafty false, and plain.
Soonest he spedes, that most can lye and fayn.
True meaning hart is had in hie disdain.
Against deceit, and cloked doublenesse,
What vaileth troth, or parfit stedfastnesse.
10 Deceaved is he, by false and crafty trayn,
That meanes no gile, and faithful doth remain
Within the trapt, without help or redresse.
But for to love (lo) such a sterne maistresse,
Where cruelty dwelles, alas it were in vain.

[76] *The lover that fled love, now*
folowes it with his harme.

Somtime I fled the fire, that me so brent,
By sea, by land, by water, and by wynde:
And now, the coales I folow, that be quent,
From Dover to Calas, with willing minde,
5   Lo, how desire is both forth sprong, and spent:
And he may see, that whilom was so blinde:
And all his labour, laughes he now to scorne,
Meashed in the breers, that erst was onely torne.

[77] *The lover hopeth of bet-*
ter chance.

He is not dead, that somtime had a fall.
The Sun returnes, that hid was under clowd.
And when Fortune hath spit out all her gall,
I trust, good luck to me shall be alowd.
5   For, I have seen a ship in haven fall,
After that storme hath broke both maste, and shroud,
The willow eke, that stoupeth with the winde,
Doth rise againe, and greater wood doth binde.

[78] *The lover compareth his*
hart to the overcharged
gonne.

The furious goonne, in his most raging yre,
When that the boule is rammed into sore:
And that the flame cannot part from the fire,
Crackes in sunder: and in the ayer do rore
5   The shevered peces. So doth my desire,
Whose flame encreaseth ay from more to more.
Which to let out, I dare not loke, nor speake:
So inward force my hart doth all to breake.

[79] *The lover suspected of change*
praieth that it be not be-
leved against him.

Accused though I be, without desert:
Sith none can prove, beleve it not for true.
For never yet, since that you had my hert,
Intended I to false, or be untrue.
5   Sooner I would of death sustayn the smart,
Than breake one word of that I promised you.
Accept therfore my service in good part.
None is alyve, that can yll tonges eschew.
Hold them as false: and let not us depart
10   Our frendship old, in hope of any new.
Put not thy trust in such as use to fayn,
Except thou minde to put thy frend to payn.

[80] *The lover abused re-*
nownseth love.

My love to skorne, my service to retayne,
Therin (me thought) you used crueltie.
Since with good will I lost my libertie,
Might never wo yet cause me to refrain,
5   But onely this, which is extremitie,
To geve me nought (alas) nor to agree,
That as I was, your man I might remain.
But since that thus ye list to order me,
That would have bene your servant true and fast:
10   Displease you not: my doting time is past.
And with my losse to leave I must agree.
For as there is a certain time to rage:
So is there time such madnes to aswage.

[81] *The lover professeth*
himself con-
stant.

Within my brest I never thought it gain,
Of gentle mynde the fredom for to lose
Nor in my hart sanck never such disdain,
To be a forger, faultes for to disclose.

5 Nor I can not endure the truth to glose,
   To set a glosse upon an earnest pain.
   Nor I am not in nomber one of those,
   That list to blow retrete to every train.

[82] *The lover sendeth his com-*
plaintes and teares to sue
for grace.

   Passe forth my wonted cries,
   Those cruel eares to pearce,
   Which in most hatefull wyse
   Doe stil my plaintes reverse.
5 Doe you, my teares, also
   So wet her barrein hart:
   That pitie there may grow,
   And crueltie depart.
      For though hard rockes among
10 She semes to have bene bred:
   And of the Tigre long
   Bene nourished, and fed.
   Yet shall that nature change,
   If pitie once win place.
15 Whom as unknowen, and strange,
   She now away doth chase.
      And as the water soft,
   Without forcing or strength,
   Where that it falleth oft,
20 Hard stones doth perse at length:
   So in her stony hart
   My plaintes at last shal grave,
   And, rygour set apart,
   Winne graunt of that I crave.
25   Wherfore my plaintes, present
   Stil so to her my sute,
   As ye, through her assent,
   May bring to me some frute.
   And as she shall me prove,
30 So bid her me regarde,
   And render love for love:
   Which is a just reward.

[83] *The lovers case can not be*
hidden how ever he
dissemble.

   Your lokes so often cast,
Your eyes so frendly rolde,
Your sight fixed so fast,
Alwaies one to behold.
5 Though hyde it fayn ye would:
It plainly doth declare,
Who hath your hart in hold,
And where good will ye bare,
   Fayn would ye finde a cloke
10 Your brennyng fire to hyde:
Yet both the flame, and smoke
Breakes out on every syde.
Yee can not love so guide,
That it no issue winne.
15 Abrode nedes must it glide,
That brens so hote within.
   For cause your self do wink,
Ye judge all other blinde:
And secret it you think,
20 Which every man doth finde.
In wast oft spend ye winde
Your self in love to quit,
For agues of that kinde
Will show, who hath the fit.
25   Your sighes you set from farre,
And all to wry your wo:
Yet are ye neare the narre,
Men ar not blinded so.
Depely oft swere ye no:
30 But all those othes ar vaine.
So well your eye doth show,
Who puttes your hart to paine.
   Think not therfore to hide,
That still it selfe betraies:
35 Nor seke meanes to provide
To darke the sunny daies.
Forget those wonted waies:
Leave of such frowning chere:
There will be found no staies
40 To stoppe a thing so clere.

[84] *The lover praieth not to be disdai-*
ned, refused, mistrusted,
nor forsaken.

    Disdaine me not without desert:
Nor leave me not so sodenly:
Since well ye wot, that in my hert
I meane ye not but honestly.
5   Refuse me not without cause why:
Nor think me not to be unjust:
Sins that by lot of fantasy,
This carefull knot nedes knit I must.
    Mistrust me not, though some there be,
10 That faine would spot my stedfastnesse:
Beleve them not, sins that ye se,
The proofe is not, as they expresse.
    Forsake me not, till I deserve:
Nor hate me not, till I offend.
15 Destroy me not, till that I swerve.
But sins ye know what I intend:
    Disdaine me not that am your own:
Refuse me not that am so true:
Mistrust me not till all be known:
20 Forsake me not, now for no new.

[85] *The lover lamenteth his estate*
with sute for grace.

    For want of will, in wo I plain:
Under colour of sobernesse.
Renewing with my sute my pain,
My wanhope with your stedfastnesse.
5 Awake therfore of gentlenesse.
Regard at length, I you require,
The swelting paines of my desire.
    Betimes who giveth willingly,
Redoubled thankes aye doth deserve.
10 And I that sue unfainedly,
In frutelesse hope (alas) do sterve.
How great my cause is for to swerve:
And yet how stedfast is my sute:
Lo, here ye see, where is the frute?
15   As hound that hath his keper lost,

Seke I your presence to obtain:
In which my hart deliteth most,
And shall delight though I be slain.
You may release my band of pain.
20 Lose then the care that makes me cry,
For want of helpe or els I dye.
        I dye, though not incontinent,
By processe yet consumingly
As waste of fire, which doth relent,
25 If you as wilfull will deny.
Wherfore cease of such cruelty:
And take me wholy in your grace:
Which lacketh will to change his place.

[86] *The lover waileth his*
changed joyes.

        If every man might him avaunt
Of fortunes friendly chere:
It was my selfe I must it graunt,
For I have bought it dere.
5 And derely have I held also
The glory of her name:
In yelding her such tribute, lo,
As did set forth her fame.
        Sometime I stoode so in her grace:
10 That as I would require,
Ech joy I thought did me embrace,
That furdered my desire.
And all those pleasures (lo) had I,
That fansy might support:
15 And nothing she did me deny,
That was unto my comfort.
        I had (what would you more perde?)
Ech grace that I did crave.
Thus fortunes will was unto me
20 All thing that I would have.
But all to rathe alas the while,
She built on such a ground:
In litle space, to great a guile
In her now have I found.
25   For she hath turned so her whele:

That I unhappy man
May waile the time that I dede fele
Wherwith she fed me than.
For broken now are her behestes:
30 And plesant lookes she gave:
And therfore now all my requestes,
From perill can not save.
　　Yet would I well it might appere
To her my chiefe regard:
35 Though my desertes have been to dere
To merite such reward.
Sith fortunes will is now so bent
To plage me thus poore man:
I must my selfe therwith content:
40 And beare it as I can.

[87] *To his love that had geven*
him answere of
refusell.

　　The answere that ye made to me my dere,
When I did sue for my poore hartes redresse:
Hath so appalde my countenance and my chere:
That is this case, I am all comfortlesse:
5 Sins I of blame no cause can well expresse.
　　I have no wrong, where I can claime no right.
Nought tane me fro, where I have nothing had,
Yet of my wo, I can not so be quite.
Namely, sins that another may be glad
10 With that, that thus in sorow makes me sad.
　　Yet none can claime (I say) by former graunt,
That knoweth not of any graunt at all.
And by desert, I dare well make avaunt,
Of faithfull will, there is no where that shall
15 Beare you more truth, more ready at your call.
　　Now good then, call againe that bitter word:
That toucht your friende so nere with panges of paine:
And say my dere that it was sayd in bord.
Late, or to sone, let it not rule the gaine,
20 Wherwith free will doth true desert retaine.

[88] *To his ladie cruel over her*
yelden lover.

Such is the course, that natures kinde hath wrought,
That snakes have time to cast away their stinges.
Against chainde prisoners what nede defence be sought:
The fierce lyon will hurt no yelden thinges:
5   Why should such spite be nursed then by thought?
Sith all these powers are prest under thy winges:
And eke thou seest, and reason thee hath taught:
What mischief malice many wayes it bringes:
Consider eke, that spight availeth naught,
10 Therfore this song thy fault to thee it singes:
Displease the not, for saiyng thus (me thought.)
Nor hate thou him from whom no hate forth springes,
For furies, that in hell be execrable,
For that they hate, are made most miserable.

[89] *The lover complaineth that deadly*
sicknesse can not helpe his
affeccion.

The enmy of life, decayer of all kinde,
That with his cold withers away the grene:
This other night, me in my bed did finde:
And offerd me to ryd my fever clene.
5   And I dyd graunt: so did dispaire me blinde.
He drew his bowe, with arrowes sharpe and kene:
And strake the place, wher love had hit before:
And drave the first dart deper more and more.

[90] *The lover rejoiceth the enjoying*
of his love.

Once as me thought, fortune me kist:
And bade me aske, what I thought best:
And I should have it as me list,
Therewith to set my hart in rest.
5   I asked but my ladies hart
To have for evermore myne owne:
Then at an end were al my smart:
Then should I nede no more to mone.

Yet for all that a stormy blast
10 Had overturnde this goodly day:
And fortune semed at the last,
That to her promise she said nay.
        But like as one out of dispayre
To sodain hope revived I.
15 Now fortune sheweth her selfe so faire,
That I content me wondersly.
        My most desire my hand may reach:
My wyll is alway at my hand.
Me nede not long for to beseche
20 Her, that hath power me to commaunde.
        What earthly thing more can I crave?
What would I wishe more at my will?
Nothing on earth more would I have,
Save that I have, to have it styll.
25   For fortune now hath kept her promesse,
In graunting me my most desire.
Of my soveraigne I have redresse,
And I content me with my hire.

        [91] *The lover complaineth the un-*
                kindnes of his love.

My lute awake performe the last
Labour that thou and I shal wast:
And end that I have now begonne:
And when this song is song and past:
5 My lute be stil for I have done.
        As to be heard where eare is none:
As lead to grave in marble stone:
My song may pearse her hart as sone.
Should we then sigh? or singe, or mone?
10 No, no, my lute for I have done.
        The rockes do not so cruelly
Repulse the waves continually,
As she my sute and affection:
So that I am past remedy,
15 Wherby my lute and I have done.
        Proude of the spoile that thou hast gotte
Of simple hartes through loves shot:
By whom unkind thou hast them wonne,

Thinke not he hath his bow forgot,
20   Although my lute and I have done.
    Vengeaunce shall fall on thy disdaine
That makest but game on earnest payne.
Thinke not alone under the sunne
Unquit to cause thy lovers plain:
25   Although my lute and I have done.
    May chance thee lie withered and olde,
In winter nightes that are so colde,
Plaining in vaine unto the mone:
Thy wishes then dare not be tolde.
30   Care then who list, for I have done.
    And then may chance thee to repent
The time that thou hast lost and spent
To cause thy lovers sigh and swowne.
Then shalt thou know beaute but lent,
35   And wish and want as I have done.
    Now cease my lute this is the last
Labour that thou and I shal wast
And ended is that we begonne.
Now is this song both song and past,
40   My lute be still for I have done.

[92] *How by a kisse he found both*
his life and death.

Nature that gave the Bee so feate a grace,
To finde hony of so wondrous fashion:
Hath taught the spider out of the same place
To fetche poyson by strange alteracion.
5   Though this be strange, it is a straunger case,
With one kisse by secret operacion,
Both these at once in those your lipps to finde,
In change wherof, I leave my hart behinde.

[93] *The lover describeth his being*
taken with sight of
his love.

    Unwarely so was never no man caught,
With stedfast loke upon a goodly face:
As I of late: for sodainely me thought,

My hart was torne out of his proper place.
5   Thorow mine eye the stroke from hers did slide,
And downe directly to my hart it ranne:
In helpe wherof the blood therto did glide,
And left my face both pale and wanne.
    Then was I like a man for wo amased:
10 Or like the fowle that fleeth into the fier.
For while that I upon her beauty gased:
The more I burnd in my desire.
    Anone the bloud start in my face againe,
Inflamde with heat, that it had at my hart.
15 And brought therwith through out in every vayne,
A quaking heate with pleasant smart.
    Then was I like the straw, when that the flame
Is driven therin, by force, and rage of winde.
I can not tell, alas, what I shall blame:
20 Nor what to seke, nor what to finde.
    But well I wot: the griefe doth hold me sore
In heat and cold, betwixt both hope and dreade:
That, but her helpe to health do me restore:
This restlesse life I may not lead.

[94] *To his lover to loke upon*
him.

Al in thy loke my life doth whole depende.
Thou hydest thy self, and I must dye therfore.
But sins thou mayst so easily helpe thy frend:
Why dost thou stick to salve that thou madest sore?
5 Why do I dye: sins thou maist me defend:
And if I dye, thy lyfe may last no more.
For eche by other doth live and have reliefe,
I in thy loke, and thou most in my griefe.

[95] *The lover excuseth him of wordes*
wherwith he was unjustly
charged.

    Perdy I sayd it not:
Nor never thought to do.
As well as I ye wot:
I have no power therto,

5 And if I did, the lot,
   That first did me enchayne:
   May never slake the knot,
   But strayght it to my payne.
      And if I did ech thing,
10 That may do harme or wo:
   Continually may wring
   My hart where so I go.
   Report may always ring
   Of shame on me for aye:
15 If in my hart did spring
   The wordes that you do say.
      And if I did ech starre,
   That is in heaven above,
   May frowne on me to marre
20 The hope I have in love.
   And if I did such warre,
   As they brought unto Troye,
   Bring all my life as farre
   From all his lust and joye.
25   And if I did so say:
   The beautie that me bounde,
   Encrease from day to day
   More cruel to my wounde:
   With al the mone that may,
30 To plaint may turne my song:
   My life may sone decay,
   Without redresse by wrong.
      If I be cleare from thought,
   Why do you then complayne?
35 Then is this thing but sought.
   To turne my hart to payne,
   Then this that you have wrought,
   You must it now redresse,
   Of ryght therfore you ought
40 Such rigour to represse.
      And as I have deserved:
   So graunt me now my hire:
   You know I never swarved.
   You never founde me lier.
45 For Rachel have I served,
   For Lea cared I never:
   And her I have reserved
   Within my hart for ever.

[96] *Of such as had forsaken him.*

Lux, my faire fawlcon, and thy felowes all:
How well pleasant it were your libertie:
Ye not forsake me, that faire mought you fal.
But they that sometime liked my company:
5 Like lice away from deade bodies they crall.
Loe, what a proofe in light adversitie?
But ye my birdes, I sweare by all your belles,
Ye be my frendes, and very few elles.

[97] *A description of such a one as*
he would love.

A face that should content me wonderous wel,
Should not be faire, but lovely to behold:
Of lively loke, all griefe for to repel:
With right good grace, so would I that it should
5 Speake without word, such wordes as none can tel.
Her tresse also should be of crisped gold.
With wit, and these perchance I might be tride,
And knit againe with knot, that should not slide.

[98] *How unpossible it is to finde*
quiet in love.

Ever my hap is slack and slowe in comming
Desire encreasyng ay my hope uncertaine:
With doubtful love that but increaseth pain
For Tigre like so swift it is in parting.
5 Alas the snow black shal it be and scalding,
The sea waterles, and fishe upon the mountaine:
The Temis shal back retourne into his fountaine:
And wher he rose the sunne shal take his lodging.
Ere I in this finde peace or quietnesse.
10 Or that love or my lady rightwisely
Leave to conspire against me wrongfully.
And if I have after such bitternesse,
One drop of swete, my mouth is out of taste:
That al my trust and travell is but waste.

[99] *Of love, fortune, and the*
lovers minde.

Love, Fortune, and my minde which do remember
Eke that is now, and that that once hath bene:
Torment my hart so sore that very often
I hate and envy them beyonde al measure.
5   Love sleeth my hart while Fortune is depriver
Of all my comfort: the folishe minde than
Burneth and plaineth: as one that very sildam
Liveth in rest. So styl in displeasure
My pleasant daies they flete away and passe.
10   And dayly doth myne yll change to the worse.
While more then halfe is runne now of my course.
Alas not of stele, but of brittle glasse,
I se that from my hand falleth my trust:
And all my thoughtes are dasshed into dust.

[100] *The lover praieth his offred*
hart to be received.

How oft have I, my deare and cruel fo:
With my great pain to get som peace or truce,
Geven you my hart? but you do not use,
In so hie thinges, to cast your minde so low,
5   If any other loke for it, as you trow,
Their vaine weake hope doth greatly them abuse.
And that thus I disdaine, that you refuse.
It was once mine, it can no more be so.
If you it chase, that it in you can finde,
10   In this exile, no maner of comfort:
Nor live alone, nor where he is calde, resort,
He may wander from his naturall kinde.
So shall it be great hurt unto us twayne,
And yours the losse, and mine the deadly payne.

[101] *The lovers life compared to*
the Alpes.

Lyke unto these unmesurable mountaines,
So is my painefull life, the burden of yre.
For hye be they, and hye is my desire.

And I of teares, and they be full of fountaines.
5 Under craggy rockes they have barren plaines,
Hard thoughtes in me my wofull minde doth tire,
Small frute and many leaves their toppes do attire,
With small effect great trust in me remaines.
The boystous windes oft their hie boughes do blast:
10 Hote sighes in me continually be shed.
Wilde beastes in them, fierce love in me is fed.
Unmoveable am I: and they stedfast.
Of singing birdes they have the tune and note:
And I alwaies plaintes passing through my throte.

[102] *Charging of his love as unpetious*
and loving other.

If amorous fayth, or if an hart unfained
A swete languor, a great lovely desire:
If honest will, kindled in gentle fire:
If long errour in a blind mase chained,
5 If in my visage ech thought distained:
Or if my sparkelyng voice, lower, or hier,
Which feare and shame, so wofully doth tyre:
If pale colour, which love alas hath stained:
If to have another then my self more dere,
10 If wailing or sighing continually,
With sorowfull anger feding busily,
If burning farre of, and if frysing nere,
Are cause that I by love my selfe destroy:
Yours is the fault, and mine the great annoy.

[103] *A renouncing of love.*

Farewell, Love, and all thy lawes for ever,
Thy bayted hookes shall tangle me no more.
Senec, and Plato call me from thy lore:
To parfit wealth my wit for to endever.
5 In blinde errour when I did parsever:
Thy sharp repulse, that pricketh aye so sore:
Taught me in trifles that I set no store:
But scape forth thence: since libertie is lever.
Therefore, farewell: go trouble yonger hartes:
10 And in me claime no more auctoritie.

With ydle youth go use thy propartie:
And theron spend thy many brittle dartes.
For, hitherto though I have lost my time:
Me list no lenger rotten bowes to clime.

[104] *The lover forsaketh his unkinde love.*

My hart I gave thee, not to do it pain:
But to preserve, lo it to thee was taken.
I served thee not that I should be forsaken:
But, that I should receive reward again,
5   I was content thy servant to remain:
And not to be repayed on this fashion.
Now, since in thee there is none other reason:
Displease thee not, if that I do refrain.
Unsaciat of my wo, and thy desire.
10   Assured by craft for to excuse thy fault.
But, sins it pleaseth thee to fain default:
Farewell, I say, departing from the fire.
For, he, that doth beleve bearing in hand:
Ploweth in the water: and soweth in the sand.

[105] *The lover describeth his restlesse state.*

The flaming sighes that boyle within my brest
Somtime breake forth and thei can well declare
The hartes unrest and how that it doth fare,
The pain therof the grief and all the rest.
5   The watred eyen from whence the teares do fall,
Do fele some force or els they would be dry:
The wasted flesh of colour ded can try,
And somtime tell what swetenes is in gall.
And he that lust to see and to disarne,
10   How care can force within a weried minde:
Come he to me I am that place assinde,
But for all this no force it doth no harme.
The wound alas happe in some other place:
From whence no toole away the skar can race.
15   But you that of such like have had your part,
Can best bejudge. Wherfore my friend so deare:

I thought it good my state should now appeare.
To you and that there is no great desart.
And wheras you in weighty matters great:
20 Of fortune saw the shadow that you know,
For trifling thinges I now am striken so
That though I fele my hart doth wound and beat:
I sit alone save on the second day:
My fever comes with whom I spend my time,
25 In burning heat while that she list assigne.
And who hath helth and libertie alway:
Let him thank God and let him not provoke,
To have the like of this my painfull stroke.

[106] *The lover lamentes the*
death of his love.

The piller perisht is wherto I lent,
The strongest stay of mine unquiet minde:
The like of it no man again can finde:
From East to West still seking though he went.
5 To mine unhappe for happe away hath rent,
Of all my joy the very bark and rinde:
And I (alas) by chance am thus assinde,
Dayly to moorne till death do it relent.
But sins that thus it is by desteny,
10 What can I more but have a wofull hart,
My penne, in plaint, my voyce in carefull cry:
My minde in wo, my body full of smart,
And I my self, my selfe alwaies to hate,
Till dreadfull death do ease my dolefull state.

[107] *The lover sendeth sighes to*
mone his sute.

Go burning sighes unto the frosen hart,
Go breake the yse with pities painfull dart.
Might never perce and if that mortall praier,
In heaven be heard, at lest yet I desire
5 That death or mercy end my wofull smart.
Take with thee pain, wherof I have my part,
And eke the flame from which I cannot start.
And leave me then in rest, I you require:

Go burning sighes fulfill that I desire.
10   I must go worke I see by craft and art,
For truth and faith in her is laid apart:
Alas, I can not therfore now assaile her,
With pitefull complaint and scalding fier,
That from my brest disceivably doth start.

[108] *Complaint of the absence*
of his love.

So feble is the threde, that doth the burden stay,
Of my poore life: in heavy plight, that falleth in decay:
That, but it have elswhere some ayde or some succours:
The running spindle of my fate anone shall end his course.
5   For sins thunhappy hower, that did me to depart,
From my swete weale: one onely hope hath staied my life, apart:
Which doth perswade such wordes unto my sored minde:
Maintain thy self, O wofull wight, some better luck to finde.
For though thou be deprived from thy desired sight:
10   Who can thee tell, if thy returne be for thy more delight?
Or, who can tell, thy losse if thou mayst once recover?
Some pleasant hower thy wo may wrap: and thee defend, and cover.
Thus in this trust as yet it hath my life sustained:
But now (alas) I see it faint: and I, by trust, am trayned.
15   The time doth flete, and I see how the howers, do bend
So fast: that I have scant the space to marke my comming end,
Westward the sunne from out the East scant shewes his light:
When in the West he hies him strayt, within the dark of night.
And comes as fast, where he began, his path awry.
20   From East to West, from West to East so doth his journey lye.
The life so short, so fraile, that mortall men live here:
So great a weight, so heavy charge the bodies that we bere:
That, when I think upon the distaunce, and the space:
That doth so farre devide me from my dere desired face:
25   I know not, how tattain the winges, that I require,
To lift me up: that I might flie, to folow my desire.
Thus of that hope, that doth my life some thing sustaine,
Alas: I feare, and partly fele: full litle doth remain.
Eche place doth bring me grief: where I do not behold
30   Those lively eyes: which of my thoughts wer wont the keys to hold,
Those thoughts wer pleasant swete: whilst I enjoyed that grace:
My pleasure past, my present pain, when I might well embrace.

And, forbecause my want should more my wo encrease:
In watch, and slepe, both day and night, my will doth never cease
35 That thing to wish: wherof sins I did lese the sight:
Was never thing that mought in ought my wofull hart delight,
Thuneasy life, I lead, doth teach me for to mete
The floodes, the seas, the land, the hilles: that doth then entermete
Twene me, and those shene lightes: that wonted for to clere
40 My darked pangs of cloudy thoughts, as bright as Phebus spere
It teacheth me also, what was my pleasant state:
The more to fele, by such record, how that my wealth doth bate.
If such record (alas) provoke thenflamed minde:
Which sprong that day, that I did leave the best of me behinde:
45 If love forget himself, by length of absence let:
Who doth me guyde (O wofull wretch) unto this bayted net?
Where doth encrease my care: much better wer for me,
As dumme, as stone, all thing forgot, still absent for to be.
Alas: the clere christall, the bright transplendant glasse
50 Doth not bewray the colours hid, which underneth it hase:
As doth thaccumbred sprite the thoughtfull throwes discover,
Of feares delite, of fervent love: that in our hartes we cover.
Out by these eyes, it sheweth that evermore delight
In plaint, and teares to seke redresse: and eke both day and night.
55 Those kindes of pleasures most wherein men so rejoyce,
To me they do redouble still of stormy sighes the voyce.
For, I am one of them, whom plaint doth well content:
It sits me well myne absent wealth me semes for to lament:
And with my teares, tassay to charge mine eyes twain:
60 Like as my hart above the brink is fraughted full of pain.
And forbecause, thereto, that those faire eyes to treate
Do me provoke: I will returne, my plaint thus to repeate.
For, there is nothing els, so toucheth me within:
Where they rule all: and I alone nought but the case, or skin.
65 Wherefore, I shall returne to them, as well, or spring:
From whom descendes my mortall wo, above all other thing.
So shall mine eyes in pain accompany my hart,
That were the guides, that did it lead of love to fele the smart.
The crisped gold, that doth surmount Apollos pride:
70 The lively streames of pleasant starres that under it doth glide:
Wherein the beames of love do still encrease their heate:
Which yet so farre touch me so nere, in cold to make me sweate.
The wise and pleasant talk, so rare, or els alone:
That gave to me the curteis gift, that erst had never none:
75 Be farre from me, alas: and every other thing

I might forbeare with better will: then this that did me bring
With pleasant woord and chere, redresse of lingred pain:
And wonted oft in kindled will to vertue me to train.
Thus, am I forst to heare, and harken after newes.
80 My comfort scant, my large desire in doutfull trust renewes.
And yet with more delite to mone my wofull case:
I must complain those hands, those armes: that firmly do embrace
Me from my self: and rule the sterne of my poore life:
The swete disdaines, the pleasant wrathes, and eke the lovely strife
85 That wonted well to tune in temper just, and mete,
The rage: that oft did make me erre, by furour undiscrete.
All this is hid fro me, with sharp, and ragged hilles:
At others will, my long abode my depe dispaire fulfils.
And if my hope sometime rise up, by some redresse:
90 It stumbleth straite, for feable faint: my feare hath such excesse.
Such is the sort of hope: the lesse for more desyre:
And yet I trust ere that I dye to see that I require:
The resting place of love: where vertue dwelles and growes
There I desire, my wery life, somtime, may take repose.
95 My song: thou shalt attain to finde that pleasant place:
Where she doth live, by whom I live: may chance to have this grace
When she hath red, and sene the grief, wherin I serve:
Betwene her brestes she shall thee put: there, shall she the reserve.
Then, tell her, that I come: she shall me shortly see:
100 And if for waighte the body fayle, the soule shall to her flee.

[109] *The lover blameth his love for
renting of the letter he
sent her.*

Suffised not (madame) that you did teare,
My woful hart, but thus also to rent
The weping paper that to you I sent,
Wherof eche letter was written with a teare.
5 Could not my present paines, alas suffise
Your gredy hart: and that my hart doth fele,
Tormentes that prick more sharper then the stele,
But new and new must to my lot arise.
Use then my death. So shall your cruelty:
10 Spite of your spite rid me from all my smart,
And I no more such tormentes of the hart:
Fele as I do. This shall you gain thereby.

[110] *The lover curseth the time when*
first he fell in love.

When first mine eyes did view, and marke,
Thy faire beawtie to behold:
And when mine eares listned to harke:
The pleasant wordes, that thou me told:
5   I would as then, I had been free,
From eares to heare, and eyes to see.
And when my lips gan first to move,
Wherby my hart to thee was knowne:
And when my tong did talk of love,
10 To thee that hast true love down throwne:
I would, my lips, and tong also:
Had then bene dum, no deale to go.
And when my handes have handled ought,
That thee hath kept in memorie:
15 And when my feete have gone, and sought
To finde and get thee companie:
I would, eche hand a foote had bene,
And I eche foote a hand had sene.
And when in minde I did consent
20 To folow this my fansies will:
And when my hart did first relent,
To taste such bayt, my life to spill:
I would, my hart had bene as thine:
Or els thy hart had bene, as mine.

[111] *The lover determineth to*
serve faithfully.

Synce love will nedes, that I shall love:
Of very force I must agree.
And since no chance may it remove:
In wealth, and in adversitie,
5 I shall alway my self apply
To serve and suffer paciently.
Though for good will I finde but hate:
And cruelty my life to wast:
And though that still a wretched state
10 Should pine my daies unto the last:
Yet I professe it willingly,

To serve, and suffer paciently.
    For since my hart is bound to serve:
And I not ruler of mine owne:
15 What so befall, till that I sterve.
By proofe full well it shall be knowne:
That I shall still my selfe apply
To serve, and suffer paciently.
    Yea though my grief finde no redresse:
20 But still increase before mine eyes:
Though my reward be cruelnesse,
With all the harme, happe can devise:
Yet I professe it willingly
To serve and suffer paciently.
25   Yea though fortune her pleasant face
Should shew, to set me up aloft:
And straight, my wealth for to deface,
Should writhe away, as she doth oft:
Yet would I still my selfe apply
30 To serve and suffer paciently.
    There is no grief, no smart, no wo:
That yet I feele, or after shall:
That from this minde may make me go,
And what so ever me befal:
35 I do professe it willingly
To serve and suffer paciently.

[112] *The lover suspected bla-*
meth yll tonges.

    Mystrustfull mindes be moved
To have me in suspect.
The troth it shalbe proved:
Which time shall once detect.
5   Though falshed go about
Of crime me to accuse:
At length I do not dout,
But truth shall me excuse.
    Such sawce, as they have served
10 To me without desart:
Even as they have deserved:
Therof God send them part.

[113] *The lover complaineth and his*
ladie comforteth.

Lover.	It burneth yet, alas my hartes desire.
Ladye.	What is the thing, that hath inflamde thy hert?
Lover.	A certain point, as fervent, as the fire.
Ladye.	The heate shall cease, if that thou wilt convert.
5 Lover.	I cannot stop the fervent raging yre.
La.	What may I do, if thy self cause thy smart?
Lo.	Heare my request, and rew with weping chere.
La.	With right good will, say on: lo, I thee here.
Lo.	That thing would I, that maketh two content.
10 La.	Thou sekest, perchance, of me, that I may not.
Lo.	Would god, thou wouldst, as thou maist, well assent.
La.	That I may not, the grief is mine: God wot.
Lo.	But I it fele, what so thy wordes have ment.
La.	Suspect me not: my wordes be not forgot.
15 Lo.	Then say, alas: shall I have helpe? or no.
La.	I see no time to answer, yea, but no.
Lo.	Say ye, dere hart: and stand no more in dout.
La.	I may not grant a thing, that is so dere.
Lo.	Lo, with delaies thou drieves me still about.
20 La.	Thou wouldest my death: it plainly doth appere.
Lo.	First, may my hart his blood, and life blede out.
La.	Then for my sake, alas, thy will forbere.
Lo.	From day to day, thus wastes my life away.
La.	Yet, for the best, suffer some small delay.
25 Lo.	Now, good, say yea: do once so good a dede.
La.	If I sayd yea: what should therof ensue?
Lo.	An hart in pain of succour so should spede.
	Twixt yea, and nay, my doute shal still renew.
	My swete, say yea: and do away this drede.
30 La.	Thou wilt nedes so: be it so: but then be trew.
Lo.	Nought would I els, nor other treasure none,
	Thus, hartes be wonne, by love, request, and mone.

[114] *Why love is blind.*

Of purpose, love chose first for to be blinde:
For, he with sight of that, that I beholde,
Vanquisht had been, against all godly kinde.
His bow your hand, and trusse should have unfolde.

5 And he with me to serve had bene assinde.
   But, for he blinde, and recklesse would him holde:
   And still, by chance, his dedly strokes bestowe:
   With such, as see, I serve, and suffer wo.

[115] *To his unkinde love.*

   What rage is this: what furor: of what kinde?
   What power, what plage doth wery thus my minde:
   Within my bones to rankle is assinde
   What poyson pleasant swete?
5   Lo, see, myne eyes flow with continuall teares:
   The body still away slepelesse it weares:
   My foode nothing my fainting strength repaires,
   Nor doth my limmes sustain.
      In depe wide wound, the dedly stroke doth turne:
10 To cureles skarre that never shall returne.
   Go to: triumph: rejoyce thy goodly turne:
   Thy frend thou doest oppresse.
      Oppresse thou doest: and hast of him no cure:
   Nor yet my plaint no pitie can procure.
15 Fierce Tigre, fell, hard rock without recure:
   Cruel rebell to Love,
      Once may thou love, never beloved again:
   So love thou styll, and not thy love obtain:
   So wrathfull love, with spites of just disdain,
20 May thret thy cruell hart.

[116] *The lover blameth his instant*
desire.

   Desire (alas) my master, and my fo:
   So sore altered thy self how mayst thou see?
   Sometime thou sekest, that drives me to and fro.
   Sometime, thou leadst, that leadeth the and me.
5 What reason is to rule thy subjectes so?
   By forced law, and mutabilitie.
   For where by thee I douted to have blame:
   Even now by hate again I dout the same.

[117] *The lover complaineth his*
estate.

    I see, that chance hath chosen me
Thus secretly to live in paine:
And to an other geven the fee
Of al my losse to have the gayn.
5 By chance assinde thus do I serve:
And other have, that I deserve.
    Unto my self sometime alone
I do lament my woful case.
But what availeth me to mone?
10 Since troth, and pitie hath no place
In them: to whom I sue and serve:
And other have, that I deserve.
    To seke by meane to change this minde:
Alas, I prove, it will not be.
15 For in my hart I cannot finde
Once to refraine, but styl agre,
As bound by force, alway to serve:
And other have, that I deserve.
    Such is the fortune, that I have
20 To love them most, that love me lest:
And to my paine to seke, and crave
The thing, that other have possest.
So thus in vain alway I serve.
And other have, that I deserve.
25   And tyll I may apease the heate:
If that my happe wyll happe so well:
To waile my wo my hart shal freate:
Whose pensif pain my tong can tell.
Yet thus unhappy must I serve:
03 And other have, that I deserve.

[118] *Of his love called*
Anna.

What word is that, that changeth not,
Though it be turned and made in twaine:
It is mine Anna god it wot.
The only causer of my paine:

5   My love that medeth with disdaine.
Yet is it loved what will you more,
It is my salve, and eke my sore.

[119] *That pleasure is mixed*
with every
paine.

Venemous thrones that are so sharp and kene,
Beare flowers we se full fresh and faire of hue.
Poison is also put in medicine.
And unto man his helth doth oft renue.
5   The fier that all thinges eke consumeth cleane
May hurt and heale: then if that this be true
I trust sometime my harme may be my health,
Sins every woe is joyned with some wealth.

[120] *A riddle of a gift geven by*
a Ladie.

A Lady gave me a gift she had not,
And I received her gift which I toke not,
She gave it me willingly, and yet she would not,
And I received it, albeit, I could not,
5   If she give it me, I force not,
And if she take it againe she cares not.
Conster what this is and tel not,
For I am fast sworne I may not.

[121] *That speaking or profering*
bringes alway
speding.

Speake thou and spede where will or power ought helpth,
Where power doth want wit must be wonne by welth.
For nede will spede, where will workes not his kinde,
And gaine, thy foes thy frendes shall cause thee finde.
5   For sute and golde, what do not they obtaine,
Of good and bad the triers are these twaine.

[122] *He ruleth not though he raigne over*
realmes that is subject to
his own lustes.

If thou wilt mighty be, flee from the rage
Of cruel will, and see thou kepe thee free
From the foule yoke of sensuall bondage,
For though thyne empyre stretche to Indian sea,
5   And for thy feare trembleth the fardest Thylee,
If thy desire have over thee the power,
Subject then art thou and no governour.
　If to be noble and high thy minde be meved,
Consider well thy ground and thy beginning:
10   For he that hath eche starre in heaven fixed,
And geves the Moone her hornes and her eclipsing:
Alike hath made the noble in his working,
So that wretched no way may thou bee,
Except foule lust and vice do conquer thee.
15   　All were it so thou had a flood of gold,
Unto thy thirst yet should it not suffice.
And though with Indian stones a thousand folde,
More precious then can thy selfe devise,
Ycharged were thy backe: thy covitise
20   And busy biting yet should never let,
Thy wretched life, ne do thy death profet.

[123] *Whether libertie by losse of life, or*
life in prison and thraldom
be to be preferred.

Lyke as the birde within the cage enclosed,
The dore unsparred, her foe the Hawke without,
Twixt death and prison piteously oppressed,
Whether for to chose standeth in dout,
5   Lo, so do I, which seke to bring about,
Which should be best by determinacion,
By losse of life libertie, or life by prison.
　O mischiefe by mischiefe to be redressed.
Where pain is best there lieth but litle pleasure.
10   By short death better to be delivered,
Than bide in painfull life, thraldome, and doler,
Small is the pleasure where much pain we suffer.

Rather therfore to chuse me thinketh wisdome,
By losse of life libertie, then life by prison.
15   And yet me thinkes although I live and suffer,
I do but waite a time and fortunes chance:
Oft many thinges do happen in one houer.
That which opprest me now may me advance.
In time is trust which by deathes grevance
20 Is wholy lost. Then were it not reason,
By death to chuse libertie, and not life by prison.
    But death wer deliverance wher life lengths pain.
Of these two ylles let see now chuse the best:
This bird to deliver that here doth plain,
25 What say ye lovers? which shall be the best?
In cage thraldome, or by the Hawke opprest.
And which to chuse make plain conclusion,
By losse of life libertie, or life by prison.

[124] *Against hourders of money.*

For shamfast harm of great, and hatefull nede:
In depe dispaire, as did a wretch go,
With ready corde, out of his life to spede:
His stumbling foote did finde an hoorde, lo,
5 Of gold, I say: where he preparde this dede:
And in eschange he left the corde, tho.
He, that had hid the gold, and found it not:
Of that, he found, he shapte his neck a knot.

[125] *Discription of a gonne.*

Vulcane begat me: Minerva me taught:
Nature, my mother: Craft nourisht me yere by yere:
Thre bodies are my foode: my strength is in naught:
Anger, wrath, wast, and noyce are my children dere,
5 Gesse friend, what I am: and how I am wraught:
Monster of sea, or of land, or of els where.
Know me, and use me: and I may thee defend:
And if I be thine enmy, I may thy life end.

[126] *Wiate being in prison, to*
Brian.

Syghes are my foode: my drink are my teares.
Clinking of fetters would such musick crave.
Stink, and close ayre away my life it weares.
Poore innocence is all the hope I have.
5   Rain, winde, or wether judge I by mine eares.
Malice assaultes, that righteousnesse should have.
Sure am I, Brian, this wound shall heale again:
But yet alas, the skarre shall still remain.

[127] *Of dissembling wordes.*

Throughout the world if it wer sought,
Faire wordes inough a man shall finde:
They be good chepe they cost right nought.
Their substance is but onely winde:
5   But well to say and so to mene,
That swete acord is seldom sene.

[128] *Of the meane and sure*
estate.

Stond who so list upon the slipper wheele
Of hye astate and let me here rejoyce.
And use my life in quietnesse eche dele,
Unknowen in court that hath the wanton toyes,
5   In hidden place my time shal slowly passe
And when my yeres be past withouten noyce
Let me dye olde after the common trace
For gripes of death doth he to hardly passe
That knowen is to all: but to him selfe alas,
10   He dyeth unknowen, dased with dreadfull face.

[129] *The courtiers life.*

In court to serve decked with fresh aray,
Of sugred meates feling the swete repast:
The life in bankets, and sundry kindes of play,
Amid the presse of worldly lookes to waste,

5   Hath with it joynde oft times such bitter taste.
    That who so joyes such kinde of life to hold,
    In prison joyes fettred with cheines of gold.

[130] *Of disapointed purpose by*
negligence.

Of Carthage he that worthy warriour
Could overcome, but could not use his chance
And I likewise of all my long endevour
The sharpe conquest though fortune did advance,
5   Ne could I use. The hold that is geven over,
    I unposest, so hangeth now in balance
    Of warre, my peace, reward of all my paine,
    At Mountzon thus I restlesse rest in Spaine.

[131] *Of his returne from*
Spaine.

Tagus farewell that Westward with thy stremes
Turnes up the graines of gold already tried,
For I with spurre and saile go seke the Temmes.
Gaineward the sunne that sheweth her welthy pride,
5   And to the town that Brutus sought by dreames,
    Like bended mone that leanes her lusty side.
    My king, my countrey, I seke for whom I live,
    O mighty Jove the windes for this me give.

[132] *Of sodaine trusting.*

Driven by desire I did this dede
To danger my self without cause why:
To trust thuntrue not like to spede,
To speake and promise faithfully:
5   But now the proofe doth verifie,
    That who so trusteth ere he know,
    Doth hurt himselfe and please his foe.

[133] *Of the mother that eat her*
childe at the seige of
Jerusalem.

In doubtfull breast whiles motherly pity
With furious famine standeth at debate,
The mother sayth: O chyld unhappy
Returne thy bloud where thou hadst milke of late
5 Yeld me those limmes that I made unto thee,
And enter there where thou were generate.
For one of body against all nature,
To an other must I make sepulture.

[134] *Of the meane and sure estate*
written to John Poins.

My mothers maides when they do sowe and spinne:
They sing a song made of the feldishe mouse:
That forbicause her livelod was but thinne,
Would nedes go se her townish sisters house,
5 She thought, her selfe endured to grevous paine,
The stormy blastes her cave so sore dyd sowse:
That when the furrowes swimmed with the raine:
She must lie colde, and wet in sory plight.
And worse then that, bare meat there did remaine
10 To comfort her, when she her house had dight:
Sometime a barly corne: sometime a beane:
For which she laboured hard both day and night,
In harvest time, while she might go and gleane.
And when her store was stroyed with the floode:
15 Then weleaway for she undone was cleane.
Then was she faine to take in stede of fode,
Slepe if she might, her honger to begile.
My sister (quod she) hath a living good:
And hence from me she dwelleth not a mile.
20 In colde and storme, she lieth warme and dry,
In bed of downe: the durt doth not defile
Her tender fote, she labours not as I,
Richely she fedes, and at the richemans cost:
And for her meat she nedes not crave nor cry.
25 By sea, by land, of delicates the most
Her cater sekes, and spareth for no perell:

She fedes on boyle meat, bake meat, and on rost:
And hath therefore no whit of charge nor travell.
And when she list the licour of the grape
30   Doth glad her hart, tyll that her belly swell.
And at this journey makes she but a jape:
So forth she goes, trusting of all this wealth,
With her sister her part so for to shape:
That if she might there kepe her self in health:
35   To live a Lady while her life doth last.
And to the dore nowe is she come by stealth:
And with her fote anone she scarpes full fast.
Thother for fear, durst not well scarse appeare:
Of every noyse so was the wretch agast.
40   At last, she asked softly who was there.
And in her language as well as she could,
Pepe (quod the other) sister I am here.
Peace (quod the towne mouse) why speakest thou so loude?
And by the hand she toke her faire and well.
45   Welcome (quod she) my sister by the rode.
She feasted her that joye it was to tell
The fare they hadde, they dranke the wine so clere:
And as to purpose now and then it fell:
She chered her, with how sister what chere?
50   Amid this joye be fell a sory chance:
That (weleaway) the stranger bought full dere
The fare she had. For as she lookt a scance:
Under a stole she spied two stemyng eyes
In a rounde head, wyth sharpe eares: in Fraunce
55   Was never mouse so ferde, for the unwise
Had not ysene such a beast before.
Yet had nature taught her after her gise,
To know her fo: and dread him evermore.
The townemouse fled: she knew whither to go:
60   The other had no shift, but wonders sore
Ferde of her life, at home she wisht her tho:
And to the dore (alas as she did skippe:
The heaven it would, lo: and eke her chance was so:
At the threshold her sely fote did trippe:
65   And ere she myght recover it againe:
The traitour cat had caught her by the hippe:
And made her there against her wyll remayne:
That had forgot her power, suerty and rest,
For seking welth, wherein she thought to raigne.

70 Alas (my Poyns) how men do seke the best,
  And finde the worst, by errour as they stray,
  And no marvell, when sight is so opprest,
  And blindes the guide, anone out of the way
  Goeth guide and all in seking quiet life.
75 O wretched mindes, there is no golde that may
  Graunt that you seke, no warre, no peace, no strife.
  No, no, although thy head were hoopt with golde,
  Sergeant with mace, with hawbart, sword, nor knife,
  Can not repulse the care that folow should.
80 Ech kinde of life hath with him his disease.
  Live in delits, even as thy lust would:
  And thou shalt finde, when lust doth most thee please:
  It irketh straight, and by it selfe doth fade.
  A small thing is it, that may thy minde appease.
85 None of you al there is, that is so madde,
  To seke for grapes on brambles, or on bryers:
  Nor none I trow that hath a wytte so badde,
  To set his haye for coneies over rivers:
  Nor ye set not a dragge net for an hare.
90 And yet the thing, that most is your desire,
  You do misseke, with more travell and care.
  Make plaine thine hart, that it be not knotted
  With hope or dreade, and se thy wil be bare
  From all affectes, whom vice hath never spotted.
95 Thy selfe content with that is thee assinde:
  And use it well that is to thee alotted,
  Then seke no more out of thy selfe to finde
  The thing that thou hast sought so long before.
  For thou shalt feele it stickyng in thy minde.
100 Madde if ye list to continue your sore:
  Let present passe, and gape on time to come,
  And depe thy selfe in travell more and more.
  Henceforth (my Poins) this shall be all and summe:
  These wretched foles shall have nought els of me:
105 But, to the great God and to his dome,
  None other paine pray I for them to be:
  But when the rage doth leade them from the right:
  That loking backward, Vertue they may se,
  Even as she is, so goodly fayre and bright.
110 And whilst they claspe their lustes in armes a crosse:
  Graunt them good Lord, as thou maist of thy might,
  To freat inwarde, for losyng such a losse.

[135] *Of the Courtiers life written*
to Jhon Poins.

Myne owne Jhon Poins: sins ye delite to know
The causes why that homeward I me draw,
And fle the prease of courtes, where so they go:
Rather then to live thrall under the awe,
5   Of lordly lokes, wrapped within my cloke,
To will and lust learning to set a law:
It is not that because I scorne or mocke
The power of them: whom fortune here hath lent
Charge over us, of ryght to strike the stroke.
10   But true it is that I have alwayes ment
Lesse to esteme them, then the common sort
Of outward thinges: that judge in their entent,
Without regarde, what inward doth resort.
I graunt, sometime of glory that the fire
15   Doth touch my hart. Me list not to report
Blame by honour, and honour to desire.
But how may I this honour now attaine?
That can not dye the colour blacke a lier.
My Poyns, I can not frame my tune to fayn:
20   To cloke the truth, for praise without desert,
Of them that list all vice for to retaine.
I can not honour them, that set their part
With Venus, and Bacchus, all their life long:
Nor holde my peace of them, although I smart.
25   I can not crouch nor knele to such a wrong:
To worship them like God on earth alone:
That are as wolves these sely lambes among.
I can not with my wordes complaine and mone,
And suffer nought: nor smart without complaynt:
30   Nor turne the word that from my mouth is gone,
I can not speake and loke like as a saint:
Use wiles for wit, and make disceyt a pleasure:
Call craft counsaile, for lucre still to paint.
I can not wrest the law to fill the coffer:
35   With innocent bloud to fede my selfe fatte:
And do most hurt: where that most helpe I offer.
I am not he, that can alow the state
Of hye Ceasar, and damne Cato to dye:
That with his death did scape out of the gate,

40 From Ceasars handes, if Livye doth not lye:
   And would not live, where libertie was lost,
   So did his hart the common wealth apply.
   I am not he, such eloquence to bost:
   To make the crow in singyng, as the swanne:
45 Nor call the lyon of coward beastes the most,
   That can not take a mouse, as the cat can.
   And he that dieth for honger of the golde,
   Call him Alexander, and say that Pan
   Passeth Appollo in musike manifold:
50 Praise syr Topas for a noble tale,
   And scorne the story that the knight tolde:
   Praise him for counsell, that is dronke of ale:
   Grinne when he laughes, that beareth al the sway:
   Frowne, when he frownes: and grone when he is pale:
55 On others lust to hang both night and day.
   None of these poyntes would ever frame in me.
   My wit is nought, I can not learne the way.
   And much the lesse of things that greater be,
   That asken helpe of colours to devise
60 To joyne the meane with ech extremitie:
   With nearest vertue ay to cloke the vice.
   And as to purpose likewise it shall fall:
   To presse the vertue that it may not rise.
   As dronkennesse good fellowship to call:
65 The frendly foe, with his faire double face,
   Say he is gentle and curties therewithall.
   Affirme that favel hath a goodly grace,
   In eloquence: And cruelty to name
   Zeale of Justice: And change in time and place.
70 And he that suffereth offence without blame:
   Call him pitifull, and him true and plaine,
   That rayleth rechlesse unto ech mans shame.
   Say he is rude, that can not lye and faine:
   The letcher a lover, and tyranny
75 To be the right of a Princes raygne.
   I can not I, no, no, it will not be.
   This is the cause that I could never yet
   Hang on their sleves, that weygh (as thou mayst se)
   A chippe of chance more then a pounde of wit.
80 This maketh me at home to hunt and hauke:
   And in fowle wether at my booke to sit:
   In frost and snow, then with my bowe to stalke.

No man doth marke where so I ride or go.
In lusty leas at libertie I walke:
85   And of these newes I fele nor weale nor wo:
Save that a clogge doth hang yet at my heele.
No force for that, for it is ordred so:
That I may leape both hedge and dike full wele,
I am not now in Fraunce, to judge the wine:
90   With savery sauce those delicates to fele.
Nor yet in Spaine where one must him incline,
Rather then to be, outwardly to seme.
I meddle not with wyttes that be so fyne,
Nor Flaunders chere lettes not my syght to deme
95   Of blacke, and white, nor takes my wittes away
Wyth beastlinesse: such do those beastes esteme.
Nor I am not, where truth is geven in pray,
For money, poyson, and treason: of some
A common practise, used nyght and day.
100   But I am here in Kent and christendome:
Among the Muses, where I reade and ryme,
Where if thou list myne owne Jhon Poyns to come:
Thou shalt be judge, how I do spende my time.

[136] *How to use the court and him*
selfe therin, written to sir
Fraunces Brian.

A spendyng hand that alway powreth out,
Had nede to have a bringer in as fast.
And on the stone that styll doth turne about,
There groweth no mosse. These proverbes yet do last:
5   Reason hath set them in so sure a place:
That length of yeares their force can never waste.
When I remember this, and eke the case,
Wherin thou standst: I thought forthwith to write
(Brian) to thee: who knowes how great a grace
10   In writyng is to counsayle man the right.
To thee therfore that trottes styll up and downe:
And never restes, but runnyng day and nyght,
From realme to realme, from citie strete, and towne.
Why doest thou weare thy body to the bones?
15   And mightest at home slepe in thy bedde of downe:
And drinke good ale so nappy for the nones:

Fede thy selfe fatte, and heape up pounde by pound.
Likest thou not this? No. Why? For swine so groines
In stye, and chaw dung moulded on the ground.
20 And drivell on pearles with heade styll in the maunger,
So of the harpe the asse doth heare the sound.
So sackes of durt be filde. The neat courtier
So serves for lesse, then do these fatted swine.
Though I seme leane and drye, withouten moysture:
25 Yet wyll I serve my prince, my lord and thyne.
And let them live to fede the paunch that list:
So I may live to fede both me and myne.
By God well said. But what and if thou wist
How to bring in, as fast as thou doest spende.
30 That would I learne. And it shal not be mist,
To tell thee how. Now harke what I intende.
Thou knowest well first, who so can seke to please,
Shall purchase frendes: where trouth shall but offend.
Flee therefore truth, it is both welth and ease.
35 For though that trouth of every man hath praise:
Full neare that winde goeth trouth in great misease.
Use vertue, as it goeth now a dayes:
In worde alone to make thy language swete:
And of thy dede, yet do not as thou saies.
40 Els be thou sure: thou shalt be farre unmete
To get thy breade, ech thyng is now so skant.
Seke styll thy profit upon thy bare fete.
Lend in no wise: for feare that thou do want:
Unlesse it be, as to a calfe a chese:
45 But if thou can be sure to winne a cant
Of halfe at least. It is not good to leese.
Learne at the ladde, that in a long white cote,
From under the stall, withouten landes or feese,
Hath lept into the shoppe: who knowes by rote
50 This rule that I have told thee here before.
Sometime also rich age beginnes to dote,
Se thou when there thy gaine may be the more.
Stay him by the arme, where so he walke or go:
Be nere alway, and if he coughe to sore:
55 What he hath spit treade out, and please him so.
A diligent knave that pikes his masters purse,
May please him so, that he withouten mo
Executour is. And what is he the wurse?
But if so chance, thou get nought of the man:

60   The wydow may for all thy paine disburse.
      A riveld skynne, a stinkyng breath, what than?
      A tothelesse mouth shall do thy lippes no harme.
      The golde is good, and though she curse or banne:
      Yet where thee list, thou mayest lye good and warme.
65   Let the olde mule bite upon the bridle:
      Whilst there do lye a sweter in thy arme.
      In this also se that thou be not idle:
      Thy nece, thy cosyn, thy sister, or thy daughter,
      If she bee faire: if handsome be her middle:
70   If thy better hath her love besought her:
      Avaunce his cause, and he shall helpe thy nede.
      It is but love, turne it to a laughter.
      But ware I say, so gold thee helpe and spede:
      That in this case thou be not so unwise,
75   As Pandar was in such a like dede.
      For he the fole of conscience was so nice:
      That he no gaine would have for all his paine.
      Be next thy selfe for frendshyp beares no price.
      Laughest thou at me, why? do I speake in vaine?
80   No not at thee, but at thy thrifty jest.
      Wouldest thou, I should for any losse or gayne,
      Change that for golde, that I have tane for best.
      Next godly thinges: to have an honest name:
      Should I leave that: then take me for a beast.
85   Nay then farewell, and if thou care for shame:
      Content thee then with honest povertie:
      Wyth free tong, what thee mislikes, to blame,
      And for thy trouth sometime adversitie.
      And therwithall this guift I shall thee give,
90   In this world now litle prosperitie:
      And coyne to kepe: as water in a sive.

                [137] *The song of Jopas unfinished.*

      When Dido feasted first the wandring Trojan knight:
      Whom Junos wrath with storms did force in Libik sands to light,
      That mighty Atlas taught, the supper lasting long,
      With crisped lockes on golden harpe, Jopas sang in song.
5   That same (quod he) that we the world do call and name:
      Of heaven and earth with all contents, it is the very frame.
      Or thus, of heavenly powers by more power kept in one,

Repugnant kindes, in mids of whom the earth hath place alone:
Firme, round, of living thinges, the mother, place and nourse:
10 Without the which in egal weight, this heven doth hold his course
And it is cald by name, the first and moving heaven,
The firmament is placed next, conteining other seven,
Of heavenly powers that same is planted full and thicke:
As shining lightes which we call stars, that therin cleve and stick.
15 With great swift sway, the first, and with his restlesse sours,
Carieth it self, and all those eyght, in even continuall cours.
And of this world so round within that rolling case,
Two points there be that never move, but firmly kepe their place.
The tone we see alway, the tother standes object
20 Against the same, deviding just the ground by line direct,
Which by imaginacion, drawen from the one to thother,
Toucheth the centre of the earth, for way there is none other.
And these be calde the Poles, descryde by starres not bright.
Artike the one northward we see: Antartike thother hight,
25 The line, that we devise from thone to thother so:
As axel is, upon the which the heavens about do go
Which of water nor earth, of ayre nor fire have kinde,
Therefore the substance of those same were hard for man to finde.
But they bene uncorrupt, simple and pure unmixt:
30 And so we say been all those starres, that in those same be fixt.
And eke those erring seven, in circle as they stray:
So calde, because against that first they have repugnant way:
And smaller bywayes to, skant sensible to man:
To busy worke for my poore harpe: let sing them he that can.
35 The wydest save the first, of all these nine above
One hundred yere doth aske of space, for one degree to move.
Of which degrees we make, in the first mooving heaven,
Three hundred and threscore in partes justly devided even.
And yet there is another betwene those heavens two:
40 Whose moving is so sly so slack: I name it not for now.
The seventh heaven or the shell, next to the starry sky,
All those degrees that gatherth up, with aged pase so sly:
And doth performe the same, as elders count hath bene,
In nine and twenty yeres complete, and daies almost sixtene:
45 Doth carry in his bowt the starre of Saturne old:
A threatner of all living things, with drought and with his cold.
The sixt whom this conteins, doth stalke with yonger pase:
And in twelve yere doth somwhat more then thothers viage was.
And this in it doth beare the starre of Jove benigne,
50 Twene Saturns malice and us men, frendly defending signe.

The fift bears bloody Mars, that in three hundred daies,
And twise eleven with one full yere, hath finisht all those waies.
A yere doth aske the fourth, and howers therto sixe,
And in the same the daies eye, the sunne, therin he stickes.
55   The third that governd is by that, that governs mee:
And love for love, and for no love provokes: as oft we see:
In like space doth performe that course, that did the tother.
So doth the next unto the same, that second is in order.
But it doth beare the starre, that cald is Mercury:
60   That many a crafty secrete steppe doth tread, as Calcars try.
That sky is last, and fixt next us, those waies hath gone,
In seven and twenty common daies, and eke the third of one:
And beareth with his sway, the divers Moone about:
Now bright, now brown, now bent, now ful, and now her light is out.
65   Thus have they of their own two movinges all these seven:
One, wherein they be caried still, eche in his severall heaven.
An other of them selves, where their bodies be layd
In bywaies, and in lesser rowndes, as I afore have sayd.
Save of them all the Sunne doth stray lest from the streight,
70   The starry sky hath but one course, that we have cald the eight.
And all these moovinges eight are ment from West to East:
Although they seme to clime aloft, I say from East to West.
But that is but by force of the first moving sky:
In twise twelve houres from East to East that carieth them by and by.
75   But marke we well also, these movinges of these seven,
Be not about the axell tree of the first moving heven.
For they have their two poles directly tone to the tother. &c.

T. WYATE the elder.

Songes and Sonettes of
Uncertain auctours.

[138] *The complaint of a lover*
      with sute to his love
          for pitie.

If ever wofull man might move your hartes to ruthe,
Good ladies here his woful plaint, whose deth shal try his truth
    And rightfull judges be on this his true report:
If he deserve a lovers name among the faithfull sort.
5   Five hundred times the Sunne hath lodged him in the West:
Since in my hart I harbred first of all the goodlyest gest,
    Whose worthynesse to shew my wits are all to faynt
    And I lack cunning of the scooles, in colours her to paynt.
    But this I briefly say in wordes of egall weight.
10 So void of vice was never none, nor with such vertues freight.
    And for her beauties prayse, no wight that with her warres.
For, where she comes, she shewes her self as sun among the starres.
    But Lord, thou wast to blame, to frame such parfitenesse:
And puttes no pitie in her hart, my sorowes to redresse.
15   For if ye knew the paines, and panges, that I have past:
A wonder would it be to you, how that my life hath last.
    When all the Gods agreed, that Cupide with his bow
Should shote his arrowes from her eies, on me his might to show
    I knew it was in vain my force to trust upon:
20 And well I wist, it was no shame, to yelde to such a one.
    Then did I me submit with humble hart and mynde,
To be her man for evermore: as by the Gods assinde.
    And since that day, no wo, wherwith love might torment,
Could move me from this faithfull band: or make me once repent.
25   Yet have I felt full oft the hottest of his fire:
The bitter teares, the scalding sighes, the burning hote desire.
    And with a sodain sight the trembling of the hart:
And how the blood doth come, and go, to succour every part.
    When that a pleasant looke hath lift me in the ayer:
30 A frowne hath made me fall as fast into a depe despayer.
    And when that I ere this, my tale could well by hart:
And that my tong had learned it, so that no word might start:
    The sight of her hath set my wittes in such a stay:
That to be lord of all the world, one word I could not say.

35   And many a sodayn cramp my hart hath pinched so:
      That for the time, my senses all felt neither weale, nor wo.
          Yet saw I never thing, that might my minde content:
      But wisht it hers, and at her will, if she could so consent.
          Nor never heard of wo: that did her will displease:
40   But wisht the same unto my self, so it might do her ease.
          Nor never thought that fayre, nor never liked face:
      Unlesse it did resemble her, or some part of her grace.
          No distance yet of place could us so farre devide,
      But that my hart, and my good will did still with her abide.
45   Nor yet it never lay in any fortunes powre,
      To put that swete out of my thought, one minute of an howre.
          No rage of drenching sea, nor woodnesse of the winde,
      Nor cannons with their thundring cracks could put her from my minde
          For when both sea and land asunder had us set:
50   My hole delite was onely then, my self alone to get.
          And thitherward to looke, as nere as I could gesse:
      Where as I thought, that she was then, that might my wo redresse.
          Full oft it did me good, that waies to take my winde:
      So pleasant ayre in no place els, me thought I could not finde.
55   I saying to my self, my life is yonder way:
      And by the winde I have her sent, a thousand sighes a day.
          And sayd unto the sunne, great giftes are geven thee:
      For thou mayst see mine earthly blisse, where ever that she be.
          Thou seest in every place, would God I had thy might:
60   And I the ruler of my self, then should she know no night.
          And thus from wish to wish, my wits have been at strife:
      And wanting all that I have wisht, thus have I led my life.
          But long it can not last, that in such wo remaines.
      No force for that: for death is swete to him, that feles such paines.
65   Yet most of all me greves: when I am in my grave,
      That she shall purchase by my death a cruel name to have.
          Wherfore all you that heare this plaint, or shall it see:
      Wish, that it may so perce her hart, that she may pitie mee.
          For and it were her will: for both it were the best,
70   To save my life, to kepe her name, and set my hart at rest.

[139] *Of the death of master Devorox*
the lord Ferres
sonne.

Who justly may rejoyce in ought under the skye?
As life, or lands: as frends, or frutes: which only live to dye,
Or who doth not well know all worldly works are vaine?
And geveth nought but to the lendes, to take the same again.
5   For though it lift some up: as we long upward all:
Such is the sort of slipper welth: all thinges do rise to fall.
Thuncerteintie is such: experience teacheth so:
That what things men do covet most, them sonest they forgo.
Lo Devorox where he lieth: whose life men held so deare
10 That now his death is sorowed so, that pitie it is to heare.
His birth of auncient blood: his parents of great fame:
And yet in vertue farre before the formost of the same,
His king, and countrye both he served to so great gaine:
That with the Brutes record doth rest, and ever shall remaine.
15 No man in warre so mete, an enterprise to take:
No man in peace that pleasurde more of enmies frends to make.
A Cato for his counsell: his hed was surely such.
Ne Theseus frendship was so great, but Devorox was as much.
A graffe of so small grothe, so much good frute to bring:
20 Is seldome heard, or never sene: it is so rare a thing.
A man sent us from God, his life did well declare,
And now sent for by God again, to teach us what we are.
Death, and the grave, that shall accompany all that live,
Hath brought him heven, though somwhat sone, which life could never give.
25 God graunt well all, that shall professe as he profest:
To live so well, to dye no worse: and send his soule good rest.

[140] *They of the meane estate*
are happiest.

If right be rackt, and overronne:
And power take part with open wrong:
If feare my force do yelde to soone,
The lack is like to last to long.
5   If God for goodes shalbe unplaced:
If right for riches lose his shape:
If world for wisdome be embraced:
The gesse is great, much hurt may hap.

Among good thinges, I prove and finde,
10   The quiet life doth most abound:
And sure to the contented minde
There is no riches may be found.
       For riches hates to be content:
Rule is enmy to quietnesse.
15   Power is most part impacient:
And seldom likes to live in pease.
       I heard a herdman once compare:
That quiet nightes he had mo slept:
And had mo mery dayes to spare:
20   Then he, which ought the beastes, he kept.
       I would not have it thought hereby
The Dolphin swimme I meane to teache:
Nor yet to learne the Fawcon fly:
I row not so farre past my reache.
25   But as my part above the rest,
Is well to wish and well to will:
So till my breath shall fail my brest,
I will not ceasse to wish you still.

[141] *Comparison of life*
and death.

The life is long, that lothsomly doth last:
The dolefull dayes draw slowly to their date:
The present panges, and painfull plages forepast
Yelde griefe aye grene to stablish this estate.
5   So that I feele, in this great storme, and strife,
The death is swete that endeth such a life.
       Yet by the stroke of this strange overthrow,
At which conflict in thraldom I was thrust:
The Lord be praised: I am well taught to know
10   From whence man came, and eke whereto he must:
And by the way upon how feble force
His terme doth stand, till death doth end his course.
       The pleasant yeres that seme, so swift that runne
The mery dayes to end, so fast that flete:
15   The joyfull nightes, of which day daweth so soone:
The happy howers, which mo do misse then mete,
Do all consume: as snow against the sunne:
And death makes end of all, that life begunne.

Since death shall dure, till all the world be wast,
20 What meaneth man to drede death then so sore?
As man might make, that life should alway last.
Without regard, the lord hath led before
The daunce of death, which all must runne on row:
Though how, or when: the Lord alone doth know.
25 If man would minde, what burdens life doth bring:
What grevous crimes to God he doth commit:
What plages, what panges, what perilles thereby spring:
With no sure hower in all his daies to sit:
He would sure think, as with great cause I do:
30 The day of death were better of the two.
Death is a port, wherby we passe to joy.
Life is a lake, that drowneth all in payn.
Death is so dere, it ceaseth all annoy.
Life is so leude, that all it yeldes is vayn.
35 And as by life to bondage man is braught:
Even so likewise by death was fredome wraught.
Wherfore with Paul, let all men wish and pray
To be dissolvde of this foule fleshy masse:
Or at the least be armde against the day:
40 That they be found good souldiers, prest to passe
From life to death: from death to life again
To such a life, as ever shall remain.

[142] *The tale of Pigmalion with con-*
clusion upon the beautie
of his love.

In Grece somtime there dwelt a man of worthy fame:
To grave in stone his cunning was: Pygmalion was his name.
To make his fame endure, when death had him bereft:
He thought it good, of his own hand some filed worke were left.
5 In secrete studie then such worke he gan devise,
As might his cunning best commend, and please the lookers eyes.
A courser faire he thought to grave, barbd for the field:
And on his back a semely knight, well armd with speare and shield:
Or els some foule, or fish to grave he did devise:
10 And still, within his wandering thoughtes, new fansies did arise.
Thus varied he in minde, what enterprise to take:
Till fansy moved his learned hand a woman fayre to make.
Whereon he stayde, and thought such parfite fourme to frame:

Whereby he might amaze all Grece, and winne immortall name.
15   Of yvorie white he made so faire a woman than:
That nature scornd her perfitnesse so taught by craft of man.
     Wel shaped were her lims, ful comly was her face:
Ech litle vain most lively coucht, eche part had semely grace.
     Twixt nature and Pigmalion, there might appere great strife,
20 So semely was this ymage wrought, it lackt nothing but life.
     His curious eye beheld his own devised work:
And, gasing oft thereon, he found much venome there to lurk.
     For all the featurde shape so did his fansie move:
That, with his idoll, whom he made, Pygmalion fell in love.
25   To whom he honour gave, and deckt with garlandes swete.
And did adourn with jewels rich, as is for lovers mete.
     Somtimes on it he fawnd: fomtime in rage would cry:
It was a wonder to behold, how fansy bleard his eye.
     Since that this ymage dum enflamde so wise a man:
30 My dere alas, since I you love, what wonder is it than?
     In whom hath nature set the glory of her name:
And brake her moulde, in great dispaire, your like she could not frame.

[143] *The lover sheweth his wofull*
state, and praieth pitie.

Lyke as the Larke within the Marlians foote
With piteous tunes doth chirp her yelden lay:
So sing I now, seyng none other boote,
My rendering song, and to your will obey.
5 Your vertue mountes above my force so hye.
And with your beautie seased I am so sure:
That there avails resistance none in me,
But paciently your pleasure to endure.
For on your will my fansy shall attend:
10 My life, my death, I put both in your choyce:
And rather had this life by you to end,
Than live, by other alwayes to rejoyce.
And if your crueltie do thirst my blood:
Then let it forth if it may do you good.

[144] *Upon consideracion of the state
of this life he wisheth death.*

The lenger lyfe, the more offence:
The more offence, the greater paine:
The greater pain, the lesse defence:
The lesse defence, the lesser gaine.
5 The losse of gayne long yll doth trye:
Wherefore come death, and let me dye.
    The shorter life, lesse count I finde:
The lesse account, the sooner made:
The count soon made, the merier minde:
10 The mery minde doth thought evade.
Short life in truth this thing doth trye:
Wherefore come death, and let me dye:
    Come gentle death, the ebbe of care,
The ebbe of care, the flood of lyfe,
15 The flood of life, the joyfull fare,
The joyfull fare, the end of strife.
The end of strife, that thing wishe I:
Wherefore come death, and let me dye.

[145] *The lover that once disdained love
is now become subject, beyng
caught in his snare.*

To thys my song geve eare, who list:
And mine intent judge, as you wyll:
The time is come, that I have mist,
The thyng, wheron I hoped styll,
5 And from the toppe of all my trust,
Myshap hath throwen me in the dust.
    The time hath bene, and that of late:
My hart and I might leape at large.
And was not shut with in the gate
10 Of loves desire: nor toke no charge
Of any thing, that dyd pertaine
As touching love in any payn.
    My thought was free, my hart was light:
I marked not, who lost, who saught.
15 I playde by day, I slept by night.
I forced not, who wept, who laught.
My thought from all such thinges was free:

And I my self at libertee.
 I toke no hede to tauntes, nor toyes:
20 As leefe to see them frowne as smile:
Where fortune laught I scornde their joyes:
I found their fraudes and every wile.
And to my self oft times I smiled:
To see, how love had them begiled.
25 Thus in the net of my conceit
I masked still among the sort
Of such as fed upon the bayt,
That Cupide laide for his disport.
And ever as I sawe them caught:
30 I them behelde, and therat laught.
 Till at the length when Cupide spied
My scornefull will and spitefull use
And how I past not who was tied,
So that my self might still live lose:
35 He set himself to lye in wait:
And in my way he threw a bait.
 Such one, as nature never made,
I dare wel say save she alone.
Such one she was as would invade
40 A hart, more hard then marble stone.
Such one she is, I know it right,
Her nature made to shew her myght.
 Then as a man even in a maze,
When use of reason is away:
45 So I began to stare, and gaze.
And sodeinly, without delay,
Or ever I had the wit to loke:
I swalowed up both bait, and hoke.
 Which dayly greves me more and more
50 By sondry sortes of carefull wo:
And none alive may salve the sore,
But onely she, that hurt me so.
In whom my life doth now consist,
To save or slay me as she list.
55 But seing now that I am caught,
And bounde so fast, I cannot flee:
Be ye by mine ensample taught,
That in your fansies fele you free.
Despise not them, that lovers are:
60 Lest you be caught within his snare.

[146] *Of Fortune and Fame.*

The plage is great, where fortune frownes:
One mischiefe bringes a thousand woes
Where trumpets geve their warlyke sownes:
The weake sustain sharp overthrowes.
5 No better life they taste, and fele:
That subject are to fortunes whele.
Her happy chance may last no time:
Her pleasure threatneth paines to come,
She is the fall of those that clime:
10 And yet her whele avanceth some.
No force, where that she hates, or loves:
Her ficle minde so oft removes.
She geves no gift, but craves as fast.
She soone repentes a thankful dede.
15 She turneth after every blast.
She helps them oft, that have no nede.
Where power dwelles, and riches rest:
False fortune is a common gest.
Yet some affirme, and prove by skyl:
20 Fortune is not as fleyng Fame,
She neither can do good, nor yll.
She hath no fourme, yet beares a name.
Then we but strive against the streames,
To frame such toyes on fansies dreames.
25 If she have shape, or name alone:
If she do rule, or beare no sway:
If she have bodie, lief, or none:
Be she a sprite I cannot say.
But well I wot, some cause there is:
30 That causeth wo, and sendeth blisse.
The cause of thinges I wil not blame:
Lest I offend the prince of pease.
But I may chide, and braule with Fame:
To make her crye, and never cease.
35 To blow the trump within her eares:
That may apease my wofull teares.

[147] *Against wicked tonges.*

O evyll tonges, which clap at every winde:
Ye slea the quick, and eke the dead defame:
Those that live well, some faute in them ye finde.
Ye take no thought, in sclandring their good name.
5   Ye put just men oft times to open shame.
Ye ryng so loude, ye sound unto the skyes:
And yet in proofe ye sowe nothing, but lies.
    Ye make great war, wher peace hath been of long
Ye bring rich realmes to ruine, and decay.
10 Ye pluck down right: ye doe enchaunce the wrong.
Ye turne swete myrth to wo, and wel away
Of myschiefes al ye are the grounde, I say.
Happy is he, that lives on such a sort:
That nedes not feare such tonges of false report.

[148] *Hell tormenteth not the damned*
ghostes so sore as unkindnesse
the lover.

The restlesse rage of depe devouryng hell,
The blasing brandes, that never do consume,
The roryng route, in Plutoes den that dwell:
The fiery breath, that from those ymps doth fume:
5   The dropsy dryeth, that Tantale in the flood
Endureth aye, all hopelesse of relief:
He hongersterven, where frute is ready food:
So wretchedly his soule doth suffer grief:
The lyver gnawne of gylefull Promethus,
10 Whych Vultures fell wyth strained talant tire:
The labour lost of wearied Sisiphus:
These hellish houndes, with paines of quenchlesse fyre,
Can not so sore the silly soules torment,
As her untruth my hart hath all to rent.

[149] *Of the mutabilitie of*
the world.

By fortune as I lay in bed, my fortune was to finde
Such fansies, as my careful thought had brought into my minde
And when eche one was gone to rest, full soft in bed to lye:

I would have slept: but then the watch did folow still mine eye.
5 And sodeinly I saw a sea of wofull sorowes prest:
Whose wicked waies of sharpe repulse bred mine unquiet rest.
I saw this world: and how it went, eche state in his degree:
And that from wealth ygraunted is, both life and libertee.
I saw, how envy it did rayne, and beare the greatest price:
10 Yet greater poyson is not found within the Cockatrice.
I saw also, how that disdain oft times to forge my wo,
Gave me the cup of bitter swete, to pledge my mortall fo.
I saw also, how that desire to rest no place could finde
But still constrainde in endlesse payn to folow natures kinde.
15 I saw also most straunge of all how nature did forsake
The blood, that in her womb was wrought: as doth the lothed snake.
I saw, how fansie would retain no lenger then her lust:
And as the winde how she doth change: and is not for to trust.
I saw, how stedfastnesse did fly with winges of often change:
20 A flying bird, but seldome seen, her nature is so strange.
I saw, how pleasant times did passe, as flowers do in the mede:
To day that riseth red as rose: to morow falleth ded.
I saw, my time how it did runne, as sand out of the glasse.
Even as eche hower appointed is from time, and tide to passe.
25 I saw the yeres that I had spent, and losse of all my gayn:
And how the sport of youthfull playes my foly did retain.
I saw, how that the litle Ant in somer still doth runne
To seke her foode, wherby to live in winter for to come,
I saw eke vertue, how she sat the threde of life to spinne.
30 Which sheweth the end of every work, before it doth beginne.
And when all these I thus beheld with many mo pardy:
In me, me thought, ech one had wrought a parfite proparty.
And then I sayd unto my self: a lesson this shalbe
For other: that shall after come, for to beware by me.
35 Thus, all the night I did devise, which way I might constrayn
To forme a plot, that wit might work these branches in my brain.

[150] *Harpalus complaint of Phillidaes*
love bestowed on Corin, who
loved her not and denied
him that loved her.

Phylida was a fayre mayde,
As fresh as any flowre:
Whom Harpalus the herdman prayde

To be his paramour.
5   Harpalus and eke Corin
Were herdmen both yfere:
And Phillida could twist and spin
And thereto sing full clere.
        But Phillida was all to coy
10   For Harpalus to winne.
For Corin was her onely joy,
Who forst her not a pinne.
        How often would she flowers twine
How often garlandes make:
15   Of Couslips and of Colombine,
And all for Corins sake.
        But Corin he had Haukes to lure
And forced more the field:
Of lovers law he toke no cure
20   For once he was begilde.
        Harpalus prevailed nought
His labour all was lost:
For he was fardest from her thought
And yet he loved her most.
25   Therfore waxt he both pale and leane
And dry as clot of clay:
His flesh it was consumed cleane
His colour gone away.
        His beard it had not long be shave,
30   His heare hong all unkempt:
A man most fit even for the grave
Whom spitefull love had spent.
        His eyes were red and all forewatched
His face besprent with teares:
35   It semde unhap had him long hatched,
In mids of his dispaires.
        His clothes were black and also bare
As one forlorne was he:
Upon his head alwaies he ware,
40   A wreath of wilow tree.
        His beastes he kept upon the hill,
And he sate in the dale:
And thus with sighes and sorowes shrill,
He gan to tell his tale.
45   O Harpalus (thus would he say,)
Unhappiest under sunne:

The cause of thine unhappy day
By love was first begunne.
    For thou wentest first by sute to seeke
50 A Tygre to make tame:
That sets not by thy love a leeke
But makes thy griefe her game.
    As easy it were for to convert
The frost into the flame:
55 As for to turne a froward hert
Whom thou so fain wouldst frame.
    Corin he liveth carelesse
He leapes among the leaves:
He eates the frutes of thy redresse
60 Thou reapes, he takes the sheaves.
    My beastes a while your foode refrain
And harke your herdmans sound:
Whom spitefull love alas hath slain
Through girt with many a wound.
65   O happy be ye beastes wilde
That here your pasture takes:
I see that ye be not begilde
Of these your faithfull makes.
    The Hart he feedeth by the Hinde
70 The Bucke hard by the Do,
The Turtle Dove is not unkinde
To him that loves her so.
    The Ewe she hath by her the Ramme
The yong Cow hath the Bull:
75 The Calf with many a lusty Lamme
Do fede their hunger full.
    But wellaway that nature wrought
Thee Phillida so faire:
For I may say that I have bought
80 Thy beauty all to deare.
    What reason is it that cruelty
With beauty should have part,
Or els that such great tyranny
Should dwell in womans hart.
85   I see therfore to shape my death
She cruelly is prest:
To thende that I may want my breath
My dayes been at the best.
    O Cupide graunt this my request

90 And do not stoppe thine eares:
    That she may feele within her brest
    The paines of my dispaires.
        Of Corin that is carelesse
    That she may crave her fee:
95 As I have done in great distresse
    That loved her faithfully.
        But sins that I shall dye her slave
    Her slave and eke her thrall:
    Write you my frendes, upon my grave
100 This chance that is befall.
        Here lieth unhappy Harpelus
    By cruell love now slaine:
    Whom Phillida unjustly thus
    Hath murdred with disdaine.

                [151] *Upon sir James Wilfordes*
                       death.

    Lo, here the end of man the cruell sisters three
    The web of Wilfords life uneth had half ysponne,
    When rash upon misdede they all accorded bee
    To breake vertues course ere half the race were ronne
5   And trip him on his way that els had won the game
    And holden highest place within the house of fame.
        But yet though he be gone, though sence with him be past
    Whych trode the even steppes that leaden to renowne
    We that remaine alive ne suffer shall to waste
10 The fame of his desertes, so shall he lose but sowne,
    The thing shall aye remaine, aye kept as fresh in store
    As if his eares shold ring of that he wrought before.
        Waile not therefore his want sithe he so left the stage
    Of care and wretched life, with joye and clap of handes
15 Who plaieth lenger partes may well have greater age
    But few so well may passe the gulfe of fortunes sandes,
    So triedly did he treade ay prest at vertues beck
    That fortune founde no place to geve him once a check.
        The fates have rid him hence, who shal not after go,
20 Though earthed be his corps, yet florish shal his fame,
    A gladsome thing it is that ere he stepte us fro,
    Such mirrours he us left our life therby to frame,
    Wherfore his praise shall last aye freshe in Brittons sight,
    Till sunne shal cease to shine, and lende the earth his light.

[152] *Of the wretchednes in this*
world.

Who list to live upright, and holde him self content,
Shal se such wonders in this world, as never erst was sent.
Such gropyng for the swete, such tastyng of the sower
Such wandring here for worldly welth that lost is in one houre.
5 And as the good or badde gette up in hie degree,
So wades the world in right or wrong it may none other be.
And loke what lawes they make, ech man must them obay,
And yoke himselfe with pacient hart to drive and draw that way.
Yet such as long ago, great rulers were assinde
10 Both lives and lawes are now forgot and worne clene out of minde,
So that by this I se, no state on earth may last
But as their times appointed be, to rise and fall as fast.
The goodes that gotten be, by good and just desart,
Yet use them so that neady handes may helpe to spend the part.
15 For loke what heape thou hordst, of rusty golde in store,
Thine enemies shall waste the same, that never swat therfore.

[153] *The repentant sinner in durance*
and adversitie.

Unto the living Lord for pardon do I pray,
From whom I graunt even from the shell, I have run stil astray.
And other lives there none (my death shal wel declare)
On whom I ought to grate for grace, as faulty folkes do fare.
5 But thee O Lord alone, I have offended so,
That this smal scourge is much to scant for mine offence I know
I ranne without returne, the way the world liekt best
And what I ought most to regard, that I respected lest
The throng wherin I thrust, hath throwen me in such case
10 That Lorde my soule is sore beset without thy greater grace.
My giltes are growen so great, my power doth so appaire
That with great force they argue oft, and mercy much dispaire.
But then with faith I flee to thy prepared store
Where there lieth helpe for every hurt, and salve for every sore.
15 My lost time to lament, my vaine waies to bewaile,
No day, no night, no place, no houre, no moment I shal faile
My soule shal never cease with an assured faith
To knock, to crave, to cal, to cry, to thee for helpe which sayth
Knocke and it shalbe heard, but aske and geven it is

20 And all that like to kepe this course, of mercy shal not misse.
    For when I call to minde how the one wandryng shepe,
    Did bring more joye with his returne, then all the flocke did kepe,
    It yeldes full hope and trust my strayed and wandryng ghost
    Shalbe received and held more dere then those were never lost.
25 O Lord my hope beholde, and for my helpe make haste
    To pardon the forpassed race that carelesse I have past.
    And but the day draw neare that death must pay the det,
    For love of life which thou hast lent and time of paiment set.
    From this sharpe shower me shielde which threatened is at hand,
30 Whereby thou shalt great power declare and I the storme withstand
    Not my will lord but thine, fulfilde be in ech case,
    To whose gret wil and mighty power al powers shal once geve place:
    My fayth my hope my trust, my God and eke my guide
    Stretch forth thy hand to save the soule, what so the body bide.
35 Refuse not to receive that thou so dere hast bought,
    For but by thee alone I know all safety in vaine is sought.
    I knowe and knowledge eke albeit very late,
    That thou it is I ought to love and dreade in ech estate.
    And with repentant hart do laud thee Lord on hye,
40 That hast so gently set me straight, that erst walkt so awry.
    Now graunt me grace my God to stand thine strong in sprite.
    And let the world then work such waies, as to the world semes mete.

[154] *The lover here telleth of his divers*
joyes and adversities in love
and lastly of his
ladies death.

    Syth singyng gladdeth oft the harts
    Of them that fele the panges of love:
    And for the while doth ease their smarts:
    My self I shall the same way prove.
5   And though that love hath smit the stroke,
    Wherby is lost my libertie:
    Which by no meanes I may revoke:
    Yet shall I sing, how pleasantly.
        Ny twenty yeres of youth I past:
10 Which al in libertie I spent:
    And so from first unto the last,
    Ere aught I knewe, what loving ment.
        And after shal I syng the wo,

The paine, the greefe, the deadly smart:
15 When love this lyfe did overthrowe,
That hydden lyes within my hart.
        And then, the joyes, that I dyd feele.
When fortune lifted after this,
And set me hye upon her whele:
20 And changde my wo to pleasant blisse,
        And so the sodeyn fall agayne
From all the joyes, that I was in.
All you, that list to heare of payne,
Geve eare, for now I doe beginne.
25   Lo, first of all, when love began
With hote desires my heart to burne:
Me thought his might availde not than
From libertie my heart to turne.
        For I was free: and dyd not knowe,
30 How much his might mannes hert may greve.
I had profest to be his fo:
His law, I thought not to beleve.
        I went untied in lusty leas,
I had my wish alwaies at will:
35 Ther was no wo, might me displease:
Of pleasant joyes I had my fill.
        No paynfull thought dyd passe my hart:
I spilt no teare to wet my brest:
I knew no sorow, sigh, nor smart,
40 My greatest griefe was quiet rest.
        I brake no slepe, I tossed not:
Nor dyd delite to syt alone.
I felt no change of colde and hote:
Nor nought a nightes could make me mone.
45   For al was joy that I did fele:
And of voide wandering I was free.
I had no clogge tied at my hele:
This was my life at libertie.
        That yet me thinkes it is a blisse,
50 To thinke upon that pleasure past.
But forthwithall I finde the misse,
For that it might no lenger last.
        Those daies I spent at my desire,
Without wo or adversitie:
55 Till that my hart was set a fire,
With love, with wrath, and jelousie.

        For on a day (alas the while)
    Lo, heare my harme how it began:
    The blinded Lord, the God of guile
60 Had list to end my fredome than.
        And through mine eye into my hart
    All sodenly I felt it glide.
    He shot his sharped fiery dart,
    So hard, that yet under my side
65   The head (alas) doth still remaine,
    And yet since could I never know,
    The way to wring it out againe:
    Yet was it nye three yere ago.
        This soden stroke made me agast:
70 And it began to vexe me sore.
    But yet I thought, it would have past,
    As other such had done before.
        But it did not that (wo is me)
    So depe imprinted in my thought,
75 The stroke abode: that yet I see,
    Me thinkes my harme how it was wrought.
        Kinde taught me streight that this was love
    And I perceived it perfectly:
    Yet thought I thus: Nought shall me move:
80 I will not thrall my libertie.
        And divers waies I did assay,
    By flight, by force, by frend, by fo,
    This firie thought to put away.
    I was so lothe for to forgo
85   My libertie: that me was lever,
    Then bondage was, where I hard say:
    Who once was bounde, was sure never
    Without great paine to scape away.
        But what for that, there is no choice,
90 For my mishap was shapen so:
    That those my dayes that did rejoyce,
    Should turne my blisse to bitter wo.
        For with that stroke my blisse toke ende.
    In stede wherof forthwith I caught,
95 Hotte burnyng sighes, that sins have brend,
    My wretched hart almost to naught.
        And sins that day, O Lord my life,
    The misery that it hath felt.
    That nought hath had, but wo and strife,

100 And hotte desires my hart to melt.
    O Lord how sodaine was the change
    From such a pleasant liberty?
    The very thraldome semed straunge
    But yet there was no remedy.
105   But I must yeld, and geve up all,
    And make my guide my chefist fo.
    And in this wise became I thrall,
    Lo, love and happe would have it so.
    I suffred wrong and held my peace,
110 I gave my teares good leave to ronne:
    And never would seke for redresse,
    But hopt to live as I begonne.
    For what it was that might me ease,
    He lived not that might it know,
115 Thus dranke I all mine owne disease:
    And all alone bewailde my wo.
    There was no sight that mighte me please,
    I fled from them that did rejoyce,
    And oft alone my hart to ease,
120 I would bewaile with wofull voyce
    My life, my state, my misery,
    And curse my selfe and al my daies.
    Thus wrought I with my fantasie,
    And sought my helpe none other waies.
125   Save sometime to my selfe alone,
    When farre of was my helpe God wot:
    Lowde would I crye: My life is gone,
    My dere, if that ye helpe me not.
    Then wisht I streight, that death might end
130 These bitter panges, and al this grief
    For nought, methought, might it amend.
    Thus in dispaire to have relief,
    I lingred forth: tyl I was brought
    With pining in so piteous case:
135 That al, that sawe me, sayd, methought:
    Lo, death is painted in his face.
    I went no where: but by the way
    I saw some sight before mine eyes:
    That made me sigh, and oft times say:
140 My life, alas I thee despyse.
    This lasted well a yere, and more:
    Which no wight knew, but onely I:

So that my life was nere for lore:
And I dispaired utterly.
145   Til on a day, as fortune would:
(For that, that shalbe, nedes must fal)
I sat me down, as though I should
Have ended then my lyfe, and al.
    And as I sat to write my playnt,
150 Meanyng to shew my great unrest:
With quaking hand, and hart full faint,
Amid my plaintes, among the rest,
    I wrote with ynk, and bitter teares:
I am not myne, I am not mine:
155 Behold my life, away that weares:
And if I dye the losse is thine.
    Herewith a little hope I caught:
That for a whyle my life did stay.
But in effect, all was for naught.
160 Thus lived I styl: tyl on a day
    As I sat staring on those eyes:
Those shining eyes, that first me bound:
My inward thought tho cryed: Aryse:
Lo, mercy where it may be found.
165   And therewithall I drew me nere:
With feble hart, and at a braide,
(But it was softly in her eare)
Mercy, Madame, was all, I sayd.
    But wo was me, when it was told,
170 For therwithall fainted my breath:
And I sate still for to beholde,
And heare the judgement of my death.
    But Love nor Hap would not consent,
To end me then, but welaway:
175 There gave me blisse: that I repent
To thinke I live to se this day.
    For after this I plained styll
So long, and in so piteous wise:
That I my wish had at my will
180 Graunted, as I would it devise.
    But Lord who ever hard, or knew
Of halfe the joye that I felt than?
Or who can thinke it may be true,
That so much blisse had ever man?
185   Lo, fortune thus set me aloft:

And more my sorowes to releve,
Of pleasant joyes I tasted oft:
As much as love or happe might geve.
    The sorowes old, I felt before
190 About my hart, were driven thence:
And for ech griefe, I felt afore,
I had a blisse in recompence.
    Then thought I all the time well spent:
That I in plaint had spent so long.
195 So was I with my life content:
That to my self I sayd among.
    Sins thou art ridde of al thine yll:
To shewe thy joyes set forth thy voyce.
And sins thou haste thy wish at will:
200 My happy hart, rejoyce, rejoyce.
    Thus felt I joyes a great deale mo,
Then by my song may well be tolde:
And thinking on my passed wo,
My blisse did double many folde.
205   And thus I thought with mannes blood,
Such blisse might not be bought to deare.
In such estate my joyes then stode:
That of a change I had no feare.
    But why sing I so long of blisse?
210 It lasteth not, that will away,
Let me therfore bewaile the misse:
And sing the cause of my decay.
    Yet all this while there lived none,
That led his life more pleasantly:
215 Nor under hap there was not one,
Me thought, so well at ease, as I.
    But O blinde joye, who may thee trust?
For no estate thou canst assure?
Thy faithfull vowes prove al unjust:
220 Thy faire behestes be full unsure.
    Good proofe by me: that but of late
Not fully twenty daies ago:
Which thought my life was in such state:
That nought might worke my hart this wo.
225   Yet hath the enemy of myne ease,
Cruell mishappe, that wretched wight:
Now when my life did most me please:
Devised me such cruel spight.

That from the hiest place of all,
230 As to the pleasing of my thought,
Downe to the deepest am I fall,
And to my helpe availeth nought,
    Lo, thus are all my joyes quite gone:
And I am brought from happinesse,
235 Continually to wayle, and mone.
Lo, such is fortunes stablenesse.
    In welth I thought such suertie,
That pleasure should have ended never.
But now (alas) adversitie,
240 Doth make my singyng cease for ever.
    O brittle joye, O welth unstable:
O fraile pleasure, O slidyng blisse,
Who feles thee most, he shall not misse,
At length to be made miserable.
245   For all must end as doth my blisse:
There is none other certeintie.
And at the end the worst is his,
That most hath knowen prosperitie.
    For he that never blisse assaied,
250 May well away with wretchednesse:
But he shall finde that hath it sayd,
A pain to part from pleasantnesse:
    As I do now, for ere I knew
What pleasure was, I felt no griefe,
255 Like unto this, and it is true,
That blisse hath brought me all this mischiefe.
    But yet I have not songen, how
This mischiefe came: but I intend
With wofull voyce to sing it now:
260 And therwithall I make an end.
    But Lord, now that it is begoon,
I fele, my sprites are vexed sore.
Oh, geve me breath till this be done:
And after let me live no more.
265   Alas, the enmy of this life,
The ender of all pleasantnesse:
Alas, he bringeth all this strife,
And causeth all this wretchednesse.
    For in the middes of all the welth,
270 That brought my hart to happinesse:
This wicked death he came by stelth,

And robde me of my joyfulnesse.
   He came, when that I litle thought
Of ought, that might me vexe so sore:
275 And sodenly he brought to nought
My pleasantnesse for evermore.
   He slew my joy (alas, the wretch)
He slew my joy, or I was ware:
And now (alas) no might may stretch
280 To set an end to my great care.
   For by this cursed deadly stroke,
My blisse is lost, and I forlore:
And no helpe may the losse revoke:
For lost it is for evermore.
285   And closed up are those faire eyes,
That gave me first the signe of grace:
My faire swete foes, mine enemies,
And earth doth hide her pleasant face.
   The loke which did my life uphold:
290 And all my sorowes did confound:
With which more blisse then may be told:
Alas, now lieth it under ground.
   But cease, for I will sing no more:
Since that my harme hath no redresse:
295 But as a wretche for evermore,
My life will waste with wretchednesse.
   And ending this my wofull song,
Now that it ended is and past:
I would my life were but as long:
300 And that this word might be my last.
   For lothsome is that life (men say)
That liketh not the livers minde:
Lo, thus I seke mine own decay,
And will, till that I may it finde.

[155] *Of his love named White.*

Full faire and white she is, and White by name:
Whose white doth strive, the lillies white to staine:
Who may contemne the blast of blacke defame:
Who in darke night, can bring day bright againe.
5 The ruddy rose inpreaseth with cleare heew,
In lips and chekes, right orient to behold:

That the nerer gaser may that bewty reew,
And fele disparst in limmes the chilling cold:
For White, all white his bloodlesse face will be:
10   The asshy pale so alter will his cheare.
But I that do possesse in full degree
The harty love of this my hart so deare:
So oft to me as she presents her face,
For joy do feele my hart spring from his place.

[156] *Of the lovers unquiet
state.*

What thing is that which I both have and lacke,
With good will graunted, yet it is denyed
How may I be received and put abacke
Alway doing and yet unoccupied,
5   Most slow in that which I have most applied,
Still thus to seke, and lese all that I win,
And that was doon is newest to begin.
In riches finde I wilfull povertie,
In great pleasure, live I in heavinesse.
10   In much freedome I lacke my libertie,
Thus am I both in joy and in distresse.
And in few wordes, if that I shall be plaine,
In Paradise I suffer all this paine.

[157] *Where good will is, some proofe
will appere.*

It is no fire that geves no heate,
Though it appeare never so hot:
And they that runne and can not sweate,
Are very leane and dry God wot.
5   A perfect leche applieth his wittes,
To gather herbes of all degrees:
And fevers with their fervent fittes,
Be cured with their contraries.
New wine will serch to finde a vent,
10   Although the caske be set so strong:
And wit will walke when will is bent,
Although the way be never so long.
The Rabbets runne under the rockes:

The Snailes do clime the highest towers:
15 Gunpowder cleaves the sturdy blockes.
A fervent will all thing devowers.
    When wit with will and diligent
Apply them selves, and match as mates,
There can no want of resident,
20 From force defend the castell gates.
    Forgetfulnesse makes litle haste,
And slouth delites to lye full soft:
That telleth the deaf, his tale doth waste,
And is full dry that craves full oft.

[158] *Verses written on the picture of sir*
James Wilford, knight.

Alas that ever death such vertues should forlet,
As compast was within his corps, whose picture is here set.
Or that it ever lay in any fortunes might,
Through depe disdain to end his life that was so worthy a wight.
5 For sithe he first began in armour to be clad,
A worthier champion then he was, yet England never had.
And though recure be past, his life to have againe,
Yet would I wish his worthinesse in writing to remaine.
That men to minde might call how farre he did excell,
10 At all assayes to wynne the fame, which were to long to tell.
And eke the restlesse race that he full oft hath runne,
In painfull plight from place to place,where service was to don.
Then should men well perceive, my tale to be of trouth,
And he to be the worthiest wight that ever nature wrought.

[159] *The ladie praieth the returne of*
her lover abiding on
the seas.

Shall I thus ever long, and be no whit the neare,
And shall I still complain to thee, the which me will not heare?
Alas say nay, say nay, and be no more so dome,
But open thou thy manly mouth, and say that thou wilt come.
5 Wherby my hart may thinke, although I see not thee,
That thou wilt come thy word so sware, if thou a live man be.
The roaring hugy waves, they threaten my poore ghost,
And tosse thee up and downe the seas, in daunger to be lost.

Shall they not make me feare that they have swalowed thee,
10 But as thou art most sure alive, so wilt thou come to me.
Wherby I shall go see thy ship ride on the strand,
And think and say lo where he comes, and sure here will he land.
And then I shalt lift up to thee my litle hand,
And thou shalt think thine hart in ease, in helth to see me stand.
15 And if thou come in dede (as Christ thee send to do,)
Those armes which misse thee yet, shall then imbrace thee to.
Ech vain to every joynt, the lively blood shall spred,
Which now for want of thy glad sight, doth show full pale and dead.
But if thou slip thy trouth and do not come at all,
20 As minutes in the clocke do strike so call for death I shall.
To please both thy false hart, and rid my self from wo,
That rather had to dye in trouth then live forsaken so.

[160] *The meane estate is best.*

The doutfull man hath fevers strange
And constant hope is oft diseasde,
Dispaire cannot but brede a change,
Nor fleting hartes cannot be pleasde.
5 Of all these bad, the best I thinck,
Is well to hope, though fortune shrinck.
Desired thinges are not ay prest,
Nor thinges denide left all unsought,
Nor new things to be loved best,
10 Nor all offers to be set at nought,
Where faithfull hart hath bene refusde,
The chosers wit was there abusde.
The wofull ship of carefull sprite,
Fleting on seas of welling teares,
15 With sailes of wishes broken quite,
Hanging on waves of dolefull feares,
By surge of sighes at wrecke nere hand,
May fast no anker hold on land.
What helps the dyall to the blinde,
20 Or els the clock without it sound.
Or who by dreames doth hope to finde,
The hidden gold within the ground:
Shalbe as free from cares and feares,
As he that holds a Wolfe by the eares.
25 And how much mad is he that thinks

To clime to heaven by the beames,
What joy alas, hath he that winks,
At Titan or his golden streames,
His joyes not subject to reasons lawes,
30   That joyeth more then he hath cause.
     For as the Phenix that climeth hye,
The sunne lightly in ashes burneth,
Againe, the Faulcon so quick of eye,
Sone on the ground the net masheth.
35   Experience therfore the meane assurance,
Prefers before the doutfull pleasance.

       [161] *The lover thinkes no paine to*
         great, wherby he may ob-
            tain his ladie.

     Sith that the way to wealth is wo,
And after paine is pleasure prest,
Why should I than dispaire so,
Ay bewailing mine unrest:
5   Or let to leade my life in paine,
So worthy a lady to obtaine.
     The fisher man doth count no care,
To cast his nets to wrack or wast,
And in reward of eche mans share.
10   A gogen gift is much imbrast,
Should I than grudge it grief or gall,
That loke at length to whelm a Whall.
     The poore man ploweth his ground for grain,
And soweth his seede increase to crave,
15   And for thexpence of all his pain,
Oft holdes it hap his seede to save,
These pacient paines my part doth show,
To long for love ere that I know.
     And take no scorne to scape from skill,
20   To spend my sprites to spare my speche,
To win for welth the want of will.
And thus for rest to rage I reche,
Running my race as rect upright:
Till teares of truth appease my plight.
25   And plant my plaint within her brest,
Who doutles may restore againe,

My harmes to helth, my ruthe to rest,
That laced is within her chaine,
For earst ne are the griefes so gret:
30 As is the joy when love is met.
      For who covets so high to clim,
As doth the bird that pitfoll toke,
Or who delightes so swift to swim,
As doth the fish that scapes the hoke,
35 If these had never entred wo:
How mought they have rejoysed so.
      But yet alas ye lovers all,
That here me joy thus lesse rejoyce,
Judge not amis what so befall.
40 In me there lieth no power of choyse,
It is but hope that doth me move:
Who standerd bearer is to love.
      On whose ensigne when I behold,
I see the shadow of her shape,
45 Within my faith so fast I fold:
Through drede I die, through hope I scape,
Thus ease and wo full oft I finde,
What will you more, she knoweth my minde.

[162] *Of a new maried student that*
plaied fast or lose.

A student at his boke so plast:
That welth he might have wonne,
From boke to wife did flete in hast,
From wealth to wo to runne.
5 Now, who hath plaied a feater cast,
Since jugling first begonne?
In knitting of him self so fast,
Him selfe he hath undonne.

[163] *The meane estate is to be*
accompted the best.

Who craftly castes to stere his boate
      and safely skoures the flattering flood:
He cutteth not the greatest waves,
      for why that way were nothing good.

5   Ne fleteth on the crocked shore
            lest harme him happe awayting lest.
    But wines away betwene them both,
            as who would say the meane is best.
    Who waiteth on the golden meane,
10   he put in point of sickernes:
    Hides not his head in sluttish coates,
            ne shroudes himself in filthines.
    Ne sittes aloft in hye estate,
            Where hatefull hartes envie his chance:
15 But wisely walkes betwixt them twaine,
            ne proudly doth himself avance.
    The highest tree in all the wood
            is rifest rent with blustring windes:
    The higher hall the greater fall
20   such chance have proude and lofty mindes.
    When Jupiter from hye doth threat
            With mortall mace and dint of thunder
    The hyest hilles bene batrid eft
            when they stand still that stoden under.
25 The man whose hed with wit is fraught
            in welth will feare a worser tide
    When fortune failes dispaireth nought
            but constantly doth still abide.
    For he that sendeth grisely stormes
30   with whisking windes and bitter blastes
    And fowlth with hayle the winters face,
            and frotes the soile with hory frostes:
    Even he adawth the force of cold
            the spring in sendes with somer hote:
35 The same full oft to stormy hartes
            is cause of bale: of joy the roote.
    Not alwaies yll though so be now
            When cloudes ben driven, then rides the racke.
    Phebus the fresh ne shooteth still,
40   somtime he harpes his muse to wake.
    Stand stif therfore, pluck up thy hart,
            lose not thy port though fortune faile.
    Againe whan winde doth serve at will,
            take hede to hye to hoyse thy saile.

[164] *The lover refused, lamenteth*
his estate.

I lent my love to losse and gaged my life in vaine,
If hate for love and death for life of lovers be the gaine.
   And curse I may by course the place eke time and howre
That nature first in me did forme to be a live creature.
5   Sithe that I must absent my selfe so secretly
In place desert where never man my secretes shall discry:
   In doling of my dayes among the beastes so brute,
Who with their tonges may not bewray the secretes of my sute.
   Nor I in like to them may once to move my minde
10 But gase on them and they on me, as beastes are wont of kinde.
   Thus ranging as refusde, to reache some place of rest,
All ruff of heare, my nayles unnocht, as to such semeth best
   That wander by their wittes, deformed so to be,
That men may say, such one may curse the time he first gan see
15   The beauty of her face, her shape in such degree,
As God himself may not discerne, one place mended to be,
   Nor place it in like place, my fansy for to please,
Who would become a heardmans hyre, one howre to have of ease.
   Whereby I might restore to me some stedfastnes,
20 That have mo thoughtes heapt in my hed then life may long disges
   As oft to throw me downe upon the earth so cold,
Wheras with teares most rufully, my sorowes do unfold.
   And in beholding them, I chiefly call to minde,
What woman could finde in her hart, such bondage for to binde.
25   Then rashly forth I yede, to cast me from that care,
Like as the bird for foode doth flye, and lighteth in the snare.
   From whence I may not meve, untill my race be roon,
So trained is my truth through her, that thinkes my life well woon.
   Thus tosse I to and fro, in hope to have reliefe,
30 But in the fine I finde not so, it doubleth but my griefe.
   Wherfore I will my want, a warning for to be,
Unto all men, wishing that they, a myrrour make of me.

[165] *The felicitie of a minde imbracing vertue,*
   that beholdeth the wretched desires
         of the worlde.

When dredful swelling seas, through boisterous windy blastes,
So tosse the ships, that all for nought, serves ancor, sail and mastes.
   Who takes not pleasure then, safely on shore to rest,
And see with drede and depe dispaire, how shipmen are distrest.
5   Not that we pleasure take, when others felen smart,
Our gladnes groweth to see their harmes, and yet to fele no part.
   Delight we take also, well ranged in aray,
When armies meete to see the fight, yet free be from the fray.
   But yet among the rest, no joy may match with this,
10 Taspyre unto the temple hye, where wisdome troned is.
   Defended with the saws of hory heades expert,
Which clere it kepe from errours mist, that might the truth pervert,
   From whence thou mayst loke down, and see as under foote,
Mans wandring wil and doutful life, from whence they take their roote.
15 How some by wit contend, by prowes some to rise,
Riches and rule to gaine and hold, is all that men devise.
   O miserable mindes, O hartes in folly drent,
Why see you not what blindnesse in this wretched life is spent?
   Body devoyde of griefe, minde free from care and drede,
20 Is all and some that nature craves, wherwith our life to feede.
   So that for natures turne few thinges may well suffice,
Dolour and grief clene to expell, and some delight surprice.
   Yea and it falleth oft, that nature more content
Is with the lesse, then when the more to cause delight is spent.

[166] *All worldly pleasures vade.*

The winter with his griesly stormes ne lenger dare abide,
The plesant grasse, with lusty grene, the earth hath newly dide:
The trees have leves, the bowes don spred, new changed is the yere:
The water brokes are cleane sonk down, the plesant banks apere.
5   The spring is come, the goodly nimphes now daunce in every place
Thus hath the yere most pleasantly of late ychangde his face.
Hope for no immortalitie, for welth will weare away,
As we may learne by every yere, yea howers of every day.
For Zepharus doth molifie the cold and blustering windes:
10 The somers drought doth take away the spring out of our mindes
And yet the somer cannot last, but once must step aside,

Then Autumn thinks to kepe his place, but Autumn cannot bide.
For when he hath brought forth his fruits and stuft the barns with corn
Then winter eates and empties all, and thus is Autumn worn.
15 Then hory frosts possesse the place, then tempests work much harm,
Then rage of stormes done make all cold, which somer had made so warm.
Wherfore let no man put his trust in that, that will decay,
For slipper wealth will not continue, pleasure will weare away.
For when that we have lost our life, and lye under a stone,
20 What are we then: we are but earth, then is our pleasure gone.
No man can tell what God almight of every wight doth cast,
No man can say to day I live, till morne my life shall last.
For when thou shalt before thy judge stand to receive thy dome,
What sentence Minos doth pronounce that must of the become.
25 Then shall not noble stocke and bloud redeme the from his hands
Nor sugred talke with eloquence shall lose thee from his bandes.
Nor yet thy life uprightly lead, can help thee out of hell,
For who descendeth down so depe, must there abide and dwell.
Diana could not thence deliver chaste Hypolitus,
30 Nor Theseus could not call to life his frende Perithous.

[167] *A complaint of the losse of li-*
bertie by love.

In seking rest, unrest I finde,
I finde that welth is cause of wo:
Wo worth the time that I inclinde,
To fixe in minde her beauty so.
5   That day be darkned as the night,
Let furious rage it cleane devour:
Ne Sunne nor Moone therin give light,
But it consume with storme and shower.
Let no small birds straine forth their voyce,
10 With pleasant tunes, ne yet no beast:
Finde cause wherat he may rejoyce,
That day when chaunced mine unrest.
Wherin alas from me was raught,
Mine own free choyce and quiet minde,
15 My life my death in balance braught
And reason rasde through barke and rinde.
And I as yet in flower of age,
Both wit and will did still advance:
Ay to resist that burning rage:

20   But when I darte then did I glaunce.
     Nothing to me did seme so hye,
    In minde I could it straight attaine:
    Fansy perswaded me therby,
    Love to esteme a thing most vaine.
25   But as the bird upon the brier,
    Doth pricke and proyne her without care:
    Not knowing alas (poore foole) how nere
    She is unto the fowlers snare.
     So I amid disceitfull trust,
30   Did not mistrust such wofull happe:
    Till cruell love ere that I wist
    Had caught me in his carefull trappe.
     Then did I fele, and partly know,
    How litle force in me did raigne:
35   So soone to yelde to overthrow,
    So fraile to flit from joy to paine.
     For when in welth will did me leade
    Of libertie to hoyse my saile:
    To hale at shete and cast my leade,
40   I thought free choyce would still prevaile.
     In whose calme streames I sayld so farre,
    No raging storme had in respect:
    Untill I raysde a goodly starre,
    Wherto my course I did direct.
45   In whose prospect in doolfull wise,
    My tackle failde, my compasse brake?
    Through hote desires such stormes did rise,
    That sterne and top went all to wrake.
     Oh cruell hap, oh fatall chaunce,
50   O Fortune why were thou unkinde:
    Without regarde thus in a traunce,
    To reue from me my joyfull minde.
     Where I was free now must I serve,
    Where I was lose now am I bound:
55   In death my life I do preserve,
    As one through girt with many a wound.

[168] *A praise of his La-*
dye.

    Geve place you Ladies and be gone,
Boast not your selves at all:
For here at hand approcheth one:
Whose face will staine you all.
5   The vertue of her lively lokes,
Excels the precious stone:
I wish to have none other bokes
To read or loke upon.
    In eche of her two cristall eyes,
10 Smileth a naked boye:
It would you all in hart suffice
To see that lampe of joye.
    I thinke nature hath lost the moulde,
Where she her shape did take:
15 Or els I doubt if nature could,
So faire a creature make.
    She may be well comparde
Unto the Phenix kinde:
Whose like was never sene nor heard,
20 That any man can finde.
    In life she is Diana chast,
In trouth Penelopey:
In word and eke in dede stedfast,
What wil you more we sey.
25   If all the world were sought so farre,
Who could finde such a wight:
Her beuty twinkleth like a starre,
Within the frosty night.
    Her rosiall colour comes and goes,
30 With such a comely grace:
More redier to then doth the rose,
Within her lively face.
    At Bacchus feast none shall her mete,
Ne at no wanton play:
35 Nor gasyng in an open strete,
Nor gadding as a stray.
    The modest mirth that she doth use,
Is mixt with shamefastnesse:
All vice she doth wholy refuse,
40 And hateth ydlenesse.

O lord it is a world to see,
How vertue can repaire:
And decke in her such honestie,
Whom nature made so faire.
45   Truely she doth as farre excede,
Our women now adayes:
As doth the Jelifloure, a wede,
And more a thousand waies.
How might I do to get a graffe:
50   Of this unspotted tree.
For al the rest are plaine but chaffe,
Which seme good corne to be.
This gift alone I shal her geve,
When death doth what he can:
55   Her honest fame shall ever live,
Within the mouth of man.

[169] *The pore estate to be holden*
for best.

E xperience now doth shew what God us taught before,
D esired pompe is vaine, and seldome doth it last:
W ho climbes to raigne with kinges, may rue his fate full sore.
A las the woful ende that comes with care full fast,
5 R eject him doth renowne, his pompe full low is caste.
D eceived is the birde by swetenesse of the call.
E xpell that pleasant taste, wherein is bitter gall.
S uch as with oten cakes in poore estate abides,
O f care have they no cure, the crab with mirth they rost,
10 M ore ease fele they then those, that from their height down slides.
E xcesse doth brede their wo, they saile in Scillas cost,
R emainyng in the stormes tyll shyp and al be lost.
S erve God therefore thou pore, for lo, thou lives in rest.
E schue the golden hall, thy thatched house is bes T.

[170] *The complaint of Thestilis*
amid the desert
wodde.

Thestilis, a sely man, when love did him forsake,
In mourning wise, amid the wods thus gan his plaint to make.
Ah woful man (quod he) fallen is thy lot to mone

And pyne away with careful thoughtes, unto thy love unknowen.
5   Thy lady thee forsakes whom thou didst honor so
That ay to her thou were a frend, and to thy selfe a foe.
Ye lovers that have lost your heartes desired choyse,
Lament with me my cruell happe, and helpe my trembling voice.
Was never man that stode so great in fortunes grace:
10   Nor with his swete alas to deare possest so high a place.
As I whose simple hart aye thought him selfe full sure,
But now I se hie springing tides they may not aye endure.
She knowes my giltelesse hart, and yet she lets it pine,
Of her untrue professed love so feble is the twine.
15   What wonder is it than, if I berent my heares,
And craving death continually do bathe my selfe in teares,
When Cresus king of Lide was cast in cruell bandes,
And yelded goodes and life also into his enemies handes.
What tong could tell his wo, yet was his griefe much lesse
20   Then mine: for I have lost my love whych might my woe redresse.
Ye woodes that shroud my limes give now your holow sound,
That ye may helpe me to bewaile the cares that me confound.
Ye rivers rest a while and stay the streames that runne,
Rew Thestilis most woful man that lives under the sunne.
25   Transport my sighes ye windes unto my plesant foe,
My tricklyng teares shal witnesse beare of this my cruel woe.
O happy man wer I if all the goddes agreed:
That now the susters three should cut in twaine my fatall threde.
Till life with love shall ende I here resigne al joy:
30   Thy pleasant swete I now lament whose lacke bredes myne anoy
Farewell my deare therfore farewell to me well knowne:
If that I die it shalbe said that thou hast slaine thine owne.

[171] *An answere of*
comfort.

Thestilis, thou sely man, why dost thou so complayne,
If nedes thy love wyll thee forsake, thy mourning is in vaine.
For none can force the streames against their course to ronne,
Nor yet unwilling love with teares or wailyng can be wonne.
5   Cease thou therefore thy plaintes, let hope thy sorowes ease,
The shipmen though their sailes be rent yet hope to scape the seas.
Though straunge she seme a while, yet thinke she wil not chaunge:
Good causes drive a ladies love, sometime to seme full straunge.
No lover that hath wit, but can forsee such happe,

10   That no wight can at wish or will slepe in his ladies lappe.
     Achilles for a time faire Brises did forgo,
     Yet did they mete with joye againe, then thinke thou maist do so.
     Though he and lovers al in love sharpe stormes do finde,
     Dispaire not thou pore Thestilis though thy love seme unkinde.
15   Ah thinke her graffed love cannot so sone decay,
     Hie springes may cease from swelling styll, but never dry away.
     Oft stormes of lovers yre, do more their love encrease:
     As shinyng sunne refreshe the fruites when raining gins to cease.
     When springes are waxen lowe, then must they flow againe,
20   So shall thy hart advaunced be, to pleasure out of paine.
     When lacke of thy delight most bitter griefe apperes,
     Thinke on Etrascus worthy love that lasted thirty yeres,
     Which could not long atcheve his hartes desired choice,
     Yet at the ende he founde rewarde that made him to rejoyce.
25   Since he so long in hope with pacience did remaine,
     Can not thy fervent love forbeare thy love a moneth or twaine?
     Admit she minde to chaunge and nedes will thee forgo,
     Is there no mo may thee delyght but she that paynes thee so?
     Thestilis draw to the towne and love as thou hast done,
30   In time thou knowest by faythful love as good as she is wonne.
     And leave the desert woodes and waylyng thus alone,
     And seke to salve thy sore els where, if all her love be gone.

¶ [172] *The lover praieth pity showing that*
nature hath taught his dog as it
were to sue for the same
by kissing his ladies
handes.

     Nature that taught my silly dog god wat:
     Even for my sake to like where I do love,
     Inforced him whereas my lady sat
     With humble sute before her fallyng flat.
5   As in his sorte he might her pray and move
     To rue upon his lord and not forgete
     The stedfast faith he beareth her and love,
     Kissing her hand whom she could not remove
     A way, that would for frowning nor for threte
10   As though he would have sayd in my behove.
     Pity my lord your slave that doth remaine,
     Lest by his death, you giltles slay us twaine.

[173] *Of his ring sent to his*
ladie.

Since thou my ring mayst go where I ne may.
Since thou mayst speake, where I must hold my peace.
Say unto her that is my lives stay,
Graven within which I do here expresse:
5   That sooner shall the sunne not shine by day,
And with the raine the floods shall waxen lesse.
Sooner the tree the hunter shall bewray,
Then I for change, or choyce of other love,
Do ever seke my fansy to remove.

[174] *The changeable state*
of lovers.

For that a restles hed must somwhat have in ure
Wherwith it may acquainted be, as falcon is with lure.
Fansy doth me awake out of my drowsy slepe,
In seing how the litle Mouse, at night begins to crepe.
5   So the desirous man, that longes to catch his pray,
In spying how to watch his time, lyeth lurking still by day.
In hoping for to have, and fearing for to finde
The salve that should recure his sore, and soroweth but the minde.
Such is the guise of love, and the uncertain state,
10   That some should have their hoped hap, and other hard estate.
That some should seme to joy in that they never had,
And some againe shall frown as fast, where causeles they be sad.
Such trades do lovers use when they be most at large,
That gide the stere when they themselves lye fettred in the barge.
15   The grenesse of my youth cannot therof expresse
The processe, for by proofe unknowen, all this is but by gesse.
Wherfore I hold it best, in time to hold my peace,
But wanton will it cannot hold, or make my pen to cease.
A pen of no availe, a fruitles labour eke,
20   My troubled hed with fansies fraught, doth pain it selfe to seke.
And if perhaps my wordes of none availe do pricke,
Such as do feele the hidden harmes, I wold not they shold kicke.
As causeles me to blame which thinketh them no harme,
Although I seme by others fire, somtime my selfe to warme.
25   Which clerely I deny, as giltles of that crime,
And though wrong demde I be therin, truth it will try in time.

[175] *A praise of Audley.*

When Audley had run out his race, and ended wer his daies,
His fame stept forth and bad me write of him som worthi praise
What life he lad, what actes he did: his vertues and good name,
Wherto I calde for true report, as witnes of the same.
5   Wel born he was, wel bent by kinde, whose minde did never swerve,
A skilfull head, a valiant hart, a ready hand to serve.
Brought up and trained in feates of war long time beyond the seas,
Cald home again to serve his prince, whom still he sought to please.
What tornay was there he refusde, what service did he shoon,
10 Where he was not nor his advice, what great exploit was doon?
In town a Lambe, in fielde full fierce, a Lion at the nede,
In sober wit a Salomon, yet one of Hectors seede.
Then shame it were that any tong shold now defame his dedes,
That in his life a mirrour was to all that him succedes.
15 No poore estate nor hie renowne his nature could pervart,
No hard mischance that him befell could move his constant hart.
Thus long he lived, loved of all, as one misliekt of none.
And where he went who cald him not the gentle Paragon.
But course of kinde doth cause eche fruite to fall when it is ripe,
20 And spitefull death will suffer none to scape his grevous gripe.
Yet though the ground received have his corps into her wombe,
This Epitaphe ygrave in brasse, shall stand upon his tombe.
Lo here he lies that hateth vice, and vertues life imbrast,
His name in earth, his sprite above, deserves to be well plast.

[176] *Time trieth truth.*

Eche thing I see hath time, which time must try my truth,
Which truth deserves a special trust, on trust gret frendship groweth.
And frendship may not faile where faithfulnesse is found,
And faithfulnesse is full of fruit, and frutefull thinges be sound.
5   And sound is good at proofe, and proofe is prince of praise,
And precious praise is such a pearle, as seldome ner decaies.
All these thinges time tries forth, which time I must abide,
How should I boldly credite crave till time my truth have tride,
For as I found a time to fall in fansies frame,
10 So I do wish a lucky time for to declare the same.
If hap may answere hope, and hope may have his hire,
Then shall my hart possesse in peace the time that I desire.

[177] *The lover refused of his love*
imbraceth death.

My youthfull yeres are past,
My joyfull dayes are gone:
My life it may not last,
My grave and I am one.
5   My mirth and joyes are fled,
And I a man in wo:
Desirous to be ded,
My mischiefe to forgo.
    I burne and am a colde,
10 I freze amids the fire:
I see she doth withold
That is my most desire.
    I see my help at hand,
I see my life also:
15 I see where she doth stand
That is my deadly fo.
    I see how she doth see,
And yet she will be blinde:
I see in helping me,
20 She sekes and will not finde.
    I see how she doth wry,
When I begin to mone:
I see when I come nye,
How faine she would begone.
25   I see what will ye more,
She will me gladly kill:
And you shall see therfore
That she shall have her will.
    I can not live with stones
30 It is to hard a foode:
I will be dead at ones
To do my lady good.

[178] *The picture of a lover.*

Behold my picture here well portrayed for the nones.
With hart consumed and falling flesh, behold the very bones,
Whose cruell chance alas and desteny is such,
Onely because I put my trust in some folke all to much.

5   For sins the time that I did enter in this pine,
    I never saw the rising sunne but with my weping eyen.
    Nor yet I never heard so swete a voice or sound,
    But that to me it did encrease the dolour of my wound.
    Nor in so soft a bedde, alas I never lay,
10 But that it semed hard to me or ever it was day,
    Yet in this body bare, that nought but life retaines,
    The strength wherof clene past away the care yet still remaines.
    Like as the cole in flame doth spend it self you se,
    To vaine and wretched cinder dust till it consumed be.
15 So doth this hope of mine inforce my fervent sute,
    To make me for to gape in vaine, whilst other eate the frute.
    And shall do till death doth geve me such a grace,
    To rid this silly wofull sprite out of this dolefull case.
    And then would God wer writ in stone or els in leade,
20 This Epitaphe upon my grave, to shew why I am dead.
    Here lyeth the lover lo, who for the love he aught,
    Alive unto his lady dere, his death therby he caught.
    And in a shielde of blacke, loe here his armes appeares,
    With weping eyes as you may see, well poudred all with teares.
25 Loe here you may behold, aloft upon his brest,
    A womans hand straining the hart of him that loved her best.
    Wherfore all you that see this corps for love that starves,
    Example make unto you all, that thanklesse lovers sarves.

                [179] *Of the death of Phillips.*

    Bewaile with me all ye that have profest,
    Of musicke tharte by touche of coarde or winde:
    Lay down your lutes and let your gitterns rest.
    Phillips is dead whose like you can not finde.
5   Of musicke much exceeding all the rest,
    Muses therefore of force now must you wrest,
    Your pleasant notes into an other sound,
    The string is broke, the lute is dispossest.
    The hand is cold, the body in the ground.
10 The lowring lute lamenteth now therfore.
    Phillips her frende that can her touche no more.

[180] *That all thing somtime finde*
ease of their paine, save
onely the lover.

I see there is no sort,
Of thinges that live in griefe:
Which at somtime may not resort,
Wheras they have reliefe.
5   The striken Dere by kinde,
Of death that standes in awe:
For his recure an herbe can finde,
The arrow to withdrawe.
The chased Dere hath soile,
10   To coole him in his heat:
The Asse after his wery toile,
In stable is up set.
The Cony hath his cave,
The litle bird his nest:
15   From heate and cold them selves to save,
At all times as they list.
The Owle with feble sight,
Lyes lurking in the leaves:
The Sparrow in the frosty night,
20   May shroude her inthe eaves.
But wo to me alas,
In sunne nor yet in shade,
I cannot finde a resting place,
My burden to unlade.
25   But day by day still beares,
The burden on my backe:
With weping eyen and watry teares,
To hold my hope abacke.
All thinges I see have place,
30   Wherein they bow or bende:
Save this alas my wofull case,
Which no where findeth ende.

[181] *Thassault of Cupide upon the fort*
where the lovers hart lay woun-
ded and how he was taken.

When Cupide scaled first the fort,
Wherin my hart lay wounded sore:
The battry was of such a sort
That I must yelde or dye therfore.
5   There saw I love upon the wall,
How he his banner did display:
Alarme alarme he gan to call,
And bad his souldiours kepe aray.
    The armes the which that Cupide bare,
10 Were pearced hartes with teares besprent:
In silver and sable to declare
The stedfast love he alwaies ment.
    There might you see his band all drest,
In colours like to white and blacke:
15 With powder and with pellets prest,
To bring the fort to spoile and sacke.
    Good will the master of the shot,
Stode in the rampyre brave and proud:
For spence of powder he sparde not,
20 Assault assault to cry aloud.
    There might you heare the cannons rore,
Eche pece discharged a lovers loke:
Which had the power to rent, and tore
In any place wheras they toke.
25   And even with the trumpets sowne,
The scaling ladders were up set:
And beauty walked up and downe
With bow in hand and arrowes whet.
    Then first desire began to scale,
30 And shrowded him under his targe,
As on the worthiest of them all,
And aptest for to geve the charge.
    Then pushed souldiers with their pikes
And holbarders with handy strokes:
35 The hargabushe in flesh it lightes,
And dims the ayre with misty smokes.
    And as it is the souldiers use,
When shot and powder gins to want:
I hanged up my flagge of truce

40 And pleaded for my lives graunt.
        When fansy thus had made her breach,
    And beauty entred with her band:
    With bag and baggage sely wretch,
    I yelded into beauties hand.
45   Then beauty bad to blow retrete,
    And every soldiour to retire.
    And mercy wilde with spede to set:
    Me captive bound as prisoner.
        Madame (quoth I) sith that this day,
50 Hath served you at all assaies:
    I yelde to you without delay,
    Here of the fortresse all the kaies.
        And sith that I have ben the marke,
    At whom you shot at with your eye:
55 Nedes must you with your handy warke,
    Or salve my sore or let me dye.

                    [182] *The aged lover renoun-*
                              ceth love.

        I lothe that I did love,
    In youth that I thought swete:
    As time requires for my behove,
    Me thinkes they are not mete.
5   My lustes they do me leave,
    My fansies all be fled:
    And tract of time begins to weave,
    Gray heares upon my hed.
        For age with steling steps,
10 Hath clawed me with his crowch:
    And lusty life away she leapes,
    As there had bene none such.
        My muse doth not delight
    Me as she did before:
15 My hand and pen are not in plight,
    As they have bene of yore.
        For reason me denies,
    This youthly idle rime:
    And day by day to me she cries,
20 Leave of these toyes in time.
        The wrinkles in my brow,

The furrowes in my face:
Say limping age will hedge him now,
Where youth must geve him place.
25   The harbinger of death,
To me I see him ride:
The cough, the cold, the gasping breath,
Doth bid me to provide.
        A pikeax and a spade,
30 And eke a shrowding shete,
A house of clay for to be made,
For such a gest most mete.
        Me thinkes I heare the clarke,
That knoles the carefull knell:
35 And bids me leave my wofull warke,
Ere nature me compell.
        My kepers knit the knot,
That youth did laugh to scorne:
Of me that clene shalbe forgot,
40 As I had not bene borne.
        Thus must I youth give up,
Whose badge I long did weare:
To them I yelde the wanton cup
That better may it beare.
45   Lo here the bared scull,
By whose balde signe I know:
That stouping age away shall pull,
Which youthfull yeres did sow.
        For beauty with her band
50 These croked cares hath wrought:
And shipped me into the land,
From whence I first was brought.
        And ye that bide behinde,
Have ye none other trust:
55 As ye of claye were cast by kinde,
So shall ye waste to dust.

[183] *Of the ladie Wentworthes
death.*

To live to dye and dye to live againe,
With good renowne of fame well led before
Here lieth she that learned had the lore,

Whom if the parfect vertues wolden daine.
5   To be set forth with foile of worldly grace,
Was noble borne and matcht in noble race,
Lord Wentworthes wife, nor wanted to attaine,
In natures giftes her praise among the rest,
But that that gave her praise above the best,
10   Not fame, her wedlocks chastnes durst distain,
Wherein with child deliveryng of her wombe,
Thuntimely birth hath brought them both in tomb
So left she life by death to live againe.

[184] *The lover accusing his love for
her unfaithfulnesse, purposeth
to live in libertie.*

The smoky sighes the bitter teares,
That I in vaine have wasted:
The broken stepes, the wo and feares,
That long in me have lasted:
5   The love and all I owe to thee,
Here I renounce and make me free.
      Which fredome I have by thy guilt,
And not by my deserving,
Since so unconstantly thou wilt
10   Not love, but still be swarvying.
To leave me oft which was thine owne,
Without cause why as shalbe knowen.
      The frutes were faire the which did grow,
Within thy garden planted,
15   The leaves were grene of every bough,
And moysture nothing wanted,
Yet or the blossoms gan to fall,
The caterpiller wasted all.
      Thy body was the garden place,
20   And sugred wordes it beareth,
The blossomes all thy faith it was,
Which as the canker wereth.
The caterpiller is the same,
That hath wonne thee and lost thy name.
25   I meane thy lover loved now,
By thy pretended folye,
Which will prove like, thou shalt finde how,

Unto a tree of holly:
That barke and bery beares alwayes,
30   The one, birdes feedes, the other slayes.
     And right well mightest thou have thy wish
Of thy love new acquaynted:
For thou art lyke unto the dishe
That Adrianus paynted:
35   Wherin were grapes portraid so faire
That fowles for foode did there repaire.
     But I am lyke the beaten fowle
That from the net escaped,
And thou art lyke the ravening owle
40   That all the night hath waked.
For none intent but to betray
The slepyng fowle before the day.
     Thus hath thy love been unto me
As pleasant and commodious
45   As was the fyre made on the sea
By Naulus hate so odious.
Therwith to train the grekish host
From Troyes return where they wer lost.

[185] *The lover for want of his de-*
sire, sheweth his death
at hand.

As Cypres tree that rent is by the roote,
As branch or slippe bereft from whence it growes
As wel sowen seede for drought that can not sprout
As gaping ground that raineles can not close
5   As moules that want the earth to do them bote
As fishe on land to whom no water flowes,
As Chameleon that lackes the aier so sote,
As flowers do fade when Phebus rarest showes,
As Salamandra repulsed from the fire:
10   So wanting my wish I dye for my desire.

[186] *A happy end excedeth all plea-*
sures and riches of the
world.

The shining season here to some,
The glory in the worldes sight,
Renowined fame through fortune wonne
The glitteryng golde the eyes delight,
5 The sensuall life that semes so swete,
The hart with joyful dayes replete,
The thyng wherto eche wight is thrall,
The happy ende exceadeth all.

[187] *Against an unstedfast*
woman.

O temerous tauntres that delights in toyes
Tumbling cockboat totring to and fro,
Janglyng jestres depravers of swete joyes,
Ground of the graffe whence al my grief doth grow,
5 Sullen serpent environned with dispite,
That yll for good at all times doest requite.

[188] *A praise of Petrarke and of Lau-*
ra his ladie.

O Petrarke hed and prince of poets al,
Whose lively gift of flowing eloquence,
Wel may we seke, but finde not how or whence
So rare a gift with thee did rise and fal,
5 Peace to thy bones, and glory immortall
Be to thy name, and to her excellence.
Whose beauty lighted in thy time and sence:
So to be set forth as none other shall.
Why hath not our pens, rimes so parfit wrought
10 Ne why our time forth bringeth beauty such
To trye our wittes as golde is by the touche,
If to the stile the matter aided ought.
But ther was never Laure more then one,
And her had Petrarke for his Paragone.

[189] *That Petrark cannot be passed*
but notwithstanding that
Lawra is far surpassed.

With Petrarke to compare ther may no wight,
Nor yet attain unto so high a stile,
But yet I wote full well where is a file
To frame a learned man to praise aright:
5 Of stature meane of semely forme and shap,
Eche line of just proporsion to her height:
Her colour fresh and mingled with such sleight:
As though the rose sate in the lilies lap.
In wit and tong to shew what may be sed,
10 To every dede she joynes a parfit grace,
If Lawra livde she would her clene deface.
For I dare say and lay my life to wed
That Momus could not if he downe discended,
Once justly say, Lo this may be amended.

[190] *Against a cruel woman.*

Cruel unkinde whom mercy cannot move,
Herbour of unhappe wher rigours rage doth raigne,
Ground of my griefe where pitie cannot prove:
Trikle to trust of all untruth the traine,
5 Thou rigorous rocke that ruth cannot remove.
Daungerous delph, depe dungeon of disdaine:
Sacke of selfe will, the chest of craft and change,
What causeth the thus causeles for to change?
    Ah piteles plante whom plaint cannot provoke.
10 Den of disceite that right doth still refuse,
Causles unkinde that cariest under cloke
Cruelty and craft me onely to abuse,
Stately and stubberne withstanding Cupides stroke,
Thou merveilouse mase that makest men to muse,
15 Solleyn by selfe wil, most stony stiffe and straunge,
What causeth thee thus causelesse for to change?
    Slipper and secrete where surety cannot sowe
Net of newelty, neast of newfanglenesse,
Spring of al spite, from whence whole fluddes do flow,
20 Thou cave and cage of care and craftinesse,
Wavering willow that every blast doth blowe,

Graffe without groth and cause of carefulnesse,
Heape of mishap of all my griefe the graunge,
What causeth thee thus causelesse for to chaunge?
25   Hast thou forgote that I was thine infeft,
By force of love haddest thou not hart at all,
Sawest thou not other for thy love were left
Knowest thou unkinde, that nothing mought befall
From out of my hart that could have the bereft.
30   What meanest thou then at ryot thus to raunge,
And leavest thine owne that never thought to chaunge.

[191] *The lover sheweth what he would*
have, if it were graunted him to
have what he would
wishe.

If it were so that God would graunt me my request,
And that I might of earthly thinges have that I liked best.
I would not wish to clime to princely hye astate,
Which slipper is and slides so oft, and hath so fickle fate.
5 Nor yet to conquere realmes with cruel sworde in hande,
And so to shed the giltlesse bloude of such as would withstand.
Nor I would not desire in worldly rule to raigne,
Whose frute is all unquietnesse, and breaking of the braine.
Nor richesse in excesse of vertue so abhorde,
10 I would not crave which bredeth care and causeth all discorde.
But my request should be more worth a thousand folde:
That I might have and her enjoye that hath my hart in hold.
Oh God what lusty life should we live then for ever,
In pleasant joy and perfect blisse, to length our lives together.
15 With wordes of frendly chere, and lokes of lively love,
To utter all our hotte desires, which never should remove.
But grose and gredie wittes which grope but on the ground,
To gather muck of worldly goodes which oft do them confounde,
Can not attaine to knowe the misteries devine
20 Of perfite love wherto hie wittes of knowledge do incline.
A nigard of his golde such joye can never have
Which gettes with toile and kepes with care and is his money slave.
As they enjoy alwayes that taste love in his kinde,
For they do holde continually a heaven in their minde.
25 No worldly goodes could bring my hart so great an ease,
As for to finde or do the thing that might my ladie please.

For by her onely love my hart should have al joye,
And with the same put care away, and all that coulde annoy.
As if that any thing should chance to make me sadde,
30   The touching of her corall lippes would straightewaies make me gladde,
And when that in my heart I fele that dyd me greve
With one imbracing of her armes she might me sone releve:
And as the Angels al which sit in heaven hye
With presence and the sight of god have their felicitie,
35   So likewyse I in earth, should have all earthly blis,
With presence of that Paragon, my god in earth that is.

[192] *The lady forsaken of her lover,*
praieth his returne, or the
end of her own life.

To love, alas, who would not feare
That seeth my wofull state,
For he to whom my heart I beare
Doth me extremely hate,
5   And why therfore I cannot tell,
He will no lenger with me dwell.
    Did you not sewe and long me serve
Ere I you graunted grace?
And will you this now from me swarve
10   That never did trespace?
Alas poore woman then alas,
A wery lyfe here must I passe.
    And shal my faith have such refuse
In dede and shall it so,
15   Is ther no choise for me to chuse
But must I leve you so?
Alas pore woman then alas,
A werye life hence must I pas.
    And is there now no remedy
20   But that you will forget her?
Ther was a time when that perdy
You would have heard her better.
But now that time is gone and past,
And all your love is but a blast.
25   And can you thus breake your behest
In dede and can you so?
Did you not sweare you loved me best,

And can you now say no?
Remember me poore wight in paine,
30   And for my sake turne once againe.
        Alas poore Dido now I fele
Thy present painful state,
When false Eneas did hym stele
From thee at Carthage gate.
35   And left thee slepyng in thy bed,
Regarding not what he had sed.
        Was never woman thus betrayed,
Nor man so false forsworne,
His faith and trouth so strongly tyed,
40   Untruth hath all totorne:
And I have leave for my good will
To waile and wepe alone my fyll.
        But since it will not better be,
My teares shal never blin:
45   To moist the earth in such degree,
That I may drowne therin:
That by my death al men may say,
Lo women are as true as they.
        By me al women may beware,
50   That see my wofull smart,
To seke true love let them not spare,
Before they set their hart.
Or els they may become as I,
Which for my truth am lyke to dye.

[193] *The lover yelden into his ladies*
handes, praieth
mercie.

        In fredome was my fantasie
Abhorryng bondage of the minde,
But now I yelde my libertie,
And willingly my selfe I binde.
5   Truely to serve with al my hart,
Whiles life doth last not to revart.
        Her beauty bounde me first of all
And forst my will for to consent:
And I agree to be her thrall,
10   For as she list I am content.

My wyll is hers in that I may,
And where she biddes I wyll obey.
 It lieth in her my wo or welth,
She may do that she liketh best,
15 If that she list I have my helth,
If she list not in wo I rest.
Sins I am fast within her bandes,
My wo and welth lieth in her handes.
 She can no lesse then pittie me,
20 Sith that my faith to her is knowne,
It were to much extremitie,
With cruelty to use her owne.
Alas a sinnefull enterprise,
To slay that yeldes at her device.
25 But I thinke not her hart so harde,
Nor that she hath such cruell lust:
I doubt nothing of her reward,
For my desert but well I trust,
As she hath beauty to allure,
30 So hath she a hart that will recure.

[194] *That nature which worketh all thinges*
for our behoofe, hath made wo-
men also for our comfort
and delight.

 Among dame natures workes such perfite law is wrought,
That things be ruled by course of kind in order as thei ought.
 And serveth in their state, in such just frame and sort,
That slender wits may judge the same, and make therof report.
5 Behold what secrete force the winde doth easely show,
Which guides the ships amid the seas if he his bellowes blow.
 The waters waxen wilde where blustering blastes do rise,
Yet seldome do they passe their bondes for nature that devise.
 The fire which boiles the leade, and trieth out the gold:
10 Hath in his power both help and hurt, if he his force unfold.
 The frost which kils the fruite, doth knit the brused bones:
And is a medecin of kinde, prepared for the nones.
 The earth in whose entrails the foode of man doth live,
At every spring and fall of leafe, what pleasure doth she give?
15 The ayre which life desires, and is to helth so swete,
Of nature yeldes such lively smelles, that comforts every sprete.

The Sunne through natures might, doth draw away the dew,
And spredes the flowers wher he is wont his princely face to shew.
The Moone which may be cald, the lanterne of the night,
20   Is halfe a guide to traveling men, such vertue hath her light.
The sters not vertuelesse are beauty to the eyes,
A lodes man to the Mariner, a signe of calmed skyes.
The flowers and fruitfull trees to man do tribute pay,
And when they have their duety done by course they fade away.
25   Eche beast both fishe and foule, doth offer life and all,
To nourish man and do him ease, yea serve him at his call.
The serpentes venemous, whose uglye shapes we hate,
Are soveraigne salves for sondry sores, and nedefull in their state.
Sith nature shewes her power, in eche thing thus at large,
30   Why should not man submit himselfe to be in natures charge?
Who thinkes to flee her force, at length becomes her thrall,
The wisest cannot slip her snare, for nature governs all.
Lo, nature gave us shape, lo nature fedes our lives:
Then they are worse then mad I think, against her force that strives.
35   Though some do use to say, which can do nought but faine,
Women were made for this intent, to put us men to paine.
Yet sure I thinke they are a pleasure to the minde,
A joy which man can never want, as nature hath assinde.

[195] *When adversitie is once fallen,*
it is to late to beware.

To my mishap alas I finde
That happy hap is daungerous:
And fortune worketh but her kinde,
To make the joyfull dolorous.
5   But all to late it comes to minde,
To waile the want that makes me blinde.
Amid my myrth and pleasantnesse,
Such chaunce is chaunced sodainly,
That in dispayre without redresse,
10   I finde my chiefest remedy.
No new kinde of unhappinesse,
Should thus have left me comfortlesse.
Who would have thought that my request,
Should bring me forth such bitter frute:
15   But now is hapt that I feard lest:
And all this harme comes by my sute,

For when I thought me happiest,
Even then hapt all my chiefe unrest.
   In better case was never none
20 And yet unwares thus am I trapt,
My chiefe desire doth cause me mone,
And to my harme my welth is hapt,
There is no man but I alone,
That hath such cause to sigh and mone.
25   Thus am I taught for to beware
And trust no more such pleasant chance,
My happy hap bred me this care,
And brought my mirth to great mischance.
There is no man whom hap will spare,
30 But when she list his welth is bare.

[196] *Of a lover that made his one-*
ly god of his love.

   All you that frendship do professe,
And of a frende present the place:
Geve eare to me that did possesse,
As frendly frutes as ye imbrace.
5 And to declare the circumstance,
There were them selves that did avaunce:
To teach me truely how to take,
A faithfull friende for vertues sake.
   But I as one of litle skill,
10 To know what good might grow therby,
Unto my welth I had no will,
Nor to my nede I had none eye,
But as the childe doth learne to go,
So I in time did learne to know,
15 Of all good frutes the world brought forth,
A faithfull frende is thing most worth.
   Then with all care I sought to finde,
One worthy to receive such trust:
One onely that was riche in minde,
20 One secrete, sober, wise, and just.
Whom riches could not raise at all,
Nor povertie procure to fall:
And to be short in few wordes plaine,
One such a frende I did attaine.

25   And when I did enjoy this welth,
       Who lived Lord in such a case,
       For to my frendes it was great helth,
       And to my foes a fowle deface,
       And to my selfe a thing so riche
30   As seke the world and finde none such.
       Thus by this frende I set such store,
       As by my selfe I set no more.
          This frende so much was my delight,
       When care had clene orecome my hart,
35   One thought of her rid care as quite,
       As never care had causde my smart.
       Thus joyed I in my frende so dere,
       Was never frende sate man so nere,
       I carde for her so much alone,
40   That other God I carde for none.
          But as it doth to them befall,
       That to them selves respect have none:
       So my swete graffe is growen to gall,
       Where I sowed mirth I reaped mone.
45   This ydoll that I honorde so,
       Is now transformed to my fo,
       That me most pleased, me most paines,
       And in dispaire my hart remaines.
          And for just scourge of such desart,
50   Thre plages I may my selfe assure,
       First of my frende to lose my part,
       And next my life may not endure,
       And last of all the more to blame,
       My soule shall suffer for the same.
55   Wherfore ye frendes I warne you all,
       Sit fast for feare of such a fall.

             [197] *Upon the death of sir An-*
                   tony Denny.

     Death and the king, did as it were contend,
     Which of them two bare Denny greatest love.
     The king to shew his love gan farre extende,
     Did him advaunce his betters farre above.
  5   Nere place, much welth, great honor eke him gave,
     To make it known what powre gret princes have.

But when death came with his triumphant gift,
From worldly cark he quit his weried ghost,
Free from the corps, and straight to heaven it lift,
10 Now deme that can who did for Denny most.
The king gave welth but fading and unsure,
Death brought him blisse that ever shall endure.

[198] *A comparison of the lo-
vers paines.*

Lyke as the brake within the riders hand,
Doth straine the horse nye wood with grief of paine,
Not used before to come in such a bande,
Striveth for griefe, although god wot in vain
5 To be as erst he was at libertie,
But force of force doth straine the contrary.
Even so since band doth cause my deadly grief,
That made me so my wofull chaunce lament,
Like thing hath brought me into paine and mischiefe,
10 Save willingly to it I did assent.
To binde the thing in fredome which was free,
That now full fore alas repenteth me.

[199] *Of a Rosemary branche
sent.*

Such grene to me as you have sent,
Such grene to you I sende againe:
A flowring hart that will not feint,
For drede of hope or losse of gaine:
5 A stedfast thought all wholy bent,
So that he may your grace obtaine:
As you by proofe have always sene,
To live your owne and always grene.

[200] *To his love of his con-
stant hart.*

As I have bene so will I ever be,
Unto my death and lenger if I myght,
Have I of love the frendly lokyng eye?

Have I of fortune favour or despite?
5 I am of rock by proofe as you may see:
Not made of waxe nor of no metall light,
As leefe to dye, by chaunge as to deceave,
Or breake the promise made. And so I leave.

[201] *Of the token which his
love sent him.*

The golden apple that the Troyan boy,
Gave to Venus the fayrest of the thre,
Which was the cause of all the wrack of Troy,
Was not received with a greater joy,
5 Then was the same (my love) thou sent to me,
It healed my sore it made my sorowes free,
It gave me hope it banisht mine annoy:
Thy happy hand full oft of me was blist,
That can geve such a salve when that thou list.

[202] *Manhode availeth not without
good Fortune.*

The Cowerd oft whom deinty viandes fed,
That bosted much his ladies eares to please,
By helpe of them whom under him he led
Hath reapt the palme that valiance could not cease.
5 The unexpert that shores unknowen neare sought,
Whom Neptune yet apaled not with feare:
In wandring shippe on trustles seas hath tought
The skill to fele that time to long doth leare.
The sporting knight that scorneth Cupides kinde,
10 With fained chere the pained cause to brede:
In game unhides the leden sparkes of minde,
And gaines the gole, where glowing flames shold spede,
Thus I see proofe that trouth and manly hart
May not availe, if fortune chaunce to start.

[203] *The constancy of all vertues*
is most worthy.

Though in the waxe a perfect picture made,
Doth shew as faire as in the marble stone,
Yet do we see it is estemed of none,
Because that fier or force the forme doth fade.
5 Wheras the marble holden is ful dere,
Since that endures the date of lenger dayes.
Of Diamondes it is the greatest praise,
So long to last and alwaies one tappere.
Then if we do esteme that thing for best,
10 Which in perfection lengest time doth last:
And that most vaine that turnes with every blast
What jewel then with tong can be exprest?
Like to that hart wher love hath framed such feth,
That can not fade but by the force of death.

[204] *The uncertaine state*
of a lover.

Lyke as the rage of raine,
Filles rivers with excesse,
And as the drought againe,
Doth draw them lesse and lesse.
5 So I both fall and clyme,
With no and yea sometime.
As they swell hye and hye,
So doth encrease my state,
As they fall drye and drye
10 So doth my wealth abate,
As yea is mixt with no,
So mirth is mixt with wo.
As nothing can endure,
That lives and lackes reliefe,
15 So nothing can stande sure,
Where chaunge doth raigne as chiefe.
Wherefore I must intende,
To bowe when others bende.
And when they laugh to smile,
20 And when they wepe to waile,
And when they craft, begile,

And when they fight, assaile,
And thinke there is no chaunge,
Can make them seme to strange.
25   Oh most unhappy slave,
What man may leade this course,
To lacke he would faynest have,
Or els to do much worse.
These be rewardes for such,
30 As live and love to much.

[205] *The lover in libertie smileth at*
them in thraldome, that some-
time scorned his
bondage.

At libertie I sit and see,
Them that have erst laught me to scorne:
Whypt with the whip that scourged me
And now they banne that they were borne.
5   I see them sit full soberlye,
And thinke their earnest lokes to hide:
Now in them selves they can not spye,
That they or this in me have spide.
     I see them sitting all alone,
10 Markyng the steppes ech worde and loke:
And now they treade where I have gone
The painfull pathe that I forsoke.
     Now I see well I saw no whit,
When they saw wel that now are blinde,
15 But happy hap hath made me quit,
And just judgement hath them assinde.
     I see them wander all alone,
And treade full fast in dredfull dout:
The selfe same pathe that I have gone,
20 Blessed be hap that brought me out.
     At libertie all this I see,
And say no word but erst among:
Smiling at them that laught at me,
Lo such is hap, marke well my song.

[206] *A comparison of his love wyth*
the faithful and painful love
of Troylus to
Creside.

I read how Troylus served in Troy,
A lady long and many a day,
And how he bode so great anoy,
For her as all the stories say.
5 That halfe the paine had never man,
Which had this wofull Troyan than.
His youth, his sport, his pleasant chere,
His courtly state and company,
In him so straungely altred were,
10 With such a face of contrary.
That every joy became a wo,
This poyson new had turnde him so.
And what men thought might most him ease,
And most that for his comfort stode,
15 The same did most his minde displease,
And set him most in furious mode.
For all his pleasure ever lay,
To thinke on her that was away.
His chamber was his comon walke,
20 Wherin he kept him secretly,
He made his bed the place of talke,
To heare his great extremity.
In nothing els had he delight,
But even to be a martyr right.
25 And now to call her by her name
And straight therwith to sigh and throbbe:
And when his fansies might not frame,
Then into teares and so to sobbe,
All in extreames and thus he lyes,
30 Making two fountaines of his eyes.
As agues have sharpe shiftes of fits
Of cold and heat successively:
So had his head like change of wits:
His pacience wrought so diversly.
35 Now up, now down, now here, now there,
Like one that was he wist not where.
And thus though he were Priams sonne
And comen of the kinges hye blood,

This care he had ere he her wonne.

40 Till she that was his maistresse good,
And lothe to see her servant so,
Became Phisicion to his wo.
      And toke him to her handes and grace,
And said she would her minde apply,
45 To helpe him in his wofull case,
If she might be his remedy.
And thus they say to ease his smart,
She made him owner of her hart.
      And truth it is except they lye,
50 From that day forth her study went,
To shew to love him faithfully,
And his whole minde full to content.
So happy a man at last was he,
And eke so worthy a woman she.
55   Lo lady then judge you by this,
Mine ease and how my case doth fall,
For sure betwene my life and his,
No difference there is at all.
His care was great, so was his paine,
60 And mine is not the lest of twaine.
      For what he felt in service true
For her whom that he loved so,
The same I fele as large for you,
To whom I do my service owe.
65 There was that time in him no paine,
But now the same in me doth raigne.
      Which if you can compare and way,
And how I stand in every plight,
Then this for you I dare well say,
70 Your hart must nedes remorce of right
To graunt me grace and so to do,
As Creside then did Troylus to.
      For well I wot you are as good,
And even as faire as ever was she,
75 And commen of as worthy blood,
And have in you as large pitie
To tender me your own true man,
As she did him her servant than.
      Which gift I pray God for my sake,
80 Full sone and shortly you me sende,
So shall you make my sorowes slake,

So shall you bring my wo to ende.
And set me in as happy case,
As Troylus with his lady was.

[207] *To leade a vertuous and*
honest life.

Flee from the prease and dwell with sothfastnes,
Suffice to thee thy good though it be small,
For horde hath hate, and climing ticklenes,
Praise hath envy, and weall is blinde in all,
5 Favour no more, then thee behove shall.
Rede well thy selfe that others well canst rede,
And trouth shall thee deliver, it is no drede.
    Paine thee not eche croked to redresse,
In hope of her that turneth as a ball,
10 Great rest standeth in litle businesse,
Beware also to spurne against a nall,
Strive not as doth a crocke against a wall,
Deme first thy selfe, that demest others dede,
And truth shall thee deliver, it is no drede.
15   That thee is sent, receive in buxomnesse,
The wrestling of this world asketh a fall:
Here is no home, here is but wildernesse.
Forth pilgryme forth, forth beast out of thy stall,
Looke up on hye, geve thankes to God of all:
20 Weane well thy lust, and honest life ay leade,
So trouth shall thee deliver, it is no dreade.

[208] *The wounded lover determineth*
to make sute to his lady
for his recure.

Sins Mars first moved warre or stirred men to strife,
Was never sene so fearce a fight, I scarce could scape with life.
Resist so long I did, till death approched so nye,
To save my selfe I thought it best, with spede away to flye.
5 In daunger still I fled, by flight I thought to scape
From my dere foe, it vailed not, alas it was to late.
For Venus from her campe brought Cupide with his bronde,
Who sayd now yelde, or els desire shall chace thee in every londe.
Yet would I not straight yelde, till fansy fiercely stroke,

10 Who from my will did cut the raines and charged me with this yoke.
Then all the daies and nightes mine eare might heare the sound,
What carefull sighes my hart would steale, to feele it self so bound.
For though within my brest, thy care I worke (he sayde)
Why for good will didst thou behold her persing eye displayd?
15 Alas the fishe is caught, through baite that hides the hooke,
Even so her eye me trained hath, and tangled with her looke.
But or that it be long, my hart thou shalt be faine,
To stay my life pray her forththrow swete lokes when I complain.
When that she shall deny, to do me that good turne,
20 Then shall she see to asshes gray, by flames my body burne.
Deserte of blame to her, no wight may yet impute,
For feare of nay I never sought, the way to frame my sute.
Yet hap that what hap shall, delay I may to long,
Assay I shall for I heare say, the still man oft hath wrong.

[209] *The lover shewing of the continuall paines*
that abide within his brest, determi-
neth to die because he can-
not have redresse.

The dolefull bell that still doth ring,
The wofull knell of all my joyes:
The wretched hart doth perce and wring,
And fils mine eare with deadly noyes.
5   The hongry Viper in my brest,
That on my hart doth lye and gnaw:
Doth dayly brede my new unrest,
And deper sighes doth cause me draw.
And though I force both hand and eye,
10   On pleasant matter to attend:
My sorowes to deceive therby,
And wretched life for to amend.
Yet goeth the mill within my hart,
Which grindeth nought but paine and wo:
15   And turneth all my joy to smart,
The evil corne it yeldeth so.
Though Venus smile with yelding eyes,
And swete musicke doth play and sing:
Yet doth my sprites feele none of these,
20   The clarke doth at mine eare so ring.
As smallest sparckes uncared for,
To greatest flames do sonest grow,

Even so did this mine inward sore,
Begin in game and end in wo.
25   And now by use so swift it goeth,
That nothing can mine eares so fill:
But that the clacke it overgoeth,
And plucketh me backe into the mill.
        But since the mill will nedes about,
30   The pinne wheron the whele doth go:
I will assay to strike it out,
And so the mill to overthrow.

[210] *The power of love over gods*
them selves.

For love Apollo (his Godhed set aside)
Was servant to the king of Thessaley,
Whose daughter was so pleasant in his eye,
That both his harpe and sawtrey he defide:
5   And bagpipe solace of the rurall bride,
Did puffe and blow, and on the holtes hy,
His cattell kept with that rude melody,
And oft eke him that doth the heavens gide,
Hath love transformed to shapes for him to base:
10   Transmuted thus somtime a swan is he,
Leda taccoy, and eft Europe to please,
A milde white bull, unwrinckled front and face,
Suffreth her play till on his back lepeth she,
Whom in great care he ferieth through the seas.

[211] *The promise of a constant lover.*

As Lawrell leaves that cease not to be grene,
From parching sunne, nor yet from winters threte:
As hardened oke that feareth no sworde so kene,
As flint for toole in twaine that will not frete.
5   As fast as rocke, or piller surely set:
So fast am I to you, and ay have bene,
Assuredly whom I cannot forget,
For joy, for paine, for torment nor for tene.
For losse, for gaine, for frowning, nor for thret,
10   But ever one, yea both in calme and blast,
Your faithfull friende, and will be to my last.

[212] *Against him that had slaundered*
a gentle woman with
him selfe.

False may be he, and by the powers above,
Never have he good spede or lucke in love,
That so can lye or spot the worthy fame,
Of her for whom thou R. art to blame.
5　For chaste Diane that hunteth still the chace,
And all her maides that sue her in the race,
With faire bowes bent and arrowes by their side,
Can say that thou in this hast falsely lide.
For never hong the bow upon the wall,
10　Of Dianes temple, no nor never shall.
Of broken chaste the sacred vow to spot,
Of her whom thou doste charge so large I wot,
But if ought be wherof her blame may rise,
It is in that she did not well advise
15　To marke thee right, as now she doth thee know
False of thy dede, false of thy talke also.
Lurker of kinde like serpent layd to bite,
As poyson hid under the suger white.
What daunger suche? So was the house defilde,
20　Of Collatine: so was the wife begilde.
So smarted she, and by a trayterous force,
The Cartage quene so she fordid her corse.
So strangled was the Rodopeian maide,
Fye traytour fye, to thy shame be it sayd,
25　Thou dunghill Crow that crokest against the rayne,
Home to thy hole, brag not with Phebe againe.
Carrion for thee, and lothsome be thy voyce,
Thy song is fowle, I weary of thy noyce.
Thy blacke fethers, which are thy wearing wede,
30　Wet them with teares, and sorow for thy dede.
And in darke caves, where yrkesome wormes do crepe,
Lurke thou all day, and flye when thou shouldest slepe.
And never light where living thing hath life,
But eat and drinke where stinche and filth is rife.
35　For she that is a fowle of fethers bright,
Admit she toke some pleasure in thy sight.
As fowle of state sometimes delight to take,
Fowle of mean sort their flight with them to make.
For play of wing, or solace of their kinde:

40 But not in sort as thou dost breake thy minde.
Not for to treade with such foule fowle as thou,
No no I sweare, and dare it here avow.
Thou never settest thy foote within her nest,
Boast not so broade then to thine owne unrest.
45 But blushe for shame, for in thy face it standes,
And thou canst not unspot it with thy handes.
For all the heavens against thee recorde beare,
And all in earth against thee eke will sweare,
That thou in this art even none other man,
50 But as the judges were to Susan than
Forgers of that wherto their lust them prickt,
Bashe, blaser then the truth hath thee convict.
And she a woman of her worthy fame,
Unspotted standes, and thou hast caught the shame.
55 And there I pray to God that it may rest,
False as thou art, as false as is the best,
That so canst wrong the noble kinde of man,
In whom all trouth first floorisht and began.
And so hath stand, till now thy wretched part,
60 Hath spotted us, of whose kinde one thou art.
That all the shame that ever rose or may,
Of shamefull dede on thee may light I say.
And on thy kinde, and thus I wishe thee rather,
That all thy seede may like be to their father,
65 Untrue as thou, and forgers as thou art,
So as all we be blamelesse of thy part.
And of thy dede. And thus I do thee leave,
Still to be false, and falsely to deceave.

[213] *A praise of maistresse R.*

I heard when fame with thundring voice did sommon to appere,
The chiefe of natures children all that kinde hath placed here.
To view what brute by vertue got their lives could justly crave,
And bad them shew what praise by truth they worthy were to have.
5 Wherewith I saw how Venus came and put her selfe in place,
And gave her ladies leave at large to stand and pleade their case.
Ech one was calde by name a row, in that assemble there,
That hence are gone or here remaines, in court or other where.
A solemne silence was proclaimde, the judges sate and herd,
10 What truth could tell, or craft could fain, and who should be preferd.

Then beauty stept before the barre, whose brest and neck was bare
With heare trust up, and on her hed a caule of gold she ware.
Thus Cupides thralles began to flock whose hongry eyes did say
That she had stayned all the dames, that present were that day.
15 For er she spake, with whispring words, the prease was fild throughout
And fansy forced common voyce, therat to give a shoute.
Which cried to fame take forth thy trump, and sound her praise on hy
That glads the hart of every wight that her beholdes with eye.
What stirre and rule (quod order than) do these rude people make,
20 We hold her best that shall deserve a praise for vertues sake.
This sentence was no soner said, but beauty therwith blusht,
The noise did cease, the hall was stil, and every thing was whusht.
Then finenesse thought by training talke to win that beauty lost,
And whet her tonge with joly wordes, and spared for no cost:
25 Yet wantonnesse could not abide, but brake her tale in hast,
And pevish pride for Pecockes plumes would nedes be hiest plast.
And therwithall came curiousnesse and carped out of frame.
The audience laught to heare the strife as they beheld the same.
Yet reason sone apesde the brute, her reverence made and doon,
30 She purchased favour for to speake, and thus her tale begoon.
Sins bounty shall the garland weare, and crowned be by fame,
O happy judges call for her, for she deserves the same.
Where temperance governs beauties flowers and glory is not sought,
And shamefast mekenes mastreth pride, and vertu dwels in thought.
35 Bid her come forth and shew her face, or els assent eche one,
That true report shall grave her name in gold or marble stone.
For all the world to rede at will, what worthines doth rest,
In perfect pure unspotted life, which she hath here possest.
Then skill rose up and sought the prease to finde if that he might,
40 A person of such honest name, that men should praise of right.
This one I saw full sadly sit, and shrinke her self aside,
Whose sober lokes did shew what giftes her wifely grace did hide.
Lo here (quod skill) good people all, is Lucrece left alive,
And she shall most excepted be, that least for praise did strive.
45 No lenger fame could hold her peace, but blew a blast so hye,
That made an eckow in the aier and sowning through the skye.
The voice was loude and thus it said come. R. with happy daies,
Thy honest life hath wonne the same and crowned thee with praies.
And when I heard my maistres name I thrust amids the throng.
50 And clapt my handes and wisht of god that she might prosper long.

[214] *Of one unjustly*
defamed.

I ne can close in short and cunning verse,
Thy worthy praise of bountie by desart:
The hatefull spite and slaunder to reherse.
Of them that see but know not what thou art,
5 For kind by craft hath wrought thee so to eye,
That no wight may thy wit and vertue spye.
But he have other fele then outward sight,
The lacke wherof doth hate and spite to trie
Thus kind thy craft is let of vertues light:
10 See how the outward shew the wittes may dull:
Not of the wise but as the most entend,
Minerva yet might never perce their scull,
That Circes cup and Cupides brand hath blend
Whose fonde affects now sturred have their braine,
15 So doth thy hap thy hue with colour staine.
Beauty thy foe thy shape doubleth thy sore,
To hide thy wit and shew thy vertue vaine,
Fell were thy fate, if wisdome were not more.
I meane by thee even G. by name,
20 Whom stormy windes of envy and disdaine,
Do tosse with boisteous blastes of wicked fame.
Where stedfastnesse as chiefe in thee doth raigne.
Pacience thy setled minde dothe guide and stere,
Silence and shame with many resteth there.
25 Till time thy mother list them forth to call,
Happy is he that may enjoye them all.

[215] *Of the death of the late countisse*
of Penbroke.

Yet once againe my muse I pardon pray,
Thine intermitted song if I repeate:
Not in such wise as when love was my pay,
My joly wo with joyfull verse to treate.
5   But now (unthanke to our desert be geven,
Which merite not a heavens gift to kepe)
Thou must with me bewaile that fate hath reven,
From earth a jewel laied in earth to slepe.
    A jewel, yea a gemme of womanhed,

10 Whose perfect vertues linked as in chaine:
    So did adorne that humble wivelyhed,
    As is not rife to finde the like againe.
        For wit and learnyng framed to obey,
    Her husbandes wil that willed her to use
15 The love he bare her chiefely as a staye,
    For al her frendes that wold her furtherance chuse.
        Wel sayd therfore a heavens gift she was,
    Because the best are sonest hence bereft:
    And though her self to heaven hence dyd passe,
20 Her spoyle to earth from whence it came she left.
        And to us teares her absence to lament,
    And eke his chance that was her make by law:
    Whose losse to lose so great an ornament,
    Let them esteme which true loves knot can draw.

[216] *That eche thing is hurt of*
it self.

    Why fearest thou thy outward fo,
    When thou thy selfe thy harme dost fede,
    Of grief, or hurt, of paine, or wo,
    Whithin eche thing is sowen the sede?
5   So fine was never yet the cloth,
    No smith so hard his yron did beate:
    But thone consumed was with moth,
    Thother with canker all to freate.
        The knotty oke and wainscot old,
10 Within doth eate the silly worme:
    Even so a minde in envy rold,
    Alwaies within it self doth burne.
        Thus every thing that nature wrought,
    Within it selfe his hurt doth beare:
15 No outward harme nede to be sought,
    Where enemies be within so neare.

[217] *Of the choise of a wife.*

    The flickeryng fame that flieth from eare to eare,
    And aye her strength encreaseth with her flight
    Geves first the cause why men to heare delight,
    Of those whome she doth note for beauty bright,

5 And with this fame that flieth on so fast,
  Fansy doth hye when reason makes no hast.
    And yet not so content they wishe to see
  And thereby know if fame have sayd aryght,
  More trustyng to the triall of their eye,
10 Then to the brute that goes of any wight,
  Wise in that point that lightly will not leve,
  Unwise to seke that may them after greve.
    Who knoweth not how sight may love allure,
  And kindle in the hart a hote desire:
15 The eye to worke that fame could not procure,
  Of greater cause there commeth hotter fire.
  For ere he wete him self he feleth warme,
  The fame and eye the causers of his harme.
    Let fame not make her knowen whom I shal know,
20 Nor yet myne eye therin to be my guyde:
  Sufficeth me that vertue in her grow,
  Whose simple life her fathers walles do hide.
  Content with this I leave the rest to go,
  And in such choise shall stand my welth and wo.

[218] *Descripcion of an ungodly*
worlde.

  Who loves to live in peace, and marketh every change,
  Shall hear such news from time to time, as seme right wondrous strange,
    Such fraud in frendly lokes, such frendship al for gaine:
  Such cloked wrath in hatefull harts, which wordly men retayne.
5   Such fayned flattering fayth, amongs both hye and low:
  Such great deceite, such subtell wittes, the pore to overthrowe.
    Such spite in sugred tonges, such malice full of pride:
  Such open wrong such great untruth, which can not go unspide.
    Such restlesse sute for roumes, which bringeth men to care:
10 Such sliding downe from slippry seates, yet can we not beware.
    Such barking at the good, such bolstring of the yll:
  Such threatnyng of the wrathe of God, such vyce embraced still.
    Such strivyng for the best, such climing to estate:
  Such great dissemblyng every where, such love all mixt with hate
15   Such traines to trap the just, such prollyng faultes to pyke:
  Such cruell wordes for speaking trouth, who ever hearde the lyke?
    Such strife for stirring strawes, such discord dayly wrought,
  Such forged tales dul wits to blind, such matters made of nought.

  Such trifles told for trouth, such credityng of lyes,
20 Such silence kept when foles do speak, such laughyng at the wise.
  Such plenty made so scarce, such crying for redresse,
  Such feared signes of our decay, which tong dares not expresse.
  Such chaunges lightly markt, such troubles still apperes,
  Which never were before this time, no not this thousand yeres.
25 Such bribyng for the purse, which ever gapes for more,
  Such hordyng up of worldly welth, such kepyng muck in store.
  Such folly founde in age, such will in tender youth,
  Such sundry sortes among great clarkes, and few that speake the truth.
  Such falshed under craft, and such unstedfast wayes,
30 Was never sene within mens hartes, as is found now adayes.
  The cause and ground of this is our unquiet minde,
  Which thinkes to take those goods away whiche wee must leve behinde.
  Why do men seke to get which they cannot possesse?
  Or breake their slepes with careful thoughtes and all for wretchednes.
35 Though one amonges a skore, hath welth and ease a while,
  A thousand want which toyleth sore and travaile many a mile.
  And some although they slepe, yet welth falles in their lap,
  Thus some be rich and some be pore as fortune geves the hap.
  Wherfore I hold him wise which thinkes him self at ease,
40 And is content in simple state both god and man to please.
  For those that live like gods and honored are to day,
  Within short time their glory falles as flowers do fade away.
  Uncertein is their lives on whom this world wyl frowne,
  For though they sit above the starres a storme may strike them downe
45 In welth who feares no fal, may slide from joy ful sone,
  There is nothing so sure on earth but changeth as the Mone.
  What pleasure hath the rich, or ease more then the pore,
  Although he have a pleasant house his trouble is the more.
  They bowe and speake him faire, which seke to suck his blood,
50 And some do wishe his soule in hell and al to have his good.
  The covetyng of the goodes doth nought but dull the spirite,
  And some men chaunce to tast the sower that gropeth for the swete.
  The rich is still envied by those which eate his bred,
  With fawning spech and flatteryng tales his eares are dayly fed,
55 In fine I see and prove the rich have many foes,
  He slepth best and careth lest that litle hath to lose.
  As time requireth now who would avoyde much strife,
  Were better live in pore estate then leade a princes life.
  To passe those troublesome times I see but little choise,
60 But helpe to waile with those that wepe and laugh when they rejoise
  For as we se to day our brother brought in care,

To morow may we have such chance to fall with him in snare.
    Of this we may be sure, who thinkes to sit most fast,
Shal sonest fal like withered leaves that cannot bide a blast.
65   Though that the flood be great, the ebbe as lowe doth ronne,
When every man hath playd his part our pagent shalbe donne.
    Who trustes this wretched worlde I hold him worse then mad,
Here is not one that fereth god, the best is all to badde.
    For those that seme as saintes are devilles in their dedes,
70 Though that the earth brings forth some flowers it beareth many wedes.
    I se no present help from mischief to prevaile,
But flee the seas of worldly cares or beare a quiet saile.
    For who that medleth lest shall save him selfe from smart,
Who styres an oare in every boate shal play a folish part.

[219] *The dispairing lover la-
menteth.*

    Walkyng the pathe of pensive thought,
I askt my hart how came this wo.
Thine eye (quod he) this care me brought,
Thy mynde, thy witte, thy wyll also
5 Enforceth me to love her ever,
This is the cause joy shal I never.
    And as I walkt as one dismaide,
Thinkyng that wrong this wo me lent:
Right, sent me worde by wrath, which said,
10 This just judgement to thee is sent:
Never to dye, but dying ever,
Till breath thee faile, joy shalt thou never.
    Sith right doth judge this wo tendure,
Of health, of wealth, of remedy:
15 As I have done so be she sure,
Of faith and trouth untill I dye.
And as this paine cloke shal I ever,
So inwardly joye shal I never.
    Gripyng of gripes greve not so sore,
20 Nor serpentes styng causeth such smart,
Nothing on earth may payne me more,
Then sight that perst my woful hart.
Drowned with cares styll to persever,
Come death betimes, joye shal I never.
25   O libertie why dost thou swerve:

And steale away thus all at ones:
And I in prison like to sterve,
For lacke of foode do gnaw on bones.
My hope and trust in thee was ever,
30   Now thou art gone, joy shall I never.
        But still as one all desperate,
To leade my life in misery:
Sith feare from hope hath lockt the gate,
Where pity should graunt remedy.
35   Despaire this lot assignes me ever,
To live in paine, joy shall I never.

[220] *The lover praieth his service to*
be accepted, and his de-
faultes pardoned.

Procryn that somtime served Cephalus,
With hart as true as any lover might,
Yet her betid in loving this unright.
That as in hart with love surprised thus,
5   She on a day to see this Cephalus,
Where he was wont to shrowde him in the shade,
When of his hunting he an end had made.
Within the woods with dredfull foote forth stalketh.
So busily love in her hed it walketh,
10   That she to sene him may her not restraine.
This Cephalus that heard one shake the leaves
Uprist all egre thrusting after pray,
With darte in hand him list no further daine,
To see his love but slew her in the greaves,
15   That ment to him but perfect love alway.
        So curious bene alas the rites all,
Of mighty love that unnethes may I thinke,
In his high service how to loke or winke.
Thus I complaine that wretchedst am of all,
20   To you my love, and soveraine lady dere,
That may my hart with death or life stere
As ye best list. That ye vouchsafe in all
Mine humble service. And if me misfall,
By negligence, or els for lacke of witte,
25   That of your mercy you do pardon it,
And think that love made Procrin shake the leves
When with unright she slain was in the greves.

[221] *Descripcion and praise of*
his love.

Lyke the Phenix a birde most rare in sight,
That nature hath with gold and purple drest:
Such she me semes in whom I most delight,
If I might speake for envy at the least.
5 Nature I thinke first wrought her in despite,
Of rose and lilly that sommer bringeth first,
In beauty sure, exceding all the rest,
Under the bent of her browes justly pight:
As Diamondes, or Saphires at the least:
10 Her glistring lightes the darknesse of the night.
Whose litle mouth and chinne like all the rest.
Her ruddy lippes excede the corall quite.
Her yvery teeth where none excedes the rest.
Fautlesse she is from foote unto the waste:
15 Her body small and straight as mast upright,
Her armes long in just proporcion cast,
Her handes depaint with veines all blew and white.
What shal I say for that is not in sight?
The hidden partes I judge them by the rest.
20 And if I were the forman of the quest,
To geve a verdite of her beauty bright,
Forgeve me Phebus, thou shouldst be dispossest,
Which doest usurpe my ladies place of right.
Here will I cease lest envy cause dispite.
25 But nature when she wrought so faire a wight,
In this her worke she surely dyd entende,
To frame a thing that God could not amende.

[222] *The lover declareth his paines*
to excede far the paines
of hell.

The soules that lacked grace,
Which lye in bitter paine:
Are not in such a place,
As foolish folke do faine.
5 Tormented all with fire,
And boile in leade againe,
With serpents full of ire,

Stong oft with deadly paine.
   Then cast in frosen pittes:
10 To freze there certaine howers:
And for their painfull fittes,
Apointed tormentours.
   No no it is not so,
Their sorow is not such:
15 And yet they have of wo,
I dare say twise as much.
   Which comes because they lack
The sight of the godhed,
And be from that kept back
20 Where with are aungels fed.
   This thing know I by love
Through absence crueltie,
Which makes me for to prove
Hell pain before I dye.
25   There is no tong can tell
My thousand part of care
Ther may no fire in hell,
With my desire compare.
   No boyling leade can pas
30 My scalding sighes in hete:
Nor snake that ever was,
With stinging can so frete
   A true and tender hert,
As my thoughtes dayly doe,
35 So that I know but smart,
And that which longes thereto.
   O Cupid Venus son,
As thou hast showed thy might,
And hast this conquest woon,
40 Now end the same aright.
   And as I am thy slave,
Contented with all this:
So helpe me soone to have
My parfect earthly blisse.

[223] *Of the death of sir Thomas*
Wiate the elder.

Lo dead he lives, that whilome lived here,
Among the dead that quick go on the ground.
Though he be dead, yet doth he quick apere,
By lively name that death cannot confound.
5 His life for ay of fame the trump shall sound.
Though he be dead, yet lives he here alive.
Thus can no death from Wiate life deprive.

[224] *That length of time consumeth*
all thinges.

What harder is then stone, what more then water soft?
Yet with soft water drops, hard stones be persed ofte.
     What geves so strong impulse,
     That stone ne may withstand?
5   What geves more weake repulse,
     Then water prest with hand?
     Yet weke though water be,
     It holowith hardest flint:
     By proofe wherof we see,
10   Time geves the greatest dint.

[225] *The beginning of the epistle of Pene-*
lope to Ulisses, made in-
to verse.

O lingring make Ulisses dere, thy wife lo sendes to thee,
Her driry plaint: write not againe, but come thy selfe to me.
Our hatefull scourge, that womans foe, proud Troy now is fordon:
We bye it derer, though Priam slaine, and all his kingdome won.
5 O that the raging surges great that lechers bane had wrought,
When first with ship he forowed seas, and Lacedemon sought,
In desert bed my shivering coarse then shold not have sought rest,
Nor take in griefe the cherefull sunne so slowly fall to west.
And whiles I cast long running nightes, how best I might begile,
10 No distaff should my widowish hand have weary made the while.
When dread I not more daungers great then are befall in dede:
Love is a carefull thing God wot, and passing full of drede.

[226] *The lover asketh pardon of his passed*
follie in love.

You that in play peruse my plaint, and reade in rime the smart,
Which in my youth with sighes full cold I harbourd in my hart,
Know ye that love in that fraile age, drave me to that distresse,
When I was halfe an other man, then I am now to gesse.
5   Then for this worke of wavering words where I now rage now rew
Tost in the toyes of troublous love, as care or comfort grew.
I trust with you that loves affaires by proofe have put in ure:
Not onely pardon in my plaint, but pitie to procure.
For now I wot that in the world a wonder have I be,
10   And where to long love made me blinde, to late shame makes me see.
Thus of my fault shame is the fruite, and for my youth thus past,
Repentance is my recompence, and this I learne at last.
Looke what the world hath most in price, as sure it is to kepe,
As is the dreame which fansie drives, while sence and reason slepe.

[227] *The lover sheweth that he was striken*
by love on good friday.

It was the day on which the sunne deprived of his light,
To rew Christs death amid his course gave place unto the night
When I amid mine ease did fall to such distemperate fits,
That for the face that hath my hart I was bereft my wits.
5   I had the bayte, the hooke and all, and wist not loves pretence,
But farde as one that fearde none yll, nor forst for no defence.
Thus dwelling in most quiet state, I fell into this plight,
And that day gan my secret sighes, when all folke wept in sight.
For love that vewed me voide of care, approcht to take his pray.
10   And stept by stelth from eye to hart, so open lay the way.
And straight at eyes brake out in teares, so salt that did declare,
By token of their bitter taste that they were forgde of care.
Now vaunt thee love which fleest a maid defenst with vertues rare,
And wounded hast a wight unwise, unweaponed and unware.

[228] *The lover describeth his whole state unto his*
love, and promising her his faith-
full good will: assureth him-
self of hers again.

The Sunne when he hath spred his raies,
And shewde his face ten thousand waies.
Ten thousand thinges do then begin,
To shew the life that they are in.
5 The heaven shewes lively art and hue,
Of sundry shapes and colours new,
And laughes upon the earth anone.
The earth as cold as any stone,
Wet in the teares of her own kinde:
10 Gins then to take a joyfull minde.
For well she feeles that out and out,
The sunne doth warme her round about.
And dries her children tenderly,
And shewes them forth full orderly.
15 The moutaines hye and how they stand,
The valies and the great maine land
The trees, the herbes, the towers strong,
The castels and the rivers long.
And even for joy thus of this heate,
20 She sheweth furth her pleasures great.
And sleepes no more but sendeth forth
Her clergions her own dere worth.
To mount and flye up to the ayre,
Where then they sing in order fayre.
25 And tell in song full merely,
How they have slept full quietly,
That night about their mothers sides.
And when they have song more besides,
Then fall they to their mothers breastes,
30 Where els they fede or take their restes.
The hunter then soundes out his horne,
And rangeth straite through wood and corne.
On hilles then shew the Ewe and Lambe,
And every yong one with his dambe.
35 Then lovers walke and tell their tale,
Both of their blisse and of their bale.
And how they serve, and how they do,

And how their lady loves them to.
Then tune the birdes their armonie.
40 Then flocke the foule in companie.
Then every thing doth pleasure finde,
In that that comfortes all their kinde.
No dreames do drench them of the night,
Of foes that would them slea or bite.
45 As Houndes to hunt them at the taile,
Or men force them through hill and dale.
The shepe then dreames not of the Woulf,
The shipman forces not the goulf.
The Lambe thinkes not the butchers knife,
50 Should then bereve him of his life.
For when the Sunne doth once run in,
Then all their gladnes doth begin.
And then their skips, and then their play
So falles their sadnes then a way.
55 And thus all thinges have comforting,
In that that doth them comfort bring.
Save I alas, whom neither sunne,
Nor ought that God hath wrought and don,
May comfort ought, as though I were
60 A thing not made for comfort here.
For beyng absent from your sighte,
Which are my joy and whole delight
My comfort and my pleasure to,
How can I joy how should I do?
65 May sick men laugh that rore for paine?
Joy they in song that do complaine?
Are martirs in their tormentes glad?
Do pleasures please them that are mad?
Then how may I in comfort be,
70 That lacke the thing should comfort me?
The blind-man oft that lackes his sight,
Complaines not most the lacke of light.
But those that knewe their perfectnes,
And then do misse ther blisfulnes,
75 In martirs tunes they syng and waile,
The want of that which doth them faile.
And hereof comes that in my braines,
So many fansies worke my paines
For when I wayghe your worthynes,

80 Your wisdome and your gentlnes,
Your vertues and your sundry grace,
And minde the countenaunce of your face,
And how that you are she alone,
To whom I must both plaine and mone.
85 Whom I do love and must do still.
Whom I embrace and ay so wil,
To serve and please you as I can,
As may a wofull faithful man.
And finde my selfe so far you fro.
90 God knowes what torment, and what wo,
My rufull hart doth then imbrace.
The blood then chaungeth in my face.
My synnewes dull, in dompes I stand.
No life I fele in fote nor hand.
95 As pale as any clout and ded,
Lo sodenly the blood orespred,
And gon againe it nill so bide.
And thus from life to death I slide
As colde sometymes as any stone,
100 And then againe as hote anone.
Thus comes and goes my sundry fits,
To geve me sundri sortes of wits.
Till that a sigh becomes my frende,
And then to all this wo doth ende.
105 And sure I thinke that sigh doth roon,
From me to you where ay you woon.
For well I finde it easeth me,
And certes much it pleaseth me,
To think that it doth come to you,
110 As would to God it could so do.
For then I know you would soone finde,
By sent and favour of the winde,
That even a martirs sigh it is,
Whose joy you are and all his blis.
115 His comfort and his pleasure eke,
And even the same that he doth seke.
The same that he doth wishe and crave,
The same that he doth trust to have.
To tender you in all he may,
120 And all your likinges to obey,
As farre as in his powre shall lye:
Till death shall darte him for to dye.

But wealeaway mine owne most best,
My joy, my comfort, and my rest.
125 The causer of my wo and smart,
And yet the pleaser of my hart.
And she that on the earth above:
Is even the worthiest for to love.
Heare now my plaint, heare now my wo.
130 Heare now his paine that loves you so.
And if your hart do pitie beare,
Pitie the cause that you shall heare.
A dolefull foe in all this doubt,
Who leaves me not but sekes me out,
135 Of wretched forme and lothsome face,
While I stand in this wofull case:
Comes forth and takes me by the hand,
And saies frende harke and understand.
I see well by thy port and chere,
140 And by thy lokes and thy manere,
And by thy sadnes as thou goest,
And by the sighes that thou outthrowest:
That thou art stuffed full of wo,
The cause I thinke I do well know.
145 A fantaser thou art of some,
By whom thy wits are overcome.
But hast thou red old pamphlets ought?
Or hast thou known how bokes have taught
That love doth use to such as thow,
150 When they do thinke them safe enow
And certain of their ladies grace?
Hast thou not sene oft times the case,
That sodenly there hap hath turnde,
As thinges in flame consumde and burnde?
155 Some by disceite forsaken right.
Some likwise changed of fansy light.
And some by absence sone forgot.
The lottes in love. Why knowest thou not?
And tho that she be now thine own:
160 And knowes the well as may be knowne.
And thinkes the to be such a one,
As she likes best to be her own.
Thinkes thou that others have not grace,
To shew and plain their wofull case.

165 And chose her for their lady now,
     And swere her trouth as well as thow.
     And what if she do alter minde?
     Where is the love that thou wouldest finde?
     Absence my frende workes wonders oft.
170 Now bringes full low that lay full loft.
     Now turnes the minde now to and fro,
     And where art thou if it were so?
     If absence (quod I) be marveilous,
     I finde her not so dangerous.
175 For she may not remove me fro,
     The poore good will that I do owe
     To her, whom unneth I love and shall,
     And chosen have above them all,
     To serve and be her own as far,
180 As any man may offer her.
     And will her serve, and will her love,
     As lowly as it shall behove.
     And dye her own if fate be so.
     Thus shall my hart nay part her fro.
185 And witnes shall my good will be,
     That absence takes her not from me.
     But that my love doth still encrease,
     To minde her still and never cease.
     And what I feele to be in me,
190 The same good will I think hath she.
     As firme and fast to biden ay,
     Till death depart us both away.
     And as I have my tale thus rold,
     Steps unto me with countenance bold:
195 A stedfast frende a counsellour,
     And namde is Hope my comfortour.
     And stoutly then he speakes and saies:
     Thou hast sayde trouth withouten nayes.
     For I assure thee even by othe,
200 And theron take my hand and trothe.
     That she is one of the worthiest,
     The truest and the faithfullest,
     The gentlest and the meekest of minde:
     That here on earth a man may finde,
205 And if that love and trouth were gone,
     In her it might be found alone.

For in her minde no thought there is,
But how she may be true iwis.
And tenders thee and all thy heale,
210   And wisheth both thy health and weale.
And loves thee even as farforth than,
As any woman may a man,
And is thine own and so she saies,
And cares for thee ten thousand waies.
215   On thee she speakes, on thee she thinkes,
With thee she eates, with thee she drinkes.
With thee she talkes, with thee she mones,
With thee she sighes, with thee she grones.
With thee she saies farewell mine own.
220   When thou God knowes full farre art gon.
And even to tell thee all aright,
To thee she saies full oft good night.
And names thee oft, her owne most dere,
Her comfort weale and al her chere.
225   And telles her pelow al the tale,
How thou hast doon her wo and bale,
And how she longes and plaines for the,
And saies why art thou so from me?
Am I not she that loves the best?
230   Do I not wish thine ease and rest?
Seke I not how I may the please?
Why art thou then so from thine ease?
If I be she for whom thou carest,
For whom in tormentes so thou farest:
235   Alas thou knowest to finde me here,
Where I remaine thine owne most dere,
Thine own most true thine owne most just,
Thine own that loves the styl and must.
Thine own that cares alone for the,
240   As thou I thinke dost care for me.
And even the woman she alone,
That is full bent to be thine owne.
What wilt thou more? what canst thou crave?
Since she is as thou wouldest her have.
245   Then set this drivell out of dore,
That in thy braines such tales doth poore.
Of absence and of chaunges straunge,
Send him to those that use to chaunge.

For she is none I the avowe,
250 And well thou maiest beleve me now.
When hope hath thus his reason said,
Lord how I fele me well apaide.
A new blood then orespredes my bones,
That al in ioy I stand at ones.
255 My handes I throw to heven above,
And humbly thank the god of love.
That of his grace I should bestow,
My love so well as I it owe.
And al the planets as they stand,
260 I thanke them to with hart and hand.
That their aspectes so frendly were,
That I should so my good will bere.
To you that are the worthiest,
The fairest and the gentillest.
265 And best can say, and best can do,
That longes me thinkes a woman to.
And therfore are most worthy far,
To be beloved as you ar.
And so saies hope in all his tale,
270 Wherby he easeth all my bale.
For I beleve and thinke it true,
That he doth speake or say of you.
And thus contented lo I stand,
With that that hope beares me in hand:
275 That I am yours and shall so be,
Which hope I kepe full sure in me.
As he that all my comfort is,
On you alone which are my blis.
My pleasure chief which most I finde,
280 And even the whole joy of my minde.
And shall so be untill the death,
Shall make me yeld up life and breath.
Thus good mine own, lo here my trust.
Lo here my truth and service just.
285 Lo in what case for you I stand.
Lo how you have me in your hand.
And if you can requite a man,
Requite me as you finde me than.

[229] *Of the troubled comon welth re-*
stored to quiet by the mighty
power of god.

The secret flame that made all Troy so hot,
Long did it lurke within the wooden horse.
The machine huge Troyans suspected not,
The guiles of Grekes, nor of their hidden force:
5 Till in their beds their armed foes them met,
And slew them there, and Troy on fire set.
    Then rose the rore of treason round about,
And children could of treason call and cry.
Wives wroung their hands, the hole fired town through out,
10 When that they saw their husbands slain them by.
And to the Gods and to the skies they shright,
Vengeance to take for treason of that night.
    Then was the name of Sinon spred and blowne,
And wherunto his filed tale did tend.
15 The secret startes and metinges then were knowne,
Of Troyan traitours tending to this end.
And every man could say as in that case:
Treason in Anthenor and Eneas.
    But all to long such wisdome was in store,
20 To late came out the name of traytour than,
When that their king the aultar lay before
Slain there alas, that worthy noble man.
Ilium on flame, the matrons crying out,
And all the stretes in streames of blood about.
25   But such was fate, or such was simple trust,
That king and all should thus to ruine roon,
For if our stories certein be and just:
There were that saw such mischief should be doon
And warning gave which compted were in sort,
30 As sad devines in matter but of sport.
    Such was the time and so in state it stoode,
Troy trembled not so careles were the men.
They brake the wals, they toke this hors for good,
They demed Grekes gone, they thought al surety then.
35 When treason start and set the town on fire,
And stroied Trojans and gave Grekes their desire.
    Like to our time, wherin hath broken out,
The hidden harme that we suspected least.
Wombed within our walles and realme about,

40 As Grekes in Troy were in the Grekish beast.
   Whose tempest great of harmes and of armes,
   We thought not on, till it did noyse our harmes.
       Then felt we well the piller of our welth,
   How sore it shoke, then saw we even at hand,
45 Ruin how she rusht to confound our helth,
   Our realme and us with force of mighty band.
   And then we heard how treason loud did rore:
   Mine is the rule, and raigne I will therefore.
       Of treason marke the nature and the kinde,
50 A face it beares of all humilitie.
   Truth is the cloke, and frendship of the minde,
   And depe it goes, and worketh secretly,
   Like to a mine that creepes so nye the wall,
   Till out breakes sulphure, and oreturneth all.
55   But he on hye that secretly beholdes
   The state of thinges: and times hath in his hand,
   And pluckes in plages, and them againe unfoldes,
   And hath apointed realmes to fall and stand:
   He in the midst of all this sturre and rout,
60 Gan bend his browes, and move him self about.
       As who should say, and are ye minded so?
   And thus to those, and whom you know I love.
   Am I such one as none of you do know?
   Or know ye not that I sit here above,
65 And in my handes do hold your welth and wo,
   To raise you now, and now to overthrow?
       Then thinke that I, as I have set you all,
   In places where your honours lay and fame:
   So now my selfe shall give you eche your fall,
70 Where eche of you shall have your worthy shame:
   And in their handes I will your fall shalbe,
   Whose fall in yours you sought so sore to see.
       Whose wisdome hye as he the same foresaw,
   So is it wrought, such lo his justice is.
75 He is the Lord of man and of his law,
   Praise therfore now his mighty name in this,
   And make accompt that this our case doth stand:
   As Israell free, from wicked Pharaos hand.

[230] *The lover to his love: having for-*
saken him, and betaken her
self to an other.

The bird that somtime built within my brest,
And there as then chief succour did receive:
Hath now els where built her another nest,
And of the old hath taken quite her leave.
5   To you mine oste that harbour mine old guest,
Of such a one, as I can now conceive,
Sith that in change her choise doth chiefe consist,
The hauke may check, that now comes fair to fist.

[231] *The lover sheweth that in dis-*
sembling his love openly
he kepeth secret his
secret good will.

Not like a God came Jupiter to woo,
When he the faire Europa sought unto.
In other forme his godly wisdome toke,
Such in effect as writeth Ovides boke.
5   As on the earth no living wight can tell:
That mighty Jove did love the quene so well.
For had he come in golden garmentes bright,
Or so as men mought have starde on the sight:
Spred had it bene both through earth and ayre,
10   That Jove had loved the lady Europa fayre.
And then had some bene angry at the hart,
And some againe as jelous for their part.
Both which to stop, this gentle god toke minde,
To shape him selfe into a brutish kinde.
15   To such a kinde as hid what state he was,
And yet did bring him what he sought to passe.
To both their joyes, to both their comfort soon,
Though knowen to none, til al the thing was don.
In which attempt if I the like assay,
20   To you to whom I do my selfe bewray:
Let it suffice that I do seke to be,
Not counted yours, and yet for to be he.

[232] *The lover disceived by his love*
repenteth him of the true
love he bare her.

   I that Ulysses yeres have spent,
To finde Penelope:
Finde well that folly I have ment,
To seke that was not so.
5 Since Troylous case hath caused me,
From Cressed for to go.
   And to bewaile Ulysses truth,
In seas and stormy skies,
Of wanton will and raging youth,
10 Which me have tossed sore:
From Scilla to Caribdis clives,
Upon the drowning shore.
   Where I sought haven, there found I hap,
From daunger unto death:
15 Much like the Mouse that treades the trap,
In hope to finde her foode,
And bites the bread that stops her breath,
So in like case I stoode.
   Till now repentance hasteth him
20 To further me to so fast:
That where I sanke, there now I swim,
And have both streame and winde:
And lucke as good if it may last,
As any man may finde.
25   That where I perished, safe I passe,
And finde no perill there:
But stedy stone, no ground of glasse,
Now am I sure to save,
And not to flete from feare to feare,
30 Such anker hold I have.

[233] *The lover having enjoyed his love, humbly*
thanketh the god of love: and avowing
his hart onely to her faithfully
promiseth utterly to for-
sake all other.

Thou Cupide God of love, whom Venus thralles do serve,
I yeld thee thankes upon my knees, as thou dost well deserve.
By thee my wished joyes have shaken of despaire,
And all my storming dayes be past, and weather waxeth faire.
5 By thee I have received a thousand times more joy,
Then ever Paris did possesse, when Helen was in Troy.
By thee have I that hope, for which I longde so sore,
And when I thinke upon the same, my hart doth leap therefore.
By thee my heapy doubtes and trembling feares are fled,
10 And now my wits that troubled wer, with plesant thoughts are fed.
For dread is banisht cleane, wherein I stoode full oft,
And doubt to speake that lay full low, is lifted now aloft.
With armes bespred abrode, with opende handes and hart,
I have enjoyed the fruite of hope, reward for all my smart.
15 The seale and signe of love, the key of trouth and trust,
The pledge of pure good will have I, which makes the lovers just:
Such grace sins I have found, to one I me betake,
The rest of Venus derlinges all, I utterly forsake.
And to performe this vow, I bid mine eyes beware,
20 That they no straungers do salute, nor on their beauties stare.
My wits I warn ye all from this time forth take hede,
That ye no wanton toyes devise my fansies new to fede.
Mine eares be ye shet up, and heare no womans voyce,
That may procure me once to smile, or make my hart rejoyce.
25 My fete full slow be ye and lame when ye should move,
To bring my body any where to seke an other love,
Let all the Gods above, and wicked sprites below,
And every wight in earth acuse and curse me where I go:
If I do false my faith in any point or case,
30 A sodein vengeance fall on me, I aske no better grace.
Away then sily rime, present mine earnest faith,
Unto my lady where she is, and marke thou what she saith.
And if she welcome thee, and lay thee in her lap,
Spring thou for joy, thy master hath his most desired hap.

[234] *Totus mundus in maligno*
positus.

Complaine we may: much is amisse:
Hope is nye gone to have redresse:
These daies ben ill, nothing sure is:
Kinde hart is wrapt in heavinesse.
5   The sterne is broke: the saile is rent:
The ship is geven to winde and wave:
All helpe is gone: the rocke present
That will be lost, what man can save?
    Thinges hard, therefore are now refused.
10 Labour in youth is thought but vaine:
Duty by (will not) is excused.
Remove the stop the way is plaine.
    Learning is lewd, and held a foole:
Wisdome is shent, counted to raile:
15 Reason is banisht out of schoole:
The blinde is bold, and wordes prevaile.
    Power, without care, slepeth at ease:
Will, without law, runth where he list:
Might without mercy can not please,
20 A wise man saith not, had I wist.
    When power lackes care and forceth not:
When care is feable and may not:
When might is slouthfull and will not:
Wedes may grow where good herbes cannot.
25   Take wrong away, law nedeth not:
For law to wrong is bridle and paine.
Take feare away, law booteth not.
To strive gainst streame, it is but vaine.
    Wyly is witty: brainsicke is wise:
30 Trouth is folly: and might is right:
Wordes are reason: and reason is lies:
The bad is good: darknesse is light.
    Wrong to redresse, wisdome dare not.
Hardy is happy, and ruleth most.
35 Wilfull is witlesse, and careth not,
Which end go first, till all be lost.
    Few right do love, and wrong refuse.
Pleasure is sought in every state.
Liking is lust: there is no chuse.
40 The low geve to the hye checke mate.

Order is broke in thinges of weight.
Measure and meane who doth not flee?
Two thinges prevaile: money, and sleight.
To seme is better then to be.
45   The bowle is round, and doth downe slide,
Eche one thrusteth: none doth uphold.
A fall failes not, where blinde is guide.
The stay is gone: who can him hold?
    Folly and falshed prayeth apace.
50   Trouth under bushell is faine to crepe.
Flattry is treble, pride singes the bace.
The meane the best part scant doth pepe.
    This firy plage the world infectes.
To vertue and trouth it geves no rest:
55   Mens harts are burnde with sundry sectes,
And to echeman his way is best.
    With floods and stormes thus be we tost,
Awake good Lord, to thee we crye.
Our ship is almost sonk and lost.
60   Thy mercy help our miserye.
    Mans strength is weake: mans wit is dull:
Mans reason is blinde. These thinges tamend,
Thy hand (O Lord) of might is full,
Awake betime, and helpe us fend.
65   In thee we trust, and in no wight:
Save us as chickens under the hen.
Our crokednesse thou canst make right,
Glory to thee for aye. Amen.

[235] *The wise trade of*
lyfe.

Do all your dedes by good advise,
Cast in your minde alwaies the end.
Wit bought is of to dere a price.
The tried, trust, and take as frend,
5   For frendes I finde there be but two:
Of countenance, and of effect.
Of thone sort there are inow:
But few ben of the tother sect.
Beware also the venym swete
10   Of crafty wordes and flattery.
For to deceive they be most mete,

That best can play hypocrisy.
Let wisdome rule your dede and thought:
So shall your workes be wisely wrought.

[236] *That few wordes shew wisdome,*
and work much quiet.

Who list to lead a quiet life,
Who list to rid him self from strife:
Geve eare to me, marke what I say,
Remember wel, beare it away.
5　Holde backe thy tong at meat and meale,
Speake but few wordes, bestrow them well.
By wordes the wise thou shalt espye,
By wordes a foole sone shalt thou trye.
A wise man can his tong make cease,
10　A foole can never holde his peace,
Who loveth rest of wordes beware.
Who loveth wordes, is sure of care.
For wordes oft many have ben shent:
For silence kept none hath repent.
15　Two eares, one tong onely thou hast,
Mo thinges to heare then wordes to wast.
A foole in no wise can forbeare:
He hath two tonges and but one eare.
Be sure thou kepe a stedfast braine,
20　Lest that thy wordes put thee to paine.
Words wisely set are worth much gold:
The price of rashnesse is sone told.
If time require wordes to be had,
To hold thy peace I count thee mad.
25　Talke onely of nedefull verities:
Strive not for trifling fantasies.
With sobernesse the truth boult out,
Affirme nothing wherin is dout.
Who to this lore will take good hede,
03　And spend no mo words then he nede,
Though he be a fole and have no braine,
Yet shall he a name of wisdome gaine.
Speake while time is or hold thee still.
Words out of time do oft things spyll.
35　Say well and do well are thinges twaine,
Twise blest is he in whom both raigne.

[237] *The complaint of a hot woer,*
delayed with doutfull
cold answers.

A kinde of coale is as men say,
    Which have assaied the same:
That in the fire will wast away,
    And outward cast no flame.
5 Unto my self may I compare,
    These coales that so consume:
Where nought is sene though men do stare,
    In stede of flame but fume.
They say also to make them burne,
10   Cold water must be cast:
Or els to ashes will they turne,
    And half to sinder wast.
As this is wonder for to se,
    Cold water warme the fire,
15 So hath your coldnesse caused me,
    To burne in my desire.
And as this water cold of kinde,
    Can cause both heat and cold,
And can these coales both breake and binde,
20   To burne as I have told.
So can your tong of frosen yse,
    From whence cold answers come:
Both coole the fire and fire entice,
    To burne me all and some.
25 Like to the corne that standes on stake,
    Which mowen in winter sunne:
Full faire without, within is black:
    Such heat therin doth runne.
By force of fire this water cold,
30   Hath bred to burne within,
Even so am I, that heat doth hold,
    Which cold did first begyn.
Which heat is stint when I do strive,
    To have some ease sometime:
35 But flame a fresh I do revive,
    Wherby I cause to clime.
In stede of smoke a sighing breath:
    With sparkes of sprinkled teares,
That I should live this livyng death,
40   Which wastes and never weares.

[238] *The answer.*

Your borrowd meane to move your mone, of fume withouten flame
Being set from smithy smokyng coale: ye seme so by the same.
To shew, what such coales use is taught by such as have assayd,
As I, that most do wish you well, am so right well apayd.
5 That you have such a lesson learnd, how either to maintaine,
Your fredome of unkindled coale, upheaped all in vaine:
Or how most frutefully to frame, with worthy workmans art,
That cunnyng pece may passe there fro, by help of heated hart.
Out of the forge wherin the fume of sighes doth mount aloft,
10 That argues present force of fire to make the metall soft,
To yelde unto the hammer hed, as best the workman likes,
That thiron glowyng after blast in time and temper strikes.
Wherin the use of water is, as you do seme to say,
To quenche no flame, ne hinder heat, ne yet to wast away:
15 But, that which better is for you, and more deliteth me,
To save you from the sodain waste, vaine cinderlike to be.
Which lastyng better likes in love, as you your semble ply,
Then doth the baven blase, that flames and fleteth by and by.
Sith then you know eche use, wherin your coale may be applide:
20 Either to lie and last on hoord, in open ayre to bide,
Withouten use to gather fat by fallyng of the raines,
That makes the pitchy jucye to grow, by sokyng in his veines,
Or lye on fornace in the forge, as is his use of right,
Wherin the water trough may serve, and enteryeld her might
25 By worke of smithes both hand and hed a cunnyng key to make,
Or other pece as cause shall crave and bid him undertake:
Do as you deme most fit to do, and wherupon may grow,
Such joy to you, as I may joy your joyfull ease to know.

[239] *An epitaph made by W. G. lying*
on his death bed, to be set upon
his owne tombe.

Lo here lieth G. under the ground,
    Among the gredy wormes,
Which in his life time never found
    But strife and sturdy stormes.
5 And namely through a wicked wife,
    As to the world apperes:
She was the shortnyng of his life
    By many dayes and yeres.

He might have lived long, god wot:
10   His yeres, they were but yong:
Of wicked wives this is the lot,
        To kill with spitefull tong.
Whose memory shall still remayne
        In writing here with me,
15   That men may know whom she hath slaine,
        And say this same is she.

[240] *An answer*

If that thy wicked wife had spon the thread,
        And were the weaver of thy wo:
Then art thou double happy to be dead,
        As happely dispatched so.
5   If rage did causelesse cause thee to complayne,
        And mad moode mover of thy mone:
If frensy forced on thy testy braine:
        Then blist is she to live alone.
So, whether were the ground of others grefe,
10   Because so doutfull was the dome:
Now death hath brought your payne a right relefe,
        And blessed be ye both become:
She, that she lives no longer bound to beare
        The rule of such a froward hed:
15   Thou, that thou livest no lenger faine to feare
        The restlesse ramp that thou hadst wed,
Be thou as glad therfore that thou art gone,
        As she is glad she doth abide:
For so ye be a sonder, all is one:
20   A badder match can not betide.

[241] *An epitaph of maister Henry*
williams.

From worldly wo the mede of misbelefe,
From cause of care that leadeth to lament,
From vaine delight the ground of greater grefe,
From feare for frendes, from matter to repent,
5   From painefull pangs last sorowe that is sent,
From dred of death sith death doth set us free:
With it the better pleased should we be.

This lothsome life where likyng we do finde,
Thencreaser of our crimes, doth us bereve
10 Our blisse that alway ought to be in minde.
This wily world whiles here we breath alive,
And flesh our fayned fo, do stifly strive
To flatter us, assuryng here the joy,
Where we, alas, do finde but great annoy.
15   Untolde heapes though we have of worldly wealth,
Though we possesse the sea and frutefull ground,
Strength, beauty, knowledge, and unharmed health,
Though at a wish all pleasure do abound.
It were but vaine, no frendship can be found,
20 When death assalteth with his dredfull dart.
No raunsome can stay the home hastyng hart.
    And sith thou has cut the lives line in twaine,
Of Henry, sonne to sir John Williams knight,
Whose manly hart and prowes none could staine,
25 Whose godly life to vertue was our light,
Whose worthy fame shall florish long by right.
Though in this life so cruell mightest thou be,
His spirite in heaven shall triumph over thee.

[242] *An other of the same.*

Stay gentle frend that passest by,
And learne the lore that leadeth all:
From whence we come with hast to hye,
To live to dye, and stand to fall.
5   And learne that strength and lusty age,
That wealth and want of worldly woe,
Can not withstand the mighty rage,
Of death our best unwelcome foe.
    For hopefull youth had hight me health,
10 My lust to last till time to dye,
And fortune found my vertue wealth:
But yet for all that here I lye.
    Learne also this, to ease thy minde:
When death on corps hath wrought his spite,
15 A time of triumph shalt thou finde,
With me to scorne him in delight.
    For one day shall we mete againe,

Maugre deathes dart in life to dwell.
Then will I thanke thee for thy paine,
20   Now marke my wordes and fare thou well.

[243] *Against women, either good*
or bad.

A man may live thrise Nestors life,
Thrise wander out Ulisses race:
Yet never finde Ulisses wife.
Such change hath chanced in this case.
5   Lesse age will serve than Paris had,
Small pein (if none be small inough)
To finde good store of Helenes trade.
Such sap the rote doth yelde the bough.
For one good wife Ulisses slew
10   A worthy knot of gentle blood:
For one yll wife Grece overthrew
The towne of Troy: Sith bad and good
Bring mischief: Lord let be thy will,
To kepe me free from either yll.

[244] *An answer.*

The vertue of Ulisses wife
Doth live, though she hath ceast her race,
And farre surmountes old Nestors life:
But now in moe than then it was.
5   Such change is chanced in this case.
Ladies now live in other trade:
Farre other Helenes now we see,
Than she whom Troyan Paris had.
As vertue fedes the roote, so be
10   The sap and rote of bough and tre.
Ulisses rage, not his good wife,
Spilt gentle blood. Not Helenes face,
But Paris eye did raise the strife,
That did the Troyan buildyng race.
15   Thus sith ne good, ne bad do yll:
Them all, O Lord, maintain my wyll,
To serve with all my force and skill.

[245] *Against a gentilwoman by whom*
he was refused.

To false report and flying fame,
Whilist my minde gave credit light,
Belevyng that her bolstred name
Had stuffe to shew that praise did hight.
5 I finde well now I did mistake,
Upon report my ground to make.
    I heard it said such one was she,
As rare to finde as parragon,
Of lowly chere, of hart so free,
10 As her for bounty could passe none.
Such one were faire though forme and face,
Were meane to passe in second place.
    I sought it neare, and thinkyng to finde
Report and dede both to agree:
15 But chaunge had tried her suttle minde:
Of force I was enforced to see,
That she in dede was nothing so:
Which made my will my hart forgo.
    For she is such, as geason none.
20 And what she most may boast to be:
I finde her matches mo then one,
What nede she so to deale with me?
Ha fleryng face, with scornefull hart,
So yll reward for good desert?
25   I will repent that I have done.
To ende so well the losse is small:
I lost her love, that lesse hath won,
To vaunt she had me as her thrall.
What though a gillot sent that note,
30 Bye cocke and pye I meant it not.

[246] *The answere.*

Whom fansy forced first to love,
Now frensy forceth for to hate:
Whose minde erst madnesse gan to move,
Inconstance causeth to abate.
5 No minde of meane, but heat of braine
Bred light love: like heate, hate againe.

What hurld your hart in so great heat?
Fansy forced by fayned fame.
Belike that she was light to get.
10   For if that vertue and good name
Moved your minde, why changed your will,
Sithe vertue the cause abideth still.
    Such, Fame reported her to be
As rare it were to finde her peere,
15   For vertue and for honestie,
For her free hart and lowly cheere.
This laud had lied if you had sped,
And fame bene false that hath ben spred.
    Sith she hath so kept her good name.
20   Such praise of life and giftes of grace,
As brute self blusheth for to blame,
Such fame as fame feares to deface:
You sclaunder not but make it plaine,
That you blame brute of brutish traine.
25   If you have found it looking neere,
Not as you toke the brute to be.
Bylike you ment by lowly cheere,
Bountie and hart that you call free,
But lewd lightnesse easy to frame,
30   To winne your will against her name.
    Nay she may deme your deming so,
A marke of madnesse in his kinde,
Such causeth not good name to go:
As your fond folly sought to finde.
35   For brute of kinde bent ill to blase,
Alway sayth ill, but forced by cause.
    The mo there be, such as is she,
More should be gods thank for his grace.
The more is her joy it to see.
40   Good should by geason, earne no place,
Nor nomber make nought, that is good.
Your strange lusting hed wants a hoode.
    Her dealing greveth you (say ye)
Byside your labour lost in vaine.
45   Her dealing was not as we see,
Sclaunder the end of your great paine,
Ha lewd lieng lips, and hatefull hart,
What canst thou desire in such desart?
    Ye will repent, and right for done.

50 Ye have a dede deserving shame.
From reasons race farre have ye ronne.
Hold your rayling, kepe your tong tame.
Her love, ye lye, ye lost it not.
Ye never lost that ye never got.
55   She reft ye not your libertie,
She vaunteth not she had your thrall.
If ought have done it, let it lye,
On rage that reft you wit and all.
What though a varlets tale you tell:
60 By cock and pye you do it well.

[247] *The lover dredding to move his sute*
for dout of deniall, accuseth
all women of disdaine
and fickle-
nesse.

To walke on doutfull ground, where daunger is unsene,
Doth double men that carelesse be in depe dispaire I wene.
For as the blinde doth feare, what footing he shall finde:
So doth the wise before he speake, mistrust the straungers minde.
5 For he that blontly runnes, may light among the breers,
And so be put unto his plunge where danger least apperes:
The bird that selly foole, doth warne us to beware,
Who lighteth not on every bush, he dreadeth so the snare.
The Mouse that shons the trap, doth shew what harme doth lye:
10 Within the swete betraying bait, that oft disceives the eye.
The fish avoydes the hooke, though hunger bids him bite,
And hovereth still about the worme, whereon is his delite.
If birdes and beastes can see, where their undoing lies:
How should a mischief scape our heades, that have both wit and eyes?
15 What madnesse may be more, then plow the barreyn fielde:
Or any frutefull wordes to sow, to eares that are unwild.
They heare and than mislike, they like and then they lothe,
They hate, thei love, thei scorn, thei praise, yea sure thei can do both.
We see what falles they have, that clime on trees unknowne:
20 As they that trust to rotten bowes, must nedes be overthrowne.
A smart in silence kept, doth ease the hart much more,
Than for to playn where is no salve, for to recure the sore.
Wherfore my grief I hide, within a holow hart:
Untill the smoke thereof be spred, by flaming of the smart.

[248] *An answere.*

To trust the fayned face, to rue on forced teares,
To credit finely forged tales, wherin there oft appeares
   And breathes as from the brest a smoke of kindled smart,
Where onely lurkes a depe deceit within the hollow hart,
5   Betrayes the simple soule, whom plaine deceitlesse minde
Taught not to feare that in it selfe, it selfe did never finde.
   Not every trickling teare doth argue inward paine:
Not every sigh doth surely shew the sigher not to faine:
   Not every smoke doth prove a presence of the fire:
10 Not every glistring geves the gold, that gredy folke desire:
   Not every wayling word is drawen out of the depe:
Not grief for want of graunted grace enforceth all to wepe.
   Oft malice makes the minde to shed the boyled brine:
And envies humor oft unlades by conduites of the eyen.
15   Oft craft can cause the man to make a seming show,
Of hart with dolour all distreined, where grief did never grow.
   As cursed Crocodile most cruelly can tole,
With truthlesse teares, unto his death, the silly pitying soule.
   Blame never those therfore, that wisely can beware
20 The guilefull man, that sutly sayth himselfe to dread the snare.
   Blame not the stopped eares against the Syrenes song:
Blame not the minde not moved with mone of falsheds flowing tong.
   If guile do guide your wit by silence so to speake,
By craft to crave and faine by fraude the cause that you wold break.
25   Great harme your suttle soule shall suffer for the same:
And mighty love will wreke the wrong, so cloked with his name.
   But we, whom you have warnde, this lesson learne by you:
To know the tree before we clime, to trust no rotten bowe,
   To view the limed bushe, to looke afore we light,
30 To shunne the perilous bayted hooke, and use a further sight.
   As do the mouse, the birde, the fish, by sample fitly show,
That wily wits and ginnes of men do worke the simples wo:
   So, simple sithe we are, and you so suttle be,
God help the Mouse, the birde, the fish, and us your sleightes to fle.

[249] *The lover complaineth his fault, that*
with ungentle writing had dis-
pleased his lady.

Ah love how waiward is his wit what panges do perce his brest
Whom thou to wait upon thy will hast reved of his rest.
The light, the darke, the sunne, the mone, the day and eke the night,
His dayly dieng life, him self, he hateth in despight,
5 Sith furst he light to looke on her that holdeth him in thrall,
His moving eyen his moved wit he curseth hart and all,
From hungry hope to pining feare eche hap doth hurle his hart,
From panges of plaint to fits of fume from aking into smart.
Eche moment so doth change his chere not with recourse of ease,
10 But with sere sortes of sorrowes still he worketh as the seas.
That turning windes not calme returnde rule in unruly wise,
As if their holdes of hilles uphurld they brasten out to rise.
And puffe away the power that is unto their king assignde
To pay that sithe their prisonment they deme to be behinde.
15 So doth the passions long represt within the wofull wight,
Breake downe the banks of all his wits and out they gushen quite.
To rere up rores now they be free from reasons rule and stay,
And hedlong hales thunruled race his quiet quite away.
No measure hath he of his ruth, no reason in his rage,
20 No bottom ground where stayes his grief, thus weares away his age
In wishing wants, in wayling woes. Death doth he dayly call,
To bring release when of relief he seeth no hope at all.
Thence comes that oft in depe despeire to rise to better state,
On heaven and heavenly lampes he layeth the faute of al his fate.
25 On God and Gods decreed dome cryeth out with cursing breath,
Eche thing that gave and saves him life he damneth of his death.
The wombe him bare, the brests he suckt, ech star that with their might,
Their secret succour brought to bring the wretch to worldly light.
Yea that to his soules perile is most haynous harme of all,
30 And craves the cruellest revenge that may to man befall:
Her he blasphemes in whom it lieth in present as she please,
To dampne him downe to depth of hell, or plant in heavens ease.
Such rage constrainde my strained hart to guide thunhappy hand
That sent unfitting blots to her on whom my life doth stand.
35 But graunt O God that he for them may beare the worthy blame
Whom I do in my depe distresse finde guilty of the same.
Even that blinde boy that blindly guides the fautles to their fall,
That laughes when they lament that he hath throwen into thral.
Or Lord, save louring lookes of her, what penance els thou please

40 So her contented will be wonne I count it all mine ease.
And thou on whom doth hang my will, with hart, with soul and care,
With life and all that life may have of well or evell fare:
Graunt grace to him that grates therfore with sea of saltish brine
By extreme heat of boylyng brest distilled through his eyen.
45 And with thy fancy render thou my self to me againe,
That dayly then we duely may employ a painelesse paine.
To yelde and take the joyfull frutes that herty love doth lend,
To them that meane by honest meanes to come to happy end.

[250] *The lover wounded of Cupide,*
wisheth he had rather ben
striken by death.

The blinded boy that bendes the bow,
To make with dint of double wound:
The stowtest state to stoupe and know:
The cruell craft that I have found.
5   With death I would have chopt a change,
To borow as by bargain made:
Ech others shaft when he did range,
With restlesse rovyng to invade,
Thunthralled mindes of simple wightes,
10 Whose giltlesse ghostes deserved not:
To fele such fall of their delightes,
Such panges as I have past God wot.
Then both in new unwonted wise,
Should death deserve a better name,
15 Not (as tofore hath bene his guise)
Of crueltie to beare the blame.
But contrary be counted kinde,
In lendyng life and sparyng space:
For sicke to rise and seke to finde,
20 A way to wish their weary race
To draw to some desired end,
Their long and lothed life to rid.
And so to fele how like a frend,
Before the bargain made he did.
25   And love should either bring againe,
To wounded wightes their owne desire:
A welcome end of pinyng payne,
As doth their cause of ruthe require:

Or when he meanes the quiet man,
30 A harme to hasten him to grefe:
A better dede he should do then,
With borrowd dart to geve relefe.
    That both the sicke well demen may,
    He brought me rightly my request:
35 And eke the other sort may say,
    He wrought me truely for the best.
        So had not fancy forced me,
        To beare a brunt of greater wo:
        Then leaving such a life may be,
40 The ground where onely grefes do grow.
    Unlucky likyng linkt my hart,
    In forged hope and forced feare:
    That oft I wisht the other dart,
    Had rather perced me as neare.
45 A fayned trust, constrayned care,
    Most loth to lack, most hard to finde:
    In sunder so my judgement tare,
    That quite was quiet out of minde.
        Absent in absence of mine ease,
50 Present in presence of my paine:
    The woes of want did much displease,
    The sighes I sought did greve againe.
        Oft grefe that boyled in my brest,
        Hath fraught my face with saltish teares,
55 Pronouncyng proves of mine unrest,
    Whereby my passed paine appeares.
        My sighes full often have supplied,
        That faine with wordes I wold have said:
        My voice was stopt, my tong was tyed,
60 My wits with wo were overwayd.
        With tremblyng soule and humble chere,
        Oft grated I for graunt of grace:
        On hope that bounty might be there,
        Where beauty had so pight her place.
65 At length I found, that I did fere,
    How I had labourde all to losse,
    My self had ben the carpenter,
    That framed me the cruell crosse.
        Of this to come if dout alone,
70 Though blent with trust of better spede:
    So oft hath moved my minde to mone,

So oft hath made my hart to blede.
    What shall I say of it in dede,
Now hope is gone mine olde relefe:
75 And I enforced all to fede,
    Upon the frutes of bitter grefe?

[251] *Of womens changeable*
will.

I wold I found not as I fele,
Such changyng chere of womens will,
By fickle flight of fortunes whele,
By kinde or custome, never still.
5   So shold I finde no fault to lay,
On fortune for their movyng minde,
So should I know no cause to say
This change to chance by course of kinde.
    So should not love so work my wo,
10 To make death surgeant for my sore,
So should their wittes not wander so,
So should I reck the lesse therfore.

[252] *The lover complayneth the losse*
of his ladye.

No joy have I, but live in heavinesse,
My dame of price bereft by fortunes cruelnesse,
My hap is turned to unhappinesse,
Unhappy I am unlesse I finde relesse.
5   My pastime past, my youthlike yeres are gone,
My mouthes of mirth, my glistring daies of gladsomnesse:
My times of triumph turned into mone.
Unhappy I am unlesse I finde relesse.
    My wonted winde to chaunt my cherefull chaunce,
10 Doth sigh that song somtime the balades of my lesse:
My sobbes, my sore and sorow do advaunce.
Unhappy I am unlesse I finde relesse.
    I mourne my mirth for grefe that it is gone,
I mourne my mirth wherof my musing mindefulnesse:
15 Is ground of greater grefe that growes theron,
Unhappy I am unlesse I finde relesse.
    No joy have I: for fortune frowardly:

Hath bent her browes hath put her hand to cruelnesse:
Hath reft my dame, constrayned me to crye,
20 Unhappy I am unlesse I finde relesse.

[253] *Of the golden meane.*

The wisest way, thy bote, in wave and winde to guie,
As neither still the trade of middle streame to trie:
Ne (warely shunnyng wrecke by wether) aye to nie,
       To presse upon the perillous shore.
5 Both clenely flees he filthe: ne wonnes a wretched wight,
In carlish coate: and carefull court aie thrall to spite,
With port of proud astate he leves: who doth delight,
       Of golden meane to hold the lore.
Stormes rifest rende the sturdy stout pineapple tre.
10 Of lofty ruing towers the fals the feller be.
Most fers doth lightenyng light, where furthest we do se.
       The hilles the valey to forsake.
Well furnisht brest to bide eche chanses changing chear.
In woe hath chearfull hope, in weal hath warefull fear,
15 One self Jove winter makes with lothfull lokes appear,
       That can by course the same aslake.
What if into mishap thy case now casten be?
It forceth not such forme of luck to last to thee.
Not alway bent is Phebus bow: his harpe and he,
20   Ceast silver sound sometime doth raise.
In hardest hap use helpe of hardy hopefull hart.
Seme bold to beare the brunt of fortune overthwart.
Eke wisely when forewinde to full breathes on thy part,
       Swage swellyng saile, and doubt decayes.

[254] *The praise of a true*
frende.

Who so that wisely weyes the profite and the price,
Of thinges wherin delight by worth is wont to rise,
Shall finde no jewell is so rich ne yet so rare,
That with the frendly hart in value may compare.
5 What other wealth to man by fortune may befall,
But fortunes changed chere may reue a man of all.
A frend no wracke of wealth, no cruell cause of wo,
Can force his frendly faith unfrendly to forgo.

    If fortune frendly fawne, and lend thee welthy store,
10 Thy frendes conjoyned joy doth make thy joy the more.
    If frowardly she frown and drive thee to distresse,
    His ayde releves thy ruthe, and makes thy sorow lesse.
        Thus fortunes pleasant frutes by frendes encreased be,
    The bitter sharp and sowre by frendes alayde to thee.
15 That when thou doest rejoyce, then doubled is thy joy,
    And eke in cause of care, the lesse is thy anoy.
        Aloft if thou do live, as one appointed here,
    A stately part on stage of worldly state to bere:
    Thy frende as only free from fraud will thee advise,
20 To rest within the rule of mean as do the wise.
        He seeketh to foresee the peril of thy fall.
    He findeth out thy faultes and warnes thee of them all.
    Thee, not thy luck he loves, what ever be thy case,
    He is thy faithfull frend and thee he doth embrace.
25   If churlish cheare of chance have thrown thee into thrall,
    And that thy nede aske ayde for to releve thy fall:
    In him thou secret trust assured art to have,
    And succour not to seke, before that thou can crave.
        Thus is thy frende to thee the comfort of thy paine,
30 The stayer of thy state, the doubler of thy gaine.
    In wealth and wo thy frend, an other self to thee,
    Such man to man a God, the proverb sayth to be.
        As welth will bring thee frendes in louring wo to prove,
    So wo shall yeld thee frendes in laughing wealth to love.
35 With wisedome chuse thy frend, with vertue him retaine:
    Let vertue be the ground, so shall it not be vaine.

      [255] *The lover lamenteth other to have*
          the frutes of his service.

    Some men would think of right to have,
    For their true meaning some reward,
    But while that I do cry and crave:
    I see that other be preferd,
5 I gape for that I am debard.
    I fare as doth the hound at hatch:
    The worse I spede, the lenger I watch.
        My wastefull will is tried by trust:
    My fond fansie is mine abuse.
10 For that I would refraine my lust:

For mine availe I cannot chuse,
A will, and yet no power to use.
A will, no will by reason just,
Sins my will is at others lust.
15   They eate the hony, I hold the hyve.
I sow the sede, they reape the corne.
I waste, they winne, I draw they drive.
Theirs is the thanke, mine is the scorne.
I seke, they spede, in waste my winde is worne.
20 I gape, they get, and gredely I snatch:
Till wurse I spede, the lenger I watch.
    I fast, they fede: they drink, I thurst.
They laugh, I wayle: they joy, I mourne.
They gayne, I lose: I have the wurst.
25 They whole, I sicke: they cold, I burne.
They leape, I lye: they slepe, I tosse and turne.
I would, they may: I crave, they have at will.
That helpeth them, lo, cruelty doth me kill.

[256] *Of the sutteltie of crafty*
lovers.

Such waiward waies have some when folly stirres their braines
To fain and plain full oft of love, when lest they fele his paines.
And for to shew a griefe such craft have they in store,
That they can halt and lay a salve wheras they fele no sore.
5 As hound unto the foote, or dog unto the bow,
So are they made to vent her out, whom bent to love they know.
That if I should discribe one hundred of their driftes,
Two hundred wits beside mine owne, I should put to their shiftes
No woodman better knowes how for to lodge his dere,
10 Nor shipman on the sea that more hath skill to guide the stere.
Nor beaten dogge to herd can warer chose his game.
Nor scholeman to his fansie can a scholer better frame.
Then one of these which have old Ovids arte in ure,
Can seke the wayes unto their minde a woman to allure.
15 As round about a hyve the Bees do swarme alway,
So round about the house they prease wherin they seke their pray.
And whom they so besege, it is a wonderous thing,
What crafty engins to assault these wily warriers bring.
The eye as scout and watch to stirre both to and fro,
20 Doth serve to stale her here and there where she doth come and go.

The tong doth pleade for right as herauld of the hart:
And both the handes as oratours do serve to point their part.
So shewes the countenance then with these fowre to agree,
As though in witnes with the rest, it would hers sworne be.
25 But if she then mistrust it would turne blacke to white,
For that the woorrier lokes most smoth when he wold fainest bite.
Then wit as counsellour a helpe for this to finde:
Straight makes the hand as secretair forthwith to write his minde.
And so the letters straight embassadours are made,
30 To treate in haste for to procure her to a better trade.
Wherin if she do thinke all this is but a shewe,
Or but a subtile masking cloke to hide a crafty shrewe:
Then come they to the larme, then shew they in the fielde,
Then muster they in colours strange, that waies to make her yeld,
35 Then shoote they batry of, then compasse they her in,
At tilt and turney oft they strive this selly soule to win.
Then sound they on their lutes, then strain they forth their song,
Then romble they with instrumentes to lay her quite a long.
Then borde they her with giftes, then do they woo and watch,
40 Then night and day they labour hard this simple hold to catch,
As pathes within a wood, or turnes with in a mase:
So then they shew of wiles and craftes they can a thousand wayes.

[257] *Of the vanitie of mans*
lyfe.

Vaine is the fleting welth,
Whereon the world stayes:
Sithe stalking time by privy stelth,
Encrocheth on our dayes.
5   And elde which creepeth fast,
To taynte us with her wounde:
Will turne eche blysse unto a blast,
Which lasteth but a stounde.
Of youth the lusty floure,
10 Which whylome stoode in price:
Shall vanish quite within an houre,
As fire consumes the ice.
Where is become that wight,
For whose sake Troy towne:
15 Withstode the grekes till ten yeres fight,
Had rasde their walles adowne?

Did not the wormes consume,
Her caryon to the dust?
Did dreadfull death forbeare his fume
20   For beauty, pride, or lust?

[258] *The lover not regarded in ear-*
nest sute, being become wi-
ser, refuseth her profred
love.

Do way your phisike I faint no more,
The salve you sent it comes to late:
You wist well all my grief before,
And what I suffred for your sake.
5   Hole is my hart I plaine no more,
Anew the cure did undertake:
Wherfore do way you come to late.
    For whiles you knew I was your own,
So long in vaine you made me gape,
10   And though my fayth it were well knowne,
Yet small regard thou toke therat,
But now the blast is overblowne.
Of vaine phisicke a salve you shape,
Wherfore do way you come to late.
15   How long or this have I bene faine,
To gape for mercy at your gate,
Untill the time I spyde it plaine,
That pitie and you fell at debate.
For my redresse then was I faine:
20   Your service cleane for to forsake,
Wherfore do way you come to late.
    For when I brent in endlesse fire,
Who ruled then but cruell hate?
So that unneth I durst desire
25   One looke, my fervent heate to slake.
Therfore another doth me hyre,
And all the profer that you make,
Is made in vayne and comes to late.
    For when I asked recompence,
30   With cost you nought to graunt God wat:
Then said disdaine to great expence,
It were for you to graunt me that.

Therfore doway your rere pretence,
That you would binde that derst you brake,
35   For lo your salve comes all to late.

[259] *The complaint of a woman*
ravished, and also mor-
tally wounded.

A cruell Tiger all with teeth bebled,
A bloody tirantes hand in eche degre,
A lecher that by wretched lust was led,
(Alas) deflowred my virginitee.
5   And not contented with this villanie,
Nor with thoutragious terrour of the dede,
With bloody thirst of greater crueltie:
Fearing his haynous gilt should be bewrayed,
By crying death and vengeance openly,
10   His violent hand forthwith alas he layed
Upon my guiltles sely childe and me,
And like the wretch whom no horrour dismayde,
Drownde in the sinke of depe iniquitie:
Misusing me the mother for a time,
15   Hath slaine us both for cloking of his crime.

[260] *The lover being made thrall by*
love, perceiveth how great
a losse is libertye.

Ah libertie now have I learnd to know,
By lacking thee what Jewell I possest,
When I received first from Cupids bow
The deadly wound that festreth in my brest.
5   So farre (alas) forth strayed were mine eyes,
That I ne might refraine them backe, for lo:
They in a moment all earthly thinges despise,
In heavenly sight now are they fixed so.
What then for me but still with mazed sight,
10   To wonder at that excellence divine:
Where love (my freedome having in despight)
Hath made me thrall through errour of mine eyen,
For other guerdon hope I not to have,
My foltring toonge so basheth ought to crave.

[261] *The divers and contrarie passi-*
ons of the lover.

Holding my peace alas how loud I crye,
Pressed with hope and dread even both at ones,
Strayned with death, and yet I cannot dye.
Burning in flame, quaking for cold that grones,
5   Unto my hope withouten winges I flye.
Pressed with dispayre, that breaketh all my bones.
Walking as if I were, and yet am not.
Fayning with mirth, most inwardly with mones.
Hard by my helpe, unto my health not nye.
10   Mids of the calme my ship on rocke it rones.
I serve unbound, fast fettred yet I lye.
In stede of milke that fede on marble stones,
My most will is that I do espye:
That workes my joyes and sorowes both at ones.
15   In contrairs standeth all my losse and gaine:
And lo the giltlesse causeth all my paine.

[262] *The testament of the haw-*
thorne.

I sely Haw whose hope is past,
In faithfull true and fixed minde:
To her whom that I served last,
Have all my joyefulnes resignde,
5   Because I know assuredly,
My dying day aprocheth nye.
    Dispaired hart the carefull nest,
Of all the sighes I kept in store:
Convey my carefull corps to rest,
10   That leaves his joy for evermore.
And when the day of hope is past,
Geve up thy sprite and sigh the last.
    But or that we depart in twaine,
Tell her I loved with all my might:
15   That though the corps in clay remaine,
Consumed to asshes pale and white.
And though the vitall powres do ceasse,
The sprite shall love her nathelesse.
    And pray my lives lady dere,

20 During this litle time and space,
     That I have to abiden here,
     Not to withdraw her wonted grace,
     In recompensing of the paine,
     That I shall have to part in twaine.
25   And that at least she will withsave,
     To graunt my just and last request:
     When that she shall behold his grave,
     That lyeth of lyfe here dispossest,
     In record that I once was hers,
30 To bathe the frozen stone with teares.
         The service tree here do I make,
     For mine executour and my frende:
     That living did not me forsake,
     Nor will I trust unto my ende,
35 To see my body well conveyde,
     In ground where that it shal be layde.
         Tombed underneth a goodly Oke,
     With Ivy grene that fast is bound:
     There this my grave I have bespoke,
40 For there my ladies name do sound:
     Beset even as my testament tels:
     With oken leaves and nothing els.
         Graven wheron shalbe exprest,
     Here lyeth the body in this place,
45 Of him that living never cest
     To serve the fayrest that ever was,
     The corps is here, the hart he gave
     To her for whom he lieth in grave.
         And also set about my hersse,
50 Two lampes to burne and not to queint,
     Which shalbe token, and rehersse
     That my good will was never spent.
     When that my corps was layd alow,
     My spirit did sweare to serve no mo.
55   And if you want of ringing bels,
     When that my corps goth into grave:
     Repete her name and nothing els,
     To whom that I was bonden slave.
     When that my life it shall unframe,
60 My sprite shall joy to heare her name.
         With dolefull note and piteous sound,
     Wherwith my hart did cleave in twaine:

With such a song lay me in ground,
My sprite let it with her remayne,
65 That had the body to commend:
Till death therof did make an end.
    And even with my last bequest,
When I shall from this life depart:
I geve to her I loved best,
70 My just my true and faithfull hart,
Signed with the hand as cold as stone:
Of him that living was her owne.
    And if he here might live agayne,
As Phenix made by death anew:
75 Of this she may assure her plaine,
That he will still be just and trew.
Thus farewell she on live my owne.
And send her joy when I am gone.

[263] *The lover in dispeire lamen-*
teth his case.

    Adieu desert, how art thou spent?
Ah dropping teares how do ye washe?
Ah scalding sighes, how be ye spent?
To pricke them forth that will not hast,
5 Ah payned hart thou gapst for grace,
Even there where pitie hath no place.
    As easy it is the stony rocke,
From place to place for to remove,
As by thy plaint for to provoke:
10 A frosen hart from hate to love,
What should I say such is thy lot,
To fawne on them that force the not.
    Thus maist thou safely say and sweare,
That rigour raighneth and ruth doth faile,
15 In thanklesse thoughts thy thoughts do wear.
Thy truth, thy faith, may nought availe,
For thy good will why should thou so,
Still graft where grace it will not grow.
    Alas pore hart thus hast thou spent,
20 Thy flowryng time, thy pleasant yeres.
With sighing voyce wepe and lament:
For of thy hope no frute apperes,

Thy true meanyng is paide with scorne,
That ever soweth and repeth no corne.
25   And where thou sekes a quiet port,
Thou dost but weigh agaynst the winde,
For where thou gladdest woldst resort,
There is no place for thee assinde.
Thy desteny hath set it so
30   That thy true hart should cause thy wo.

[264] *Of his maistresse. m.B.*

In Bayes I boast whose braunch I beare,
    Such joy therin I finde:
That to the death I shall it weare,
    To ease my carefull minde.
5 In heat, in cold, both night and day,
    Her vertue may be sene:
When other frutes and flowers decay,
    The bay yet growes full grene.
Her berries fede the birdes full oft,
10   Her leves swete water make:
Her bowes be set in every loft,
    For their swete favours sake.
The birdes do shrowd them from the cold,
    In her we dayly see:
15 And men make arbers as they wold,
    Under the pleasant tree.
It doth me good when I repayre,
    There as these bayes do grow:
Where oft I walke to take the ayre,
20   It doth delight me so.
But loe I stand as I were dome,
    Her beauty for to blase:
Wherwith my sprites be overcome,
    So long theron I gase.
25 At last I turne unto my walk,
    In passing to and fro:
And to my self I smile and talk,
    And then away I go.
Why smilest thou say lokers on,
30   What pleasure hast thou found?
With that I am as cold as stone,

And ready for to swound.
Fie fie for shame sayth fansy than,
    Pluck up thy faynted hart:
35 And speke thou boldly like a man,
    Shrinke not for little smart.
Wherat I blushe and change my chere,
    My senses waxe so weake:
O god think I what make I here,
40   That never a word may speake,
I dare not sigh lest I be heard,
    My lokes I slyly cast:
And still I stand as one were scarde,
    Untill my stormes be past.
45 Then happy hap doth me revive,
    The blood comes to my face:
A merier man is not alive,
    Then I am in that case.
Thus after sorow seke I rest,
50   When fled is fansies fit.
And though I be a homely gest,
    Before the bayes I sit,
Where I do watch till leaves do fall,
    When winde the tree doth shake:
55 Then though my branch be very small,
    My leafe away I take.
And then I go and clap my hands,
    My hart doth leape for joy.
These bayes do ease me from my bands,
60   That long did me annoy:
For when I do behold the same,
    Which makes so faire a show:
I finde therin my maistresse name,
    And se her vertues grow.

      [265] *The lover complaineth his harty*
         love not requited.

    When Phebus had the serpent slaine,
He claymed Cupides boe:
Which strife did turne him to great paine,
The story well doth prove.
5 For Cupide made him fele much woe,

In sekyng Dephnes love.
    This Cupide hath a shaft of kinde,
Which wounded many a wight:
Whose golden hed had power to binde,
10 Ech hart in Venus bandes.
This arrow did on Phebus light,
Which came from Cupides handes.
    An other shaft was wrought in spite,
Which headed was with lead:
15 Whose nature quenched swete delight,
That lovers most embrace.
In Dephnes brest this cruell head,
Had found a dwellyng place.
    But Phebus fonde of his desire,
20 Sought after Dephnes so:
He burnt with heat, she felt no fire,
Full fast she fled him fro.
He gate but hate for his good will,
The gods assigned so.
25   My case with Phebus may compare,
His hap and mine are one,
I cry to her that knowes no care,
Yet seke I to her most:
When I approche then is she gone,
30 Thus is my labour lost.
    Now blame not me but blame the shaft,
That hath the golden head,
And blame those gods that with their craft
Such arrowes forge by kinde.
35 And blame the cold and heavy lead,
That doth my ladies minde.

[266] *A praise of m. .M.*

In court as I behelde, the beauty of eche dame,
Of right my thought from all the rest should M. steale the same.
But, er I ment to judge: I vewed with such advise
As retchelesse dome should not invade: the boundes of my devise.
5 And, whiles I gased long: such heat did brede within,
As Priamus towne felt not more flame, when did the bale begin.
By reasons rule ne yet by wit perceve I could,
That M, face of earth yfound: enjoy such beauty should.

And fansy doubted that from heaven had Venus come,
10 To norish rage in Britaynes harts, while corage yet doth blome,
Her native hue so strove, with colour of the rose,
That Paris would have Helene left, and .M. beauty chose.
A wight farre passyng all, and is more faire to seme,
Then lusty May the lodg of love: that clothes the earth in grene.
15 So angell like she shines: she semeth no mortall wight,
But one whom nature in her forge, did frame her self to spight.
Of beauty princesse chiefe: so makelesse doth she rest,
Whose eye would glad an heavy wight: and pryson payne in brest,
I waxe astonied to see: the feator of her shape,
20 And wondred that a mortal hart: such heavenly beames could scape
Her limmes so answeryng were: the mould of her faire face,
Of Venus stocke she semde to spring, the rote of beauties grace.
Her presens doth pretende: such honour and estate,
That simple men might gesse her birthe: if folly bred debate.
25 Her lokes in hartes of flint: would such affectes imprese,
As rage of flame not Nilus stremes: in Nestors yeres encrease.
Within the subtill seat, of her bright eyen doth dwell,
Blinde Cupide with the pricke of paine: that princes fredom sell.
A Paradice it is: her beauty to behold,
30 Where natures stuffe so full is found, that natures ware is sold.

[267] *An old lover to a yong*
gentilwoman.

Ye are to yong to bryng me in,
And I to old to gape for flies:
I have to long a lover bene,
If such yong babes should bleare mine eyes,
5 But trill the ball before my face,
I am content to make you play:
I will not se, I hide my face,
And turne my backe and ronne away.
But if you folowe on so fast,
10 And crosse the waies where I should go,
Ye may waxe weary at the last,
And then at length your self orethrow.
I meane where you and all your flocke,
Devise to pen men in the pound:
15 I know a key can picke your locke,
And make you runne your selves on ground.

Some birdes can eate the strawie corne,
And flee the lime that fowlers set,
And some are ferde of every thorne,
20 And so therby they scape the net.
But some do light and never loke,
And seeth not who doth stand in waite,
As fish that swalow up the hoke,
And is begiled through the baite.
25 But men can loke before they leape,
And be at price for every ware,
And penyworthes cast to bye good cheape,
And in ech thyng hath eye and care.
But he that bluntly runnes on hed,
30 And seeth not what the race shal be:
Is like to bring a foole to bed,
And thus ye get no more of me.

[268] *The lover forsaketh his*
unkinde love.

Farewell thou frosen hart and eares of hardned stele,
Thou lackest yeres to understand the grefe that I did fele,
The gods revenge my wrong, with equall plage on thee,
When plesure shal prick forth thy youth, to learn what love shalbe.
5 Perchance thou provest now, to scale blinde Cupides holde,
And matchest where thou maist repent, when al thy cards are told.
But blush not thou therfore, thy betters have done so,
Who thought they had retaind a dove, when they but caught a cro.
And some do lenger time, with lofty lokes we see,
10 That lights at length as low or wors then doth the betell bee.
Yet let thy hope be good, such hap may fall from hye:
That thou maist be if fortune serve, a princesse er thou dye.
If chance prefer thee so, alas poore sely man,
Where shall I scape thy cruell handes, or seke for succour than?
15 God shild such greedy wolves, should lap in giltlesse bloode,
And send short hornes to hurtful heads, that rage like lyons woode.
I seldome se the day, but malice wanteth might,
And hatefull harts have never hap, to wreke their wrath aright.
The madman is unmete, a naked sword to gide,
20 And more unfit are they to clime, that are orecome with pride.
I touch not thee herein, thou art a fawcon sure,
That can both soer and stoupe sometime, as men cast up the lure.

The pecock hath no place, in thee when thou shalt list,
For some no soner make a signe, but thou percevest the fist.
25   They have that I do want, and that doth thee begilde,
The lack that thou dost se in me, doth make thee loke so wilde.
My luryng is not good, it liketh not thine eare,
My call it is not half so swete, as would to god it were.
Well wanton yet beware, thou do no tiryng take,
30   At every hand that would thee fede, or to thee frendship make,
This councell take of him that ought thee once his love,
Who hopes to mete thee after this among the saintes above.
But here within this world, if he may shonne the place,
He rather asketh present death, then to beholde thy face.

[269] *The lover preferreth his lady*
above all other.

Resigne you dames whom tikelyng brute delight,
The golden praise that flatteries tromp doth sownd
And vassels be to her that claims by right,
The title just that first dame beauty found.
5   Whose dainty eyes such sugred baits do hide,
As poyson harts where glims of love do glide.
Come eke and see how heaven and nature wrought,
Within her face where framed is such joy:
As Priams sonnes in vaine the seas had sought,
10   If halfe such light had had abode in Troy.
For as the golden sunne doth darke ech starre,
So doth her hue the fayrest dames as farre.
Ech heavenly gift, ech grace that nature could,
By art or wit my lady lo retaynes:
15   A sacred head, so heapt with heares of gold,
As Phebus beames for beauty farre it stayns,
A sucred tong, where eke such swetenesse snowes,
That well it semes a fountain where it flowes.
Two laughyng eyes so linked with pleasyng lokes,
20   As wold entice a tygers hart to serve:
The bayt is swete but eager be the hookes,
For Dyane sekes her honour to preserve.
Thus Arundell sits, throned still with fame,
Whom enmies trompe can not attaynt with shame.
25   My dased head so daunted is with heapes,
Of giftes divine that harber in her brest:

Her heavenly shape, that lo my verses leaps,
And touch but that wherin she clowds the rest.
For if I should her graces all recite,
30   Both time should want, and I should wonders write.
      Her chere so swete, so christall is her eyes,
Her mouth so small, her lips so lively red:
Her hand so fine, her wordes so swete and wise,
That Pallas semes to sojourne in her hed.
35   Her vertues great, her forme as farre excedes,
As sunne the shade that mortall creatures leades.
      Would God that wretched age would spare to race,
Her lively hew that as her graces rare:
Be goddesse like, even so her goddesse face,
40   Might never change but still continue faire
That eke in after time ech wight may see,
How vertue can with beauty beare degree.

[270] *The lover lamenteth that he
would forget love, and
can not.*

      Alas when shall I joy,
When shall my wofull hart,
Cast forth the folish toy
That breadeth all my smart.
5   A thousand times and mo,
I have attempted sore:
To rid this restlesse wo,
Which raigneth more and more.
      But when remembrance past,
10   Hath laid dead coales together:
Old love renewes his blast,
That cause my joyes to wither.
Then sodaynely a spark,
Startes out of my desire:
15   And lepes into my hart,
Settyng the coles a fire.
      Then reason runnes about,
To seke forgetfull water:
To quench and clene put out,
20   The cause of all this matter.
And saith dead flesh must nedes,

Be cut out of the core,
For rotten withered wedes,
Can heale no grevous sore.
25   But then even sodaynely,
The fervent heat doth slake:
And cold then straineth me,
That makes my bodie shake.
Alas who can endure,
30 To suffer all this paine,
Sins her that should me cure,
Most cruell death hath slaine.
    Well well, I say no more,
Let dead care for the dead,
35 Yet wo is me therfore,
I must attempt to lead,
One other kinde of life,
Then hitherto I have:
Or els this paine and strife,
40 Will bring me to my grave.

¶ Songes written by N. G.

[271] *Of the ix. Muses.*

Imps of king Jove, and quene Remembrance lo,
The sisters nyne, the poets pleasant feres.
Calliope doth stately stile bestow,
And worthy praises paintes of princely peres.
5 Clio in solem songes reneweth all day,
With present yeres conjoyning age bypast.
Delitefull talke loves Comicall Thaley:
In fresh grene youth, who doth like laurell last.
With voyces Tragicall sowndes Melpomen,
10 And, as with cheins, thallured eare she bindes.
Her stringes when Terpsichor doth touche, even then
She toucheth hartes, and raigneth in mens mindes,
Fine Erato, whose looke a lively chere
Presents, in dauncing keepes a comely grace.
15 With semely gesture doth Polymnie stere:
Whose wordes holle routes of rankes doo rule in place,
Uranie, her globes to view all bent,

The ninefold heaven observes with fixed face.
The blastes Eutrepe tunes of instrument,
20   With solace sweet hence heavie dumps to chase.
Lord Phebus in the mids (whose heavenly sprite
These ladies doth enspire) embraceth all.
The graces in the Muses weed, delite
To lead them forth, that men in maze they fall.

[272] *Musonius the Philosophers*
saying.

In working well, if travell you sustain:
Into the winde shall lightly passe the paine:
But of the dede the glory shall remain,
And cause your name with worthy wights to raign.
5   In working wrong, if pleasure you attaine:
The pleasure soon shall vade, and voyde, as vaine:
But of the deed, throughout the life, the shame
Endures, defacing you with fowl defame:
And still tormentes the minde, both night and day:
10   Scant length of time the spot can wash away.
Flee then ylswading pleasures baits untrew:
And noble vertues fair renown purseew.

[273] *Description of Ver-*
tue.

What one art thou, thus in torn weed yclad?
Vertue, in price whom auncient sages had.
Why, poorely rayd? For fading goodes past care.
Why doublefaced? I marke ech fortunes fare.
5   This bridle, what? Mindes rages to restrain.
Tooles why beare you? I love to take great pain.
Why, winges? I teache above the starres to flye.
Why tread you death? I onely cannot dye.

[274] *Praise of measure-
keping.*

The auncient time commended, not for nought,
The mean: what better thing can ther be sought?
In meane, is vertue placed: on either side,
Both right, and left, amisse a man shall slide.
5 Icar, with sire hadst thou the mid way flown,
Icarian beck by name had no man known.
If middle path kept had proud Phaeton,
No burning brand this earth had fallne upon.
Ne cruel powr, ne none to soft can raign:
10 That kepes a mean, the same shall still remain.
Thee, Julie, once did too much mercy spill:
Thee, Nero stern, rigor extreem did kill.
How could August so many yeres well passe?
Nor overmeek, nor overferse he was.
15 Worship not Jove with curious fansies vain,
Nor him despise: hold right atween these twain.
No wastefull wight, no greedy goom is prayzd.
Stands largesse just, in egall balance payzd.
So Catoes meal, surmountes Antonius chere,
20 And better fame his sober fare hath here.
To slender building, bad: as bad, to grosse:
One, an eyesore, the tother falls to losse.
As medcines help, in measure: so (God wot)
By overmuch, the sick their bane have got.
25 Unmeet mee seems to utter this, mo wayes:
Measure forbids unmeasurable prayse.

[275] *Mans life after Possidonius,
or Crates.*

What path list you to tread? what trade will you assay?
The courts of plea, by braul, and bate, drive gentle peace away.
In house, for wife, and childe, there is but cark and care:
With travail, and with toyl ynough, in feelds we use to fare.
5 Upon the seas lieth dreed: the rich in foraine land,
Doo fear the losse: and there, the poore, like misers poorely stand.
Strife, with a wife, without, your thrift full hard to see:
Yong brats, a trouble: none at all, a maym it seems to bee:
Youth, fond: age hath no hert, and pincheth all to nye.
10 Choose then the leefer of these twoo, no life, or soon to dye.

[276] *Metrodorus minde to the*
contrarie.

What race of life ronne you? what trade will you assay?
In courts, is glory got, and wit encreased day by day.
At home, wee take our ease, and beak our selves in rest:
The feeldes our nature doo refresh with pleasures of the best.
5   On seas, is gayn to get: the straunger, hee shall bee
Estemed: having much: if not, none knoweth his lack, but hee.
A wife will trim thy house: no wyfe? then art thou free.
Brood is a lovely thing: without, thy life is loose to thee.
Yong bloods be strong: old sires in double honour dwell.
10 Doway that choyse, no life, or soon to dye: for all is well.

[277] *Of frendship.*

Of all the heavenly giftes, that mortall men commend,
What trusty treasure in the world can countervail a frend?
Our helth is soon decayd: goodes, casuall, light, and vain:
Broke have we sene the force of powre, and honour suffer stain.
5   In bodies lust, man doth resemble but base brute:
True vertue gets, and keeps a frend, good guide of our pursute:
Whose harty zeale with ours accords, in every case:
No terme of time, no space of place, no storme can it deface.
When fickle fortune failes, this knot endureth still:
10 Thy kin out of their kinde may swarve, when frends owe the good will.
What sweter solace shall befall, than one to finde,
Upon whose brest thou mayst repose the secretes of thy minde?
He wayleth at thy wo, his teares with thine be shed:
With thee doth he all joyes enjoy: so leef a life is led.
15 Behold thy frend, and of thy self the patern see:
One soull, a wonder shall it seem, in bodies twain to bee.
In absence, present, rich in want, in sicknesse sound,
Yea after death alive, mayst thou by thy sure frend be found.
Eche house, eche towne, eche realm by stedfast love doth stand:
20 Where fowl debate breeds bitter bale, in eche devided land.
O frendship, flowr of flowrs: O lively sprite of life,
O sacred bond of blisfull peace, the stalworth staunch of strife:
Scipio with Lelius didst thou conjoyn in care,
At home, in warrs, for weal and wo, with egall faith to fare.
25 Gesippus eke with Tite, Damon with Pythias,
And with Menetus sonne Achill, by thee combined was.
Euryalus, and Nisus gave Virgil cause to sing:

Of Pylades doo many rimes, and of Orestes ring.
Down Theseus went to hell, Pirith, his frend to finde:
30 O that the wives, in these our daies, wer to their mates so kinde.
Cicero, the frendly man, to Atticus, his frend,
Of frendship wrote: such couples lo doth lot but seldome lend.
Recount thy race, now ronne: how few shalt thou there see,
Of whom to say: This same is he, that never fayled mee.
35 So rare a jewell then must nedes be holden dere:
And as thou wilt esteem thy self, so take thy chosen fere.
The tirant, in dispaire, no lacke of gold bewayls.
But, Out I am undoon (sayth he) for all my frendship fails.
Wherfore sins nothing is more kindely for our kinde:
40 Next wisdome thus that teacheth us, love we the frendful minde.

[278] *The death of Zoras, an Egyp-*
tian Astonomer, in the
first fight, that Alex-
ander had with
the Persi-
ans.

Now clattering armes, now ragyng broyls of warre,
Gan passe the noyes of dredfull trompets clang:
Shrowded with shafts, the heven: with clowd of darts,
Covered the ayre: against full fatted bulls,
5 As forceth kindled yre the Lyons keen:
Whose greedy gutts the gnawyng honger pricks:
So Macedoins against the Persians fare.
Now corpses hide the purpurde soyl with blood:
Large slaughter, on ech side: but Perses more
10 Moyst feelds be bledd: their harts, and nombers bate.
Fainted while they geve back, and fall to flight:
The lightening Macedon, by swoords, by gleaves,
By bands and trowps, of fotemen with his garde,
Speeds to Darie: but him, his nearest kyn,
15 Oxate preserves, with horsemen on a plump
Before his carr: that none the charge could geve.
Here grunts, here grones, echwhere strong youth is spent:
Shakyng her bloody hands, Bellone, among
The Perses, soweth all kynde of cruel death.
20 With throte ycutt, he roores: he lieth along,
His entrails with a lance through girded quite:

Him smites the club, him wounds farstrikyng bow,
And him the sling, and him the shinyng swoord:
Hee dieth, he is all dead, he pants, he rests.
25 Right overstood, in snowwhite armour brave,
The Memphite Zoroas, a cunning clarke:
To whom the heaven lay open, as his boke:
And in celestiall bodies he could tell
The movyng, metyng, light, aspect, eclips,
30 And influence, and constellacions all:
What earthly chances would betide: what yere
Of plenty, storde, what signe forwarned derth:
How winter gendreth snow, what temperature
In the primetide doth season well the soyl:
35 Why somer burns, why autumne hath ripe grapes:
Whether the circle, quadrate may become:
Whether our tunes heavens harmony can yelde:
Of four begins, among them selves how great
Proporcion is: what sway the erryng lightes
40 Doth send in course gayn that first movyng heaven:
What grees, one from another distant be:
What starre doth let the hurtfull sire to rage,
Or him more milde what opposition makes:
What fire doth qualify Mavorses fire:
45 What house ech one doth seke: what planet raignes
Within this hemisphere, or that, small things
I speake, whole heaven he closeth in his brest.
This sage then, in the starres had spied: the fates
Threatned him death, without delay: and sithe
50 He saw, he could not fatall order change:
Forward he preast, in battayle that he might
Mete with the ruler of the Macedoins:
Of his right hand desirous to be slayne,
The boldest beurn, and worthiest in the felde:
55 And, as a wight now weary of his life,
And sekyng death: in first front of his rage,
Comes desperatly to Alexanders face:
At him, with darts, one after other, throwes:
With reckles wordes, and clamour him provokes:
60 And faith, Nectanabs bastard, shamefull stain
Of mothers bed: why losest thou thy strokes,
Cowards among? Turne thee to me, in case
Manhod there be so much left in thy hart:
Come fight with me: that on my helmet weare

65 Appolloes laurell, both for learnings laude,
    And eke for martiall praise: that, in my shield,
    The sevenfold sophie of Minerve contein:
    A match, more meet, sir king, than any here.
    The noble prince amoved, takes ruthe upon
70 The wilfull wight: and with soft wordes, ayen,
    O monstrous man (quod he) what so thou art,
    I pray the, lyve: ne do not, with thy death,
    This lodge of lore, the Muses mansion marr.
    That treasure house this hand shall never spoyl:
75 My sword shall never bruse that skilfull braine,
    Long gatherd heapes of science sone to spyll.
    O, how faire frutes may you to mortall men
    From wisdomes garden geve? How many may
    By you the wiser and the better prove?
80 What error, what mad moode, what phrensy thee
    Perswades to be downe sent to depe Averne:
    Where no arts florish, nor no knowledge vails?
    For all these sawes, when thus the soverain sayd,
    Alighted Zoroas: with sword unsheathed,
85 The careles king there smot, above the greve,
    At thopenyng of his quishes: wounded him
    So that the blood down reyled on the ground.
    The Macedon, perceivyng hurt, gan gnash:
    But yet his minde he bent, in any wise,
90 Him to forbear: set spurs unto his stede,
    And turnde away: lest anger of his smart
    Should cause revenger hand deale balefull blowes.
    But of the Macedonian chieftains knights
    One, Meleager, could not beare this sight:
95 But ran upon the said Egyptian renk:
    And cut him in both knees: he fell to ground:
    Wherwith a whole rout came of souldiers stern,
    And all in pieces hewed the silly seg.
    But happily the soule fled to the starres:
100 Where, under him, he hath full sight of all,
    Wherat he gased here, with reaching looke.
    The Persians wailde such sapience to forgo:
    The very fone, the Macedonians wisht,
    He would have lived: King Alexander self
105 Demde him a man, unmete to dye at all:
    Who won like praise, for conquest of his yre,
    As for stout men in field that day subdued:

Who princes taught, how to discerne a man,
That in his hed so rare a jewell beares.
110 But over all, those same Camenes, those same
Devine Camenes, whose honour he procurde,
As tender parent doth his daughters weal:
Lamented: and for thankes all that they can,
Do cherish him deceast, and set him free,
115 From dark oblivion of devouring death.

[279] *Marcus Tullius Ciceroes*
death.

Therfore, when restlesse rage of winde, and wave
Hee saw: By fates, alas calld for (quod hee)
Is haplesse Cicero: sayl on, shape course
To the next shore, and bring me to my death.
5   Perdy these thanks, reskued from civill swoord,
Wilt thou my countrey paye? I see mine end:
So powers divine, so bid the gods above,
In citie saved that Consul Marcus shend.
Speakyng no more, but drawyng from deep hart
10 Great grones, even at the name of Rome rehearst:
His eies and chekes, with showrs of teares, he washt.
And (though a rout in dayly daungers worne)
With forced face, the shipmen held their teares:
And, strivyng long the seas rough floods to passe,
15 In angry windes, and stormy showres made way:
And at the last, safe ancred in the rode
Came heavy Cicero a land: with pain,
His fainted lims the aged sire doth draw:
And, round about their master, stood his band:
20 Nor greatly with their owne hard hap dismayd,
Nor plighted fayth, prove in sharp time to break:
Some swordes prepare: some their dere lord assist:
In littour layd, they lead him unkouth wayes:
If to deceave Antonius cruell gleaves
25 They might, and threats of folowyng routs escape.
Thus lo, that Tullie, went, that Tullius,
Of royall robe, and sacred senate prince:
When he a far the men approch espieth,
And of his sone the ensignes doth aknow:
30 And, with drawn swoord, Popilius threatning death:

Whose life, and holl estate, in hazard once,
Hee had preservde: when Room as yet to free
Herd him, and at his thundring voyce amazde.
Herennius eek, more eyger than the rest,
35 Present enflamde with furie, him purseews.
What might hee doo? Should hee use in defense
Disarmed hands? or pardon ask, for meed?
Should he with wordes attempt to turn the wrath
Of tharmed knight, whose safegard hee had wrought?
40 No, age forbids, and fixt within depe brest
His countryes love, and falling Romes image.
The charret turn, sayth hee, let loose the rayns:
Roon to the undeserved death: mee, lo,
Hath Phebus fowl, as messenger forwarnd:
45 And Jove desires a neew heavensman to make.
Brutus, and Cassius soulls, live you in blisse:
In case yet all the fates gaynstrive us not,
Neither shall we perchaunce dye unrevenged.
Now have I lived, O Room, ynough for mee:
50 My passed life nought suffreth me to dout
Noysom oblivion of the lothesome death.
Slea mee: yet all the offspring to come shall know:
And this deceas shall bring eternall life.
Yea, and (onlesse I fayl, and all in vain
55 Room, I soomtime thy Augur chosen was)
Not evermore shall frendly fortune thee
Favour, Antonius: once the day shall coom:
When her deare wights, by cruell spight, thus slain,
Victorious Room shall at thy hands require.
60 Me likes, therwhile, go see the hoped heaven.
Speech had he left: and therwith hee, good man,
His throte preparde, and held his hed unmoved.
His hasting to those fates the very knightes
Be lothe to see: and, rage rebated, when
65 They his bare neck beheld, and his hore heyres:
Scant could they hold the teares, that forth gan burst:
And almost fell from bloody hands the swoords.
Onely the stern Herennius, with grym looke,
Dastards, why stand you still? he sayth: and straight,
70 Swaps of the hed, with his presumptuous yron.
Ne with that slaughter yet is he not fild:
Fowl shame on shame to heape is his delite.
Wherefore the handes also doth hee of smyte,

Which durst Antonius life so lively paynt.
75 Him, yeldyng strayned goste, from welkin hye,
With lothy chere, lord Phebus gan behold:
And in black clowd, they say, long hid his hed.
The latine Muses, and the Grayes, they wept:
And, for his fall, eternally shall weep.
80 And lo, hertpersing Pitho (straunge to tell)
Who had to him suffisde both sense, and words,
When so he spake: and drest, with nectar soote,
That flowyng toung: when his windpipe disclosde,
Fled with her fleeyng frend: and (out alas)
85 Hath left the earth, ne will no more return.
Popilius flyeth, therwhile: and, leaving there
The senslesse stock, a grizely sight doth bear
Unto Antonius boord, with mischief fed.

[280] *Of M.T. Cicero.*

For Tullie, late, a tomb I gan prepare:
When Cynthie, thus, bad mee my labour spare:
Such maner things becoom the ded, quoth hee:
But Tullie lives, and styll alyve shall bee.

N.G.

*Imprinted at London in flete
strete within Temple barre, at the
sygne of the hand and starre,
by Richard Tottell
the.xxxi. day of July.
An. 1557.*

*Com privilegio ad impri-
mendum solum.*

ANNOTATIONS AND GLOSSARY

5.8   rote] s., root; *see also* 243.8; 244.10; memory 136.49; 266.22.

9.4   **tickell**] adj., gratifying; *see also* tickleness 207.3; tikelyng 269.1.

9.8   **geason**] adj., rare; rarity; *see also* 245.19; 246.40.

9.14   **all to shaken**] phr., completely and utterly shaken.

10.3   **tickell**] adj., fickle; *see also* 207.3; 269.1; uncertain, Chaucer, *Canterbury Tales*, Miller's Tale 3428.

15.6   **hove**] v., wait, linger; Chaucer, *Troilus and Creseyde* 5.33.

15.44 **Upsupped**] pp., drunk.

15.46 **fere**] s., mate, companion; *see also* 29.1; 29.22; 271.2; 277.36.

18.4   **hye**] v., hasten; *see also* 163.44; 217.6; 242.3.

19.33 **uneth**] unneath, adv., 151.2; 228.177; 258.24; unnethes, adv., in difficult circumstances 220.17.

21.3   **neck**] s., a move to cover check in a game of chess.

21.12 **ferse**] s., Queen in a game of chess; Chaucer, *Book of the Duchess*, 654 f.

23.5   **glimsing**] pres. p., glancing; n. glimpse; Chaucer, *Canterbury Tales*, Merchant's Tale 2383.

25.11 **pese**] s., one pea.

25.23 **ure**] s., use, practise; *see also* 16.28; 25.23; 63.17; 171.1; 226.7; 256.13.

28.13 **drive**] v., thrive; hold one's course toward.

29.60 **stale**] s., decoy-bird; 256.20, decoy, v.

30.32 **grave**] v., engrave, carve; *see also* 91.7; 142.2, 9; 213.36; Chaucer, *Canterbury Tales*, Physician's Tale 15; *Troilus and Creseyde* 3.1462.

30.37, **riveth**] v., destroys; Chaucer, ryve, v., pierce, cleave, *Canterbury Tales*, Pardoner's Tale 828; *Troilus and Creseyde* 5.1560.

30.59 **refarde**] pp., referred, conveyed back.

31.5   **egall**] adj., well-matched; equal; *see also* 137.10; 138.9; 274.18; 277.25; Chaucer, *Boece*, 2. M7 2/16; *Troilus and Creseyde* 3.137

32.4   freat] v., rage, fume; *see also* 36.13; 69.85; 117.27; 134.112; 216.8.

32.8 glome] v., gloom, frown.

32.11   clives] s., cliffs; *see also* 232.11.

32.20   ryft] v. phr., take in a ryft (reef) or sail.

36.1   rife] adj., common; *see also* 212.34; easy 215.12; rifest, adj., most fre-
quently 163.18; 253.9.

37.9   scace] adv., scarcely.

38.16   chewes] s., jaws.

39.01   *Bonum est mihi quod humiliasti me]* Heading. KJV Psalm 119:71: "It
is good for me that I have been afflicted"; Vulgate Psalm 118:71.

39.4   determed] pp. adj., determined.

40.1   Ratclif] Thomas Radcliffe, third earl of Sussex (b. 1526?), who par-
ticipated in the military operations of Surrey in France.

41.12   Bullayn] Boulogne, France.

45.2   vaileth] aphetic form of 'availeth;' *see also* 68.7; 75.1,9.

49.8   Brunet] Anne Boleyn.

52.14   glead] s., fire; gle(e)d(e), glowing coal; Chaucer, *Canterbury Tales*,
Knight's Tale 1997; Parson's Tale 548; *Troilus and Creseyde* 4.337.

53.12   shright] inf., to shriek; v., shrieked 229.11.

57.12   small] adj., slender, slim; *see also* 139.19; 221.15; 264.55. Chaucer,
Canterbury Tales, Miller's Tale; 3234; Wife of Bath's Tale 261; Merchant's
Tale 1602.

58.3   boordes] s., jests; *see also*, bordes 71.12; bord 87.18; borde, v., trick
256.39.

60.6   That of my health is very crop, and roote] *see* Chaucer, *Troilus and
Creseyde* 5.1245, 'crop and roote': the whole, everything.

68.8   eschue] s., avoidance; eschew, v., shun 79.8.

69.2   acited] v., summoned.

69.84   daskard] s., dastard.

69.85   Atride] n., Agamemnon.

83.26   all to wry] conceal, misinterpret, twist aside; Chaucer, *Book of the
Duchess* 628; *Troilus and Creseyde* 3.620; turn aside 177.21.

83.27   narre] adv., never.

91.34   beaute] n. beauty; beautee, Chaucer, *Canterbury Tales*, Knight's Tale
1114; *Troilus and Creseyde* 1.102.

95.45–46   Rachel, Lea] Genesis 29–35.

103.11　ydle] adj., pointless, empty; Chaucer, *Canterbury Tales*, Pardoner's Tale 638; lazy, Physician's Tale 57; ydleness 169.40; idelnesse, n., indolence; Knight's Tale 1940.

126.01; 136.01　Sir Frances Brian] Courtier and opportunist who had been a favorite of Henry VIII, as well as the Protector Somerset.

130.8　Mountzon] Spain, where, in 1537, Wyatt was Henry VIII's ambassador to Emperor Charles V.

131.4　gaineward] prep., towards, facing.

134.01; 135.01　*John Poins*] member of a distinguished Essex family and relation to Sir Francis Poyntz (1528) and Sir Anthony Poyntz (1533), diplomats in the service of Henry VIII. A painting of John Poins by Holbein portrays a man of scholarship and intelligence.

134.64　sely] adj., hapless, unfortunate, insignificant, innocent, 135.27; 170.1; 171.1; 181.43; 259.11; 262.1; 268.13; selly, 247.7; 256.36; sily 233.31; silly 148.13; 172.1; 178.18; 216.10; 249.18; 279.98.

134.105　dome] aphetic form of 'kingdome.'

135.40　Livye] Fragment 32.

135.50　Syr Topas] The moral tale of Syr Topaz was told by Chaucer's narrator of the *Canterbury Tales*.

135.65　double] adj., duplicitous; *see also* 247.2.

135.67　favel] s., flattery; could be a proper name.

135.94　lettes] v., hinders, obstructs; Chaucer, *Canterbury Tales*, Knight's Tale 889.

136.21　asse] Boethius, *Consolation of Philosophy*, 1 pr. 4

137　Vergil, *Aeneid* 1, 740–746.

137.45　bowt] s., circuit, orbit

137.60　Calcars] astrologers

139.01–03　*Master Devorox, the lord Ferres sonne*] Richard Devereux, eldest son of Walter Devereux, third Baron of Ferrers, died in 1547, leaving a son Walter, who later became the father of Penelope Devereux, Sir Philip Sidney's 'Stella.'

139.4　lendes] pl., loins; Chaucer, *Canterbury Tales*, Miller's Tale 3237.

139.19　graffe] n., plant, shoot; *see also* 168.49; 187.4; 190.22; 196.43.

140.20　ought] v., owned; owed 268.31.

141.38　dissolvde] Philippians 1:23

142.4　filed] pp. adj., polished, finished; false 229.14.

143.1　Marlian] v., merlin; small falcon.

143.2   yelden] pp., pp. adj., yolden, submissive. *see also* 88.01, 4; 143.2; 193.01.

148.9   The lyver ... Prometheus] In the tragedy by Aeschylus, Prometheus pities frail and vulnerable man by giving him fire, defying the law of heaven and invoking the wrath of Zeus who enchains Prometheus on a rock where immortal suffering is inflicted upon him when his liver is eaten each day by birds and is restored at night.

148.14   all to rent] phr., completely and utterly torn apart.

149.27   Ant] Proverbs 6:6–8.

150.6   yfere] adv., together.

151.01; 158.02   *Wilford*] Sir James Wilford (b. circa 1516). As a career soldier, Wilford fought against France, 1544–1545, against the Scots, under Protector Somerset, and was knighted in 1547. He also fought under Lord Grey de Wilton at Haddington, where as Governor, he withstood sieges by the Scots and French, and was later captured while attacking Dunbar Castle. After his release, Wilford died in 1550.

151.17   triedly] adv., in an experienced manner.

153.19   knocke . . . aske] Matthew 7:7; Luke 11:19.

153.21   shepe] Luke 15:4–7.

155.5   inpreaseth] v., mingles with.

160.24   Wolfe] Varro, *De lingua Latina* 7.21.4.

160.34   masheth] v., enmeshes, catches in a net

161.10   gogen gift] s., a gift to a credulous or gullible person.

162.1, 3   boke] s., book; *see also* 168.7; 185.5; 228.148; 231.4; 278.27.

163.33   adawth] v., subdueth; awake, Chaucer, *Troilus and Criseyde* 3.1120.

165.7   aray] s., military order; *see also* 181.8.

166.24   Minos] Ovid, *Metamorphoses*, 8, 1–210.

166.29   Diana, Hypolitus] Ovid, *Metamorphoses*, 15. 470–578; Horace, *Odes* 4.7. 25–28.

166.30   Theseus, Perithous] Pirithous; Ovid, *Metamorphoses*, 12.180–367; Horace, *Odes* 4.7. 27–28.

168.47   Jeliflowre] Gillyflower.

169.9   crab] s., crab-apple.

169.11   Scillas cost] Ovid, *Metamorphoses*, 8.1–174; 13.929–310; 14.1–100.

170.01; 171.1   *Thestilis*] In Theocritus, *Idyll* II, and Virgil, *Eclogue* II, Thestilis is a shepherdess, but in these poems by Uncertain Auctours, Thestilis is the name of the lamenting male lover.

170.16   **craving**] v., carving.

170.17   **Cresus, king of Lide**] Croesus, Lydian king.

170.21   **limes, lims**] s., limbs; *see also* 142.17; 279.18.

171.11   **Achilles and Brises**] Briseis was awarded to Achilles after a raid on Lyrnessus during which he killed her husband, Mynes, king of Lyrnessus. Agamemnon took her from Achilles when he had to forgo his own captive, Chryseis, at Apollo's command. Briseis was restored to Achilles untouched after the death of Patroclus.

171.15   **graffed**] pp., adj., grafted

171.22   **Etrascus**] In Melbanck's *Philotimus*, 1583, we hear about Etrascus's achievement in love after thirty years of disappointment.

175.01   *Audley*] Thomas: captain at Guisnes, lieutenant of the Old Man in Boulogne, Gentleman Usher to Henry VIII, who willed him 200 marks, eventually captured Ket, the rebel of the north, and for that received 100 pounds by the Privy Council in 1548.

175.11   **at the nede**] n. phr., when necessary.

177.21 **wry**] v., turn aside.

179.01   *Phillips*] Philip van Wilder, appointed lutenist by Henry VIII and Keeper of His Majesty's musical instruments in 1538, was made a Gentleman of the Privy Chamber by Edward VI in 1550.

181.18   **rampyre**] s., rampart.

183.01   *ladie Wentworth*] Lady Mary Wentworth, daughter of Sir John Wentworth, of Gosfield, Essex, married Baron Thomas Wentworth of Nettlestead, Suffolk, and died bearing her first still borne child in 1555.

184.18, 23   **caterpiller**] cf. Isaiah 33:4.

184.34   **Adrainus**] The poet substitutes this name for Zeuxis, a Greek painter at the close of the 5th century B.C., who in a contest painted grapes so lifelike that birds came and pecked at them.

184.46   **Naulus**] Nauplis's son, Palmendes, was betrayed in the Trojan war by Odysseus. When Nauplis was refused satisfaction, he misled the Greeks, who were returning home from the war in their ships, by lighting huge beacon fires on the coast of Euboea, which caused the ships to dash against the rocks.

189.13   **Momus**] according to Hesiod, the son of night, and a personification of mockery, ridicule and censure.

190.6   **delph**] s., pit.

190.23   **graunge**] n., storehouse

190.25   **infeft**] pp., abandoned entirely to you.

192.44   blin] v., cease.

197.01   *Sir Anthony Denny*] (b. 1501; d. 1549). Educated at St. Paul's School, London, and St. John's College, Cambridge, Knighted by Henry VIII in 1544, and later appointed an executor of Henry's will. Deny became a councilor to Edward VI, was dedicated to the Reformation, and thus highly admired by Roger Ascham and Sir John Cheke.

207.11   nall] n., an awl.

210.11   taccoy] inf., to accoy, seduce.

212.20   Collatine] The husband of Lucrece who took her own life following her rape by Tarquin.

212.22   Cartage quene] The story of Dido, Queen of Carthage, is told in Book 4 of Virgil's *Aeneid*.

212.23   The Rodopeian maide] When Demophoon failed to come to marry Phyllis, daughter of King Sithon, she hanged herself and was metamorphosed into an almond tree: Ovid, *Heroides*, 2.1.

212.50   Susan] Daniel, 13:1–63; Chaucer, *Canterbury Tales*, Man of Law's Tale 639; Parson's Tale 797.

213.01   Maistresse R] Q1 reads *maistresse Ryce*, possibly a lady of the court eulogized by Thomas Churchyard.

215.02   Countess of Pembroke] Ann Parr, sister of Catherine Parr, the sixth wife of Henry VIII, married to Sir William Herbert, the Earl of Pembroke, in 1534, and died 20 February 1551/52.

217.6   hye] v., hasten.

220.1   Procryn and Cephalus] Ovid, *Metamorphoses*, 7.700–865.

222.20   aungels fed] cf. Psalm 78:25.

225]   The source is Ovid, *Heroides* 1.1–12.

227.1–2   sunne] Matthew 27:45, Mark 15:33, Luke 23:44.

228.22   clergions] s., young song-birds.

229.18   Anthenor and Eneas] Aeneas allegedly betrayed the Trojans to the Greeks because of his hatred of Paris. Anthenor arranged with Agamemnon and Odysseus to deliver Troy into their hands.

229.78   Israel and the wicked Pharoas] Exodus 6–12.

231.4   Ovid's boke] The story of Jupiter and Europa is told in Ovid, *Metamorphoses*, 2. 845–875.

234.tit.]   1 John 5:18 (Vulgate).

234.57–60]   Matthew 8:25, Mark 4:38, Luke 8:24.

234.66   chickens] Matthew 23:37.

238.18   **baven blase]** s. phr., brushwood fire.

239.01   **W.G**] Possible manuscript sources suggest that the initials refer to William Gray (d. February 1557), a writer of ballads and a favorite attendant of Protector Somerset; *see also* 214.19.

241.01   *Henry Williams*] Henry's father, Sir John Williams, was an ardent supporter of Mary I in the Northumberland—Lady Jane Grey rebellion. Henry married Anne Stafford, daughter of the first Baron Stafford, and died without issue, 20 August 1551.

240.16.   **ramp]** s., vulgar woman.

248.17   **tole]** v., allure.

248.21   **Syrenes]** Ulysses stopped his ears so as not to hear the Sirens' song, Homer, *Odyssey* 12.39 ff.

245.29   **gillot]** s., wanton woman.

254.31   **other self]** Aristotle, *Nicomachean Ethics* 9.4.5.

256.13   **Ovid's arte]** Publius Ovidius Naso, 43 B.C.–A.D. 17, was well known for his *Ars Amatoria*, the art of love, and *Amores*, a collection of love poems.

264.01   *m. B*] The poem suggests that the lover's mistress was named Bayes. Richard Edward's *The Paradise of daynty devices* (1576) has an imitation of this poem.

266.01   *m. M*] In Thomas Proctor's *A gorgeous gallery of gallant inventions* (1578), a poem is titled: "In the prayse of a beautiful and vertuous Virgin, whose name begins with M."

269.23   **Arundell]** Possibilities include Elizabeth Arundell (b. 1526), Cecilia Arundell (b. 1527), and Mary (b. 1529), of Lanherne, Cornwall, England. One of these women is listed in the accounts of Mary I's funeral. Mary Arundell became the wife of Thomas Howard, Duke of Norfolk. George Turbervile praises Elizabeth Arundell in *Epitaphes, Epigrams, Songs and Sonets* (1567).

270.34   **dead]** Matthew 8:22, Luke 9:60.

272.01   *Musonius*] Rufus Musonius (30–101 A.D.) a popular Stoic philosopher whose interests included the relation between the individual and the state.

274.6   **Icarian beck]** The Icarian sea into which Icarus fell when he tried to fly too close to the sun.

274.11   **Julie]** Julius Caesar was merciful toward Cassius and Brutus after the battle of Pharsalia in which they supported Pompey, though they eventually assassinated him.

274.14   **overferse]** adj., overfierce

274.12–13   Nero, August] Where Nero committed suicide to escape public execution, Augustus Caesar lived moderately from 63 B.C. to A.D. 14.

274.19   Catoes meal, Antonius chere] Cato the Elder, sometimes called 'the Censor,' attempted to restore the integrity of morals and the simplicity of manners prevalent in the early days of the Republic. Marcus Antonius, Roman politician, orator, and censor, was put to death by an opposing political party in 87 B.C.

275.01–02   *Possidonius or Crates*] The former was a Greek Stoic philosopher, reputed the most learned in the 1st century B.C., educated at Athens, who later had Cicero as one of his pupils, and Marius and Pompey as his friends. He headed the school of Stoic philosophy at Rhodes. The latter was a Greek Cynic philosopher, borne at Thebes (c. 320 B.C.), who became a disciple of Diogenes.

276.01   *Metrodorus*] Metrodorus of Chios (4th century B.C.) atomist philosopher.

277.16   bodies twain] Ovid, *Tristia*, 4.4.72.

277.23   Scipio with Lelius] Scipio Africanus, the younger, was a constant friend of Gaius Laelius, both of whom are featured in Cicero's *De Amicitia*, where Laelius laments the death of Scipio in 129 B.C.

277.25   Damon with Pythias] Pythagorean philosophers of Syracuse in the first half of the 4th century B.C. who were celebrated for their friendship.

277.25   Gesippus, Tite] Boccaccio's *Decameron* 10.8. celebrates the friendship of Gisippus and Titus Quintus Fulvius.

277.26   Menetus sonne] Homer's *Iliad* tells of the friendship between Patroclus, Menoetius's son, and Achilles.

277.27   Euryalus and Nisus] Virgil's *Aeneid* 9.176–180, tells of their friendship at Troy and their escape with Aeneas to Italy where Euryalus died at the hands of the Rutulians.

277.27   Pylades and Orestes] Pylades, a son of Strophius, king of Phocus, and of Agamemnon's sister. When Orestes was brought to Stophius' court to protect him from the evil designs of Aegisthus, Pylades became his intimate and faithful friend.

277.29   Pirith and Theseus] When Pirithous, a Lapith prince, confronted Theseus, instead of fighting him he acknowledged the latter's valor, a gesture which bound the two in lifelong friendship. Theseus was sadly unable to rescue his friend from the underworld: Horace, *Odes* 4.7.27–28.

277.31   Cicero and Atticus] Cicero dedicated *De Amicitia* and *De Senectute* to Titus Pomponius Atticus, a Roman scholar and bibliophile, who died in 32 B.C. Cicero also addressed 16 volumes of letters to Atticus who edited and published them.

278.11   **Camenes]** In Italian mythology, four prophetic nymphs, identified by Roman poets with the Muses.

278.12   **gleaus]** s., gleaves, glaives, swords; *see also* 279.24.

278.15   **Oxate]** Oxathres, also called Exacreus, defended his brother, Darius III, against Alexander.

278.26   **Memphite Zoroas]** Zoroas, of Memphis, Egypt, was a great prophet and imminent foe of Alexander.

278.36   **quadrate]** adj., square.

278.44   **Mavorses]** Mavors, an old Latin name for Mars, the Roman god of war.

278.60   **Nectanab's bastard]** According to legend, Nectanebo was the last Pharaoh and the real father of Alexander the Great by Olympias, wife of Philip II of Macedonia, the reputed father of Alexander.

278.67   **Sophie of Minerve]** "the sevenfold sophie of Minerve." Sophia (Greek for 'wisdon') in Roman mythology was the goddess of wisdom and inventiveness, and patron of the arts, including sculptors, artists, actors, poets, physicians, teachers and students. Minerva was the virgin daughter of Jupiter, the supreme god.

278.86   **quishes]** s., cuisses, thigh-armor.

278.98   **seg]** s., segge man.

279.8   **Consul Marcus]** obscure translation of Beza's *Sylva* 2.7–8: *seruata ut Consul in urbe Tullius intereat.* The reference is to Cicero. shend, v., be destroyed.

279.30, 86   **Pompilius]** Gaius Popilius Laenas of Picenum, defended in the courts by Cicero.

279.57, 74, 88.   **Antonius]** Mark Anthony.

279.68   **Herennius]** On 3 December 43 B.C. Cicero was apprehended and murdered near Gaeta, by centurions, led by Herennius.

279.80   **Pitho]** In Greek mythology, Peitho, an attendant of Aphrodite, is the goddess of persuasion.

Appendix 1

Possible Manuscript Sources for Poems in Q2

No.	Possible MSS.

Poems by Surrey

1. Arundel Harington, fol. 49.
   Add. 36529, fol. 50r–v.
3. Add. 36529, fol. 54.
4. Arundel Harington, ff. 50–1.
   Add. 36529, fol. 53 (lines 1–30, 33–50).
   Blage, fol. 178r–v.
6. Add. 36529, fol. 55v.
7. Add. 36529, fol. 56.
8. Add. 36529, fol. 55.
9. Arundel Harington, fol. 212v.
11. Add. 36529, fol. 54.
12. Add. 36529, fol. 57.
13. Add. 36529, f. 55.
15. Add. 36529, fol. 51r–v.
16. Osborn
17. Add. 30513, ff. 107–8
    Devonshire, fol. 55r–v.
    Harl. 78, fol. 30v.
    PRO. SP, ff. 31v–2v.
18. Osborn, fol. 41v.
    Royal, app. fol. 52.
19. Arundel Harington, fol. 54r–v.
24. Add. 36529, fol. 53v.
27. Arundel Harington, fol. 37.
29. Arundel Harington, ff. 51–52.
30. Ash. 176, fol. 97r–v.
    Library Stowe 389, fol. 120.
    Osborn, fol. 22.

No.	Possible MSS.

31. Add. 30513, fol. 65v.
    Add. 36529, fol. 54v.
    Cotton Titus A. 24, fol. 80.
32. Harl. 78, fol. 29.
33. Add. 36529, fol. 56.
    Egerton, fol. 85v.
34. Add. 36529, fol. 57.
35. Harl. 78
36. Add. 36529, fol. 56v.
37. Add. 36529, fol. 56v.
38. Arundel Harington, fol. 50 (lines 1–12).
    Cotton Titus A. 24, fol. 83.
232. Harl. 78, fol. 30v.

Poems by Wyatt

42. Egerton, fol. 5r–v.
    Arundel Harington, fol. 63.
43. Egerton, fol. 11.
    Arundel Harington, fol. 63r–v.
44. Egerton, fol. 14v.
    Devonshire, fol. 19v.
    Arundel Harington, fol. 60v; ff. 65v–6.
    Blage, fol. 174.
45. Egerton, fol. 32v.
    Devonshire, fol. 36v.
    Arundel Harington, fol. 67 (bis).

No.	Possible MSS.	No.	Possible MSS.
46.	Egerton, fol. 38.	63.	Egerton, fol. 17.
	Devonshire fol. 31.		Blage, fol. 98.
	Arundel Harington, fol. 67	64.	Egerton, fol. 17v.
	(bis).		Devonshire, fol. 72.
47.	Egerton, fol. 54.	65.	Egerton, fol. 19
	Arundel Harington, fol. 67	66.	Egerton, fol. 12.
	(bis).	67.	Egerton, fol. 7v.
48.	Egerton, fol. 64v.		Devonshire, fol. 18.
	Arundel Harington, ff. 67 (bis)	68.	Egerton, fol. 66.
	v–68.		Blage, fol. 73.
49.	Egerton, fol. 66v.	69.	Egerton, ff. 8–10v.
	Arundel Harington, fol. 68.		Arundel Harington, fol.
50.	Egerton, ff. 4v–5.		102r–v.
	Devonshire, fol. 70.	70.	Egerton, fol. 35r–v.
51.	Egerton, fol. 11v.		Devonshire, fol. 16v.
	Devonshire, fol. 75v.	71.	Egerton, fol. 36r–v.
	Arundel Harington, fol. 63v.		Arundel Harington, fol. 78r–v.
52.	Egerton, fol. 19v.	72.	Egerton, fol. 37.
	Arundel Harington, fol. 66.		Devonshire, fol. 73.
53.	Egerton, fol. 20.		Arundel Harington, fol. 68v.
	Arundel Harington, fol. 66r–v.	73.	Egerton, fol. 29v.
54.	Egerton, fol. 20v.		Devonshire, fol. 73.
	Devonshire, fol. 82r–v.		Arundel Harington, fol. 68.
	Add. 36529, fol. 32.	74.	Egerton, fol. 4.
55.	Egerton, fol. 21v.		Devonshire, fol. 69v.
	Arundel Harington, fol. 66v.	75.	Egerton, fol. 4.
56.	Egerton, fol. 22.	76.	Egerton, fol. 40.
	Arundel Harington, fol. 67.		Devonshire, fol. 38v.
57.	Egerton, fol. 26v.		Arundel Harington, fol. 68v.
	Devonshire, ff. 69v–70.		Harl. 78, fol. 27.
58.	Egerton, fol. 24v.	77.	Egerton, fol. 40.
	Blage, fol. 128.		Devonshire, fol. 74.
59.	Egerton, fol. 31.		Add. 37529, fol. 32.
	Arundel Harington, fol. 63v.	78.	Egerton, fol. 40v.
60.	Egerton, fol. 32.		Arundel Harington, fol. 68v.
	Devonshire, fol. 35v.	79.	Blage, fol. 70.
	Add. 36529, fol. 32v.	80.	Devonshire, fol. 79v.
61.	Egerton, fol. 33.	82.	Blage, fol. 148.
	Arundel Harington, fol. 68r–v.	83.	Blage, fol. 104.
62.	Egerton, fol. 33.	84.	Add. 18752, fol. 163v.
	Arundel Harington, fol. 67	87.	Egerton, fol. 63r–v.
	(bis).	89.	Egerton, fol. 42v.

No.	Possible MSS.
90.	Egerton, fol. 42v–3; ff. 73v–4.
	Devonshire, fol. 71v.
91.	Egerton, ff. 43v–4.
	Devonshire, ff. 14v–15.
	Blage, fol. 125.
92.	Egerton, fol. 45.
	Devonshire, fol. 71v.
	Blage, fol. 129v.
	Harl. 78, fol. 27.
93.	Devonshire, fol. 32.
94.	Devonshire, fol. 69.
95.	Devonshire, ff. 70v–1.
	Blage, fol. 145.
	Osborn, fol. 31v.
96.	Add. 36529, fol. 32v.
97.	Add. 36529, fol. 32v.
	Blage, fol. 72.
98.	Egerton, fol. 22v.
	Arundel Harington, fol. 67.
99.	Egerton, fol. 23
	Arundel Harington, fol. 67r–v.
100.	Egerton, fol. 23v.
	Arundel Harington, ff. 67v.
101.	Egerton, fol. 24.
	Arundel Harington, ff. 67v–67 (bis).
102.	Egerton, fol. 12v.
	Arundel Harington, fol. 65.
103.	Egerton, fol. 13.
	Devonshire, fol. 75.
	Arundel Harington, fol. 65v.
104.	Egerton, fol. 3.
	Devonshire, fol. 3; fol. 75v.
	Arundel Harington, fol. 65v.
105.	Arundel Harington, fol. 216v.
106.	Arundel Harington, fol. 60v.
107.	Egerton, fol. 16v.
	Devonshire, fol. 61v.
108.	Egerton, ff. 67–8v.
	Devonshire, ff. 49–50v
	Arundel Harington, ff. 97v–8v.
114.	Egerton, fol. 69.

No.	Possible MSS.
115.	Egerton, fol. 69v.
116.	Egerton, fol. 50.
	Devonshire, fol. 73.
118.	Egerton, fol. 33v.
	Arundel Harington, fol. 67 (bis).
119.	Egerton, fol. 50
	Devonshire, fol. 72v.
	Add. 36529, fol. 32.
	Harl. 78, fol. 27.
120.	Arundel Harington, fol. 60v.
	Rawl. Poet 172, fol. 3v.
123.	Parker 168, Corpus Christi College, Cambridge, no. 21.
125.	Egerton, fol. 70.
	Harl. 78, fol. 29v.
126.	Harl. 78, fol. 27.
128.	Arundel Harington, fol. 216v.
130.	Egerton, fol. 54.
131.	Egerton, fol. 69.
132.	Devonshire, fol. 81v (7 lines).
	Blage, fol. 87 (31 lines).
133.	Egerton, fol. 54v.
134.	Egerton, ff. 50v–2v.
	Devonshire, f. 87.
	Arundel Harington, ff. 100–1v.
135.	Egerton, ff. 49r–v (lines 52–103).
	Devonshire, ff. 85v–7 (lines 1–27, 31–103).
	Arundel Harington, ff. 64–5 (lines 1–17, 20–8, 32–103).
	Add. 36529, ff. 30–1 (lines 1–17, 20–8, 32–103).
	Parker 168, Corpus Christi College, Cambridge 168, no. 22.
136.	Egerton, ff. 56–7v.
	Arundel Harington, ff. 99 (bis)–100).
137.	Egerton, ff. 100–1.
	Arundel Harington, fol. 99r–v.

No.	Possible MSS.

Poems by Uncertain Auctours

27. Arundel Harington, fol. 37.
139. Cotton Titus A. 24, ff. 80v–r.
140. Arundel Harington, fol. 22r–v.
     Blage, fol. 179.
141. Arundel Harington, fol. 23v–24.
     Ash. 48, ff. 24v–5.
142. Arundel Harington, fol. 101v.
144. Add. 26737, fol. 108v (lines
     10–21).
     Rawl. Poet 85, fol. 115v.
     Sloane 159, fol. 23.
145. Arundel Harington, fol. 20v–21v.
149. Arundel Harington, fol. 180–1.
152. Cotton Titus A. 24, fol. 81r–v.
153. Arundel Harington, fol. 37v.
156. Arundel Harington, fol. 217.
     Harl. 78, fol. 29v.
166. Cotton Titus A. 24, ff. 81v–2v.
169. Arundel Harington, fol. 210v.
175. Add. 23971, ff. 37v–9.
176. Arundel Harington, fol. 210v.
177. Devonshire, fol. 68–68v.
182. Ash. 48, ff. 23v–4r.
186. Arundel Harington, fol. 182v–
     183v (48 lines).
187. Arundel Harington, fol. 212v.

No.	Possible MSS.

189. Arundel Harington, fol. 59v.
195. Blage, fol. 172.
     Devonshire, fol. 42r–v.
196. Arundel Harington, ff. 22v–23v.
197. Landsdowne 98, fol. 206v.
207. Arch. Seld. B.10, ff. 201v–2.
212. Arundel Harington, fol. 168v–9v.
214. Arundel Harington, fol. 60.
218. Add. 15225, ff. 56–58
     Add. 28539, fol. 12.
     Sloane 1896, ff. 35v–38
222. Arundel Harington, ff. 179–179v.
227. Arundel Harington, fol. 60.
229. Arundel Harington, ff. 211v–212v.
232. Harl. 78, fol. 30.
234. Add. 60577, ff. 57v–58v.
     Rawl. Poet. 82, ff. 1v–2v.
239. Landsdowne 98, ff. 206.
     Sloane 1207, ff. 9–10.
240. Landsdowne 98, fol. 206
242. Arundel Harington, ff. 212v–213.
     Cotton Titus A. 24, fol. 9v.
243. Cotton Titus A. 24, fol. 80v.
254. Sloane 1896, ff. 40v–42.
255. Blage, fol. 154.
257. PRO. SP, ff. 18v–19.
     Sloane 1896, fol. 42.

Appendix 2

Poems in Q3 Significantly Changed from Q2

[5] *Complaint of a lover, that defied*
love, and was by love after
the more tor-
mented.

When sommer toke in hand the winter to assail,
With force of might, and vertue gret, his stormy blasts to quail,
    And when he clothed faire the earth about with grene,
And every tree new garmented, that pleasure was to sene:
5   Mine hart gan new revive, and changed blood did stur
Me to withdrawe my winter woes, that kept within the dore.
    Abrode, quod my desire: assay to set thy fote,
Where thou shalt finde the savour swete: for sprong is every rote.
    And to thy health, if thou were sick in any case,
10 Nothing more good, than in the spring the aire to fele a space.
    There shalt thou heare and se all kindes of birdes ywrought,
Well tune their voice with warble smal, as nature hath them tought.
    Thus pricked me my lust the sluggish house to leave:
And for my health I thought it best such counsail to receave.
15   So on a morow furth, unwist of any wight,
I went to prove how well it would my heavy burden light.
    And when I felt the aire so pleasant round about,
Lord, to my self how glad I was that I had gotten out.
    There might I se how Ver had every blossom hent:
20 And eke the new betrothed birdes ycoupled how they went.
    And in their songes me thought they thanked nature much,
That by her licence all that yere to love their happe was such,
    Right as they could devise to chose them feres throughout:

With much rejoysing to their Lord thus flew they al about.
25   Which when I gan resolve, and in my head conceave,
What pleasant life, what heapes of joy these litle birdes receave,
    And saw in what estate I wery man was brought,
By want of that they had at will, and I reject at nought:
    Lord how I gan in wrath unwisely me demeane.
30   I cursed love and him defied: I thought to turne the streame.
    But when I well beheld he had me under awe,
I asked mercy for my fault, that so transgrest his lawe.
    Thou blinded God (quod I) forgeve me this offence,
Unwittingly I went about, to malice thy pretence.
35   Wherwith he gave a beck, and thus me thought he swore,
Thy sorowe ought suffice to purge thy fault, if it were more.
    The vertue of which sound mine hart did so revive,
That I, me thought, was made as whole as any man alive,
    But here I may perceive mine errour all and some,
40   For that I thought that so it was: yet was it still undone.
    And all that was no more but mine expressed minde,
That faine would have some good reliefe, of Cupide well assinde.
    I turned home forthwith, and might perceve it well,
That he agreved was right sore with me for my rebell.
45   My harmes have ever since, encreased more and more,
And I remaine without his help, undone for evermore,
    A mirror let me be unto ye lovers all:
Strive not with love, for if ye do, it will ye thus befall.

[7] *Complaint of the lover disdained.*

In Ciprus, springes (where as dame Venus dwelt)
A Well so hotte is, that whoso tastes the same,
Were he of stone, as thawed yse should melt,
And kindeled finde his brest with fired flame.
5   Whose moist poyson dissolved hath my hate.
This crepyng fire my colde lyms so opprest,
That in the hart that harborde freedome late,
Endlesse dispaire long thraldome hath imprest.
An other so colde in frozen yse is founde,
10   Whose chilling venome of repugnant kinde
The fervent heat doth quenche of Cupides wounde:
And with the spot of change infectes the minde:
Whereof my dere hath tasted, to my paine.
My service growes is growen into disdaine.

[8] *Description and praise of his*
love Geraldine.

From Tuskane came my Ladies worthy race:
Faire Florence was sometime her auncient seate:
The Western yle, whose pleasant shore doth face
Wilde Cambers clifs, did gyve her lively heate:
5 Fostred she was with milke of Irishe brest:
Her sire, an Earle: her dame, of princes blood.
From tender yeres, in Britain she doth rest,
With kinges child, where she tasteth costly food.
Honsdon did first present her to mine iyen:
10 Bright is her hewe, and Geraldine she hight.
Hampton me taught to wishe her first for mine:
And Windsor, alas, doth chase me from her sight.
Her beauty of kinde, her vertues from above.
Happy is he, that can obtaine her love.

[13] *Complaint that his ladie after she*
knew of his love kept her face
alway hidden from
him.

I never saw my Ladie laye apart
Her cornet blacke, in cold nor yet in heate,
Sith first she knew my griefe was growen so great,
Which other fansies driveth from my hart.
5 That to my selfe I do the thought reserve,
The which unwares did wounde my woful brest,
But on her face mine eyes mought never rest,
Yet, sins she knew I did her love and serve,
Her golden tresses clad alway with blacke,
10 Her smiling lokes that hid thus evermore,
And that restraines which I desire so sore.
So doth this cornet governe me alacke:
In somer, sunne: in winters, breath a frost:
Wherby the light of her faire lokes I lost

[228] *The lover describeth his whole state unto his*
love, and promising her his faith-
full good will: assureth him-
self of hers again.

The Sunne when he hath spred his raies,
And shewde his face ten thousand waies.
Ten thousand thinges do then begin,
To shew the life that they are in.
5 The heaven shewes lively art and hue,
Of sundry shapes and colours new,
And laughes upon the earth anone.
The earth as cold as any stone,
Wet in the teares of her own kinde:
10 Gins then to take a joyfull minde.
For well she feeles that out and out,
The sunne doth warme her round about.
And dries her children tenderly,
And shewes them forth full orderly.
15 The moutaines hye and how they stand,
The valies and the great maine land
The trees, the herbes, the towers strong,
The castels and the rivers long.
And even for joy thus of this heate,
20 She sheweth furth her pleasures great.
And sleepes no more but sendeth forth
Her clergions her own dere worth.
To mount and flye up to the ayre,
Where then they sing in order fayre.
25 And tell in song full merely,
How they have slept full quietly,
That night about their mothers sides.
And when they have song more besides,
Then fall they to their mothers breastes,
30 Where els they fede or take their restes.
The hunter then soundes out his horne,
And rangeth straite through wood and corne.
On hilles then shew the Ewe and Lambe,
And every yong one with his dambe.
35 Then lovers walke and tell their tale,
Both of their blisse and of their bale.
And how they serve, and how they do,
And how their lady loves them to.

Then tune the birdes their armonie.
40 Then flocke the foule in companie.
Then every thing doth pleasure finde,
In that that comfortes all their kinde.
No dreames do drench them of the night,
Of foes that would them slea or bite.
45 As Houndes to hunt them at the taile,
Or men force them through hill and dale.
The shepe then dreames not of the Woulf,
The shipman forces not the goulf.
The Lambe thinkes not the butchers knife,
50 Should then bereve him of his life.
For when the Sunne doth once run in,
Then all their gladnes doth begin.
And then their skips, and then their play
So falles their sadnes then a way.
55 And thus all thinges have comforting,
In that that doth them comfort bring.
Save I alas, whom neither sunne,
Nor ought that God hath wrought and don,
May comfort ought, as though I were
60 A thing not made for comfort here.
For beyng absent from your sighte,
Which are my joy and whole delight
My comfort and my pleasure to,
How can I joy how should I do?
65 May sick men laugh that rore for paine?
Joy they in song that do complaine?
Are martirs in their tormentes glad?
Do pleasures please them that are mad?
Then how may I in comfort be,
70 That lacke the thing should comfort me.
The blind-man oft that lackes his sight,
Complaines not most the lacke of light.
But those that knewe their perfectnes,
And then do misse ther blisfulnes,
75 In martirs tunes they syng and waile,
The want of that which doth them faile.
And hereof comes that in my braines,
So many fansies worke my paines
For when I wayghe your worthynes,
80 Your wisdome and your gentlnes,
Your vertues and your sundry grace,

And minde the countenaunce of your face,
And how that you are she alone,
To whom I must both plaine and mone.
85   Whom I do love and must do still.
Whom I embrace and ay so wil,
To serve and please you as I can,
As may a wofull faithful man.
And finde my selfe so far you fro.
90   God knowes what torment, and what wo,
My rufull hart doth then imbrace.
The blood then chaungeth in my face.
My synnewes dull, in dompes I stand.
No life I fele in fote nor hand.
95   As pale as any clout and ded,
Lo sodenly the blood orespred,
And gon againe it nill so bide.
And thus from life to death I slide
As colde sometymes as any stone,
100 And then againe as hote anone.
Thus comes and goes my sundry fits,
To geve me sundri sortes of wits.
Till that a sigh becomes my frende,
And then to all this wo doth ende.
105 And sure I thinke that sigh doth roon,
From me to you where ay you woon.
For well I finde it easeth me,
And certes much it pleaseth me,
To think that it doth come to you,
110 As would to God it could so do.
For then I know you would soone finde,
By sent and favour of the winde,
That even a martirs sigh it is,
Whose joy you are and all his blis.
115 His comfort and his pleasure eke,
And even the same that he doth seke.
The same that he doth wishe and crave,
The same that he doth trust to have.
To tender you in all he may,
120 And all your likinges to obey,
As farre as in his powre shall lye:
Till death shall darte him for to dye.
But wealeaway mine owne most best,
My joy, my comfort, and my rest.

125 The causer of my wo and smart,
And yet the pleaser of my hart.
And she that on the earth above:
Is even the worthiest for to love.
Heare now my plaint, heare now my wo.

130 Heare now his paine that loves you so.
And if your hart do pitie beare,
Pitie the cause that you shall heare.
A dolefull foe in all this doubt,
Who leaves me not but sekes me out,

135 Of wretched forme and lothsome face,
While I stand in this wofull case:
Comes forth and takes me by the hand,
And saies frende harke and understand.
I see well by thy port and chere,

140 And by thy lokes and thy manere,
And by thy sadnes as thou goest,
And by the sighes that thou outthrowest:
That thou art stuffed full of wo,
The cause I thinke I do well know.

145 A fantaser thou art of some,
By whom thy wits are overcome.
But hast thou red old pamphlets ought?
Or hast thou known how bokes have taught
That love doth use to such as thow,

150 When they do thinke them safe enow.
And certain of their ladies grace:
Hast thou not sene oft times the case,
That sodenly there hap hath turnde,
As thinges in flame consumde and burnde?

155 Some by disceite forsaken right.
Some likwise changed of fansy light.
And some by absence sone forgot.
The lottes in love. Why knowest thou not?
And tho that she be now thine own:

160 And knowes the well as may be knowne.
And thinkes the to be such a one,
As she likes best to be her own.
Thinkes thou that others have not grace,
To shew and plain their wofull case.

165 And chose her for their lady now,
And swere her trouth as well as thow.
And what if she do alter minde?

Where is the love that thou wouldest finde?
Absence my frende workes wonders oft.
170 Now bringes full low that lay full loft.
Now turnes the minde now to and fro,
And where art thou if it were so?
If absence (quod I) be marveilous,
I finde her not so dangerous.
175 For she may not remove me fro,
The poore good will that I do owe
To her, whom unneth I love and shall,
And chosen have above them all,
To serve and be her own as far,
180 As any man may offer her.
And will her serve, and will her love,
As lowly as it shall behove.
And dye her own if fate be so.
Thus shall my hart nay part her fro.
185 And witnes shall my good will be,
That absence takes her not from me.
But that my love doth still encrease,
To minde her still and never cease.
And what I feele to be in me,
190 The same good will I think hath she.
As firme and fast to biden ay,
Till death depart us both away.
And as I have my tale thus told,
Steps unto me with countenance bold:
195 A stedfast frende a counsellour,
And namde is Hope my comfortour.
And stoutly then he speakes and saies:
Thou hast sayde trouth withouten nayes.
For I assure thee even by othe,
200 And theron take my hand and trothe.
That she is one of the worthiest,
The truest and the faithfullest,
The gentlest and the meekest of minde:
That here on earth a man may finde,
205 And if that love and trouth were gone,
In her it might be found alone.
For in her minde no thought there is,
But how she may be true iwis.
And tenders thee and all thy heale,
210 And wisheth both thy health and weale.

And loves thee even as farforth than,
As any woman may a man,
And is thine own and so she saies,
And cares for thee ten thousand waies.
215   On thee she speakes, on thee she thinkes,
With thee she eates, with thee she drinkes.
With thee she talkes, with thee she mones,
With thee she sighes, with thee she grones.
With thee she saies farewell mine own.
220   When thou God knowes full farre art gon.
And even to tell thee all aright,
To thee she saies full oft good night.
And names thee oft, her owne most dere,
Her comfort weale and al her chere.
225   And telles her pelow al the tale,
How thou hast doon her wo and bale,
And how she longes and plaines for the,
And saies why art thou so from me?
Am I not she that loves the best?
230   Do I not wish thine ease and rest?
Seke I not how I may the please?
Why art thou then so from thine ease?
If I be she for whom thou carest,
For whom in tormentes so thou farest:
235   Alas thou knowest to finde me here,
Where I remaine thine owne most dere,
Thine own most true thine owne most just,
Thine own that loves the styl and must.
Thine own that cares alone for the,
240   As thou I thinke dost care for me.
And even the woman she alone,
That is full bent to be thine owne.
What wilt thou more? what canst thou crave?
Since she is as thou wouldest her have.
245   Then set this drivell out of dore,
That in thy braines such tales doth poore.
Of absence and of chaunges straunge,
Send him to those that use to chaunge.
For she is none I the avowe,
250   And well thou maiest beleve me now.
When hope hath thus his reason said,
Lord how I fele me well apaide.
A new blood then orespredes my bones,

That al in ioy I stand at ones.
255 My handes I throw to heven above,
And humbly thank the god of love.
That of his grace I should bestow,
My love so well as I it owe.
And al the planets as they stand,
260 I thanke them to with hart and hand.
That their aspectes so frendly were,
That I should so my good will bere.
To you that are the worthiest,
The fairest and the gentillest.
265 And best can say, and best can do,
That longes me thinkes a woman to.
And therfore are most worthy far,
To be beloved as you ar.
And so saies hope in all his tale,
270 Wherby he easeth all my bale.
For I beleve and thinke it true,
That he doth speake or say of you.
And thus contented lo I stand,
With that that hope beares me in hand:
275 That I am yours and shall so be,
Which hope I kepe full sure in me.
As he that all my comfort is,
On you alone which are my blis.
My pleasure chief which most I finde,
280 And even the whole joy of my minde.
And shall so be untill the death,
Shall make me yeld up life and breath.
Thus good mine own, lo here my trust.
Lo here my truth and service just.
285 Lo in what case for you I stand.
Lo how you have me in your hand.
And if you can requite a man,
Requite me as you finde me than.

List 1

Substantive Variants between Q1 and Q2

The lemmata are those of the edited text (Q2 unless noted otherwise); the reading to the right of the bracket is the reading of Q1, unless otherwise noted. On the left of the page, the number of the poem is followed by the number of the line where substantives occur. To determine whether a change of word is a genuine substantive or the correction of a misprint resulting from foul case or compositorial error has not always been straightforward; yet I thought it more prudent to include rather than exclude all such instances.

Title page: *Cum privilegio ad impri | mendum Solum*] *Cum privilegio*

Preface:

| | 04 | *To the reder*] *The Printer to the | Reader* |
| | 2 | workes] Q1; woorkers Q2 |

Poem	Line	
1.	*Heading*	*as* Q1
	2	Twise] And
	4	ones] new
	5	Sins] Since
	43	sprites] spretes
2.	*Heading*	*as* Q1
	1	soote] Q1; foote Q2
		forth] furth
	8	flete] flote
3.	*Heading*	*as* Q1
	2	had made me runne] me causde to ronne
	18	of their request] that was their quest
	24	To . . . fled] The woe wherin my hart was fed

Renaissance and English Text Society Volume XXXII

Richard Tottel's Songes and Sonettes: The Elizabethan Version. MRTS Vol. 338, Tempe, AZ, 2007.

Poem	Line	
4.	*Heading*	*as* Q1
	3	is] Q1; in Q2
	5	He causeth thone] He makes the one
	14	sute] suite
	32	his[1]] the
	38	ones] once
5.	*Heading*	*as* Q1
	6	woes] woe
	7	A brode] Abrode
	11	heare] here
	22	love] Q1; leve Q2
	34	Unwittingly] Unwillingly
	38	whole] hole
	39	I] ye
	41	expressed] empressed
6.	*Heading*	*as* Q1
	7	restraine] refraine
7.	*Heading*	*as* Q1
	2	hotte . . . same] hote, that whoso tastes thesame
	5	hart] hate
	6	With] This
		ar supprest] so opprest
	7	Feeleth] That in
		smart] late
	9	well of] so colde in
	14	Wherby . . . growes] My service thus is growen
8.	*Heading*	*as* Q1
	4	furst gave] did gyve
	7	did she] she doth
	8	With a] With
		who] where she
		ghostly] costly
9.	*Heading*	*as* Q1
10.	*Heading*	*as* Q1
11.	*Heading*	*as* Q1
	3	The] Q1; Set Q2
		plots] plot
	14	me] we
12.	*Heading*	*as* Q1
	1	doth] Q1; do Q2
13.	*Heading*	*as* Q1
	7	For] But

Poem	Line	
13.	8	Sins that] Yet, sins
	9	tresse is clad] tresses cladde
	10	to hide] that hid
	12	corner] cornet
		my] me
	13	winter] *edd.*; winters Q2. Q1
		of] a
14.	*Heading*	*as* Q1
	9	Garret] Ladie
15.	*Heading*	*as* Q1
	4	feastes] feast
	40	nightes] night
16.	Heading	*as* Q1
17.	Heading	*as* Q1
	36	ware] waxe
18.	*Heading*	*as* Q1
	80˚	belongeth] belonged
19.	*Heading*	*as* Q1
20.	*Heading*	*as* Q1
21.	*Heading*	*as* Q1
	10	folish] foolish
	18	in the felde] the in feeld
22.	*Heading*	*as* Q1
	7	my] Q1; my well Q2
23.	*Heading*	*as* Q1
	27	troubles] Q1; troules Q2
24.	*Heading*	*The lover describes his	restlesse state* Q1
	22	one] on
25.	*Heading*	*as* Q1
	12	prise] price
	22	winde] Q1; win Q2
26.	*Heading*	*as* Q1
	1	walke] Q1; walkt Q2
	13	thee] the
	14	grow] go
27	*Heading*	*Of the dissembling lover.* Q1, no. 243.
28.	*Heading*	*as* Q1, no. 262.
29.	*Heading*	*as* Q1, no. 264.
	21	Doway] Do way
	22	thee] the
	39	so dyed] likewise
	56	would] should

Poem	Line	
29.	63	rue] ruse
	64	Thus] This
		bote] bode
	66	A] I
30.	*Heading*	*as* Q1, no. 265.
	2	not I] I not
	7	serve] Q1; serves Q2
	55	breath] brethe
31.	*Heading*	*as* Q1, no. 27.
32.	*Heading*	*as* Q1, no. 28.
33.	*Heading*	*as* Q1, no. 29.
34.	*Heading*	*as* Q1, no. 30.
	8	With] Wepe
35.	*Heading*	*as* Q1, no. 31.
36.	*Heading*	*A praise of sir Thomas wyate thelder	for his excellent learning.* Q1, no. 263.
37.	*Heading*	*as* Q1, no. 32.
38.	*Heading*	*as* Q1, no. 33.
	4	dyd] doth
	20	belief] Q1; belife Q2
39.	*Heading*	*as* Q1, no. 34.
40.	*Heading*	*as* Q1, no. 35.
	1	retchlesse] rechlesse
41.	*Heading*	*as* Q1, no. 36.
42.	*Heading*	*as* Q1, no. 37.
43.	*Heading*	*as* Q1, no. 38.
	4	hath] have
44.	*Heading*	*as* Q1, no. 39.
	7	lost] Q1; last Q2
45.	*Heading*	*as* Q1, no. 40.
	9	one] on
	10	crying] errying
46.	*Heading*	*as* Q1, no. 41.
47.	*Heading*	*as* Q1, no. 42.
48.	*Heading*	*as* Q1, no. 43.
49.	*Heading*	*as* Q1, no. 44.
50.	*Heading*	*as* Q1, no. 45.
51.	*Heading*	*as* Q1, no. 46.
52.	*Heading*	*as* Q1, no. 47.
53.	*Heading*	*as* Q1, no. 48.
54.	*Heading*	*as* Q1, no. 49.
	11	thus I] Q1; *omit* thus Q2

Poem	Line	
55.	*Heading*	*as* Q1, no. 50.
56.	*Heading*	*Of douteous love.* Q1, no. 51.
	5	his] this
57.	*Heading*	*as* Q1, no. 52.
58.	*Heading*	*as* Q1, no. 53.
59.	*Heading*	*as* Q1, no. 54.
60.	*Heading*	*as* Q1, no. 55.
61.	*Heading*	*as* Q1, no. 56.
62.	*Heading*	*as* Q1, no. 57.
	4	Though he] *edd;* Though thee Q2; Thought he Q1
63.	*Heading*	*as* Q1, no. 58.
64.	*Heading*	*as* Q1, no. 59.
	6	ruth] such
65.	*Heading*	*as* Q1, no. 60.
	21	of] of thy
66.	*Heading*	*as* Q1, no. 61.
67.	*Heading*	*as* Q1, no. 62.
68.	*Heading*	*as* Q1, no. 63.
69.	*Heading*	*as* Q1, no. 64.
	10	fiercely] *edd.*; fircly Q2; fierly Q1
	43	through] thorough
	84	Whereas] Where:as
	89	honour] nurture
	90	actes] honor
		lift them up] bring them
	106	deceites] Q1; diceites Q2
70.	*Heading*	*as* Q1, no. 65.
71.	*Heading*	*as* Q1, no. 66.
72.	*Heading*	*as* Q1, no. 67.
	3	heard] herd
73.	*Heading*	*as* Q1, no. 68.
	1	heard] hard
74.	*Heading*	*as* Q1, no. 69.
75.	*Heading*	*as* Q1, no. 70.
	12	trapt] trap
76.	*Heading*	*as* Q1, no. 71.
	5	forth] furth
77.	*Heading*	*as* Q1, no. 72.
78.	*Heading*	*as* Q1, no. 73.
79.	*Heading*	*as* Q1, no. 74.
80.	*Heading*	*as* Q1, no. 75.
81.	*Heading*	*as* Q1, no. 76.

Poem	Line	
81.	2	mynde] Q1; mindes Q2
82.	*Heading*	*as* Q1, no. 77.
	2	eares] Q1; cares Q2
83.	*Heading*	*as* Q1, no. 78.
	27	neare] nere
84.	*Heading*	*The lover praieth not to be disdai-* | *ned, refused, mis-* *trusted,* | *nor forsaken.* Q1, no. 79.
	01	to be] Q1; *be* Q2
	3	Since] Sins
	6	Nor] Q1; For Q2
	20	now] ne
85.	*Heading*	*as* Q1, no. 80.
	7	The] Q1; My Q2
86.	*Heading*	*as* Q1, no. 81.
	1	every] ever
	16	unto] to
87.	*Heading*	*as* Q1, no. 83.
88.	*Heading*	*as* Q1, no. 84.
	3	Against] Q3; Ainst Q2, Q1
	5	by] Q3; thy Q2; in thy Q1
89.	*Heading*	*as* Q1, no. 85.
90.	*Heading*	*as* Q1, no. 86.
	10	day] Q1; nay Q2
	12	nay] Q1; day Q2
	25	now hath] hath
91.	*Heading*	*as* Q1, no. 87.
	28	Plaining] Playning
92.	*Heading*	*as* Q1, no. 88.
93.	*Heading*	*as* Q1, no. 89.
	4	his proper] Q1; *omit* proper Q2
	6	And . . . ranne] Directly downe into . . . ranne
94.	*Heading*	*as* Q1, no. 90.
	4	dost] doest
95.	*Heading*	*as* Q1, no. 91.
	43	swarved] swerved
96.	*Heading*	*as* Q1, no. 92.
97.	*Heading*	*as* Q1, no. 93.
	6	Her] The
98.	*Heading*	*How unpossible it is to finde* | *quiet in his love.* Q1, no. 94.
	02	in] in his

Poem	Line	
98.	3	With . . . pain] That love or wait it, alike doth me payne.
	4	For] And
	13	One drop of] Any thing
99.	*Heading*	*as* Q1, no. 95.
	5	is] Q1; his Q2
	7	that very] that
	8	So styl] Still
100.	*Heading*	*as* Q1, no. 96.
101.	*Heading*	*as* Q1, no. 97.
102.	*Heading*	*as* Q1, no. 98.
	12	farre . . . nere] a farre of, and fre syng nere
	13	that . . . destroy] that by love my selfe I stroy
103.	*Heading*	*as* Q1, no. 99.
104.	*Heading*	*as* Q1, no. 100.
	6	on] after
	7	there . . . other] is there none nother
	11	sins] since
105.	*Heading*	*as* Q1, no. 101.
	8	somtime] somthing
106.	*Heading*	*as* Q1, no. 102.
	9	sins] since
107.	*Heading*	*as* Q1, no. 103.
	2	with] which
	4	heard] herd
	12	now assaile] assaile
108.	*Heading*	*as* Q1, no. 104.
	5	sins] since
	18	hies] hides
	35	sins] since
		lese] leese
	55	Those] These
	61	that] of
	63	so toucheth me within] that toucheth me so within
	87	fro me] me fro
109.	*Heading*	*as* Q1, no. 105.
	12	shall you] shalt thou
110.	*Heading*	*as* Q1, no. 106.
	16	thee] thy
111.	*Heading*	*as* Q1, no. 107.
	26	aloft] *edd.*; a loft Q2, Q1
112.	*Heading*	*as* Q1, no. 108.

Poem	Line	
113.	*Heading*	*as* Q1, no. 109.
	7	and rew with] *edd*.; and rew Q2; alas, with Q1
	12	the] thy
114.	*Heading*	*as* Q1, no. 110.
115.	*Heading*	*as* Q1, no. 111.
116.	*Heading*	*as* Q1, no. 112.
	4	the] thee
117.	*Heading*	*as* Q1, no. 113.
	2	secretly] Q3; secertly Q2; secretely Q1
118.	*Heading*	*as* Q1, no. 266.
119.	*Heading*	*as* Q1, no. 267.
	1	thrones] thornes
120.	*Heading*	*as* Q1, no. 268.
121.	*Heading*	*as* Q1, no. 269.
	1	helpth] helpthe
	2	wit] will
122.	*Heading*	*as* Q1, no. 270.
	4	thyne] thy
	10	heaven] heanen
	13	may thou] thou may
123.	*Heading*	*as* Q1, no. 271.
	11	doler] dolore
	23	ylles] evyls
	24	plain] playne
124.	*Heading*	*as* Q1, no. 114.
125.	*Heading*	*as* Q1, no. 115.
126.	*Heading*	*as* Q1, no. 116.
	4	Poore] Pore
127.	*Heading*	*as* Q1, no. 117.
128.	*Heading*	*as* Q1, no. 118.
129.	*Heading*	*as* Q1, no. 119.
	4	worldly] lordly
130.	*Heading*	*as* Q1, no. 120.
	6	unposest] Q1; unposess Q2
		now in] in
131.	*Heading*	*as* Q1, no. 121.
132.	*Heading*	*as* Q1, no. 122.
133.	*Heading*	*as* Q1, no. 123.
	7	of one] Q1; one of Q2
134.	*Heading*	*as* Q1, no. 124.
	37	scarpes]scrapes
	69	seking] semyng

Poem	Line	
134.	69	raigne] raine
	71	worst] Q1; worse Q2
	81	delits] delite
	87	a] his
	94	never] ever
	100	Madde] Q1; Made Q2
	102	thy] your
135.	Heading	*as Q1, no. 125.*
	7	not that] not
	21	vice] nice
	62-63	*These lines are repeated in Q1, not in Q2. One set appears at the bottom of L_3^v, while the other set is found at the top of L_4^r.*
136.	Heading	*as Q1, no. 126.*
	24	moysture] Q1; moyster Q2
	39	thy] the
	45	But if thou can . . . cant] By which returne . . . cant
	60	paine disburse] charge deburs
	66	thy] thine
	67	se that] se
	68	thy sister] Q1; sister Q2
	72	it ²] Q1; thou it Q2
	89	guift] thing
137.	Heading	*as Q1, no. 127.*
	54	he] her
	71	to] to the
	77	to the] tothe
138.	Title	*Songes and Sonettes of	Uncertain auctours.] Uncertain auctours.*
	Heading	*as Q1, no. 168.*
	56	her] here
139.	Heading	*as Q1, no. 169.*
140.	Heading	*as Q1, no. 170.*
	3	my] by
	17	heard] hard
141.	Heading	*as Q1, no. 171.*
	18	makes] wakes
	38	fleshy] Q1; fleshly Q2
142.	Heading	*as Q1, no. 172.*
	2	cunning] connyng
	6	cunning] conning
	32	dispaire] dispayre

Poem	Line	
	Poem	**Line**
143.	*Heading*	*as* Q1, no. 173.
144.	*Heading*	*as* Q1, no. 174.
	01	state	of this] Q3; *state*	this Q2, Q1
145.	*Heading*	*as* Q1, no. 175.
146.	*Heading*	*as* Q1, no. 176.
147.	*Heading*	*as* Q1, no. 177.
	10	enchaunce] enhaunce
148.	*Heading*	*as* Q1, no. 179,
149.	*Heading*	*as* Q1, no. 180.
150.	*Heading*	*as* Q1, no. 181.
	2	As] And
	48	begunne] begone
	68	makes] face
	87	breath] breathe
	102	By . . . slaine] Whom . . . hath slayne
	103	Whom] By
	104	Hath . . . disdaine] Murdred with false disdaine
151.	*Heading*	*as* Q1, no. 182.
	21	stepte] step
152.	*Heading*	*as* Q1, no. 183.
	4	worldly] wordly
	9	Yet] For
153.	*Heading*	*as* Q1, no. 184.
	14	Where] Q1; Whe[n] Q2 *damaged*
	26	forpassed] Q1; for passed Q2
	28	love] lone
154.	*Heading*	*as* Q1, no. 185.
	86	hard] heard
	143	for lore] forlore
	162	Those shining] I mean, those
	177	plained] playned
	181	hard] heard
	225	myne] my
	226	Cruell mishappe] Mishappe I meane
	233	quite gone] gone
	241	O welth unstable] O slidyng blisse
	242	O slidying blisse] O welth unstable
	265	this] my
	299	would] wold
155.	*Heading*	*as* Q1, no. 186.
	7	nerer] nere
156.	*Heading*	*Of the lovers unquiet*	*state.* Q1, no. 187.

Poem	Line	
156.	02	*state*] Q1; *stare* Q2
	7	doon] ready
157.	*Heading*	*Where good will is some profe	will appere.* Q1, no. 188.
	10	set] never
	21	makes] Q1; make Q2
158.	*Heading*	*as* Q1, no. 189.
	4	to end his life] his life to traine
	10	fame] praise
	12	don] doon
159.	*Heading*	*as* Q1, no. 190.
	2	heare] here
	6	a live] *edd.*; a lives Q2, Q1
	7	poore] pore
	15	thee] the
	16	yet] now
160.	*Heading*	*as* Q1, no. 191.
161.	*Heading*	*as* Q1, no. 192.
	2	paine is] paynes
	11	Should] Sould
	13	poore] pore
	17	doth] do
	20	sprites] spirites
	29	griefes] grieves
162.	*Heading*	*Of a new maried Student.* Q1, no. 193.
163.	*Heading*	as Q1, no. 194.
	39	shooteth] shoteth
164.	*Heading*	*as* Q1, no. 195.
	4	live] *edd.*; lives Q2, Q1
	8	sute] fate
	24	hart] heart
	25	forth] furth
	29	to^1] too
165.	*Heading*	*as* Q1, no. 196.
	10	Taspyre] Tasapyre
	19	drede] dreede
166.	*Heading*	*All worldly pleasures fade.* Q1, no. 197
	1	ne] no
	13	forth] furth
	14	Then] the
	26	sugred] surged
		bandes] bendes
167.	*Heading*	*as* Q1, no. 198.

Poem	Line	
167.	8	storme] Q1; streame Q2
	15	my ²] Q1; me Q2
	27	(poore foole)] pore fole
	36	So] Q1; Do Q2
	52	from] fro
168.	*Heading*	*as* Q1, no. 199.
169.	*Heading*	*as* Q1, no. 200.
	14	bes T] best
170.	*Heading*	*as* Q1, no. 201.
	16	craving] Q1; carving Q2
	24	lives . . . sunne] liveth under sunne
171.	*Heading*	*A comfort to the complaynt* | *of Thestilis.* Q1, no. 234.
	32	where] Q1; were Q2
172.	*Heading*	*as* Q1, no. 202.
	5	pray] play
	9	Away] Q1; A way Q2
173.	*Heading*	*as* Q1, no. 203.
	4	within] the within
174.	*Heading*	*as* Q1, no. 204.
	15	grenesse] grenes
	16	proofe] profe
	25	clerely] Q3; clcrcly Q2; clercly Q1
175.	*Heading*	*as* Q1, no. 205.
	5	swerve] swarve
	15	poore] pore
176.	*Heading*	*as* Q1, no. 206.
	3	found] Q1; sound Q2
177.	*Heading*	*as* Q1, no. 207.
	24	begone] be gone
178.	*Heading*	*as* Q1, no. 208.
	2	behold] lo here
	5	sins] since
	12	remaines.] Q1; remaine Q2
	17	till death doth] *edd.*; the death Q2; the death do Q1
	18	sprite] spirite
179.	*Heading*	*as* Q1, no. 209.
180.	*Heading*	*as* Q1, no. 210.
	18	Lyes] Lieth
181.	*Heading*	*as* Q1, no. 211.
	11	silver] Q1; *corr.*; sliver Q2 *unc.*
	54	your] youe
182.	*Heading*	*as* Q1, no. 212.

Poem	Line	
182.	10	crowch] cowche
183.	*Heading*	*as* Q1 no. 213.
	6	matcht] Q1; match Q2
184.	*Heading*	*as* Q1, no. 214.
	10	arvyng] Q1; swering Q2
	11	oft] Q1; of Q2
	17	to fall] Q1; fall Q2
	26	pretended] Q1; pretented Q2
	36	repaire] repayre
185.	*Heading*	*as* Q1, no. 215.
	7	Chameleon] Q1; Thameleon Q2
186.	*Heading*	*as* Q1, no. 216.
187.	*Heading*	*as* Q1, no. 217.
188.	*Heading*	*as* Q1, no. 218.
	13	Laure] Laura
189.	*Heading*	*as* Q1, no. 219.
190.	*Heading*	*as* Q1, no. 220.
	1	unkinde] and unkind
	3	Ground] The ground
	4	Trikle] To tickle
	7	Sacke] The sacke
	8	causeles] Q3; causels Q2; so causels Q1
	10	Den] Darke den
	19	al spite] very spite
	23	Heape] The heape
	27	for] that for
	29	of my] of
191.	*Heading*	*as* Q1, no. 221.
192.	*Heading*	*as* Q1, no. 222.
	13-18	*Added in* Q2.
	27	loved] loude
	33	false] salse
	39	tyed] tayed
193.	*Heading*	*as* Q1, no. 223.
194.	*Heading*	*as* Q1, no. 224.
	11	kils] kilith
	19	Moone] Mone
195.	*Heading*	*as* Q1, no. 225.
196.	*Heading*	*as* Q1, no. 226.
	1	you] yon
197.	*Heading*	*as* Q1, no. 227.
	8	quit] Q3; quite Q2, Q1

Poem	Line	
198.	*Heading*	*as* Q1, no. 228
199.	*Heading*	*as* Q1, no. 229.
200.	*Heading*	*as* Q1, no. 230.
	4	favour or despite] the favour or the spite
201.	*Heading*	*as* Q1, no. 231.
202	*Heading*	*as* Q1, no. 232.
	1	The] Tho
203.	*Heading*	*as* Q1, no. 233.
204.	*Heading*	*The uncertain state of*	*a lover.* Q1, no. 235.
205.	*Heading*	*as* Q1, no. 236.
206.	*Heading*	*as* Q1, no. 237.
	01	*Troylus to*] Q1; *Troylusto* Q2
	20	secretly] seretely
	66	raigne] raine
207.	*Heading*	*as* Q1, no. 238.
	15	thee] the
	16	asketh] axith
	18	forth², forth beast] forth² beast
	19	hye] high
	21	thee] the
208.	*Heading*	*as* Q1, no. 239.
	5	flight] fiight
	8	thee] the
	18	forththrow] furthrowe
209.	*Heading*	*as* Q1, no. 240.
	4	eare] care
	18	doth] both
	20	clarke] clacke
	22	do] dothe
	26	eares] cares
210.	*Heading*	*as* Q1, no. 241.
211.	*Heading*	*as* Q1, no. 244.
	3	feareth] fearth
	10	and] or
212.	*Heading*	*as* Q1, no. 245.
	1	may be he] Q1; may be Q2
	8	lide] lied
	15	thee] the
	16	dede] dedes
	23	Rodopeian maide] R. so depe can avoyde
	27	thee] the
	42	dare] I dare

Poem	Line	
212.	58	floorisht] floorist
	59	thy] the
	62	shamefull] shamefall
213.	*Heading*	*A praise of maistresse	Ryce. Q1, no. 246.*
	2	hath] had
	7	a row] arowe
	9	herd] heard
	22	The . . . stil] The audience ceased with the same
	24	tonge] tonges
	30	for] Q1; [f]or Q2 *damaged*
	31	weare] were
	41	aside] a side
	44	least] lest
	47	R.] Rise
214.	*Heading*	*as Q1, no. 247.*
215.	*Heading*	*Of the death of the late county	of Penbroke. Q1, no. 248.*
	01	*countisse] county*
216	*Heading*	*as Q1, no. 249.*
	3	or wo] of wo
	15	outward] cutward
217.	*Heading*	*as Q1, no. 250.*
218.	*Heading*	*as Q1, no. 251.*
	2	seme right wondrous] semeth wonderous
	64	withered] wethered
	73	lest] least
219.	*Heading*	*as Q1, no. 252.*
	25	swerve] swarve
	36	paine] payne
		joy] Joee
220.	*Heading*	*as Q1, no. 259.*
	8	forth] she
	21	my] myne
	23	me] that me
221.	*Heading*	*as Q1, no. 260.*
	2	That . . . drest] With golde and purple that nature hath drest
	9	Diamondes] polisht Diamondes
222.		*not in Q1*
223.		*not in Q1*
224.		*not in Q1*
	2	ofte] *edd.*; softe Q2
225.		*not in Q1*

Poem	Line	
226.		*not in* Q1
	10	me see] Q3; mese Q2
227.		*not in* Q1
228.		*not in* Q1
	88	may] *corr.*; nay *unc.*
	175	me] Q3; ire Q2
	201	one of] *edd.*; *omit* of Q2
229.		*not in* Q1
230.		*not in* Q1
231.		*not in* Q1
232.		*not in* Q1
233.		*not in* Q1
	23	shet] *edd.*; shit Q2
	32	[t]hou Q2 *faded ink*
234.		*not in* Q1
	64	fend] *edd.*; send Q2
235.		*not in* Q1
236.		*not in* Q1
237.		*not in* Q1
238.		*not in* Q1
	14	hinder.] *corr.* Q2; hinde *unc.*
	28	ease] *edd.*; case Q2
239.	Heading	*An epitaphe written by w. G.	to be set upon his owne	grave.* Q1, no. 255.
	15	slaine] Q1; slayns Q2
240.	Heading	*as* Q1, no. 256.
	20	can] cad
241.	Heading	*as* Q1, no. 253.
	4	for] from
	12	stifly] stifely
	18	a] our
	22	thou has cut] Q1; thou cut Q2
242.		*not in* Q1
243.	Heading	*as* Q1, no. 257.
244.	Heading	*as* Q1, no. 258.
	10	rote] frute
	14	buildyng] buildyngs
245.	Heading	*as* Q1, no. 254.
	2	Whilist] While erst
	6	ground] gounde
	11	were faire] sofaire
	13	and thinkyng] *omit* and

Poem	Line	
246.		*not in* Q1
	5	but] Q3; dut Q2
247	Heading	Not to trust to much but beware | by others calamat-ies. Q1, no. 178.
	17	heare] here
	24	spred] spied
248	Heading	*An answere to a song before im-| printed beginnyng. To | walke on doutfull | grounde.* Q1, no. 261.
	17	tole] toll
249.		*not in* Q1
	34	unfitting] *edd.*; unsitting Q2
250.		*not in* Q1
	5	have] *edd.*; had Q2
	28	[t]heir Q2 *damaged*
251.		*not in* Q1
252.		*not in* Q1
	13	mourne] Q3; mo[ ]e Q2 *damaged*
	19	reft] *edd.*; rest Q2
253.		*not in* Q1
	5	Both] *corr.*; Bath *unc.*
254.		*not in* Q1
255.	Heading	*as* Q1, no. 82.
256.	Heading	*as* Q1, no. 242.
	7	one] on
	16	the] that
	18	What] hat *missing* W
	32	crafty shrewe] craft ye shrewe
257 to 270		*not in* Q1
270.	28	bodie] Q3; bodies Q2
271.	Title	*Songes written by N. G. | Songes written by Nicolas Grimald.*
	Heading	*The Muses.* Q1, no. 133.
	5	all] old
	16	rankes] renkes
272.	Heading	*as* Q1, no. 134.
273.	Heading	*as* Q1, no. 149.
274.	Heading	*as* Q1, no. 150.
	14	overmeek] onermeek
275.	Heading	*as* Q1, no. 151.
276.	Heading	*as* Q1, no. 152.
277.	Heading	*as* Q1, no. 154.
278.	Heading	*as* Q1, no. 165.

Poem	Line	
278.	2	dredfull trompets] taratantars
	10	be bledd] bebledd
	12	gleaves] *edd.*; gleaus Q2, Q1
	19	kynde] kindes
	22	smites] down
		wounds] beats
	23	shinyng] shinand
	47	whole] holl
	57	Alexanders] Alisanders
	66	martiall] Martiall
	91	his] the
	95	renk] Q1; reuk Q2
	99	soule] soll
279.	*Heading*	*as* Q1, no. 166.
	10	Rome] Room
	15	showres] stowrs
	21	prove] prone
	24	to] *edd.*; so Q2, Q1
	27	senate] Senate
	41	Romes] Rooms
280.	*Heading*	*as* Q1; no. 167

List 2
Substantive Variants between Q2 and Q3

The lemmata are those of the edited text (Q2 unless noted otherwise); the reading to the right of the bracket is the reading of Q3 (unless noted otherwise). Where appropriate, the rejected reading of Q2 concludes the entry. The number of the poem is followed by the number of the line where substantives occur. To determine whether a change of word is a genuine substantive or the correction of a misprint resulting from foul case or compositorial error has not always been straightforward; yet I thought it more prudent to include rather than exclude all such instances.

Preface	.2	workes] Q1; woorkers Q2; workers Q3

Poem	Line	
1.	1	furth] forth
2.	1	soote] Q3, Q1; foote Q2
4.	3	is] Q3, Q1; in Q2
4.	26	furth] forth
5.	7	A brode] Abrode Q3, Q1
	18	self] Q3, Q1; seif Q2
	23	them] Q3, Q1; thein Q2
	46	remaine] Q3, Q1; reinaine Q2
7.	2	who] whoso Q3, Q1
	5	hart] hate Q3, Q1
	6	With] This Q3, Q1
		ar supprest] so opprest Q3, Q1
	7	Feeleth] That in Q3, Q1
		smart] late Q3, Q1
	9	well of] so colde in Q3, Q1
	14	Whereby . . . growes] My service thus is grown Q3, Q1
8.	4	furst gave] did gyve Q3, Q1

Poem	Line	
8.	7	did she] she doth Q3, Q1
	8	With a] *omit* a Q3, Q1
		who] where she Q3, Q1
		ghostly] costly Q3, Q1
11.	3	The] Q3, Q1; Set Q2
		plots] plot Q3, Q1
12.	1	doth] Q3, Q1; do Q2
	8	heares] heeres Q3, Q1
13.	7	For] But Q3, Q1
	8	Sins that] Yet, sins Q3, Q1
	9	tresse is] tresses cladde] Q3, Q1
	10	to hide] that hid Q3, Q1
	12	corner] cornet Q3, Q1
		my] me Q3, Q1
	13	winter] *edd*.; winters Q1–3
		of] a Q3, Q1
14.	9	Garret] Ladie Q3, Q1
15.	4.	feastes] feast Q3, Q1
	13	where] were Q3, Q1
	40	nightes] night Q3, Q1
17.	36	ware] waxe Q3, Q1
19.	34	Sum] Some Q3, Q1
20.	30	sonne] sunne
21.	10	folish] foolish Q3, Q1
	12	your] you
23.	2	herd] hard
26.	1	walke] Q3, Q1; walkt Q2
29.	57	Nature] nature Q3, Q1
	64	boote] bote Q3; bode Q1
	70	ye] you Q3, Q1
30.	5	have] hath
	45	an] and ² Q3, Q1
31.	8	continuance] continnance
33.	3	dan] Dan
53.	13	outstart] out start
58.	01	*ladie*] *Lady*
62.	2	thee] the
63.	16	suretie] suerte
66.	14	a part] apart
69.	01	*Love	to Reason: . . . with Loves*] love to	reason with loves
	10	fiercely] *edd*.; firely Q3; fircly Q2
	106	deceites] Q3, Q1; diceites

Poem	Line	
82.	13	that] not
86.	37	Sith] Sins
88.	3	Against] Q3; Ainst Q2, Q1
	5	by] Q3; thy Q2
90.	2	bade] bad
	12	nay] Q3, Q1; day Q2
94.	5	sins] since
95.	46	Lea] Leo
99.	5	is] Q1; his Q3, Q2
108.	5	sins] since Q3, Q1
	97	red] read
111.	26	aloft] *edd*.; a loft Q1–Q3
117.	2	secretly] Q3; secertly Q2; secretely Q1
119	1	thrones] thornes Q3, Q1
121.	1	helpth] helpeth Q3; helpthe Q1
	2	wit] will Q3, Q1
126.	5	mine] my
128.	8	to] do
133.	7	one of] of one Q3, Q1
134.	35	doth] do
	37	scarpes] scrapes Q3, Q1
137.	69	lest] least
141.	25	bring] know
146.	32	pease] peace
153.	14	Where] Q1; When Q3, Whe[n] *damaged in* Q2
	39	do] to
154.	73	did] dit
	140	thee] the
		for lore] forlore Q3, Q1
156.	02	*state*] Q3, Q1; *stare* Q2
	7	doon] done Q3, ready Q1
157.	10	set] never Q3, Q1
159.	6	a live] *edd*., a lives Q3–Q1
161.	13	poore] pore Q3, Q1
162.	02	*or*] *and*
163.	13	aloft] a loft
	20	have] hath
164.	4	a live] *edd*.; a lives Q3–Q1
165.	14	take] taye
167.	36	So] Q1; Do Q3, Q2
	42	No raging] Nor aging
	52	reue] rue

Poem	Line	
168.	19	heard] hard
169.	14	bes T] best Q3, Q1
170.	21	limes] limmes
171.	32	where] Q3, Q1; were Q2
172.	2	like] licke
	9	A way] Away Q3, Q1
174	16	proofe] profe Q3, Q1
	25	clerely] Q3; clcrcly Q2; clercly Q1
175.	5	swerve] swarve Q3, Q1
176.	3	found] Q3, Q1; sound Q2
	8	have] hath
177.	18	be] me
	24	begone] be gone Q3, Q1
178.	5	sins] since Q3, Q1
	28	sarves] serves
181.	11	silver] Q3, Q1; sliver Q2
	30	his] her
	31	on] one
184.	25	thy] the
	26	pretended] Q1; pretented Q3, Q2
185.	2	bereft] better
	6	water] waters
186.	3	through] though
188.	4	thee] the
	5	bones] boues
190.	4	untruth] Q3, Q1; but truth Q2
	5	ruth] truth
	8	causeles] Q3; causels Q2; so causels Q1
191.	25	hart] heart
192.	22	heard her] her heard
193.	11	is] his
	13	It] At
	21	It were to] At to were
197.	8	quit] Q3; quite Q2
206.	66	raigne] raine Q3, Q1
208.	18	forththrow] forth throw Q3; furthrowe Q1
209.	20	clarke] clacke Q3, Q1
212	22	Cartage] cartage
	62	shamefull] shamfull Q3; shamefall Q1
213.	15	prease] pase
	41	aside] a side Q3, Q1
218.	72	cares] care

Poem	Line	
218.	73	lest] least] Q3, Q1
226.	10	me see] Q3; mese Q2
	12	your] you
228.	88	may] Q3; nay Q2
	152	oft] of
	173	If absence] Q3; Ifbasence Q2
	175	me] Q3; ire Q2
	193	rold Q2] told Q3, Q1
229.	9	hole] whole
232.	1	have] hath
233.	17	sins] since
234.	34	is] his
	53	firy] fiery
235.	2	minde] mide
236.	6	bestrow] bestow
241.	1	mede] ende
243.	8	rote] roote
244.	10	rote] roote Q3; frute Q1
246.	5	but] Q3; dut Q2
250.	20	A way] Away
	56	paine] paines
251.	4	or] of
254.	17	Aloft] A loft
258.	15	or] to
	34	derst] erst
262.	25	withsave] witsave
	71	the hand] hand
	75	she] ye
266.	2	my] me
268.	29	no] not
269.	2	sownd] *edd.*; sown Q2; sound Q3
270.	28	bodie] Q3; bodies Q2
	40	me . . . my grave] my . . . me grace
271.	5	Clio] Clion
272.	4	raign] raine
274.	9	raign] rain
277.	40	Next] Vext
278.	70	wordes] workes
	95	renk] Q1; reuk] Q3, Q2
279.	24	to] *edd.*; so Q3–Q1
	42	sayth] sith
	65	heyres] heares

List 3

Emendations of Accidentals

This list includes the emendations of accidentals made from Q1 to Q2 and from Q2 to the edited text. The lemmata are those of the edited text. If this text diverges from the Q2 copy text, the source of the emendation is given next; if no source is given, the emendation is editorial. Then follows the rejected reading of Q2 or Q1, or both. Where the edited text adopts the corrected form of a press variant, no entry is given here.

	lemma] rejected reading
Preface	
.9	english] English Q1
Poem / line no.	
1.5	harm,] ~ ˄ Q1
1.10	hart,] ~ ˄ Q1
1.17	trie:] ~ , Q1
1.26	fate:] ~ . Q1
1.30	then ˄] ~ , Q1
1.34	pace,²] *corr.*, Q1; ~ . *unc.*
1.40	sometime,] ~ ˄ Q1
1.41	porte:] ~ , Q1
1.47	flee,] ~ ˄ Q1
1.51	tene.] ~ ˄ Q1
1.52	I, alas,] Q1; I 'alas, Q2. *Turned sort prints as a reversed apostrophe.*
2.2	hill,] ~ ˄ Q1
2.3	nightingale,] ~ ˄ Q1
2.13	things,] ~ ˄ Q1
3.2	runne:] ronne, Q1

3.3	backe,] back ˄ Q1
3.5	desire,] ~ ˄ Q1
3.7	eyen,] ~ ˄ Q1
3.9	day ˄] ~ , Q1
3.10	game:] ~ , Q1
3.14	sowen:] ~ ˄ Q1
3.18	request ˄] quest , Q1
3.19	renew ˄] ~ . Q1
3.26	new:] ~ , Q1
3.27	see ˄] ~ , Q1
3.30	secretely,] ~ : Q1
3.31	flame:] ~ , Q1
4.01	Desciption] Description Q1
	affec- | tions,] affections ˄ Q1
	panges,] ~ ˄ Q1
4.2	stand:] ~ , Q1
4.4	hartes,] ~ ˄ Q1
4.11	withholdes,] ~ ˄ Q1
	place:] ~ , Q1
4.12	grace.] ~ : Q1
4.14	lost,] ~ ˄ Q1

4.16	returne.] ~ , Q1
4.17	lust:] ~ , Q1
4.30	devise,] ~ ₐ Q1
4.32	pleasures,] ~ ₐ Q1
	eye,] ~ ₐ Q1
4.33	foe:] ~ , Q1
4.37	splene,] ~ ₐ Q1
4.41	fire,] ~ ₐ Q1
	freze:] ~ . Q1
4.42	burne:] ~ , Q1
	wast:] ~ , Q1
4.45	gall:] ~ , Q1
5.18	self] Q1; seif Q2
5.23	them] Q1; thein Q2
5.30	love ₐ] ~ , Q1
5.33	God] god
5.34	about,] ~ ₐ Q1
5.38	alive,] ~ . Q1
5.40	undone.] ~ : Q1
5.41	but] Q1; bnt Q2
5.42	reliefe,] ~ ₐ Q1
5.45	since,] ~ ₐ Q1
5.46	remaine ₐ] reinaine ₐ Q2; remaine, Q1
5.48	befall.] ~ , Q1
6.7	shadow ₐ] ~ , Q1
6.9	love] Love Q1
6.14	love.] ~ , Q1
7.1	where as] whereas Q1
7.2	Well] well Q1
	the same,] ~ . Q2; thesame, Q1
8.13	kinde,] ~ ₐ Q1
10.11	by and by] byandby Q1
10.12	sting.] ~ , Q1
11.8	rakehell life] Q1; rakehell-life Q2 *corr.*; rakchelllife Q2 *unc.*
12.1	Sunne] sunne Q1
12.12	good,] ~ . Q1
13.4	hart.] ~ ₐ Q1
13.8	serve,] ~ ₐ Q1
13.13	winter,] winters ₐ Q2, Q1

	breath ₐ] ~ , Q2, Q1
14.1	geve ₐ] ~ , Q1
14.3	beleve,] Q1; ~ . Q2
15.2	joy,] Q1; ~ . Q2
15.9	hewe:] Q1; ~ ₐ Q2
15.15	ball ₐ] ~ , Q1
15.35	accord,] ~ : Q1
	delight:] ~ , Q1
16.6	death.] ~ : Q1
16.12	Gods] goddes Q1
17.14	me ₐ] ~ , Q1
17.18	yet] Q1; y[et] Q2 *copy smudged*
17.28	Mariner] mariner Q1
17.30	rise ₐ] ~ , Q1
18.7	plaint] Q1; plai[nt] Q2 *copy damaged*
18.8	attaint] Q1; attai[nt] Q2 *copy damaged*
18.12	lesse,] ~ . Q1
18.14	mone,] ~ . Q1
18.20	write thou] writethou Q1
18.22	bound,] ~ ₐ Q1
18.27	ran.] ~ , Q1
18.46	content ₐ] ~ . Q1
18.53	clene,] ~ : Q1
18.55	defence,] ~ . Q1
18.56	shepheard ₐ] shephard, Q1
	hence ₐ] ~ : Q1
18.62	said ₐ] ~, Q1
18.68	sight,] ~ . Q1
18.71	drede ₐ] dread, Q1
	dolour,] ~ ₐ Q1
18.75	Then ₐ] ~ , Q1
18.78	Creseids] Chreseids Q1
18.80	And ₐ] ~ , Q1
18.81	soule ₐ] ~, Q1
	angels] Angels Q1
19.1	Ladies:] ~ , Q1
19.5	desire,] ~ ₐ Q1
19.8	define,] ~ . Q1
19.9	lorde ₐ] ~ , Q1
19.13	send,] ~ . Q1

19.16	payne,] ~ . Q1		27.4	appere.] ~ ‸ Q2, Q1
19.21	An other] Another Q1		27.6	sterne,] ~ . Q2, Q1
19.31	dreme:] ~ , Q1		27.12	hand.] ~ ‸ Q1
20.01	*reproveth*] *teproveth* Q1		27.13	declare] Q1; de clare Q2
20.02	*that*] *tha* Q1		27.16	smoke,] ~ . Q1
21.01	*ladie*] *Ladie* Q1		29.6	be,] ~ . Q1
21.1	*Indentations are edd., except*		29.9	Wolfe] wolfe Q1
	for first lines of the last two		29.13	her feete] herfeete Q1
	quatrains.		29.22	thee.] the: Q1
21.2	hard,] ~ . Q1		29.55	might,] ~ ‸ Q1
21.9	you ‸] ~ , Q1		29.57	Nature] nature Q1
21.10	verse,] ~ : Q1		29.64	no] ne Q1
21.12	ferse,] ~ . Q1		29.72	say,] ~ . Q1
22.7	frend,] ~ . Q1		29.74	refrain,] ~ ‸ Q1
22.13	power,] ~ . Q2, Q1		29.75	game,] Q1; ~ . Q2
23.5	glimsing] glisming Q2; gl-		30.3	amongst] amongest Q1
	siming Q1		30.6	Asse] asse Q1
23.27	troubles] Q1; troules Q2			Oxe] oxe Q1
23.32	within] Q1; with in Q2		30.8	shipboy] shyp boy Q1
23.39	aloft,] ~ . Q1			and] Q1; aud Q2
24.8	payne.] paine, Q1		30.15	cannot] can not Q1
24.23	away,] ~ ‸ Q1		30.24	smart.] ~ ‸ Q1
24.24	unrest.] Q1; ~ ˙ Q2 *sort is*		30.27	paine,] ~ . Q1
	turned		30.31	have.²] ~ , Q1
25.22	blusteryng] blustring Q1		30.38	within] Q1; with in Q2
	winde,] Q1; win Q2		30.39	devide,] ~ . Q2, Q1
25.26	churlish] chorlish Q1		30.42	just,] ~ . Q1
25.28	unbinde.] ~ , Q1		30.47	watery] watry Q1
25.33	all,] ~ . Q1		30.55	breath,] brethe. Q1
25.43	can not] cannot Q1		30.57	smart,] ~. Q1
25.45	fire,] ~ ‸ Q1		30.58	wyll,] ~ ‸ Q2, Q1
26.01	*man* ‸] ~ , Q2, Q1		33.13	Gods] gods Q1
26.02	*describing* ‸] ~ , Q2, Q1		35.27	loft] lost Q1
26.13	so,] ~ . Q1		35.28	mischaunce,] ~ . Q1
26.16	relief,] ~ ‸ Q1		35.32	manhodes ‸ shape,] ~, ~ ‸ Q1
	gaine ‸] ~ , Q1		36.9	In] Q1; Ia Q2
26.20	bent,] ~ ‸ Q1			Wiates] wyates Q1
26.21	to ‸] ~ . Q1		37.01	*Sardanapalus*] *Sardinapalus*
	still,] ~ ‸ Q1			Q1
26.23	made,] ~ ‸ Q1		37.13	Proud ‸] ~ . Q2, Q1
26.26	devise,] ~ ‸ Q1		38.7	opprest ‸] ~ . Q1
27.3	list] Q1; l[ ] Q2 *copy*		38.10	so much] somuch Q1
	smudged		39.01	*est*] *cst* Q1

39.3	fore knowne] foreknowne Q1		*Love* ^] ~ [,] Q2 *copy smudged;* ~ , Q1
39.14	(alas)] (alas, Q1	69.7	seketh.] Q1; ~ ͵ Q2
43.11	relief,] ~ . Q1	69.21	just] Q1; jnst Q2
43.12	otherwise] Q1; other wise Q2	69.36	where ͵] ~ , Q2, Q1
45.3	hart ͵] ~ , Q1	69.46	seas,] Q1 ~ . Q2
45.10	there,] ~ . Q1	69.54	Gods] goddes Q1
46.5	begone] be gone Q1	69.64	For ͵] ~ , Q1
47.1	dreame ͵] ~ , Q1	69.65	resident ͵] ~ , Q1
47.8	timbrace,] ~ . Q1	69.66	threaten,] ~ . Q1
47.12	into] in to Q1	69.70	tother.] Q1; ~ , Q2
48.1	abundance,] ~ . Q1	69.82	now ͵] ~ , Q1
48.4	observaunce.] ~ : Q1	69.84	sit.] Q1; ~ ͵ Q2
48.8	advance,] ~ . Q1	69.101	still ͵] ~ , Q1
49.12	all ͵] ~ : Q1	69.104	learned ͵] ~ , Q1
49.13	wel worthy] welworthy Q1	69.105	repenteth ͵] ~ , Q1
49.14	day.] Q1; ~ , Q2	69.106	These ͵] ~ , Q1
50.5	out shit] outshyt Q1	69.126	gain.] Q1; ~ , Q2
52.1	be ͵] ~ , Q1	69.129	honour ͵] ~ , Q1
52.12	eyen] eyn Q1	69.134	sayd ͵] ~ , Q1
56.7	himself] Q2 *corr.;* him self Q2 *unc.;* Q1	69.135	But ͵] ~ , Q1
56.10	inflame] Q2 *corr.;* in flame Q2 *unc.;* Q1	69.137	cry.] ~ : Q1
		69.138	by ͵²] ~ , Q1
56.11	wo ͵] ~, Q1	70.03	(Souche)] *Souche* Q1
	earnest ͵] ~ , Q1	70.1	no more] nomore Q1
56.13	hardinesse,] ~ . Q1	70.4	never] Q1; n[ever] Q2 *copy damaged*
57.16	gentlenesse,] ~ . Q1	70.5	hart ͵] ~ , Q1
59.4	meanes ͵] ~ , Q1	70.25	yet ͵] ~ , Q1
60.6	roote,] ~ . Q1	70.27	And ͵] ~ , Q1
62.4	deliteth:] ~ , Q1	70.28	Then ͵] ~ , Q1
65.6	enwrapt ͵] ~ , Q1	71.24	saith] sayeth Q1
65.17	under.] ~ , Q1	71.41	life,] Q1; ~ ͵ Q2
65.18	smile.] Q1; ~ , Q2	71.42	salve,] Q1; ~ ͵ Q2
66.02	*love.*] Q1; ~ ͵ Q2	73.3	more¹] ~ , Q1
66.4	tragedy,] ~ . Q1	73.4	sit ͵] ~ , Q1
66.15	astart,] ~ . Q1	74.01	*Cupide* ͵] ~ , Q1
67.7	thee forsake] Q1; theefor- sake Q2	75.1	payn ͵] ~ ? Q1
		76.01	*love,*] ~ ͵ Q1
67.11	fold,] Q1; ~. Q2	78.1	yre,] Q1; ~ . Q2
69.01	*Wiates*] *wiates* Q2, Q1	78.2	into] in to Q1
		79.6	you .] Q1; ~ ͵ Q2
		79.8	can] Q1; cau Q2

80.9	true ˌ] ~ , Q1		108.22	bodies ˌ] ~ , Q2, Q1
81.2	lose ˌ] ~ . Q1		108.33	forebecause] for because Q1
81.8	train.] Q1; ~ , Q2		108.34	day ˌ] ~ , Q1
83.14	winne.] Q1; winnne. Q2		108.40	spere ˌ] ~ . Q1
83.22	quit,] ~ : Q1		108.45	absence ˌ] ~ , Q1
84.01	*praieth*] Q1; *ptaieth* Q2		108.46	net?] ~ : Q1
85.24	relent,] ~ . Q2, Q1		108.53	delight ˌ] ~ . Q2, Q1
86.11	embrace,] Q1; ~ . Q2		108.58	well ˌ] ~ : Q1
87.7	had,] ~ . Q1		108.67	hart,] ~ : Q1
88.8	bringes:] ~ . Q1		108.76	bring ˌ] ~ . Q1
88.13	execrable,] Q1; ~ . Q2		108.84	strife ˌ] ~ : Q1
90.24	have[1]] Q1; hane Q2		108.96	chance ˌ] ~ , Q1
91.1	awake] ˋ~ Q1		109.2	rent ˌ] ~ : Q2, Q1
91.26	withered] witherd Q1		109.3	sent,] ~ . Q2, Q1
91.34	beaute] beauty Q1		109.5	suffise ˌ] ~ . Q2; ~ , Q1
91.36	last ˌ] ~ , Q2, Q1		111.11	willingly,] ~ . Q1
91.37	wast ˌ] ~ , Q1		111.24	serve ˌ] ~ , Q1
95.16	say.] ~ ˌ Q2, Q1		113.18	dere.] Q1; ~ ˌ Q2
98.3	pain ˌ] ~ . Q1		113.21	out.] ~ ˌ Q2, Q1
99.01	*love*] *Love* Q1		113.27	spede.] ~ , Q1
	fortune] *Fortune* Q1		113.31	none,] ~ . Q1
99.6	than ˌ] ~ : Q2, Q1		113.32	request,] ~ ˌ Q1
99.7	plaineth] plainth Q2;		114.01	*Why*] *why* Q2, Q1
	playneth Q1		114.6	he blinde] Q1; heblinde Q2
	sildam ˌ] Q1; ~ . Q2		115.7	repaires] repayres Q1
100.4	low,] ~ . Q1		115.10	returne] Q1; returue Q2
102.11	busily,] Q1; ~ ˌ Q2		116.1	my ˌ²] ~ : Q1
102.12	frysing] fre syng Q1		116.3	fro.] ~ ˌ Q1
104.01	*forsaketh*] Q1; *forsakerh* Q2		116.4	the ˌ] thee, Q1
104.02	*unkinde*] Q1; *uukinde* Q2		117.18	have,] Q1; ~ ˌ Q2
	love.] ~ , Q1		118.01	*called* ˌ] ~ . Q1
104.2	But ˌ] ~ , Q1		119.2	hue.] *corr.* Q2; ~ , Q2 *unc.*;
104.6	And ˌ] ~ , Q1			hue: Q1
105.8	And] and Q1		119.6	true ˌ] ~ . Q2, Q1
105.11	assinde,] ~ . Q1		122.13	bee,] Q1; ~ . Q2
105.16	bejudge.] be judge ˌ Q1		122.21	life,] ~ ˌ Q1
105.27	God] god Q1		123.01	*Whether*] *whether* Q2, Q1
106.12	smart,] ~ . Q1		123.2	Hawke] hawke Q1
107.4	desire ˌ] ~ . Q2, Q1		123.11	doler,] dolore. Q1
108.10	delight?] ~ : Q1		123.26	Hawke] hawke Q1
108.11	recover?] ~ . Q1		124.6	eschange ˌ] ~ , Q1
108.12	cover.] Q1; ~ ˌ Q2		125.1	Vulcane] Vvulcane Q1
108.16	end,] ~ . Q1			

125.4   Anger] A ng er Q2; Angre
         Q1
         dere,] ~ . Q1
126.01   *Wiate*] *wiate* Q2, Q1
126.2   musick] Musick Q1
128.1   wheele ₐ] ~ , Q2, Q1
129.01   *life.*] Q1; ~ ₐ Q2
131.1   Westward] westward Q1
131.3   Temmes.] temmes. Q2, Q1
132.6   know,] ~ . Q1
132.7   himselfe] him self Q1
         foe.] Q1; ~ , Q2
134.53   eyes ₐ] ~ . Q1
134.62   And] Q1; Aud Q2
134.96   alotted,] ~ . Q1
134.99   minde.] ~, Q1
134.100 Madde ₐ] Q1; Made, Q2
134.101 come,] ~ : Q1
134.103 summe:] ~ ₐ Q2, Q1
135.01   *Jhon*] *John* Q1
135.10   is ₐ] ~ , Q1
135.45   most,] ~ . Q2, Q1
135.95   blacke,] ~ ₐ Q1
135.98   poyson,] ~ . Q1
         of some] Q1; ofsome Q2
135.100 Kent] kent Q2, Q1
135.102 *Jhon*] *John* Q1
136.79   vaine?] ~ : Q1
136.91   kepe:] ~ , Q1
137.2   light,] ~ ₐ Q2, Q1
137.7   one,] ~ ₐ Q2, Q1
137.9   mother,] ~ ₐ Q1
137.18   place.] ~ ₐ Q1
137.20   direct,] ~ . Q2, Q1
137.21   thother,] ~ ₐ Q2, Q1
137.24   hight,] ~ . Q1
137.27   kinde,] ~ . Q1
137.54   eye,] ~ ₐ Q2, Q1
137.55   third ₐ] ~ , Q1
137.65   seven:] ~ ₐ Q2, Q1
137.71   West to East] west to east
         Q1

137.72   East to West] East to west
         Q2; east to west Q1
137.74   East to East] east to east Q2,
         Q1
         by.²] Q1; ~ ₐ Q2
137.76   axell tree] Q1; axelltree Q2
138.03   *pity.*] *pitye-* Q1
138.5   Sunne] sonne Q1
138.6   gest,] ~ . Q2, Q1
138.11   wight ₐ] ~ , Q2, Q1
138.12   starres.] Q1; ~ ₐ Q2
138.21   hart ₐ] ~ , Q1
138.31   I ₐ] ~ , Q1
138.43   devide,] ~ : Q1
138.61   wish²,] ~ ₐ Q1
139.12   same,] ~ . Q1
139.19   grothe,] ~ ₐ Q1
139.21   declare,] ~ : Q1
139.22   God] god Q1
139.24   give.] ~ ₐ Q2, Q1
141.9   know ₐ] ~ , Q1
141.13   runne ₐ] ~ : Q1
141.15   soone:] Q1; ~ . Q2
141.16   misse ₐ] ~ , Q1
141.19   wast,] ~ . Q2, Q1
141.24   when:] ~ , Q1
         Lord] lord Q1
141.26   God] god Q1
141.37   Paul,] ~ ₐ Q1
         wish ₐ] ~ , Q1
142.19   nature ₐ] ~ , Q1
142.25   swete.] ~ , Q1
143.1   Larke] larke Q1
         Marlians] marlians Q1
143.14   forth ₐ] ~ , Q1
145.02   *subject,*] ~ ₐ Q2, Q1
145.33   tied,] ~ . Q1
145.41   know ₐ] ~ , Q2, Q1
146.01   *Fortune* ₐ] ~ , Q1; *Fottune,*
         Q2
146.9   those ₐ] ~ , Q2, Q1
146.18   gest.] ~ , Q2, Q1
147.8   long ₐ] ~ , Q1

147.11 wel away] welaway Q1
148.14 all to rent] alltorent Q1
149.2 my¹] wy Q1
149.8 life ˏ] ~ , Q1
149.18 doth change] Q1; doth-change Q2
149.25 yeres ˏ] yeares, Q1
149.27 Ant] ant Q1
149.35 constrayn ˏ] ~ . Q2, Q1
150.03 *not* ˏ] Q1; ~ : Q2
150.04 *him* ˏ] ~ , Q2, Q1
150.60 reapes,] ~ ˏ Q1
150.75 Calf] calf Q1
151.01 *Wilfordes*] wilfordes Q2, Q1
151.10 sowne,] ~ . Q1
151.16 sandes,] ~ ˏ Q2, Q1
152.10 minde,] ~ ˏ Q2, Q1
152.14 part.] ~ ˏ Q2, Q1
153.10 grace.] ~ ˏ Q1
153.16 day,] ~ ˏ Q1
       night,] ~ ˏ Q1
       place,] ~ ˏ Q1
       houre,] ~ ˏ Q1
153.18 cal,] ~ ˏ Q1
       cry,] ~ ˏ Q1
153.20 misse.] ~ ˏ Q2, Q1
153.22 kepe,] ~ . Q2, Q1
153.30 withstand ˏ] ~ . Q1
153.32 place:] ~ ˏ Q2, Q1
154.43 colde ˏ] ~ , Q1
154.61 hart ˏ] ~, Q1
154.103 straunge ˏ] ~ : Q1
154.118 rejoyce,] ~ . Q1
154.130 griefe ˏ] ~ . Q1
154.160 day ˏ] ~ , Q1
154.161 *indented*] Q1; *unindented* Q2
154.165 *indented*] Q1; *unindented* Q2
154.169 told,] ~ . Q1
154.170 breath:] ~ . Q1
154.205 And] Q1; Aud Q2
154.243 misse,] ~ ˏ Q1
154.254 was,] ~ : Q1
154.264 more.] ~ , Q1

154.276 evermore.] ~ , Q1
155.01 *White*] white Q2, Q1
156.2 graunted,] ~ ˏ Q1
156.9 pleasure,] ~ ˏ Q1
       heavinesse.] ~ , Q1
157.01 *Where*] where Q2, Q1
       is,] ~ ˏ Q1
157.4 wot.] Q1; ~ , Q2
157.13 Rabbets] rabbets Q1
       rockes:] ~ , Q1
157.14 Snailes] snailes Q1
157.15 blockes.] ~ , Q1
158.02 *Wilford,*] wilford ˏ Q2, Q1
158.6 was,] ~ ˏ Q1
158.12 don.] doon ˏ Q1
159.10 alive,] ~ ˏ Q1
159.12 land.] Q1; ~ . Q2 *sublinear point.*
160.3 cannot] can not Q1
160.4 cannot] can not Q1
160.20 sound.] ~ , Q1
160.24 Wolfe] wolfe Q1
161.3 so,] ~ . Q1
161.4 unrest:] ~ , Q1
161.6 obtaine.] ~ , Q1
161.12 Whall] whall Q1
161.15 paine,] ~ . Q1
161.27 rest,] ~ . Q2, Q1
161.33 swim,] ~ . Q1
162.01 *studient*] *Student* Q1
162.2 wonne,] ~ : Q1
163.3 waves,] ~ ˏ Q1
163.6 lest.] ~ , Q1
163.16 avance.] ~ ˏ Q2, Q1
163.24 under.] ~ ˏ Q1
163.31 face,] ~ ˏ Q1
163.32 frostes:] ~ ˏ Q1
163.34 hote:] ~ ˏ Q1
163.38 driven,] ~ ˏ Q1
       racke.] ~ ˏ Q1
163.39 still,] ~ ˏ Q1
163.40 wake.] ~ ˏ Q1
163.41 therfore,] ~ ˏ Q1

163.42   faile.] ~ ‸ Q1
163.43   will,] ~ ‸ Q1
164.01   *refused,*] ~ ‸ Q1
164.4   creature.] ~ ‸ Q1
164.6   discry:] ~ ‸ Q1
164.7   brute,] ~ ‸ Q1
164.10   and] aud Q1
         me,] ~ ‸ Q1
         kinde.] ~ ‸ Q1
164.11   refused,] ~ ‸ Q1
164.12   best ‸] ~ . Q2, Q1
164.16   God] god Q1
         be,] ~ . Q2, Q1
164.18   hyre,] ~ ‸ Q1
164.19   restore ‸] ~ , Q2, Q1
164.20   disges ‸] ~ . Q1
165.1   blastes,] ~ ‸ Q1
165.12   pervert,] ~ ‸ Q2 ; ~ . Q1
165.15   contend,] ~ ‸ Q1
         rise,] ~ ‸ Q1
165.16   hold,] ~ ‸ Q1
165.17   mindes,] ~ ‸ Q1
         drent,] ~ ‸ Q1
165.18   spent?] ~ . Q1
165.19   griefe,] ~ ‸ Q1
         drede,] dreede ‸ Q1
165.20   nature] Q1; natute Q2
         craves,] ~ ‸ Q1
165.21   suffice,] ~ ‸ Q1
165.22   expell,] ~ ‸ Q1
         surprice.] ~ : Q1
165.23   oft,] ~ ‸ Q1
166.2   dide:] ~ ‸Q2; ~ . Q1
166.3   yere:] ~ ‸Q2; ~ . Q1
166.10   mindes ‸] ~ . Q1
166.13   corn ‸] ~ , Q1
166.16   warm.] ~ ‸ Q2, Q1
166.20   then:] ~, Q1
166.21   God] god Q1
166.25   hands ‸] ~ , Q1
167.1   rest,] ~ ‸ Q1
167.7   Sunne] sunne Q1
         Moone] moone Q1

167.10   tunes,] ~ ‸ Q1
167.14   minde,] ~ : Q1
167. 28 snare.] ~ , Q1
167.40   prevaile.] ~ ‸ Q1
167.46   failde,] ~ ‸ Q1
         brake?] ~ : Q1
167.49   hap,] happe ‸ Q1
168.3   one:] ~ Q1 *suad in place of*
         colon.
168.53   geve,] ~ ‸ Q1
169.5   renowne,] ~ ‸ Q2, Q1
169.6   call.] ~ ‸ Q2, Q1
169.10   slides.] ~ ‸ Q2, Q1
169.14   bes T.] best. Q1
170.1   Thestilis,] ~ ‸ Q2, Q1
170.2   make.] Q1; ~ ‸ Q2
170.4   unknowen.] Q1; ~ ^ Q2
170.19   wo,] ~ ‸ Q1
         lesse ‸] ~: Q1
170.20   mine:] ~ ‸ Q1
170.31   knowne:] ~ ‸ Q1
171.1   Thestilis,] ~ ‸ Q2, Q1
171.6   seas.] ~ ‸ Q2, Q1
171.7   chaunge:] ~ ‸ Q2, Q1
171.16   away.] ~ ‸ Q2, Q1
171.26   twaine?] ~ . Q1
172.8   remove ‸] Q1; ~, Q2
172.12   death,] ~ ‸ Q1
173.2   speake,] ~ ‸ Q1
173.3   stay,] ~ . Q1
173.8   change,] ~ ‸ Q1
174.4   Mouse] mouse Q1
174.8   minde.] ~ , Q1
175.1   race,] ~ ‸ Q1
175.2   him som] hi some Q1
         praise ‸] ~ . Q1
175.5   was,] ~ ‸ Q1
         swerve,] ~ ‸ Q2, swarve ‸ Q1
175.7   seas,] ~ ‸ Q1
175.8   prince,] ~ ‸ Q1
175.10   doon?] done, Q1
175.11   Lambe,] lambe ‸ Q1
         fierce,] ~ ‸ Q1

Lion] lyon Q1
175.13 dedes,] ~ . Q2; ~ ˄Q1
175.17 lived,] ~ ˄Q1
all,] ~ ˄Q1
175.22 Epitaphe] epitaphe Q1
175.24 earth,] ~ ˄Q1
above,] ~ ˄Q1
176.1 time,[1]] ~ ˄Q1
176.2 groweth.] ~ ˄Q1
176.6 pearle,] ~ ˄Q1
177.25 more,] ~ ˄Q2, Q1
177.32 lady] Lady Q1
178.01 *picture*] *Picture* Q1
178.1 nones.] ~ , Q1
178.2 bones,] ~ . Q2, Q1
178.10 day,] ~ . Q1
178.11 bare,] ~ ˄Q1
178.12 remaines.] Q1; remaine ˄Q2
179.3 rest.] ~ , Q1
179.8 dispossest.] ~ , Q1
179.10 therfore.] ~ , Q1
180.5 Dere] dere Q1
180.9 Dere] dere Q1
180.11 Asse] asse Q1
180.13 Cony] conye Q1
180.17 Owle] owle Q1
180.19 Sparrow] sparrow Q1
180.22 shade,] ~ . Q1
181.8 souldiours] Q1; souldiou s Q2
aray.] Q1; ~ , Q2
181.9 bare,] ~ ˄Q1
181.21 rore,] ~ ˄Q1
181.30 targe,] ~ : Q1
181.39 truce ˄] ~ , Q1
181.41 breach,] ~ ˄Q1
181.45 retrete,] ~ . Q1
181.55 warke,] Q1; wark[e] Q2
copy smudged
181.56 dye.] Q1; ~ , Q2
182.3 behove,] ~ ˄Q1
182.4 mete.] ~ , Q1

182.5 My] Q1 *indented*; ~ *not in-*
dented Q2
183.01 *Wentworthes*] wentworthes
Q2, Q1
183.1 dye ˄[1]] ~ , Q1
183.7 attaine,] ~ ˄Q1
183.9 best,] ~ ˄Q2, Q1
183.10 fame,] ~ ˄Q1
distain,] ~ ˄Q1
184.9 wilt ˄] ~ , Q1
184.23 caterpiller] cater piller Q2, Q1
185.9 Salamandra] salamandra Q1
185.10 desire.] ~ ˄Q2, Q1
186.01 *plea-| sures*] *plea,* | *sures* Q1
186.03 *world.*] ~ , Q1
186.4 delight,] ~ . Q1
187.4 grow,] ~ ˄Q1
188.7 sence:] ~ ˄Q1
188.9 pens,] ~ ˄Q1
188.14 Petrarke] petrarke Q1
Paragone] paragone Q1
189.01 *Petrark*] *petrark* Q2, Q1
surpassed.] Q1; ~ , Q2
189.1 Petrarke] petrarke Q1
189.3 file ˄] ~ . Q2; ~ .. Q1 *double*
pointed
189.14 say,] ~ ˄Q1
190.6 delph,] ~ ˄Q2, Q1
190.7 will,] ~ ˄Q2, Q1
190.8 change?] ~ . Q1
190.13 Cupides] cupides Q1
190.16 change?] ~ .
190.17 *line unindented in Q1.*
sowe,] ~ ˄Q2, Q1
190.20 craftiness,] ~ ˄Q2; craftin
esse ˄Q1
190.21 blowe,] ~ ˄Q2, Q1
190.22 carefulnesse,] ~ . Q1
190.24 chaunge?] ~ . Q1
191.02 *have,*] ~ ˄Q1
191.7 raigne,] Q1; ~ . Q2
191.17 ground,] ~ . Q2, Q1
191.18 confounde,] ~ . Q2, Q1

191.34	felicitie,] ~ . Q1
191.36	Paragon] paragon Q1
192.20	her?] ~ , Q1
192.36	sed.] Q1; ~ , Q2
192.41	will ∧] ~ , Q1
192.47	say,] Q1; ~ . Q2
193.17	bandes,] Q1; ~ . Q2
194.2	ought.] ~ ∧ Q1
194.9	leade,] ~ ∧ Q1
194.10	hurt,] ~ ∧ Q1
194.11	fruite,] ~ ∧ Q1
194.12	kinde,] ~ ∧ Q1
194.14	leafe,] ~ ∧ Q1
	give?] ~ . Q1
194.15	desires,] ~ ∧ Q1
194.16	smelles,] ~ ∧ Q1
194.17	Sunne] sonne Q1
	might,] ~ ; Q2; ~ ∧ Q1
194.18	shew.] ~ ∧ Q1
194.19	cald,] ~ ∧ Q1
194.20	men,] ~ ∧ Q1
194.22	Mariner,] mariner ∧ Q1
194.26	ease,] ~ ∧ Q1
194.30	charge?] ~ ∧ Q1
194.34	strives.] Q1; ~ ∧ Q2
195.01	*When*] *when* Q2, Q1
195.5	late it comes] Q1; lat[ ]omes Q2 *copy smudged*
195.6	blinde.] ~ , Q1
195.15	lest:] ~ , Q1
195.17	happiest,] Q1; ~ ∧ Q2
196.01	*one-* | *ly; one-* | *lye* Q1
196.02	*god*] *God* Q1
196.14	know,] ~ . Q1
196.15	forth,] Q1; ~ . Q2
196.22	fall:] ~ , Q1
196.30	such.] sich ∧ Q1
196.31	store,] Q1; ~ . Q2
196.37	dere,] ~ ∧ Q1
196.44	mone.] ~ ∧ Q1
196.47	pleased,] ~ ∧ Q1
196.56	fall.] ~ , Q1
197.1	king,] ~ ∧ Q1
198.4	vain ∧] ~. Q1
200.2	myght,] ~ . Q1
200.3	eye?] ~ , Q1
202.7	tought ∧] ~ , Q1
202.13	hart ∧] ~ , Q1
203.02	*worthy.*] Q1; ~ ∧ Q2
203.3	none,] Q1; ~ . Q2
203.7	praise,] Q1; ~ . Q2
204.1	raine,] Q1; ~ . Q2
204.11	no,] Q1 ~ . Q2
204.16	chiefe.] Q1; ~ , Q2
205.3	me ∧] ~ , Q1
205.24	hap,] ~ ∧ Q1
206.13	ease,] ~ ∧ Q1
206.23	delight,] Q1, ~ . Q2
206.43	grace,] ~ . Q1
206.59	great,] ~ ∧ Q1
206.64	owe.] ~ , Q1
207.02	*life.*] ~ , Q1
207.3	hate,] ~ ∧ Q1
207.4	all,] ~ Q1
207.7	deliver,] ~ ∧ Q1
207.8	redresse,] ~ ∧ Q1
207.13	dede,] ~ ∧ Q1
207.19	God] god Q1
208.10	yoke.] ~ ∧ Q1
208.12	steale,] ~ ∧ Q1
	bound.] ~ ∧ Q1
208.13	(he sayde) ∧] he sayde, Q1
208.14	displayd?] ~ , Q2; ~ . Q1
208.15	baite ∧] ~ , Q1
210.4	defide:] ~ . Q1
210.6	blow,] ~ ∧ Q1
210.8	gide,] ~ . Q1
210.9	base:] ~ ∧ Q2, Q1
211.2	threte:] Q1; ~ ∧ Q2
211.5	rocke,] ~ ∧ Q1
	set:] ~ ∧ Q1
211.6	you,] ~ ∧ Q1
	bene,] ~ . Q1
211.7	cannot] can not Q1
211.9	thret,] ~ . Q1
212.6	race,] ~ . Q2, Q1

212.10 temple,] ~ ‸ Q1
212.12 wot,] ~ . Q1
212.15 right,] ~ ‸ Q1
        know ‸] ~ , Q1
212.16 dede,] dedes ‸ Q1
212.20 Collatine:] Collatiue: Q2, Q1
212.23 maide,] ~ .Q1
212.25 Crow] crowe Q1
212.28 fowle,] ~ ‸ Q1
212.30 teares,] ~ ‸ Q1
212.35 bright,] ~ . Q1
212.39 wing,] ~ ‸ Q1
212.42 sweare,] ~ ‸ Q1
212.45 shame,] ~ ‸ Q1
212.48 sweare,] ~ . Q1
212.59 stand,] ~ ‸ Q1
212.60 us,] ~ ‸ Q1
213.01 R.] *Ryce* Q1
213.1 appere,] ~ ‸ Q1
213.8 remaines,] ~ ‸ Q1
213.10 tell,] ~ ‸ Q1
213.12 up,] ~ ‸ Q1
213.14 dames,] ~ ‸ Q1
213.15 spake,] ~ ‸ Q1
213.16 voyce,] ~ ‸ Q1
213.21 said,] ~ ‸ Q1
213.24 cost:] ~ . Q1
213.26 Pecockes] pecockes Q1
213.29 brute,] Q1; ~ ‸ Q2
213.30 speake,] ~ ‸ Q1
        begoon.] ~ , Q1
213.32 her,] ~ ‸ Q1
213.33 sought,] ~ ‸ Q1
213.34 pride,] ~ ‸ Q1
        thought.] ~ ‸ Q1
213.35 face,] ~ ‸ Q1
213.37 will,] ~ ‸ Q1
213.38 life,] ~ ‸ Q1
213.40 name,] ~ ‸ Q1
213.41 sit,] ~ ‸Q1
213.42 hide.] ~ ‸ Q1

213.43 (quod skill) good people all, is] (quod skill, good people all) is Q2, Q1
213.44 be,] ~ ‸ Q1
213.46 That] Q1; Th[at] Q2 *badly inked.*
        Eckow] Q1; e[ck]ow Q2 *badly inked.*
213.49 heard] Q1; [h]eard Q2 *badly inked.*
213.50 handes] Q1; [h]andes Q2 *badly inked.*
215.8 slepe.] Q1; ~ , Q2
215.9 jewel,] Q1; ~ ‸ Q2
215.16 chuse.] Q1; ~ ‸ Q2
216.3 paine,] Q1; ~ ‸ Q2
216.4 sede?] ~ . Q1
217.8 aryght,] ~ . Q1
217.12 greve.] Q1; ~ , Q2
218.2 Shall] Q1; shall Q2
        strange,] ~ . Q1
218.16 lyke?] ~ . Q1
218.18 nought.] ~ ‸ Q1
218.28 truth.] ~ ‸ Q2, Q1
218.33 possesse?] ~ , Q1
218.45 fal,] ~ ‸ Q1
218.47 rich,] ~ ‸ Q1
218.52 swete.] ~ ‸ Q2, Q1
218.54 fed,] ~ . Q1
218.62 snare.] ~ , Q1
218.68 god,] ~ ‸ Q2, Q1
218.69 dedes,] ~ : Q1
219.3 brought,] ~ . Q1
219.24 betimes,] Q1; ~ ‸ Q2
        never.] Q1; ~ , Q2
219.25 swerve:] swarve, Q1
219.30 gone,] ~ ‸ Q2, Q1
219.36 paine,] payne. Q1
220.1 somtime] some tyme Q1
220.8 stalketh.] ~ , Q1
220.9 walketh,] ~ . Q2, Q1
220.11 leaves ‸] ~ , Q1
220.18 winke.] ~ , Q1

220.20	love,] ~ ∧ Q1
220.24	witte,] Q1; ~ . Q2
220.26	leves ∧] ~ , Q1
221.5	despite,] Q1; ~ . Q2
221.7	sure,] ~ ∧ Q1
221.15	upright,] ~ . Q1
221.22	Forgeve] Q1; Forgeve Q2
222.20	fed.] ~ ∧ Q2
223.02	*Wiate*] wiate Q2
223.4	confound.] ~ ∧ Q2
223.7	Wiate ∧] ~ ; Q2
225.2	plaint:] ~ ∧ Q2
225.3	scourge,] ~ ∧ Q2
	foe,] ~ ∧ Q2
	fordon:] ~ ∧ Q2
226.2	hart,] ~ ∧ Q2
228.70	me?] ~ . Q2
228.112	winde,] ~ . Q2
228.150	enow ∧] ~ Q2
228.151	grace?] ~: Q2
228.176	good] goo[d] Q2 *copy damaged.*
229.19	wisdome] wis dome Q2
229.57	unfoldes,] ~ . Q2
231.18	don.] ~ ∧ Q2
233.04	*promiseth* ∧] ~ , Q2
233.16	just:] ~ ∧ Q2
233.31	rim[e,] Q2 *copy smudged*
236.32	gaine.] ~ ∧ Q2
238.11	likes,] ~ . Q2
239.01	W.] w. Q2, Q1
239.1	ground ,] Q1; ~ ∧ Q2
239.2	wormes,] ~ : Q1
239.3	found ∧] ~ , Q1
239.9	wot:] ~ , Q1
239.10	yeres,] ~ ∧ Q1
239.13	remayne ∧] ~ , Q1
239.14	me,] ~ : Q1
239.15	slaine,] slayns, Q2; slaine. Q1
240.13	She,] ~ ∧ Q1
240.15	Thou,] ~ ∧ Q1
240.16	wed,] ~ . Q1
241.9	crimes,] ~ : Q1
	bereve ∧] ~ , Q1
241.13	us,] ~ ∧ Q1
241.14	we, alas,] we ∧ alas ∧ Q1
241.24	staine,] ~ . Q2, Q1
243.01	*women,*] ~ ∧ Q1
243.12	Troy:] ~ . Q1
244.16	Lord,] Q1; ~ ∧ Q2
245.9	chere,] ~ ∧ Q1
245.12	place.] Q1; ~ , Q2
245.15	minde:] ~ , Q1
245.17	so:] ~ , Q1
245.19	such,] ~ ∧ Q1
	none.] ~ , Q1
245.23	face,] ~ ∧ Q1
245.25	done.] ~ , Q1
245.26	small:] ~ , Q1
246.6	againe.] ~ ∧ Q2
246.48	desart?] ~ ∧ Q2
247.2	wene.] ~ , Q1
247.9	Mouse] mouse Q1
247.14	eyes?] ~. Q1 *point is sublinear.*
247.18	both.] ~ ∧ Q2, Q1
248.6	selfe,¹] ~ ∧ Q1
248.15	show,] ~ ∧ Q1
248.24	break.] ~ : Q1
248.31	sample] Q1; samply Q2
248.34	Mouse] mouse Q1
249.28	light.] ~ ∧ Q2
255.1	have,] ~ ^ Q1
255.2	reward,] ~ . Q1
255.4	preferd,] ~ ∧ Q1
256.2	love,] ~ ∧ Q1
256.6	out,] ~ ∧ Q1
256.7	driftes,] ~ ∧ Q1
256.8	owne,] ~ ∧ Q1
256.9	dere,] ~ ∧ Q1
256.11	game.] ~ , Q1
256.15	Bees] bees Q1
256.20	go.] ~ , Q1
256.24	rest,] ~ ∧ Q1
256.28	minde.] ~ ∧ Q1

256.34   strange,] ~ ‸ Ql
            yeld,] ~ ‸ Q2, Ql
256.37   lutes,] Lutes ‸ Ql
256.39   giftes,] ~ ‸ Ql
257.16   adowne?] ~ ‸ Q2
258.6   Anew] A new Q2
262.18   nathelesse] natrelesse Q2
263.15   wear.] ~ ‸ Q2
266.3   advise ‸] ~ . Q2
266.30   sold.] ~ , Q2
268.6   told.] ~ ‸ Q2
268.8   cro.] ~ ‸ Q2
269.2   sownd] sown Q2
269.29   recite,] ~ . Q2
271.5   songes ‸] ~ , Ql
274.2   sought?] ~ : Ql
274.19   meal,] ~ ‸ Ql
275.3   cark ‸] ~ , Ql
275.9   fond:] Ql; ~ , Q2
276.10   Doway] Doo waye Ql
277.18   Yea ‸] ~ , Ql
277.28   Pylades] Ql; *broken staff in*
            Q2, *looks like* Dylades
277.37   bewayls.] ~ : Ql
277.38   (sayth he)] Ql; (saith he ( )
            Q2
277.40   wisdome ‸] ~ , Ql
278.1   warre,] ~ ‸ Ql
278.4   Covered ‸] ~ , Ql
278.13   bands ‸] ~ , Ql
278.32   plenty,] ~ ‸ Ql
278.33   snow,] ~ : Ql
278.35   burns,] ~ : Ql
278.46   that,] ~ : Ql
278.47   speake,] ~ : Ql
278.58   other,] Ql; ~ ‸ Q2
278.70   and ‸] ~ , Ql
278.78   may ‸] ~ , Ql
278.79   you ‸] ~ , Ql
278.88   Macedon,] Ql; ~ ‸ Q2
278.94   One,] Ql; ~ ‸ Q2
278.100 Where,] Ql; ~ ‸ Q2
278.103 wisht,] Ql; ~ .Q2

278.114 free,] ~ ‸ Ql
279.6   thou ‸] ~ , Ql
            countrey ‸] ~ , Ql
279.27   senate] Senate Ql
279.40   age ‸] ~ , Q2, Ql
279.44   messenger ‸] ~ , Ql
279.66   burst:] Ql; ~ ‸ Q2
279.72   heape ‸] Ql; ~ , Q2
279.75   hye,] Ql; ~ . Q2
279.76   lothy] lothly

LIST 4
PRESS VARIANTS IN Q2

Copies Collated: British Museum Library (BML) Shelf Mark: G11170; Henry
E. Huntington Library (HNL) Shelf Mark: 59482.
    The lemmata are those of the corrected state; readings of the uncorrected
state follow.

SHEET A (inner forme)
Corrected: HL
Uncorrected BML
Sig. A$_2$^{r}.
(poem/line)
    1.34.   pace,] ~ .
Sig. A$_4$^{r}.
    5.25.   canceaue] conceaue

SHEET B (inner forme)
Corrected: BML
Uncorrected: HNL
Sig. B$_2$^{r}.
    11.8.   rakehelllife] rakchelllife

SHEET C (outer forme)
Corrected: HNL
Uncorrected: BML
Sig. C$_1$^{r}.
    Page.   Fo.9.] ^
Sig. C$_4$^{v}.
    25.16.   well.] ~ :

SHEET C (inner forme)
Corrected: BML
Uncorrected: HNL
Sig. C$_1$^{v}.
    19.10.   of] af
Sig. C$_4$^{r}.
    Page.   ^] Fol. 12.

SHEET D (inner forme)
Corrected: BML
Uncorrected: HNL
Sig. D$_3$^{v}.
    Catchword: Martiall.] ~ ,

SHEET D (outer forme)
Corrected: BML
Uncorrected: HNL
Sig. D$_4$^{v}.
    Running Title: Songes ^] ~ .

SHEET E (inner forme)
Corrected: BML
Uncorrected: HNL
Sig. E$_2$^{r}.
Signature: E.ii.] E,ii.

SHEET F (outer forme)
Corrected: BML
Uncorrected: HNL
Sig. F$_4$^{v}.
65.10.   yet] y t

SHEET G (outer forme)
Corrected: HNL
Uncorrected: BML
Sig. G$_2$^{v}.
69.110.   further.] ~ ,

SHEET G (inner forme)
Corrected: BML
Uncorrected: HNL
Sig. G$_3$^{v}.
70.31.   chance,] ~ .

SHEET H (inner forme)
Corrected: HNL
Uncorrected: BML
Sig. H$_4$^{r}.
86.02.   ioyes.] ~ ·
catchword   And] ^

SHEET H (outer forme)
Corrected: HNL
Uncorrected: BML
Sig. H$_4$^{v}.
87.1.   The an∫were] Thean∫were

SHEET I (outer forme)
Corrected: BML
Uncorrected: HNL
Sig. J$_2$^{v}.
94.2.   therfore.] ~ ,

SHEET L (inner forme)
Corrected: BML
Uncorrected: HNL
Sig. L$_2$^{r}
117.4.   haue] hane
.5.   ∫erue] ∫e rue

SHEET L (outer forme)
Corrected: HNL
Uncorrected: BML
Sign. L$_2$^{v}
119.2.   hue.] ~ ,

SHEET L (outer forme)
Corrected: BML
Uncorrected: HNL
Sig. L$_3$^{v}
123.18.   aduance] adnance

SHEET M (inner forme)
Corrected: BML
Uncorrected: HNL
Sig. M$_1$^{v}
134.24.   craue] crane

SHEET Q (outer forme)
Corrected: BML
Uncorrected: HNL
Sig. Q$_3$^{r}
160.30.   That] Thar

SHEET R (inner forme)
Corrected: HNL
Uncorrected: BML
Sig. R_2^r
page: Fo. 66.] Fo 66.

SHEET S (inner forme)
Corrected: BML
Uncorrected: HNL
Sig. S_3^v
181.11.   ſiluer] ſliuer

SHEET U (inner forme)
Corrected: HNL
Uncorrected: BML
Sig. U_2^r
196.8.   vertues] vertnes

SHEET X (outer forme)
Corrrected: BML
Uncorrected: HNL
Sig. X_4^v.
213.5. Wherewith] Wherwith

SHEET Y (inner forme)
Corrected: BML
Uncorrected: HNL
Sig. Y_1^v
215.7.   me] aie
216.01   eche] cche

SHEET Z (outer forme)
Corrected: HNL
Uncorrected: BML
Sig. Z_1^r
224.2.   ſoft] ~ ,
Sig. Z_2^r.
227.9.   his] hi s

SHEET Z (inner forme)
Corrected: HNL
Uncorrected: BML
Sig. Z_3^r
228.88. may] nay

SHEET Aa (outer forme)
Corrected: HNL
Uncorrected: BML
Sig. Aa_3^r
231.5   tell:] ~ .

SHEET Bb (outer forme)
Corrected: BML
Uncorrected: HNL
Sig. Bb_2^v
238.14. hinder] hinde.
Sig. Bb_3^r
241.13. uſ,] ~ ^
Sig. Bb_4^v
246.5.   meane] meaRe

SHEET Bb (inner forme)
Corrected: BML
Uncorrected: HNL
Sig. Bb_3^v
243.02   or] . ~

SHEET Cc (outer forme)
Corrected: BML
Uncorrected: HNL
Sig. Cc_1^r
catchword.   Her] Hee
Corrected: HNL
Uncorrected: BML
Sig. Cc_4^v
253.5.   Both] Bath

SHEET Dd (inner forme)
Corrected: HNL
Uncorrrected: BML
Sig. Dd$_1^v$
  255.21   lenger] lengev

SHEET Ff (inner forme)
Corrected: HNL
Uncorrected: BML
Sig. Ff$_1^v$
  272.1.   working] work ing
Sig. Ff$_4^r$
  278.100. full] fnll

INDEX 1

SEQUENCE OF POEMS IN Q1 (FIRST LINES) WITH THE NUMBERS OF POEMS IN Q2 (IN PARETHESES)

1. The sonne hath twise brought furth his tender grene (1)
2. The soote season, that bud and blome furth bringes (2)
3. When youth had led me halfe the race (3)
4. Suche waiward waies hath love, that most part in discord (4)
5. When sommer toke in hand the winter to assail (5)
6. Love, that liveth, and reigneth in my thought (6)
7. In Ciprus, springes (whereas dame Venus dwelt) (7)
8. From Tuskane came my Ladies worthy race (8)
9. Brittle beautie, that nature made so fraile (9)
10. Alas so all things nowe doe holde their peace (10)
11. When Windsor walles susteyned my wearied arme (11)
12. Set me wheras the sunne doth parche the grene (12)
13. I never sawe my Ladye laye apart (13)
14. The golden gift that nature did thee geve (14)
15. So cruell prison how coulde betide, alas (15)
16. When ragyng love with extreme payne (16)
17. O happy dames, that may embrace (17)
18. In winters just returne, when Boreas gan his raigne (18)
19. Good Ladies, ye that have your pleasures in exile (19)
20. Geve place ye lovers, here before (20)
21. Although I had a check (21)
22. To dearely had I bought my grene and youthfull yeres (22)
23. O lothsome place where I (23)
24. As oft as I behold and se (24)
25. Though I regarded not (25)
26. Wrapt in my carelesse cloke, as I walke to and fro (26)
27. Martiall, the things that do attayn (31)
28. Of thy lyfe, Thomas, this compasse well mark (32)
29. The great Macedon, that out of Persie chased (33)
30. Dyvers thy death doe diversly bemone (34)
31. W. resteth here, that quick could never rest (35)
32. Thassirian king in peace, with foule desire (37)

33. Layd in my quiet bed, in study as I were (38)

34. The stormes are past these cloudes are overblowne (39)

35. My Ratclif, when thy rechlesse youth offendes (40)

36. The fansy, which that I have served long (41)

37. The longe love, that in my thought I harber (42)

38. Yet was I never of your love agreved (43)

39. Was never file yet half so well yfiled (44)

40. The lively sparkes, that issue from those eyes (45)

41. Such vain thought, as wonted to mislead me (46)

42. Unstable dreame, accordyng to the place (47)

43. Yet that in love finde luck and swete abundance (48)

44. If waker care: if sodayn pale colour (49)

45. Cesar, when that the traytour of Egypt (50)

46. Eche man me telth, I change most my devise (51)

47. Some fowles there be, that have so perfit sight (52)

48. Because I still kept thee fro lyes, and blame(53)

49. I find no peace, and all my warre is done (54)

50. My galley charged with forgetfulnesse (55)

51. Avisyng the bright beames of those fayre eyes (56)

52. They flee from me, that somtime did me seke (57)

53. Madame, withouten many wordes (58)

54. Alas, Madame, for stealing of a kisse (59)

55. The wandring gadling, in the sommer tyde (60)

56. What nedes these threatnyng woordes, and wasted wynd (61)

57. Right true it is, and sayd full yore ago (62)

58. It may be good like it who list (63)

59. Resownde my voyce ye woodes, that heare me plaine (64)

60. In fayth I wot not what to say (65)

61. Farewell the hart of crueltie (66)

62. The restfull place, renewer of my smart (67)

63. From these hie hilles as when a spring doth fall (68)

64. Myne olde dere enmy, my froward maister (69)

65. Marvell nomore altho (70)

66. Where shall I have, at myne owne wyll (71)

67. She sat, and sowed: that hath done me the wrong (72)

68. What man hath hard such cruelty before (73)

69. Behold, Love, thy power how she despiseth (74)

70. What vaileth troth: or by it, to take payn (75)

71. Somtime I fled the fire, that me so brent (76)

72. He is not dead, that somtime had a fall (77)

73. The furious goonne, in his most ragyng yre (78)

74. Accused though I be, without desert (79)

75. My love to skorne, my service to retayne (80)

76. Within my brest I never thought it gain (81)

77. Passe forth my wonted cryes (82)

78. Your lokes so often cast (83)

79. Disdaine me not without desert (84)
80. For want of will, in wo I playne (85)
81. If ever man might him avaunt (86)
82. Some men would thinke of right to have (255)
83. The answere that ye made to me my deare (87)
84. Such is the course, that natures kinde hath wrought (88)
85. The enmy of life, decayer of all kinde (89)
86. Once as me thought, fortune me kist (90)
87. My lute `awake performe the last (91)
88. Nature that gave the Bee so feat a grace (92)
89. Unwarely so was never no man caught (93)
90. Al in thy loke my life doth whole depende (94)
91. Perdy I sayd it not (95)
92. Lux, my faire fawlcon, and thy felowes all (96)
93. A face that should content me wonderous well (97)
94. Ever my hap is slack and slowe in commyng (98)
95. Love, fortune, and my minde which do remember (99)
96. How oft have I, my deare and cruell fo (100)
97. Lyke unto these unmesurable mountaines (101)
98. If amourous fayth, or if an hart unfained (102)
99. Farewell, Love, and all thy lawes for ever (103)
100. My hart I gave thee, not to do it pain (104)
101. The flaming sighes that boyle within my brest (105)

102. The piller perisht is wherto I lent (106)
103. Go burning sighes unto the frosen hart (107)
104. So feble is the threde, that doth the burden stay (108)
105. Suffised not (madame) that you did teare (109)
106. When first mine eyes did view, and marke (110)
107. Synce love wyll nedes, that I shall love (111)
108. Mystrustfull mindes be moved (112)
109. It burneth yet, alas, my hartes desire (113)
110. Of purpose, love chose first for to be blinde (114)
111. What rage is this: what furor: of what kinde (115)
112. Desire (alas) my master, and my fo (116)
113. I see, that chance hath chosen me (117)
114. For shamefast harm of great, and hatefull nede (124)
115. Vuulcane begat me: Minerva me taught (125)
116. Syghes are my foode: my drink are my teares (126)
117. Through out the world if it wer sought (127)
118. Stond who so list upon the slipper whele (128)
119. In court to serve decked with freshe a ray (129)
120. Of Carthage he that worthy warriour (130)
121. Tagus farewel that westward with thy stremes (131)
122. Driven by desire I did this dede (132)
123. In doubtfull breast whiles motherly pity (133)

124. My mothers maides when they do sowe and spinne (134)

125. Myne owne John Poyns: sins ye delite to know (135)

126. A spendyng hand that alway powreth out (136)

127. When Dido feasted first the wanderyng Troian knight (137)

128. What sweet releef the showers to thirstie plants we see (*not in* Q2)

129. Phebe twise took her horns, twise layd them by (*not in* Q2)

130. Lovers men warn the corps be-loved to flee (*not in* Q2)

131. Sythe, Blackwood, you have mynde to wed a wife (*not in* Q2)

132. Sythe, Vincent, I have minde to wed a wife (*not in* Q2)

133. Imps of king Jove, and quene Re-membrance lo (271)

134. In workyng well, if travell you sustaine (272)

135. Who wold beleeve mans life like yron to bee (*not in* Q2)

136. One is my fire: my soons, twise fix they bee (*not in* Q2)

137. By heavens hye gift, incase re-vived were (*not in* Q2)

138. A heavy hart, with wo en-creaseth every smart (*not in* Q2)

139. Charis the fourth, Pieris the tenth, the second Cypris, Jane (*not in* Q2)

140. What cause, what reason moveth me: what fansy fils my brains (*not in* Q2)

141. Deserts of Nymphs, that aun-cient Poets showe (*not in* Q2)

142. Now flaming Phebus, passing through his heavenly region hye (*not in* Q2)

143. So happy bee the course of your long life (*not in* Q2)

144. To you, madame, I wish, bothe now, and eke from yere to yere (*not in* Q2)

145. As this first daye of Janus youthe restores unto the yere (*not in* Q2)

146. Gorgeous attire, by art made trym, and clene (*not in* Q2)

147. To you this present yere full fay-re, and fortunable fall (*not in* Q2)

148. No image carved with coonnyng hand, no cloth of purple dye (*not in* Q2)

149. What one art thou, thus in torn weed yclad (273)

150. The auncient time commended, not for nought (274)

151. What path list you to tred: what trade will you assaye (275)

152. What race of life ronne you: what trade will you assaye (276)

153. When princes lawes, with rever-end right, do keep the commons under (*not in* Q2)

154. Of all the heavenly gifts, that mortall men commend (277)

155. The issue of great Jove, draw nere you, Muses nine (*not in* Q2)

156. The worthy Wilfords body, which alyve (*not in* Q2)

157. For Wilford wept first men, then ayr also (*not in* Q2)

158. Man, by a woman lern, this life what we may call (*not in* Q2)

159. Myrrour of matrones, flowr of spouslike love (*not in* Q2)

160. Now, blythe Thaley, thy feastfull layes lay by (*not in* Q2)

161. Why, Nicolas, why doest thou make such haste (*not in* Q2)

162. Yea, and a good cause why thus should I playn (*not in* Q2)

163. The noble Henry, he, that was the lord Mautravers named (*not in* Q2)

164. Mee thought, of late when lord Mautravers dyed (*not in Q2*)
165. Now clattering arms, now ragyng broyls of ware (278)
166. Therfore, when restlesse rage of wynde, and wave (279)
167. For Tullie, late, a toomb I gan prepare (280)
168. If ever wofull man might move your hartes to ruthe (138)
169. Who justly may rejoyce in ought under the skye (139)
170. If right be rackt, and overronne (140)
171. The lyfe is long, that lothsumly doth last (141)
172. In Grece sometime there dwelt a man of worthy fame (142)
173. Lyke as the lark within the marlians foote (143)
174. The lenger lyfe, the more offence (144)
175. To this my song geue eare, who list (145).
176. The plage is great, where fortune frownes (146)
177. O evyll tonges, which clap at every winde (147)
178. To walke on doubtfull ground, where danger is unseen (247)
179. The restlesse rage of depe devouryng hell (148)
180. By fortune as I lay in bed, my fortune was to fynde (149)
181. Phylida was a fayer mayde (150)
182. Lo, here the end of man the cruell sisters three (151)
183. Who list to live upright, and holde him self content (152)
184. Unto the livyng Lord for pardon do I pray (153)
185. Sythe singyng gladdeth oft the hartes (154)
186. Full faire and white she is, and White by name (155)
187. What thing is that which I bothe have and lacke (156)
188. It is no fire that geves no heate (157)
189. Alas that ever death such vertues should forlet (158)
190. Shall I thus ever long, and be no whit the neare (159)
191. The doutfull man hath fevers strange (160)
192. Sith that the way to welth is woe (161)
193. A student at his boke so plast (162)
194. Who craftly castes to stere his boate (163)
195. I lent my love to losse and gaged my life in vaine (164)
196. When dredful swelling seas, through boisterous windy blastes (165)
197. The winter with his griesly stormes no lenger dare abyde (166)
198. In sekyng rest unrest I finde (167)
199. Geve place you Ladies and be gon (168)
200. Experience now doth shew what God us taught before (169)
201. Thestilis a sely man, when love did him forsake (170)
202. Nature that taught my silly dog god wat (172)
203. Since thou my ring mayst goe where I ne may (173)
204. For that a restles head must somewhat have in ure (174)
205. When Audley had runne out his race and ended wer his days (175)
206. Eche thing I se hath time which time must trye my truth (176)
207. My youthfull yeres are past (177)

208. Behold my picture here well portrayed for the nones (178)
209. Bewaile with me all ye that have profest (179)
210. I see there is no sort (180)
211. When Cupide scaled first the fort (181)
212. I lothe that I did love (182)
213. To live to dye, and dye to live againe (183)
214. The smoky sighes the bitter teares (184)
215. As Cypres tree that rent is by the roote (185)
216. The shinyng season here to some (186)
217. O temerous tauntres that delights in toyes (187)
218. O petrarke hed and prince of poets all (188)
219. With Petrarke to compare there may no wight (189)
220. Cruell and unkind whom mercy cannot move (190)
221. If it were so that God would graunt me my request (191)
222. To love, alas, who would not feare (192)
223. In fredome was my fantasie (193)
224. Among dame natures workes such perfite lawe is wrought (194)
225. To my mishap alas I fynde (195)
226. Al you that frendship do professe (196)
227. Death and the kyng did as it were contende (197)
228. Lyke as the brake within the riders hande (198)
229. Suche grene to me as you have sent (199)
230. As I have bene so will I ever be (200)

231. The golden apple that the Troyan boy (201)
232. Tho Cowerd oft whom deinty viandes fed (202)
233. Though in the waxe a perfect picture made (203)
234. Thestilis thou sely man, why dost thou so complaine (171)
235. Lyke as the rage of raine (204)
236. At libertie I sit and see (205)
237. I read how Troylus served in Troy (206)
238. Flee from the prese and dwell with sothfastnes (207)
239. Sins Mars first moved warre or stirred men to strife (208)
240. The dolefull bell that still dothe ring (209)
241. For love Appollo (his Godhead set aside) (210)
242. Such waiward waies have some when folly stirres their braines (256)
243. Girt in my giltlesse gowne as I sit here and sow (27)
244. As Lawrell leaves that cease not to be grene (211)
245. False may he be, and by the powers above (212)
246. I heard when fame with thundryng voice did sommon to appere (213)
247. I ne can close in short and cunning verse (214)
248. Yet once againe my muse I pardon pray (215)
249. Why fearest thou thy outward foe (216)
250. The flickeryng fame that flieth from eare to eare (217)
251. Who loves to live in peace, and marketh every change (218)
252. Walkyng the pathe of pensive thought (219)

253. From worldly wo the mede of misbeliefe (241)
254. To false report and flying fame (245)
255. Lo here lieth G. under the grounde (239)
256. If that thy wicked wife had spon the thred (240)
257. A man may live thrise Nestors life (243)
258. The vertue of Ulisses wife (244)
259. Procryn that some tyme served Cephalus (220)
260. Lyke the Phenix a birde most rare in sight (221)
261. To trust the fayned face, to rue on forced teares (248)
262. Syns fortunes wrath envieth the welth (28)

263. In the rude age when knowledge was not rife (36)
264. Eche beast can chose hys fere according to his minde (29)
265. If care do cause men cry, why do not I complaine (30)
266. What word is that, that changeth not (118)
267. Venemous thornes that are so sharp and kene (119)
268. A lady gave me a gift she had not (120)
269. Speake thou and spede where will or power ought helpthe (121)
270. If thou wilt mighty be, flee from the rage (122)
271. Lyke as the birde within the cage enclosed (123)

Index 2

Alphabetical Sequence of Headings in Q2 with the Number of Poem Following

A carelesse man scorning and describing the suttle usage of women to warde their lovers (26)

A comparison of his love wyth the faithful and painful love of Troylus to Creside (206)

A comparison of the lovers paines (198)

A complaint by night of the lover not beloved (10)

A complaint of the losse of libertie by love (167)

A description of such a one as he would love (97)

A happy end excedeth all pleasures and riches of the world (186)

A praise of Audley (175)

A praise of his Ladye (168)

A praise of his love: wherin he reproveth them that compare their Ladies with his (20)

A praise of m. M. (266)

A praise of maistresse R (213)

A praise of Petrarke and of Laura his ladie (188)

A renouncing of hardly escaped love (66)

A renouncing of love (103)

A riddle of a gift geven by a Ladie (120)

A song written by the earle of Surrey to a ladie that refused to daunce with him (29)

A warning to the lover how he is abused by his love (22)

Against a cruel woman (190)

Against a gentilwoman by whom he was refused (245)

Against an unstedfast woman (187)

Against him that had slaundered a gentle woman with him selfe (212)

Against his tonge that failed to utter his sutes (53)

Against hourders of money (124)

Against wicked tonges (147)

Against women, either good or bad (243)

All worldly pleasures vade (166)

An answer (240)

An answer (244)

An answer in the behalfe of a woman of an uncertain aucthor (27)

An answere (248)

An answere of comfort (171)

An epitaph made by W. G. lying on his death bed, to be set upon his owne tombe (239)

An epitaph of maister Henry Williams (241)

An old lover to a yong gentilwoman (267)

An other of the same (242)

Bonum est mihi quod humiliasti me (39)

Charging of his love as unpetious and loving other (102)

Comparison of life and death (141)

Comparison of love to a streame falling from the Alpes (68)

Complaint for true love unrequited (75)

Complaint of a diyng lover refused upon his ladies injust mistaking of his writing (18)

Complaint of a lover rebuked (6)

Complaint of a lover, that defied love, and was by love after the more tormented (5)

Complaint of the absence of her lover being upon the sea (19)

Complaint of the absence of her lover being upon the sea (17)

Complaint of the absence of his love (108)

Complaint of the lover disdained (7)

Complaint that his ladie after she knew of his love kept her face alway hidden from him (13)

Desciption of the fickle affections, panges, and sleightes of love (4)

Descripcion and praise of his love (221)

Descripcion of an ungodly worlde (218)

Descripcion of the restlesse state of a lover, with sute to his ladie, to rue on his diyng hart (1)

Description and praise of his love Geraldine (8)

Description of Spring, wherin eche thing renewes, save onely the lover (2)

Description of the contrarious passions in a lover (54)

Description of the restlesse state of a lover (3)

Description of Vertue (273)

Discription of a gonne (125)

Exhortacion to learne by others trouble (40)

Harpalus complaint of Phillidaes love bestowed on Corin, who loved her not and denied him that loved her (150)

He ruleth not though he raigne over realmes that is subject to his own lustes (122)

Hell tormenteth not the damned ghostes so sore as unkindnesse the lover (148)

How by a kisse he found both his life and death (92)

How eche thing save the lover in spring reviveth to pleasure (11)

How no age is content with his owne estate, and how the age of children is the happiest, if they had skill to understand it (38)

How the lover perisheth in his delight, as the flie in the fire (52)

How to use the court and him selfe therin, written to sir Frauences Brian (136)

How unpossible it is to finde quiet in love (98)

Manhode availeth not without good Fortune (202)

Mans life after Possidonius, or Crates (275)

Marcus Tullius Ciceroes death (279)

Metrodorus minde to the contrarie (276)

Musonius the Philosophers saying (272)

Of M.T. Cicero (280)

Of a lover that made his onely god of his love (196)

Of a new maried student that plaied fast or lose (162)

Of a Rosemary branche sent (199)

Of change in minde (51)

Of disapointed purpose by negligence (130)

Of dissembling wordes (127)

Of doutful love (56)

Of Fortune and Fame (146)

Of frendship (277)

Of his love called Anna (118)

Of his love named White (155)

Of his love that pricked her finger with a nedle (72)

Of his maistresse. m.B. (264)

Of his returne from Spaine (131)

Of his ring sent to his ladie (173)

Of love, fortune, and the lovers minde (99)

Of one unjustly defamed (214)

Of others fained sorrow, and the lovers fained mirth (50)

Of Sardanapalus dishonorable life, and miserable death (37)

Of sodaine trusting (132)

Of such as had forsaken him (96)

Of the choise of a wife (217)

Of the Courtiers life written to Jhon Poins (135)

Of the death of master Devorox the lord Ferres sonne (139)

Of the death of Phillips (179)

Of the death of sir Thomas Wiate the elder (223)

Of the death of the late countisse of Penbroke (215)

Of the death of the same sir T.w. (34)

Of the fained frend (62)

Of the golden meane (253)

Of the ix. Muses (271)

Of the Jelous man that loved the same woman and espied this other sitting with her (60)

Of the ladie Wentworthes death (183)

Of the lovers unquiet state (156)

Of the meane and sure estate (128)

Of the meane and sure estate written to John Poins (134)

Of the mother that eat her childe at the seige of Jerusalem (133)

Of the mutabilitie of the world (149)

Of the same (73)

Of the same (36)

Of the same (35)

Of the sutteltie of crafty lovers (256)

Of the token which his love sent him (201)

Of the troubled comon welth restored to quiet by the mighty power of god (229)

Of the vanitie of mans lyfe (257)

Of the wretchednes in this world (152)

Of womens changeable will (251)

Praise of certaine psalmes of David, translated by sir T.w. the elder (33)

Praise of meane and constant estate (32)

Praise of measure keping (274)

Prisoned in windsor, he recounteth his pleasure there passed (15)

Request to Cupide for revenge of his unkinde love (74)

Request to his love to joyne bountie with beautie (14)

Thassault of Cupide upon the fort where the lovers hart lay wounded and how he was taken (181)

That all thing somtime finde ease of their paine, save onely the lover (180)

That eche thing is hurt of it self (216)

That few wordes shew wisdome, and work much quiet (236)

That length of time consumeth all things (224)

¶The lover praieth pity showing that nature hath taught his dog as it were to sue for the same by kissing his ladies handes (172)

That nature which worketh all thinges for our behoofe, hath made women also for our comfort and delight (194)

That Petrark cannot be passed but notwithstanding that Lawra is far surpassed (189)

That pleasure is mixed with every paine (119)

That speaking or profering bringes alway speding (121)

The abused lover seeth his folie, and entendeth to trust no more (44)

The aged lover renounceth love (182)

The answer (238)

The answere (246)

The beginning of the epistle of Penelope to Ulisses, made into verse (225)

The changeable state of lovers (174)

The complaint of a hot woer, delayed with doutfull cold answers (237)

The complaint of a lover with sute to his love for pitie (138)

The complaint of a woman ravished, and also mortally wounded (259)

The complaint of Thestilis amid the
    desert wodde (170)
The constancy of all vertues is most wor-
    thy (203)
The constant lover lamenteth (28)
The courtiers life (129)
The death of Zoras, an Egyptian Astono-
    mer, in the first fight, that Alexander
    had with the Persians (278)
The dispairing lover lamenteth (219)
The divers and contrarie passions of the
    lover (261)
The faithfull lover declareth his paines
    and his uncertein joyes, and with
    only hope recomforteth somwhat his
    wofull heart (30)
The fansie of a weried lover (41)
The felicitie of a minde imbracing vertue,
    that beholdeth the wretched desires of
    the worlde (165)
The forsaken lover describeth and for-
    saketh love (23)
The frailtie and hurtfulnes of beautie (9)
The ladie praieth the returne of her lover
    abiding on the seas (159)
The lady forsaken of her lover, praieth
    his returne, or the end of her own life
    (192)
The lover abused renownseth love (80)
The lover accusing his love for her un-
    faithfulnesse, purposeth to live in lib-
    ertie (184)
The lover asketh pardon of his passed
    follie in love (226)
The lover being made thrall by love, per-
    ceiveth how great a losse is libertye
    (260)
The lover blameth his instant desire (116)
The lover blameth his love for renting of
    the letter he sent her (109)
The lover comforteth himselfe with the
    worthinesse of his love (16)
The lover compareth his hart to the over-
    charged gonne (78)

The lover compareth his state to a ship in
    perilous storme tossed on the sea (55)
The lover complaineth and his ladie
    comforteth (113)
The lover complaineth himself forsaken
    (71)
The lover complaineth his estate (117)
The lover complaineth his fault, that
    with ungentle writing had displeased
    his lady (249)
The lover complaineth his harty love not
    requited (265)
The lover complaineth that deadly sick-
    nesse can not helpe his affeccion (89)
The lover complaineth that his love doth
    not pitie him (64)
The lover complaineth the unkindnes of
    his love (91)
The lover complayneth the losse of his
    ladye (252)
The lover confesseth him in love with
    Phillis (49)
The lover curseth the time when first he
    fell in love (110)
The lover declareth his paines to excede
    far the paines of hell (222)
The lover describes his restlesse state (24)
The lover describeth his being striken
    with sight of his love (45)
The lover describeth his being taken with
    sight of his love (93)
The lover describeth his restlesse state
    (104)
The lover describeth his whole state unto
    his love, and promising her his faith-
    full good will: assureth himself of hers
    again (228)
The lover determineth to serve faithfully
    (111)
The lover disceived by his love repenteth
    him of the true love he bare her (232)
The lover dredding to move his sute for
    dout of deniall, accuseth all women of
    disdaine and ficklenesse (247)

The lover excuseth him of wordes wher-with he was unjustly charged (95)

The lover excuseth himself of suspected change (25)

The lover for shamefastnesse hideth his desire within his faithfull hart (42)

The lover for want of his desire, sheweth his death at hand (185)

The lover forsaketh his unkinde love (268)

The lover forsaketh his unkinde love (104)

The lover having dreamed enjoying of his love, complaineth that the dreame is not either longer or truer (47)

The lover having enjoyed his love, hum-bly thanketh the god of love: and avowing his hart onely to her faith-fully promiseth utterly to forsake all other (233)

The lover here telleth of his divers joyes and adversities in love and lastly of his ladies death (154)

The lover hopeth of better chance (77)

The lover in dispeire lamenteth his case (263)

The lover in libertie smileth at them in thraldome, that sometime scorned his bondage (205)

The lover lamentes the death of his love (106)

The lover lamenteth his estate with sute for grace (85)

The lover lamenteth other to have the frutes of his service (255)

The lover lamenteth that he would forget love, and can not (270)

The lover not regarded in earnest sute, being become wiser, refuseth her prof-red love (258)

The lover praieth his offred hart to be received (100)

The lover praieth his service to be ac-cepted, and his defaultes pardoned (220)

The lover praieth not to be disdained, re-fused, mistrusted, nor forsaken (84)

The lover preferreth his lady above all other (269)

The lover professeth himself constant (81)

The lover refused of his love imbraceth death (177)

The lover refused, lamenteth his estate (164)

The lover rejoiceth the enjoying of his love (90)

The lover rejoyseth against fortune that by hindering his sute had happily made him forsake his folly (65)

The lover sendeth his complaintes and teares to sue for grace (82)

The lover sendeth sighes to mone his sute (107)

The lover sheweth his wofull state, and praieth pitie (143)

The lover sheweth how he is forsaken of such as he somtime enjoyed (57)

The lover sheweth that he was striken by love on good friday (227)

The lover sheweth that in dissembling his love openly he kepeth secret his secret good will (231)

The lover sheweth what he would have, if it were graunted him to have what he would wishe (191)

The lover shewing of the continuall paines that abide within his brest, determineth to die because he cannot have redresse (209)

The lover suspected blameth yll tonges (112)

The lover suspected of change praieth that it be not beleved against him (79)

The lover taught, mistrusteth allure-mentes (63)

The lover that fled love, now folowes it with his harme (76)

The lover that once disdained love is now become subject, beyng caught in his snare (145)

The lover thinkes no paine to great, wherby he may obtain his ladie (161)

The lover to his bed, with describing of his unquiet state (67)

The lover to his love: having forsaken him, and betaken herself to an other (230)

The lover unhappy biddeth happy lovers rejoice in Maie, while he waileth that month to him most unlucky (48)

The lover waileth his changed joyes (86)

The lover waxeth wiser, and will not die for affeccion (43)

The lover wounded of Cupide, wisheth he had rather ben striken by death (250)

The lover yelden into his ladies handes, praieth mercie (193)

The lovers case can not be hidden how ever he dissemble (83)

The lovers life compared to the Alpes (101)

The lovers sorowfull state maketh him write sorowfull songes, but (Souche) his love may change the same (70)

The meane estate is best (160)

The meane estate is to be accompted the best (163)

The meanes to attain happy life (31)

The picture of a lover (178)

The pore estate to be holden for best (169)

The power of love over gods them selves (210)

The praise of a true frende (254)

The promise of a constant lover (211)

The repentant sinner in durance and adversitie (153)

The song of Jopas unfinished (137)

The tale of Pigmalion with conclusion upon the beautie of his love (142)

The testament of the hawthorne (262)

The uncertaine state of a lover (204)

The wavering lover willeth, and dreadeth, to move his desire (46)

The wise trade of lyfe (235)

The wounded lover determineth to make sute to his lady for his recure (208)

They of the meane estate are happiest (140)

Time trieth truth (176)

To a ladie to answer directlie with yea or naie (58)

To his ladie cruel over her yelden lover (88)

To his love from whom he had her gloves (61)

To his love of his constant hart (200)

To his love that had geven him answere of refusell (87)

To his love whom he had kissed against her will (59)

To his lover to loke upon him (94)

To his unkinde love (115)

To leade a vertuous and honest life (207)

To the ladie that scorned her lover (21)

Totus mundus in maligno positus (234)

Upon consideracion of the state of this life he wisheth death (144)

Upon sir James Wilfordes death (151)

Upon the death of sir Antony Denny (197)

Verses written on the picture of sir James Wilford, knight (158)

Vow to love faithfullie howsoever he be rewarded (12)

When adversitie is once fallen, it is to late to beware (195)

Where good will is, some proofe will appere (157)

Whether libertie by losse of life, or life in prison and thraldom be to be preferred (123)

Why love is blind (114)

Wiate being in prison, to Brian (126)

Wiates complaint upon Love to Reason: with Loves answere (69)

Index 3

Alphabetical Sequence of Poems in Q2 (First Lines) with Number Following

A cruell Tiger all with teeth bebled (259)

A face that should content me wonderous wel (97)

A kinde of coale is as men say (237)

A Lady gave me a gift she had not (120)

A man may live thrise Nestors life (243)

A spendyng hand that alway powreth out (136)

A student at his boke so plast (162)

Accused though I be, without desert (79)

Adieu desert, how art thou spent (263)

Ah libertie now have I learnd to know (260)

Ah love how waiward is his wit what panges do perce his brest (249)

Al in thy loke my life doth whole depende (94)

Alas so all things now do hold their peace (10)

Alas that ever death such vertues should forlet (158)

Alas when shall I joy (270)

Alas, Madame, for stealing of a kisse (59)

All you that frendship do professe (196)

Although I had a check (21)

Among dame natures workes such perfite law is wrought (194)

As Cypres tree that rent is by the roote (185)

As I have bene so will I ever be (200)

As Lawrell leaves that cease not to be grene (211)

As oft as I behold and see (24)

At libertie I sit and see (205)

Avisyng the bright beames of those fayre eyes (56)

Because I stil kept thee fro lyes, and blame (53)

Behold my picture here well portrayed for the nones (178)

Behold, Love, thy power how she despiseth (74)

Bewaile with me all ye that have profest (179)

Brittle beautie, that nature made so fraile (9)

By fortune as I lay in bed, my fortune was to finde (149)

Cesar, when that the traitour of Egipt (50)

Complaine we may: much is amisse (234)

Cruel unkinde whom mercy cannot move (190)

Death and the king did as it were contend (197)

Renaissance and English Text Society Volume XXXII

Richard Tottel's Songes and Sonettes: The Elizabethan Version. MRTS Vol. 338, Tempe, AZ, 2007.

Desire (alas) my master, and my fo (116)

Disdaine me not without desert (84)

Do all your dedes by good advise (235)

Do way your phisike I faint no more (258)

Driven by desire I did this dede (132)

Dyvers thy death do diversly bemone (34)

Eche beast can chose his fere according to his minde (29)

Eche man me telth, I change most my devise (51)

Eche thing I see hath time, which time must try my truth (176)

Ever my hap is slack and slowe in coming (98)

Experience now doth shew what God us taught before (169)

False may be he, and by the powers above (212)

Farewell the hart of crueltie (66)

Farewell thou frosen hart and eares of hardned stele (268)

Farewell, Love, and all thy lawes for ever (103)

Flee from the prease and dwell with sothfastnes (207)

For love Apollo (his Godhed set aside) (210)

For shamfast harm of great, and hatefull nede (124)

For that a restles hed must somwhat have in ure (174)

For Tullie, late, a tomb I gan prepare (280)

For want of will, in wo I plain (85)

From these hie hilles as when a spring doth fall (68)

From Tuskane came my Ladies worthy race (8)

From worldly wo the mede of misbelefe (241)

Full faire and white she is, and White by name (155)

Geve place ye lovers, here before (20)

Geve place you Ladies and be gone (168)

Girt in my giltles gowne as I sit here and sow (27)

Go burning sighes unto the frosen hart (107)

Good Ladies: ye that have your pleasures in exile (19)

He is not dead, that somtime had a fall (77)

Holding my peace alas how loud I crye (261)

How oft have I, my deare and cruel fo (100)

I finde no peace, and all my warre is done (54)

I heard when fame with thundring voice did sommon to appere (213)

I lent my love to losse and gaged my life in vaine (164)

I lothe that I did love (182)

I ne can close in short and cunning verse (214)

I never saw my Ladie laye apart (13)

I read how Troylus served in Troy (206)

I see there is no sort (180)

I see, that chance hath chosen me (117)

I sely Haw whose hope is past (262)

I that Ulysses yeres have spent (232)

I wold I found not as I fele (251)

If amorous fayth, or if an hart unfained (102)

If care do cause men cry, why do not I complaine (30)

If ever wofull man might move your hartes to ruthe (138)

If every man might him avaunt (86)

If it were so that God would graunt me my request (191)

If right be rackt, and overronne (140)

If that thy wicked wife had spon the thread (240)

If thou wilt mighty be, flee from the rage (122)

If waker care: if sodayn pale colour (49)

Imps of king Jove, and quene Remembrance lo (271)

In Bayes I boast whose braunch I beare (264)

In Ciprus, springes (where as dame Venus dwelt) (7)

In court as I behelde, the beauty of eche dame (266)

In court to serve decked with fresh aray (129)

In doubtfull breast whiles motherly pity (133)

In faith I wot not what to say (65)

In fredome was my fantasie (193)

In Grece somtime there dwelt a man of worthy fame (142)

In seking rest, unrest I finde (167)

In the rude age when knowledge was not rife (36)

In winters just returne, when Boreas gan his raigne (18)

In working well, if travell you sustain (272)

It is no fire that geves no heate (157)

It may be good like it who list (63)

It was the day on which the sunne deprived of his light (227)

Layd in my quiet bed, in study as I were (38)

Lo dead he lives, that whilome lived here (223)

Lo here lieth G. under the ground (239)

Lo, here the end of man the cruell sisters three (151)

Love, Fortune, and my minde which do remember (99)

Love, that liveth, and raigneth in my thought (6)

Lover. It burneth yet, alas my hartes desire (113)

Lux, my faire fawlcon, and thy felowes all (96)

Lyke as the birde within the cage enclosed (123)

Lyke as the brake within the riders hand (198)

Lyke as the Larke within the Marlians foote (143)

Lyke as the rage of raine (204)

Lyke the Phenix a birde most rare in sight (221)

Lyke unto these unmesurable mountaines (101)

Madame, withouten many wordes (58)

Martial, the thinges that do attain (31)

Marvell no more altho (70)

Mine old dere enmy, my froward maister (69)

My galley charged with forgetfulnesse (55)

My hart I gave thee, not to do it pain (104)

My love to skorne, my service to retayne (80)

My lute awake performe the last (91)

My mothers maides when they do sowe and spinne (134)

Myne owne Jhon Poins: sins ye delite to know (135)

My Ratclif, when thy retchlesse youth offendes (40)

My youthfull yeres are past (177)

Mystrustfull mindes be moved (112)

Nature that gave the Bee so feate a grace (92)

Nature that taught my silly dog god wat (172)

No joy have I, but live in heavinesse (252)

Not like a God came Jupiter to woo (231)

Now clattering armes, now ragyng broyls of warre (278)

O evyll tonges, which clap at every winde (147)

O happy dames, that may embrace (17)

O lingring make Ulisses dere, thy wife lo sendes to thee (225)

O lothsome place where I (23)

O Petrarke hed and prince of poets al (188)

O temerous tauntres that delights in toyes (187)

Of all the heavenly giftes, that mortall men commend (277)

Of Carthage he that worthy warriour (130)

Of purpose, love chose first for to be blinde (114)

Of thy life, Thomas, this compasse wel mark (32)

Once as me thought, fortune me kist (90)

Passe forth my wonted cries (82)

Perdy I sayd it not (95)

Phylida was a fayre mayde (150)

Procryn that somtime served Cephalus (220)

Resigne you dames whom tikelyng brute delight (269)

Resownde my voyce ye woodes, that heare me plain (64)

Right true it is, and sayd full yore ago (62)

Set me wheras the Sunne do parche the grene (12)

Shall I thus ever long, and be no whit the neare (159)

She sat, and sowed: that hath done me the wrong (72)

Since thou my ring mayst go where I ne may (173)

Sins fortunes wrath envieth the wealth (28)

Sins Mars first moved warre or stirred men to strife (208)

Sith that the way to wealth is wo (161)

So cruell prison how could betide, alas (15)

So feble is the threde, that doth the burden stay (108)

Some fowles there be that have so perfit sight (52)

Some men would think of right to have (255)

Somtime I fled the fire, that me so brent (76)

Speake thou and spede where will or power ought helph (121)

Stay gentle frend that passest by (242)

Stond who so list upon the slipper wheele (128)

Such grene to me as you have sent (199)

Such is the course, that natures kinde hath wrought (88)

Such vain thought, as wonted to mislead me (46)

Such waiward waies hath love, that most part in discord (4)

Such waiward waies have some when folly stirres their braines (256)

Suffised not (madame) that you did teare (109)

Syghes are my foode: my drink are my teares (126)

Synce love will nedes, that I shall love (111)

Syth singyng gladdeth oft the harts (154)

Tagus farewell that Westward with thy stremes (131)

Thassirian king in peace, with foule desire (37)

The answere that ye made to me my dere (87)

The auncient time commended, not for nought (274)

The bird that somtime built within my brest (230)

The blinded boy that bendes the bow (250)

The Cowerd oft whom deinty viandes fed (202)

The dolefull bell that still doth ring (209)

The doutfull man hath fevers strange (160)

The enmy of life, decayer of all kinde (89)

The fansy, which that I have served long (41)

The flaming sighes that boyle within my brest (105)

The flickeryng fame that flieth from eare to eare (217)

The furious goonne, in his most raging yre (78)

The golden apple that the Troyan boy (201)

The golden gift that nature did thee geve (14)

The great Macedon, that out of Persie chased (33)

The lenger lyfe, the more offence (144)

The life is long, that lothsomly doth last (141)

The lively sparkes, that issue from those eyes (45)

The long love, that in my thought I harber (42)

The piller perisht is wherto I lent (106)

The plage is great, where fortune frownes (146)

The restfull place, renewer of my smart (67)

The restlesse rage of depe devouryng hell (148)

The secret flame that made all Troy so hot (229)

The shining season here to some (186)

The smoky sighes the bitter teares (184)

The soote season, that bud and blome forth brings (2)

The soules that lacked grace (222)

The stormes are past these cloudes are overblowne (39)

The sunne hath twise brought furth his tender grene (1)

The Sunne when he hath spred his raies (228)

The vertue of Ulisses wife (244)

The wandring gadling, in the summer tide (60)

The winter with his griesly stormes ne lenger dare abide (166)

The wisest way, thy bote, in wave and winde to guie (253)

Therfore, when restlesse rage of winde, and wave (279)

Thestilis a sely man, when love did him forsake (170)

Thestilis thou sely man, why dost thou so complayne (171)

They flee from me, that sometime did me seke (57)

Thou Cupide God of love, whom Venus thralles do serve (233)

Though I regarded not (25)

Though in the waxe a perfect picture made (203)

Throughout the world if it wer sought (127)

To dearely had I bought my grene and youthfull yeres (22)

To false report and flying fame (245)

To live to dye and dye to live againe (183)

To love, alas, who would not feare (192)

To my mishap alas I finde (195)

To thys my song geve eare, who list (145)

To trust the fayned face, to rue on forced teares (248)

To walke on doutfull ground, where daunger is unsene (247)

Unstable dreame according to the place (47)

Unto the living Lord for pardon do I pray (153)

Unwarely so was never no man caught (93)

Vaine is the fleting welth (257)

Venemous thornes that are so sharp and kene (119)

Vulcane begat me: Minerva me taught (125)

Walkyng the pathe of pensive thought (219)

Was never file yet half so well yfiled (44)

What harder is then stone, what more then water soft (224)

What man hath heard such cruelty before (73)

What nedes these threatning wordes, and wasted wynd (61)

What one art thou, thus in torn weed yclad (273)

What path list you to tread? What trade will you assay (275)

What race of life ronne you? What trade will you assay (276)

What rage is this: what furor: of what kinde (115)

What thing is that which I both have and lacke (156)

What vaileth troth? or by it, to take payn (75)

What word is that, that changeth not (118)

When Audley had run out his race, and ended wer his daies (175)

When Cupide scaled first the fort (181)

When Dido feasted first the wandring Trojan knight (137)

When dredful swelling seas, through boisterous windy blastes (165)

When first mine eyes did view, and marke (110)

When Phebus had the serpent slaine (265)

When raging love with extreme payne (16)

When sommer toke in hand the winter to assail (5)

When Windsor walles susteyned my wearied arme (11)

When youth had led me half the race (3)

Where shall I have, at mine owne wyll (71)

Who craftly castes to stere his boate (163)

Who justly may rejoyce in ought under the skye (139)

Who list to lead a quiet life (236)

Who list to live upright, and holde him self content (152)

Who loves to live in peace, and marketh every change (218)

Who so that wisely weyes the profite and the price (254)

Whom fansy forced first to love (246)

Why fearest thou thy outward fo (216)

W. resteth here, that quick could never rest (35)

With Petrarke to compare ther may no wight (189)

Within my brest I never thought it gain (81)

Wrapt in my carelesse cloke, as I walke to and fro (26)

Ye are to yong to bryng me in (267)

Ye that in love finde luck and swete abundance (48)

Yet once againe my muse I pardon pray (215)

Yet was I never of your love agreved (43)

You that in play peruse my plaint, and reade in rime the smart (226)

Your borrowd meane to move your mone, of fume withouten flame (238)

Your lokes so often cast (83)